Fifth Edition

AMERICAN SPORTS
From the Age of Folk Games
to the Age of Televised Sports

Benjamin G. Rader
University of Nebraska—Lincoln

Prentice
Hall

Upper Saddle River, New Jersey 07458

Library of Congress Cataloging-in-Publication Data

Rader, Benjamin G.
   American sports: from the age of folk games to the age of televised sports / Benjamin G.
Rader.—5th ed.
     p. cm.
   Includes bibliographical references and index.
   ISBN 0-13-097750-0
    1. Sports—United States—History.   2. Sports—Social aspects—United States.   I. Title.

GV583.R3 2004
796'.0973—dc21

To Barbara Koch Rader

Editorial director: Charlyce Jones Owen
Acquisitions editor: Charles Cavaliere
Associate editor: Emsal Hasan
Production editor: Edie Riker
Cover art director: Jayne Conte
Cover photo credit: "Lawn Tennis" 1886 painting. Library of Congress
Prepress and Manufacturing buyer: Sherry Lewis
Director of marketing: Beth Gillet Mejia
Editorial assistant: Adrienne Paul
Cover design: Lisa Boylan

This book was set in 10/12 Palatino by Lithokraft
and it was printed and bound by Hamilton Printing.
The cover was printed by Coral Graphics.

© 2004, 1999, 1996, 1990, 1983 by Pearson Education
Upper Saddle River, New Jersey 07458

Printed in the United States of America

10 9 8 7 6 5 4 3

ISBN 0-13-097750-0

Pearson Education LTD., *London*
Pearson Education Australia PTY, Limited, *Sydney*
Pearson Education Singapore, Pte. Ltd
Pearson Education North Asia Ltd, *Hong Kong*
Pearson Education Canada, Ltd., *Toronto*
Pearson Educacíon de Mexico, S.A. de C.V.
Pearson Education—Japan, *Tokyo*
Pearson Education Malaysia, Pte. Ltd
Pearson Education, *Upper Saddle River, New Jersey*

CONTENTS

PREFACE

Those readers familiar with the first and second editions of *American Sports* will notice a subtle but significant shift in emphases in the third through the fifth editions. The original edition (and to a lesser extent the second as well) focused on major changes in sports. The narrative's overall coherence relied mainly upon a concept of stages in the development of sports as we know them today. While not neglecting important new developments in sports over time nor the technological, material, social, and cultural forces that induced them, these revisions give greater attention to continuities in the American sporting experience.

In this edition, I have continued my quest to present the relationships between sport, society, and culture with greater clarity. Thus I have sought to be more explicit about the connections between the great social and cultural divisions in the United States and sport. The major cleavages that I tried to keep in mind throughout the narrative are gender, class, race, ethnicity, religion, and region. At the same time, I have tried to consider how sport may transcend these fundamental social categories, how the experience of sport either as a player or a fan may bind diverse groups together. This has led me to give greater attention to layers of association. For instance, persons divided by gender, ethnicity, religion, region—or all four of these at once—may share a common experience in watching the Super Bowl on television but never enjoy a round of golf together on the local country club course.

Apart from recognizing the sheer joy of engaging in or watching athletic contests, I have in addition sought to provide some of the possible meanings of sporting experiences within specific historical contexts. Sports are frequently played for sheer fun, but they may also present an individual an opportunity to display her or his athletic skills. The athlete may thereby win the esteem of others; the display may be accompanied by improved status, feelings of personal empowerment, autonomy, and perhaps even wealth. Moreover, athletic performances may serve as a "text," a text that can be "read" or understood in ways similar to how one reads a novel or watches television. Indeed, since the experience of sports entails "real" drama, it provides a particularly powerful text for viewers and athletes alike. As a text, sports send messages regarding fundamental beliefs, customs, and values. For example, that black and white baseball players in the age of segregation rarely played against one another or on the same teams may have confirmed and reinforced the nation's racial apartheid. Put somewhat differently, it suggested to those who watched baseball games that Jim Crow was an appropriate way of dealing with the nation's race relations. Given power in this vital sense, sports have never been immune from conflict. Paradoxically, at the same time, the sporting principle of a "level playing field," the idea that all have the right to compete equally in sports, may have helped to encourage social and cultural change.

Readers of this edition will find a considerable body of new material and the reshaping of old materials. Influenced by the recent publication of a remarkable set of scholarly books and articles on the history of American sports, I have revised, deleted, and added material in every chapter. Especially noteworthy in this regard are a major revision of Chapter 11, "Intercollegiate Football Spectacles"; greater emphasis in Chapter 7 on the role of sports in the forging of an American upper class; new sections on the "new" middle class, consumer culture, and the quest for excitement (Chapter 8); female cheerleading (Chapter 13); and the new individualism and sports (Chapter 14). Finally, I have updated Chapters 14 through 21. References to the works shaping these revisions can be found in the footnotes of individual chapters.

As with earlier revisions, I have tried to give special attention to the needs of neophyte readers. Without sacrificing the fundamental substance or complexity of the subject, I have been acutely sensitive to clarity and style. To aid reader comprehension, separate conclusions are presented in each chapter. Each chapter also includes updated bibliographical information.

ACKNOWLEDGMENTS

My list of those who should be acknowledged for assistance in writing this book has grown ever longer. It includes a substantial number of the members of the North American Society of Sport History, a group which warmly welcomed a stranger into their midst more than two decades ago. For fear that I will overlook someone who made a valuable suggestion, corrected an error, or directed me to an important source, I hope they will understand why I do not attempt to list all of them here. Yet allow me to mention specifically with respect to this edition Robert Barnett, Richard Crepeau, Richard Davies, Andy Doyle, Mark Dyreson, Gerald Early, Donald Fisher, Gerald Gems, Larry Gerlach, Pamela Grundy, Wendy Katz, George Kirsch, Renee Laegreid, Charles Martin, Patrick Miller, Timothy Mahoney, Michael Oriard, Gustavo Paz, Samuel Regalado, Steven Riess, Nancy Struna, Ahati Toure, Kenneth Winkle, David Zang, and the members of the University of Nebraska's Reading Group; and Prentice Halls' reviewer, John Neuenschwander at Carthage College. My footnotes reflect debts to many others.

More than any other single person, Barbara Koch Rader aided in the formation of many of the ideas that have found their way into this book. For that and much more, I remain profoundly grateful to her.

Benjamin G. Rader
Lincoln, Nebraska

1
SPORTS IN EARLY AMERICA

*B*efore dawn on Christmas Day 1621, William Bradford, the doughty governor of the tiny Plymouth colony, called his able-bodied men to their work. Bradford's summons came as no surprise to most of the settlers. As a separatist Protestant group (later called Pilgrims), they rejected the idea of Christmas as a holiday. Therefore, they expected to work on that day. Yet a few recent arrivals from England objected to Bradford's order. Their consciences, they informed the governor, forbade them from toiling on Christmas Day. Bradford disagreed with the newcomers, but, as daylight hours were precious, he decided to wait until later to convince them of their errors. So he then departed with the remaining men to take up the work at hand.

When Bradford and his workmen returned at noon, he found that the new men were shouting, laughing, and running about in Plymouth's single street "openly at play." "Some were pitching the bar," Bradford later wrote, "and some [were playing] at stool-ball."[1] Bradford knew well these folk games of seventeenth-century Britain. But the governor was furious. He seized the players' "implements" and ordered them off the street. As work on Christmas Day violated the newcomers' consciences, Bradford said, merrymaking on Christ's birthday violated the conscience of the governor.

This incident, though inconsequential in itself, illustrates several fundamental forces that helped shape the sports of the British colonists in North America. Like the newcomers at Plymouth, most of the colonists would have preferred to continue playing the same games that they had left behind in Britain. Throughout the colonial era (from the settlement of Jamestown in 1607 to the Declaration of Independence in 1776), the settlers' memories of the past plus their continuing interactions with the Mother Country encouraged their retention of traditional sports.

Yet, the Christmas Day controversy at Plymouth also reveals that no simple transfer of culture from the Old to the New World was possible. William Bradford was only one of many religious zealots who warred against Britain's traditional festive culture. Apart from religious suspicion, if not outright hostility, toward the older culture, those who sought to transplant British sporting traditions to North America encountered other difficulties. Except in New England (where settlers resided mostly in towns), the colonists lived on the land that they farmed. Their dispersal across vast spaces worked against the re-creation of the village life that many of them had left behind. Neither did the colonists duplicate the British system of social ranks. Britain was a rank-ordered society headed by the monarch and a powerful nobility. Few of its landed aristocrats came to the colonies (and those who did remained only briefly). Until a native colonial gentry developed in the eighteenth century, efforts to copy upper-class British sporting life went mostly for naught.

The net effect of these considerations was a sporting world in the colonies that, though broadly similar to that of Britain, differed in significant ways. Only with a growth in wealth, population, and towns in the eighteenth century were the colonists able to reproduce even an approximation of the remarkable range of games regularly played in Great Britain. Sharp regional differences also marked colonial sporting life. The expressive, socially stratified sporting ways of the South shared little with the far more restrained, "lawful sport and recreation" of the New England colonists in the North.

BRITAIN'S FESTIVE CULTURE

Central to comprehending the place of sports in seventeenth- and eighteenth-century Britain is what Richard Holt has aptly termed a "festive culture."[2] Britain's festive culture grew out of pagan customs, religious practices, and the circumstances of daily life. That most of the people in Britain lived in tiny agricultural villages encouraged face-to-face relations and communal festivities. Typically scattered three or four miles apart, the villages served as homes for tradesmen, craftsmen, and farmers. The villagers invariably concluded their harvest season with a festival of thanks accompanied by hearty eating, drinking, dancing, and game playing.

In addition, the ecclesiastical (or church) calendar freed people from work so they could honor the parish's patron saint, celebrate the major events in the life of Christ, and commemorate numerous other saints and martyrs. Celebrations frequently entailed both Christian and pagan customs. For instance, May Day, perhaps the favorite holiday of the English countryside, originated as a rite of spring. Fertility and the return of spring, their ancestors had believed, depended upon the proper veneration of a phallic symbol. Accordingly, the young people trekked to the woods after midnight on May first, cut down a tree, and brought it back to the village. There they erected a maypole amid much ceremony, fastened long ribbons to the top of the pole, and danced about it merrily. Critics saw the ancient rite as a form of idolatry and loose morals. "Of forty, three-score, or a hundred maids going to the wood over night," Philip Stubbes, an archenemy of the custom reported (with probable exaggeration), "there have been scarcely the third part of them returned home again undefiled."[3]

The villagers celebrated other holidays. One of the most popular was the annual parish feast, often called a wake or revel, a respite from work in which the entire community gathered to eat, drink, dance, and compete in the folk games of their ancestors. Seasonal holidays, which were equally popular, included the Christmas season, Plough Monday, Shrove Tuesday, and the Easter season. Country fairs, which mingled business with pleasure, added to the long list of opportunities for the ordinary people to engage in merrymaking. Combining Sundays, holy days, and seasonal holidays, nearly one holiday for each two days of work was available for festivities.

Folk games invariably accompanied observances. Many parishes enjoyed stoolball, foot races, quoits (in which a contestant attempted to throw an iron ring over a peg), and skittles or ninepins (both forms of bowling). The games could furnish young men with opportunities to display their physiques and skills to the marriageable young women in the village. In some places, games served a similar purpose for women; they too engaged in foot races. "Nothing is more usual than for a nimble-footed wench to get a husband at the same time as she wins a smock," observed Joseph Addison about the Bath wakes in the early eighteenth century.[4]

Britons took a special delight in violent games and spectacles. They relished contests of brute strength, especially wrestling and cudgeling. In cudgeling the combatant, while employing a wicker shield for protection, used a long stick to "break the head" or draw blood from his opponent. Such violent contests affirmed a masculine ethos of individual prowess and physical courage. Throwing stones at cocks was a popular contest on Shrove Tuesday; contestants paid a fee that allowed them to throw stones at a rooster tethered by a string. The thrower who delivered the lethal blow thereby gained the right to carry the trophy of his triumph home for his supper. Cockfighting was an even more common pastime; excited spectators usually wagered on the outcome. Believing that baiting a bull improved the quality of the meat, bulldogs would be unleashed upon a tethered bull. The dogs would try to seize the bull by the nape of the neck or the scrotum; if successful, they would hold on until forced to let go by pouring flour into their nostrils. Admiration for the characteristics of the bulldog led to that animal's becoming a national symbol of Britain's tenacity.

No contests excited the villagers more than "football." Unlike modern football (soccer), rugby, or American football, all of which are offsprings of the medieval game, the village sport had no common rules. Depending on time and place, it might be an ad hoc affair with an unspecified number of players or it might be an annual contest between the residents of two villages. Depending upon local customs, it might emphasize kicking, running, or throwing the ball. The football, which was normally an inflated animal bladder, was sometimes encased in leather. The ostensible purpose of the game was to move the ball across a previously defined goal line.

VILLAGE FOOTBALL This drawing of a village football contest suggests that the play-ers enjoyed the brutality and the expression of uninhibited emotions as much as the game itself. Apparently one of the players has been victimized by a kick in the shin or perhaps the groin.
(Getty Images Inc.)

In some places, the game had sophisticated rules and strategies for de-ceiving the opposition. In Cornwall, for example, custom required that each play-er pair off with another, attempting to block his opponent's advance. This feature, along with an offside rule, made it similar to modern American football. On the other hand, in many places football seems to have been little less than an unregu-lated brawl. The players kicked, wrestled, and sometimes struck their opponents with their fists. Damaged property, torn clothing, bloodied bodies, and sometimes death accompanied these contests. Citing football's contribution to social disorder, between 1314 and 1617 English monarchs and local magistrates banned the game on at least 30 separate occasions. None of these measures permanently impeded football's popularity.

Games and revelries helped satisfy particular needs of seventeenth- and eighteenth-century Britons. In the first place, festivities relieved some of the grim-ness of life which routinely included early death from disease and famine. Second, as revealed in the celebration of May Day, festivals frequently provided a setting for mating rituals. Third, they allowed for the symbolic and thereby safe expres-sion of resentments arising from the social structure. For example, bachelors, de-nied the opportunity for marriage until much later than today, frequently engaged in a pageant of "misrule"; the spectacle might entail public mockery of superiors in social rank, married men, the church, and even the monarch. Finally, such violent games as football helped to promote village unity. "At the seasons of football and cockfighting" many parishes, according to a report in 1712, "reassume their . . . hatred of each other. My tenant in the country is verily persuaded that the parish of the enemy hath not one honest man in it."[5]

Sports in Britain also mirrored the nation's social hierarchy. Although society was marked by shifting gradations in rank, the monarch stood at the top, followed in descending order by an aristocracy of the hereditary nobility, the gentry, a middling class, and at the bottom the dregs of society. While the privileged upper ranks frequently patronized and mingled with the common people in their pastimes, they also set aside certain sports to themselves. Hunting was an important entitlement of the well-born; only the monarchs, the nobility, and the gentry were allowed to hunt deer, for example. They employed both hounds and hawks to ferret out their prey. "When we do not hunt, we hawk," Viscount Conway explained to a friend in 1638, "the rest of the time is spent in tennis, chess, and dice, and in a word we eat and drink and rise to play . . . for what is a gentleman but his pleasure."[6] Indeed, the freedom and the wealth to spend one's time in play provided visible proof of one's superior social standing; devotion to a life of conspicuous leisure served to separate the upper strata from the lower social ranks.

In the eighteenth century, yet another world of sport began to emerge in Britain's rapidly growing cities. In particular, London witnessed the growth of sports tied neither to the exclusivity of the upper ranks nor to the festivities of rural villages. Certain sports stood alone; they became part of a burgeoning world of commercialized leisure. Inn- or tavernkeepers played a critical role in this development; they promoted and profited from prizefights, cockfights, bearbaitings, and dozens of other contests. Many of these contests involved the spilling of blood, and hence the contemporary term "blood sports" to describe them. They attracted men of all sorts—workingmen, merchants, aristocrats—both as spectators and bettors. Yet it would be a mistake to think of eighteenth-century urban-commercialized sport in completely modern terms. For example, the practice of charging gate fees to watch sports awaited the nineteenth century, and major sporting events in the eighteenth century continued to require the patronage of the wealthy.

THE PURITAN ASSAULT UPON BRITAIN'S FESTIVE CULTURE

Not everyone in Great Britain looked favorably upon the typical diversions of the upper ranks or the nation's traditional festive culture. During the late sixteenth and early seventeenth centuries, even before the first permanent British settlements in North America, recreation became a focal point of controversy. Protestant reformers, commonly called Puritans, thought that Henry VIII had not gone far enough when he broke with Rome and established a separate Church of England. They sought to purify and reform the Church of England by wiping out all remnants of the holy days, rituals, pageantry, and symbols associated with the Roman Catholic Church.

Sunday merriments especially enraged the Puritans. Throughout England in the early years of the seventeenth century, the Puritans mounted campaigns to suppress public recreation on the Sabbath. But they encountered opposition—not only from the common people, but also from the upper social ranks, high authorities in the Church of England, and the king himself. In response to the attacks by the Puritans on Sunday festivities in Lancastershire, King James I issued a Declaration (Book) of Sports in 1618, which was to be read from every pulpit in England.

The royal declaration sanctioned specific Sunday pastimes as well as other customs arising from the festive culture.[7] "After the end of divine service our good people [must] not be disturbed ... or discouraged from any lawful recreation, nor from having of May-games, Whitson Ales, and Morris-dances, and the setting up of May-poles and other sports." James rhetorically asked: "For when shall the common people have leave to exercise if not upon Sunday and holidays, seeing they must apply their labor and win their living in all working days?" Those clergymen who declined to read the royal proclamation from their pulpits found themselves censured, suspended, or deprived of their positions. Yet in those parishes where Puritans gained the upper hand politically, they successfully suppressed traditional festivities.

Parliament, the majority of whose members were at odds with both James I and his successor Charles I, repeatedly tried to rescind the Book of Sports, only to be blocked by the kings. Finally, in 1641, during the Puritan Revolution, Parliament imposed a rigid Sabbath on all of Britain. Restoration of the monarchy in 1660 brought a return of the earlier festive culture and the traditional Sunday. Yet Britons never celebrated Sunday with quite the same gusto as before; the Puritan Revolution bequeathed to Britain "the peculiar British Sunday," one devoid of much of the holiday spirit that had prevailed before the revolution and stood in sharp contrast with the practices of the continental countries of Europe.

Puritans in the New World also tried to exterminate traditional convivialities. In seventeenth-century New England, where the Puritans were particularly strong, they abrogated the Church of England's calendar of feasts and saints' days. They celebrated none of the traditional religious holidays. For example, in 1640 Massachusetts levied a fine upon anyone who fasted, feasted, or refused to work on Christmas Day. In Pennsylvania, the Quakers, another group of Protestant reformers, adopted similar laws.

The New England colonies established an unusually stern Sabbath. Beginning on Saturday night and ending at sundown on Sunday, the colonies forbade work, recreation, travel, idle conversation, sexual intercourse, and even "unnecessary and unreasonable walking in the streets and fields." In 1656 a Captain Kemble of Boston had to sit in the stocks for two hours for "lewd and unseemly conduct." After having been at sea for three years the indiscreet captain had publicly kissed his wife on the Sabbath. Even as late as the 1730s, when stringent control of personal behavior had noticeably relaxed in colonial Massachusetts, Joseph Bennett, an English traveler, observed that in Boston the Lord's Day was the "strictest kept that ever I yet saw anywhere."[8]

Other colonies enacted strict Sabbatarian laws, albeit, with the exception of the Quaker colonies, either not as sweeping or as rigorously enforced as in New

England. The Sabbatarian legislation of colonial America left an enduring legacy, one that was reinforced periodically by religious revivals. It was not until the 1930s, for example, that Pennsylvania dropped bans on Sunday baseball games. Even to this day in some parts of the United States local ordinances prohibit certain activities on Sunday.

"LAWFUL SPORT" IN NEW ENGLAND AND THE MIDDLE COLONIES

In both Old and New England, the Puritans objected more to Britain's festive culture than to the specific games associated with that culture. Indeed, the Puritans extended their approval to what Richard Baxter, a prominent divine, called "lawful sport or recreation." To be lawful, a sport had to be dissociated from traditional revelries. Furthermore, a lawful sport should refresh the participants so that they could better execute their worldly and spiritual "callings" or duties. "We daily need some respite and diversion, without which we dull our powers; a little intermission sharpens 'em again," wrote one Puritan minister. Recreation, wrote another minister, "must tend also to glorify God . . . the scope and end of all recreation is, that God may be honored in and by them."[9]

    To meet the standards of lawful sport required constant vigilance, an undeviating attention to the consequences of engaging in diversions. If a sport became an all-absorbing activity, an end in itself without thought of one's higher duties, then one should stop playing it. If the sport stimulated the passions, entailed deceit, or resulted in idleness, gambling, excessive drinking, or sexual immorality, then it should also be avoided. Believing that all time was sacred (and therefore one's use of it was accountable to God), conscientious Puritans approached all forms of play with excruciating caution.

    Consistent with their notions of lawful sport, seventeenth-century New England Puritans expressly condemned certain sports. They castigated animal baiting, fighting, and all games associated with gambling or immoderate drinking. The colonial assemblies specifically legislated against "unlawful games at cards, dice, etc." and fined innkeepers who permitted gambling of any kind. To the Puritans, gambling was not only a form of idleness; it also mocked God whom they believed controlled all things.

    The Puritans also sought to discourage horse racing. For example, anyone "convicted of running races upon horses . . . in the streets of Ipswich, or for abetting and encouraging others of laying wagers on any side should pay 40 shillings," an extraordinarily severe fine.[10] Such legal strictures did not completely suppress racing; later in the eighteenth century Boston newspapers even openly advertised races held outside the city's environs. Yet, unlike the southern colonies, horse racing never occupied a central place in New England's recreational life.

    While censuring blood sports and gambling, the New England authorities specifically endorsed other sports. They permitted fishing and hunting if those activities were pursued for food, to refresh the body, or to rid the colony of vermin.

Towns even paid bounties to those killing foxes, wolves, and bears. New Englanders exempted children from rigid strictures on play. Children played with toys and, when orderly, they were allowed to swim in the summer and skate in the winter. Boys and young men also played football and bat-and-ball games. Since "several persons . . . received hurt by boys and young men playing at football in the streets," Boston's selectmen prohibited the game in 1657. But the ban must not have been completely effective, for it was republished in 1677 and again in 1701. An English traveler, John Dutton, reported witnessing "a great game of football" between young men on the beach near Rowley, Massachusets, in 1685, but, given the paucity of evidence for similar contests elsewhere, this game must have been unusual.[11]

Although New Englanders abolished holy days and enforced a strict Sabbath, they constructed their own kind of communal rites. Church services on Sunday, lecture days, election days, thanksgiving days, Harvard commencements, public punishments, and funerals drew people together at a single place. But, when compared with the festive culture of the Mother Country, colonial New England's holidays were tame affairs. Dancing, heavy drinking (except at funerals), mockery of church officials or those in the higher social ranks, and the playing of games rarely accompanied these public events.

Training days represented something of an exception. Law required that all men between the ages of 16 and 60 meet for military training on a regular basis. Martial arts were an important part of this training. In the afternoons, the officers frequently scheduled contests among their men. Troops competed in wrestling, foot races, jumping, horse racing, and shooting-at-the mark. Even Samuel Sewall, a conscientious Puritan and an officer in the Massachusetts militia, reported in his diary in 1702 that he had awarded a silver cup to the winner of a shooting-at-the-mark match. Similarly, in Connecticut, according to a traveler in 1704, the victor in a target-shooting contest on training day won several yards of red ribbon and a "great applause, as even the winner of the Olympic games."[12]

Although New Englanders were among the earliest English settlers on Long Island and Manhattan, they were unable to impose their cultural hegemony over that region. In 1664, the English forcibly took the colony from the original Dutch settlers, made the Church of England the official church, and ordered the toleration of religious dissenters. With an ethnically polyglot population, New York was a remarkably cosmopolitan colony.

New York's sporting ways reflected the city's cultural heterogeneity. The Dutch settlers bowled, held boat races, and played *kolven*, which some authorities translate as "golf." Apparently a version of *kolven* was still being played a century later, for in 1766 James Rivington advertised for sale "gouff clubs," as well as shuttlecocks, cricket balls, and racquets. While condemned by local Puritans, the royal governor, his entourage, and prosperous merchants patronized other diversions. In 1664, the governor established the first organized horse races at the Newmarket course on Hempstead Plains, Long Island, and, in 1736, wealthy sportsmen built America's first circular track for racing. In addition, cockfighting and animalbaiting became common occurrences in the New York colony.

Farther south and west, in the middle colonies of New Jersey and Pennsylvania, another group of Protestant reformers, the Quakers, were far less tolerant of sport than the New Yorkers. For reasons similar to the Puritans', the first Quakers specifically banned "all prizes, stage plays, cards, dice, may games, masques, revels, bull-baiting, cock-fighting, bear-baitings and the like." On the other hand, they specifically encouraged "useful" and "needful" recreation. Quaker schools set aside times for physical exercises and both youngsters and adults swam in the summer and skated in the winter. Hunting and fishing, if engaged in for subsistence, and gardening also met with Quaker approval. William Penn, the colony's founder, summed up the Quaker attitude in an epigram. "The best recreation," he wrote, "is to do good."[13]

Like the Puritans in New York, the Quakers encountered difficulties in enforcing their notions of lawful sport. In the eighteenth century they had to contend with a huge influx of non-Quaker immigrants, including not only non-Quaker English but Scots-Irish and Germans as well. Each ethnic group had its own recreational traditions. Furthermore, by the middle of the eighteenth century, the Quakers were losing political and cultural power to a new and more secular gentry class. The new group had little or no sympathy with Penn's idea of a Godly Commonwealth. Emulating counterparts in London, the local gentry in Philadelphia formed exclusive clubs—the Mount Regal Fishing Club, the Society of the Sons of St. Tammany, and the Hunting Club, for example—and shared a rich associative life that revolved around leisure activities.[14]

Quaker and Puritan notions of lawful sport persisted long after the colonial era. Even for those who had rejected Puritan or Quaker theology but who were products of its culture, engagement in uninhibited play was likely to result in guilt feelings. "I was not sent into this world to spend my days in sports, diversions, and pleasures," wrote John Adams in the middle of the eighteenth century. "I was born for business; for both activity and study."[15] Heirs of the Puritan tradition never engaged in sport for the sheer pleasure that it afforded to the participants or the spectators. They needed a larger justification, such as a belief that the activity glorified God or renewed and strengthened the body for more important tasks before they could feel comfortable about engaging in sports. In addition, in New England and those areas later settled by New Englanders (mainly a tier of northern states extending westward to the Pacific) sports were for the most part more restrained than in the South.

SPORTING WAYS OF THE SOUTHERN COLONIES

A strikingly different world of sport emerged in the southern colonies.[16] Although the leaders of struggling early settlements sought to curb excessive behavior of all sorts, in the end the South developed a far less restrictive way of life than the North. One reason was religious. Southern sport did not have to contend with powerful Puritan or Quaker groups; the far more tolerant Church of England enjoyed a near-monopoly over the region's religious life. Until a religious revival (the Great Awakening) swept into the area the 1740s, southerners could normally express their emotions, drink, and gamble without incurring the wrath of the clergy. Neither did personal moral scruples preclude horse racing or blood sports. Indeed, southern sportsmen liked nothing better than to race horses, chase foxes, hunt stags, or fight cocks. Finally, southern sports reflected that region's greater disparities in wealth, its more rigid social stratification, and the great racial chasm separating whites and blacks.

Central to southern sporting life was the growth of a powerful landed gentry. Comprised mostly of the younger sons of eminent English families who had been unable to inherit their families' estates, a small group of men in Virginia (and later in other southern colonies as well) in the last half of the seventeenth century obtained huge land grants from the royal governor and used either the labor of indentured servants or African slaves to become great tobacco planters.

The great southern planters sought to imitate the lifestyle of the English country gentry. They built splendid mansions that often included special rooms for dancing and billiard playing; they ate with silver decorated with the family's coat of arms. They frequently sent their sons to England to acquire the culture, the tastes, and the skills of a "gentlemen." For example, upon returning to the family's estate in Virginia after having been educated in England, William Byrd II enthusiastically played all the games that he had encountered in the Mother Country. These included billiards, bowls, ninepins, skittles, and even a version of cricket.

As in Britain, certain sports separated the southern gentry from the lower social ranks. In Britain, stalking the stag was a sport of kings and noblemen; likewise in colonial Virginia, only the gentry, accompanied by much pomp and ceremony, hunted deer. Fox chasing was also a sport of the upper ranks. When the indigenous grey fox proved to be too elusive, Virginians imported red foxes from England. The much cited case of James Bullocke, a common tailor, provides striking evidence of how the gentry perceived certain sports as a privilege exclusive to their rank. In 1674 Bullocke entered his mare in a race against a horse owned by Dr. Matthew Slader, a "gentleman," for 2,000 pounds of tobacco. For such a presumption the county court fined Bullocke 200 pounds of tobacco and asserted that horse racing was "a sport for gentlemen only."[17]

No pastimes ignited the passions of the southern gentry more than horse racing and gambling. Wherever a few great planters gathered, someone nearly always produced a deck of cards, a backgammon board, or a pair of dice. They sometimes made extravagant and ruinous bets on dice, cards, cocks, or horses. Since gambling was restricted by law to men of property, it reinforced the South's system of social ranks. The gentry believed that the results of gambling provided clues to a man's fortune or standing in the cosmos. If one won, then the mysterious powers that governed the universe looked upon one favorably. The converse was true if one lost. Similar beliefs, though frequently unconscious, have linked gambling and sport in other cultures.

Until the mid-eighteenth century, horse racing was usually an impromptu affair. Young bloods might challenge one another to a race on Saturday afternoons, after church services, or on court days. Bets would be placed on the respective steeds, the owners would mount, a gun would be fired, and the horses would sprint down a quarter mile dirt track. "If you happened to be looking the other way," Thomas Anburey wrote, "the race is terminated before you can turn your head."[18] Virginians bred a special horse, the quarter horse, a particularly wiry animal with powerful hindquarters, for this kind of race.

In the last half of the eighteenth century, the great planters turned from the native quarter horse to the English thoroughbred. Thoroughbred racing tested "bottom," the ability to race over a mile or several miles rather than a quarter mile. In contrast to England, the colonial gentry apparently encouraged thoroughbred racing as a public spectacle. In England, the straightaway courses permitted exciting perspectives only in the vicinity of the finish line and only the upper strata attended the races. But the colonial gentry raced their horses on mile-long oval tracks, which afforded a good view to all the spectators. Men of all ranks attended the races.

After mid-eighteenth century, thoroughbred racing took on many of the qualities of modern sport. Horse owners formed jockey clubs in Maryland, Virginia, and South Carolina; the clubs built fenced tracks and charged admission. The clubs kept careful records of bloodlines and races and the participants began to don colorful apparel that separated them from one another. Under the gentry's tutelage, racing exceeded all other sports in popularity and in the degree to which it was organized, a position of eminence that it would continue to hold into the nineteenth century.

As T. H. Breen and Nancy Struna have demonstrated in separate essays, the planters' absorption in games and gambling held a wider meaning for southern society.[19] First, as previously suggested, displaying the emblems of higher rank helped men to achieve the social positions they sought. Sports nurtured a body of social conventions that set the gentry apart from the more boisterous games of the lower social ranks and the slaves. Although the great planters extolled reckless courage and physical prowess, in the eighteenth century they replaced brawling with more genteel forms of boxing or the potentially deadly duel. Properly fought duels embodied cool restraint rather than the uninhibited rough-and-tumble fighting of the lower ranks. Such conventions not only reinforced gentry values but may also have served as behavioral guides for nineteenth- and twentieth-century sporting elites.

Second, by promoting great public displays, such as horse racing, the planters helped convince subordinate groups that gentry life was something to be esteemed. By conceding the superiority of the gentry's lifestyle, the other members of the society were more likely to acquiesce to the gentry's control of the political and economic life of the colonies. Finally, sport was a ritual of manhood. Exhibitions of courage, recklessness, and defiance in sports attested to a man's worthiness. Indeed, full acceptance among his peers might require a man to engage in raucous sports.

The lower social ranks (excepting slaves) in the South also enjoyed a fuller sporting life than counterparts in the North. Although handicapped by the dispersal of settlers over the countryside and far less wealth than the great planters, the common white people attempted to re-create the festive culture that they had left behind in Britain. For example, the Hanover County Fair in Virginia, established in 1737, included a great feast accompanied by the music of drums, trumpets, and oboes. The fair sponsored contests with a wide variety of prizes: five pounds for a horse race, a hat for a cudgeling match, a violin for a fiddling contest, a quire of ballads to be sung for, a pair of silver buckles for a wrestling match, and "a pair of handsome silk stockings . . . [to] be given to the handsomest young country maid that appears in the field."[20] By arranging target, wrestling, running, and cudgeling contests as well as providing prizes, the southern gentry (as in Britain) frequently patronized the amusements of those lower in the social order. As Gordon Wood has observed, the clarity of social relationships in this era permitted a familiarity between social ranks that would surprise later generations.[21]

The common people in the southern colonies loved blood sports. Ganderpulling was a favorite. Usually staged on Easter Monday, a day of boisterous celebration in the Chesapeake Bay region, the neck of a goose was liberally greased and the hapless animal was hung by its feet from a rope stretched between two trees or tied to a tree limb. The contestants mounted their horses and as they galloped by at full speed they attempted to jerk the goose's head off. As a prize, the winner got the blood-soaked goose for his supper.

GANDERPULLING *A popular pastime in many parts of colonial America, ganderpulling reflected a pre-modern absence of concern about the suffering or fate of animals.*
(UPI/Corbis)

Men, both high and low, frequented the cockpits. One traveler's account described a cockpit as "surrounded by many genteel people, promiscuously mingled with the vulgar and the debased. Exceedingly beautiful cocks were produced, armed with long, sharp, steel-pointed gaffs." Men placed their bets. The cocks then went at each other furiously, "not the least disconcerted by the crowd or the shouting."[22] Even after having been pierced repeatedly by the gaffs, the cocks continued to fight as long as they were able to crawl. After the middle of the eighteenth century, cockfighting increasingly came under the patronage of the gentry. Then newspapers announced the greater matches, many of which were scheduled on major holidays.

In the South, as well as elsewhere in the colonies, the ubiquitous tavern, or "ordinary," served as an important site for pastimes. Scattered a few miles apart, the taverns offered food, drink, and sleeping quarters for weary travelers. Planters, merchants, artisans, and ordinary workingmen also gathered at taverns to discuss topics of mutual interest or to escape daily cares. Convivial drinking of tea, coffee, or light alcoholic beverages was an especially popular form of release.

Although most of the colonies had specific laws prohibiting certain kinds of "inn games," tavern patrons frequently combined games with wagering, drinking, and lively conversation. Taverns have "become the common . . . rendezvous of the very dregs of people," complained a Virginia clergyman in 1751, "where not only time and money are vainly and unprofitably squandered away, but (what is yet

SKITTLES *Skittles was a folk game initially played outdoors, usually next to colonial taverns. Modern ten-pin bowling had its origins in skittles and similar games.*
(Library of Congress)

worse) where prohibited and unlawful games, sports, and pastimes are used, followed and practiced almost without intermission, namely cards, dice, horse-racing, and cock-fighting, together with vices and enormities of every other kind."[23] The horrified clergyman might have added animalbaiting, skittles, and fights of various sorts to his list of popular tavern amusements. Close links between drinking establishments and sports continued into the nineteenth century and, albeit in different ways, persist to this day.

THE BACKCOUNTRY'S SPORTING WAYS

The southern backcountry, a vast region consisting originally of the mountains of Appalachia but in the nineteenth century extending west and south into the Mississippi Valley and the Ozark Plateau, developed yet another pattern of sport. Backcountry sport was a product of both the rugged frontier environment and the violent traditions of its predominately north Britain (northern English, Scots, and Scots-Irish) settlers.[24] For centuries north Britain had been racked by almost continuous warfare. Drawing upon this violent past and from the insecurities of backcountry life, the residents adhered to a warrior ethic. In particular, they nurtured in their male children ferocious fighting skills.

One form of combat was wrestling ("wrasslin" or "russlin" as it was commonly pronounced there). Wrestling required the burly contestants to begin by facing one another with their arms locked around each other's bodies and their chins tucked under their opponent's right shoulder. The wrestlers then maneuvered in crablike motions before suddenly striking quickly; a flurry of motion usually left one man thrown to the ground. When any part of the body of a wrestler other than his feet touched the ground, the bout ended.

Another form of backcountry combat, "rough-and-tumble" fighting, was far more savage. Rough-and-tumble fights usually began with bouts of drinking and bragging; an insult or a slight then led to a challenge. Spectators placed wagers on the respective fighters. No rules restrained the fight; consequently the combatants bit, scratched, kicked, and gouged out eyes. Around the beginning of the nineteenth century, "gouging" became the ultimate badge of success in rough-and-tumble fighting; according to Elliott Gorn, it was the equivalent of the knock-out punch in modern boxing.

While the incidence of rough-and-tumble fighting has been exaggerated by travelers' accounts and folklore, the practice was not an occasional oddity of backcountry life. Presiding over a court in South Carolina's backcountry, Judge Aedamus Burke recalled: "Before God . . . I never saw such a thing before in the world. There is a plaintiff with an eye out! A juror with an eye out! And two witnesses with an eye out!"[25]

Other backcountry sports prepared the competitors for warfare in far less brutal ways. Carnival-like festivities surrounded competitions in running, jumping, and leaping as well as throwing axes, sledges, long bullets, and spears. The young Andrew Jackson first gained prominence as a runner and leaper. (Later he achieved recognition for his fighting cocks and race horses as well.) Above all, backcountry people admired shooting skills. They acquired enduring reputations for their astonishing feats of marksmanship. The precise shooting of the "hunters from Kentucky" reputedly accounted for American success against the British at the Battle of New Orleans in 1815.

PASTIMES IN THE REVOLUTIONARY ERA

In the 1730s and 1740s, the Great Awakening, a revival of unprecedented proportions, swept through all of the colonies. If anything, the evangelicals, as the revival converts came to be known, were more suspicious of sport than the first Puritans. The evangelicals insisted upon a searing conversion experience and an absolute submission of the self to a demanding and an omnipotent God. After spiritual rebirth, the evangelicals embarked on crusades against the evils of the secular world. They demanded a complete purity in the church and in individual behavior.

Everywhere the evangelicals tried to suppress or at the least restrain the more boisterous sporting ways. Perhaps a typical instance occurred in 1739, when the Great Awakening's most renowned evangelist, George Whitefield, met with the governor, local ministers, and several gentlemen in Annapolis, Maryland. "Some of the company, I believe, thought I was too strict, and were very strenuous in defense of what they called innocent diversions," Whitefield reported, "but when I told them everything was sinful which was not done with a single eye to God's glory, and that such entertainment not only discovered [reflected] a levity of mind, but were contrary to the whole tenor of the Gospel of Christ, they seemed somewhat convinced."[26]

Throughout the balance of the eighteenth century and into the nineteenth century, evangelical Protestants continued to mount campaigns for the reform of leisure activities. In 1774, 35 years after Whitefield had lectured the Annapolis gentry on the evils of so-called innocent diversions, a Virginia planter explained the abiding effects of evangelicalism. "The Anabaptists [an evangelical group] in Louden County are growing very numerous and seem to be growing in afluence [influence?] . . . quite destroying pleasure in the country; for they encourage ardent pray'r; strong and constant faith & the entire banishment of gaming [gambling], dancing & Sabbath-day diversions."[27] In response to the assaults of the evangelicals, sportsmen throughout the colonies voiced similar complaints.

Republicanism, the fighting faith of the American Revolution (1775–1783), also tended to inhibit sports. The republicans believed that a successful republic— a state with sovereignty residing in the citizenry rather than a hereditary aristocracy or a monarchy—could *not* be founded upon the idle amusements of the decadent monarchies of Europe. For the American republic to survive and prosper, the citizens needed to be especially virtuous and abstemious; they had to abstain from luxury, practice frugality, and avoid dissipation.

Republicanism and evangelical Protestantism joined forces in encouraging the revolutionary governments to suppress popular pastimes. The First Continental Congress, meeting in 1774 when war with the Mother Country loomed on the horizon, resolved that the colonies "discountenance and discourage every species of extravagance and dissipation, especially all horse-racing, and all kinds of gaming, cock fighting, exhibition of shows, plays, and other expensive diversions and amusements."[28] Wherever they could, the Sons of Liberty, an extralegal citizens organization, tried to impose such strictures on the population for the duration of the Revolution. During the Revolution, all the States likewise adopted sumptuary laws designed to curtail personal extravagance. As Samuel Adams, both a product of Puritan New England and an ardent republican, put it, each state ought to strive to become a "Christian Sparta."

Thomas Jefferson, republicanism's leading champion, blamed the English gentry for the tendency of young American "gentlemen" to gamble, drink excessively, engage in riotous sports, and patronize prostitutes. If the young American "goes to England," Jefferson wrote, "he learns drinking, horse racing, and boxing." In addition, "he is led, by the strongest of human passions, into a spirit of female intrigue . . . or a passion for whores, destructive of his health, and both cases learns to consider fidelity to the marriage bed as an ungentlemanly practice."[29] In this letter Jefferson aptly spelled out a fundamental republican fear, namely that the indulgences of the European monarchies and upper classes threatened to spread like a cancer, destroying in the new nation the virtue and simplicity essential to the republic's existence. Nothing haunted the imaginations of the republicans more than an idle, pleasure-loving aristocracy.

In the end, the republican goal of abstemious behavior failed to achieve fulfillment. Even during the revolution, many ignored the demands for frugality and self-denial. General George Washington himself instructed his officers to encourage innocent "games of exercise for amusement" among the troops in the Continental Army. Soldiers bowled (sometimes using cannonballs) and played wicket (a form of cricket), shinny (a game similar to field hockey), fives (a form of handball), and football (the medieval version of the game). At the same time Washington directed his subordinates to suppress gambling, an order just as frequently ignored as obeyed.

Indeed, during the last half of the eighteenth century, America increasingly became an integral part of a larger "North Atlantic market" of commercial leisure. After mid-century itinerant theater troops from London began to stage plays in cities along the Atlantic coast from Boston to Charleston. As early as the 1750s English equestrians and acrobats regularly visited the colonies, including the "celebrated" Anthony Joseph Dugee, who performed "on a slack wire scarcely perceptible with and without the balance." During the last two decades of the eighteenth century, the incidence of cockfighting as well as other kinds of diversions apparently increased.[30] Instead of implanting a new respect for simplicity, frugality, selflessness, and order, as many of the Revolution's leaders had hoped for, the Revolution and its accompanying ideology fostered at least an equal amount of disorder and extravagance.

CONCLUSION

First played in provincial outposts of the British Empire and then in a new republic, American sports were the product of the interaction between the customs that the people brought with them and New World circumstances. The dispersion of the settlers, the need for hard work, and religious persuasions prevented the complete transfer of Britain's sporting ways to the colonies. In particular, Puritan and Quaker notions of "lawful sports" shaped leisure patterns in New England, New Jersey, and Pennsylvania. On the other hand, in the coastal South the creation of a more hierarchical society eventually resulted in a sporting life in many ways strikingly similar to Great Britain's. In the southern backcountry a heritage of violence brought from northern Britain and dangerous frontier conditions encouraged warlike sports. At most, the Great Awakening and the republicanism accompanying the American Revolution seem only to have temporarily dampened sporting enthusiasm. What no one could foresee at the end of the eighteenth century were the revolutionary changes—changes that would have far-reaching consequences for the history of American sports—that lay ahead.

NOTES

1. William Bradford, *Of Plymouth Plantation, 1620–1647* (New York: Alfred A. Knopf, 1952), 97. The most analytical treatment of sports in early Anglo-America is Nancy Struna, *People of Prowess: Sport, Leisure, and Labor in Early Anglo-America* (Urbana: University of Illinois Press, 1996).

2. See apart from Struna, *People of Prowess*, chap. 1, Richard Holt, *Sport and the British* (Oxford: Oxford University Press, 1989).

3. Quoted in W.U. Solberg, *Redeem the Time* (Cambridge, MA: Harvard University Press, 1977), 48.

4. Quoted in Holt, *Sport and the British*, 4.

5. Quoted in R.W. Malcolmson, *Popular Recreations in British Society, 1700–1850* (Cambridge: Cambridge University Press, 1975), 83.

6. Quoted in Hans-Peter Wagner, *Puritan Attitudes Towards Recreation in Early Seventeenth-Century New England* (Frankfurt am Main, Germany: Lang, 1982), 21–22.

7. Quoted in ibid., 7.

8. Quoted in John C. Miller, *The First Frontier* (New York: Dell, 1966), 87.

9. Wagner, *Puritan Attitudes*, 48; Perry Miller and T.H. Johnson, eds., *The Puritans*, 2 vols. (New York: Harper, 1963), I, 392. Apart from Struna, *People of Prowess*, see also Bruce C. Daniels, *Puritans at Play: Leisure and Recreation in Colonial New England* (New York: St. Martin's, 1995).

10. Quoted in David H. Fischer, *Albion's Seed: Four British Folkways in America* (New York: Oxford University Press, 1989), 148.

11. Wagner, *Puritan Attitudes*, 34; and A.B. Hart, *Commonwealth History of Massachusetts*, 5 vols. (New York: Historical Society, 1927–30), II, 280.

12. Wagner, *Puritan Attitudes*, 105–06; S.K. Knight, *The Journal of Madam Knight* (Boston: Massachusetts Historical Society, 1971), 20. See also H.T. Mook, "Training Days in New England," *New England Quarterly* 11 (1938), 687–97.

13. Quotations in Fischer, *Albion's Seed*, 552, 555. See J.T. Jable, "Pennsylvania's Blue Laws: A Quaker Experiment in the Suppression of Sport and Amusements," *Journal of Sport History* 1 (1974), 107–21.

14. See Stephen Brobeck, "Revolutionary Change in Colonial Philadelphia: The Brief Life of the Proprietary Gentry," *William and Mary Quarterly* 33 (1976), 410–34.

15. John Adams, *The Work of John Adams*, 5 vols. (Boston: Charles C. Little and James Brown, 1840), II, 125–26.

16. For recreation in the southern colonies, see T.H. Breen, "Horses and Gentlemen: The Cultural Significance of Gambling among the Gentry in Virginia," *William and Mary Quarterly* 34 (1977), 239–57; Struna, *People of Prowess*, chap. 5; Jane Carson, *Colonial Virginians at Play* (Williamsburg, VA: Colonial Williamsburg, 1965); and C.R. Barnett, "Recreational Patterns of the Colonial Virginia Aristocrat," *Journal of the West Virginia Historical Association* 2 (1978), 1–11. For the contrast between southern and northern life, see C. Van Woodward's classic essay, "The Southern Ethic in a Puritan World," in his *American Counterpoint* (Boston: Little, Brown, 1971).

17. Quoted in Breen, "Horses and Gentlemen," 250.

18. Quoted in Fischer, *Albion's Seed*, 361.

19. See note 16.

20. Quoted in Edmund S. Morgan, *Virginians at Home* (New York: Holt, Rinehart and Winston, 1962), 88.

21. Gordon S. Wood, *The Radicalism of the American Revolution* (New York: A.A. Knopf, 1991), 41.

22. Quoted in Rhys Isaac, *The Transformation of Virginia* (Chapel Hill: University of North Carolina Press, 1982), 102.

23. Quoted in Morgan, *Virginians at Home*, 87. See also Struna, *People of Prowess*, chap. 7.

24. See Elliott J. Gorn, " 'Gouge and Bite, Pull Hair and Scratch:' The Social Significance of Fighting in the Southern Backcountry," *American Historical Review* 90 (1985), 18–43; and Fischer, *Albion's Seed*, 735–40.

25. Quoted in Gorn, " 'Gouge and Bite,' " 33.

26. Quoted in Philip Greven, *The Protestant Temperament* (New York: A.A. Knopf, 1977), 145.

27. H.D. Farish, ed., *Journal & Letters of Philip Vickers Fithian*, (Williamsburg, VA: Colonial Williamsburg, 1943), 96.

28. H.S. Commager, ed., *Documents in American History*, 2 vols. (Englewood Cliffs, NJ: Prentice Hall, 1973), I, 86.

29. H.S. Commager, ed., *Living Ideas in America*, new ed. (New York: Harper & Row, 1964), 555–56.

30. See especially Struna, *People of Prowess*, chap. 8, and the data in Struna, "Gender and Sporting Practices in Early America, 1750–1810," *Journal of Sport History* 18 (1991), 13ff, as well as R.E. Powell, "Sport, Social Relations and Animal Husbandry: Early Cock-fighting in North America," *International Journal of Sport History* 5 (1993), 361–81.

2
THE SETTING FOR NINETEENTH-CENTURY SPORTS

*I*n the greater New York City area baseball excitement reached a fever pitch in 1858. That year an all-star Brooklyn nine met the New York all-stars in a two-best-of-three game series. At stake were bragging rights: Who produced the best ballplayers—Brooklyn or New York City?

The issue was to be resolved at the Fashion Race Course (a horse racing track with a stone grandstand) on Long Island. Despite a 50¢ admission charge, fans came to the first game in droves; 1,500 of them crowded into carriages, omnibuses, and the special trains of the Flushing Railroad. According to a press report, the spectators included "a galaxy of youth and beauty in female form, who . . . nerved the players to their task."[1] Perhaps female loveliness steeled the resolve of the New York nine the most, for they won the first game, 22–18. In the second game, Brooklyn evened the series, 29–8, but the New Yorkers captured the championship in the third contest, 29–18.

Elsewhere one could have witnessed a quite different kind of ballgame. For decades, boys had gathered for impromptu contests on empty city lots, town greens, or local cow pastures. The boys sometimes made a ball on the spot; one youngster might offer a woolen sock to be unraveled and wound around a cork or a bullet. The number of potential players and the available space rather than written rules might dictate the number of bases and the distance between them. There would be no umpire. The object of the pitcher was to throw a ball so that it could be hit by the batter. None but the players usually watched these contests, the results were rarely known outside that circle, and no one bothered to keep records.

The contrast between these two bat-and-ball games suggested the importance of both the old and the new in the history of nineteenth-century American sports.[2] Throughout the century, boys continued to play various informal bat-and-ball games as they had done in the past; indeed, even to this day, children engage in such games. Likewise, traditional amusements such as cockfighting, animal-baiting, and horse racing persisted. Yet, the all-star baseball series of 1858 reflected something decidedly new—the transformation of what had previously been exclusively a boys' game into an organized contest of men. Furthermore, the all-star series was only one among many signs of the growth in sports during the middle decades of the nineteenth century.

The purpose of this chapter is to examine the enormous changes in nineteenth-century American life that most directly affected sports. These included revolutions in communication and transportation, rising per capita incomes, and the rapid growth of cities. Simultaneously, radical changes in society and work undercut traditional sources of excitement, job satisfaction, and sense of belonging. These conditions plus the sporting ways of the past spawned the particular sporting forms of the nineteenth century.

Not all Americans looked favorably upon the new sporting ways. In the minds of many, especially those residing in the North, the Puritan and Quaker legacies of "lawful sports" as well as republican austerity lingered on. During the nineteenth century, these older suspicions of sport received an added impetus from converts to evangelical Protestantism and from those who were absorbed in the pursuit of wealth and respectability. Sometimes labeled collectively as "Victorian" and sometimes as a "new middle class," an assortment of industrious laborers, merchants, businessmen, and industrialists frowned on all "idle" amusements, including sport when engaged in for its own sake or when associated with uninhibited display, drinking, and gambling. Throughout much of the nineteenth century, the more ardent of the Victorians waged an unrelenting war against both traditional pastimes and the rapidly developing newer forms of organized sports.

CONQUERING SPACE AND TIME

During the nineteenth century, improvements in communication and transportation plus the growth of cities abetted the growth of sports.[3] Although American sports continued to have deep roots in rural life and in smaller towns, it was in the cities that sports grew most rapidly. Not only could people gather more easily in cities for playing and watching games, but news of sporting events could also be conveyed far more quickly than in the countryside. By preserving elements of the older, festive culture in a new urban setting, games helped to compensate for some of the impersonality and loneliness of modern life. By the end of the nineteenth century, sports teams and athletic heroes had become powerful urban symbols as well. Sports united heterogenous populations and deepened the emotional existences of cities. There, entrepreneurs quickly seized upon the opportunities to profit from sport.

Great waves of improvements in transportation likewise fostered the proliferation of sports. First was the steamboat, which after 1815 began to prove its value on western rivers and lakes. By 1860 more than a thousand paddle wheelers carried freight and passengers up and down the Mississippi River. For a time, as steamboat captains tried to demonstrate the superiority of their respective boats and their personal skills, steamboat racing itself was a sport, albeit a terribly dangerous one since overheated engines frequently exploded, killing passengers and crewmen alike. Steamers carried horses and fans to racing tracks, and they transported crowds to prizefight rings staked out alongside rivers away from the vigilance of local legal authorities. For example, in 1842, five steamers bore some 2,000 spectators to the New York Narrows to watch Yankee Sullivan vanquish Tom Secor.

Railroads soon supplanted steamers in importance. In 1830 travel from Detroit to New York had taken at least two weeks; by 1857 the trip required only an overnight train ride. By tying nearly every hamlet in the nation into a giant transportation grid, railroads sharply reduced the importance of space and time to the growth of sports. As early as 1842, the Long Island Railroad reportedly carried some 30,000 passengers to the Fashion-Peytona horse race. The infant sport of baseball especially benefited from the railway system. In the summer of 1860, the Excelsiors of Brooklyn toured upper New York State by rail and then made their way south to Philadelphia and Baltimore. Only a rapidly expanding railway network permitted the founding of the National League of professional baseball in 1876, which included franchises as spatially far-flung as Boston and St. Louis. Major league teams continued to travel by train until the 1950s when trains were replaced by air travel.

Equally rapid improvements in communication encouraged the sporting revolution. The mass production of watches in the early nineteenth century permitted the scheduling and advertising in advance the precise starting times for sporting events. To learn the results of contests instantly, fans turned to the newly invented telegraph. In 1867, for example, Philadelphians, "some of them venerable in years," jammed the telegraph and newspaper offices to find out if their beloved Athletics had crushed the Unions of Morrisania, New Jersey, in a baseball match.

Two kinds of print media stimulated public interest in sports: the regular daily newspaper and the weekly specialized sheet devoted to covering all aspects of nineteenth-century leisure life. At first aimed specifically at the wealthy who sought to ape the upper-class pastimes of the English gentry, the weeklies carried news of the theater, odd happenings, and sporting contests. Modeled upon *Bell's Life in London*, William Trotter Porter's *Spirit of the Times*, a weekly which began publication in 1831, was for a time the nation's premier sporting sheet; by 1856 it claimed to have 40,000 subscribers scattered across the nation. Unpaid, largely untutored authors sent in reports to Porter of sports, games, and curiosities.

In the last half of the century, other specialized sporting sheets appeared. The *New York Clipper* (1853) and the *Sporting News* (1886) popularized baseball while Henry Kyle Fox's *National Police Gazette* (1845), which gaudily covered all forms of entertainment, became the nation's widest-selling weekly. Most sporting sheets appeared briefly and sporadically, but their sheer numbers increased from 3 in the 1840s to 48 in the 1890s. That nearly all of the weeklies devoted more space to the theater than to sports suggests the close connections between all forms of nineteenth-century commercial leisure.

Rising literacy rates, along with new printing technology, broadened the potential market for sporting journalism. A new kind of daily that cost merely a penny first appeared in the 1830s; papers like the Boston *Transcript*, the *Baltimore Sun*, and, above all, the *New York Herald* of James Gordon Bennett ignored Victorian proprieties to report crime, gossip, scandals, and sports. When Fashion met Peytonia in an 1842 horse race, the *Herald* sent eight reporters to cover the event. As interest in sport increased sharply in the 1850s, the dailies provided additional coverage, but it was not until the 1880s that newspapers recognized the value of continuous sports reporting. In the 1880s and 1890s, the great circulation wars between the dailies, especially in New York City, encouraged "yellow journalism," the sensational reporting of crime and sports. Yet, most daily papers did not set aside a regular section for sports until the 1920s.

THE RISE OF MIDDLE-CLASS VICTORIAN CULTURE

The new technology helped to overcome the obstacles presented by space and time to the rapid growth of nineteenth-century sports. But, in the development of a powerful new middle-class culture, sportsmen confronted an equal, or perhaps an even more, formidable challenge.[4] (This culture is also sometimes labeled *Victorian* or *bourgeois*, thereby implying that the middle classes throughout the Western World shared a common set of values, attitudes, and behaviors.) Evangelical Protestantism and above all a rapidly growing economy contributed to the formation of the nineteenth-century's middle class. Occupationally, the class included successful farmers, merchants, professionals, independent artisans or craftsmen, and small manufacturers. Many of them were self-made men who resided in the northern half of the country. They urged upon the nation a new moral discipline, a regimen particularly antithetical to commercial sport.

Soaring material aspirations encouraged the middle-class or Victorian virtues of self-restraint and hard work. While the typical colonist had little reason to believe that the future would be very different from the past, many in the nineteenth century came to expect a better standard of living and improved status for themselves and their children. The opening of vast new territories in the West, the construction of a national system of transportation, and the sudden growth in agriculture, commerce, and industry fed material hopes. Alexis de Tocqueville, the perceptive French aristocrat who visited the United States in 1831 to 1832, was astonished. "We are most certainly in another world here," he exclaimed. "Political passions are only on the surface. The profound passion, the only one which profoundly stirs the human heart, the passion of all days, is the acquisition of riches."[5] Those who were caught up in the frenzied pursuit of material gain recognized that the ceaseless practice of such traditional Protestant virtues as self-control, frugality, and hard work might aid their cause. The marketplace, they further believed, would automatically reward moral fitness while punishing those weak in moral character.

Victorian culture received an additional transfusion of energy and ardor from evangelical Protestantism. Building on the first Great Awakening of the eighteenth century, great revivals (sometimes collectively called the Second Great Awakening) swept the country at the beginning of the nineteenth century, the decades of the 1820s, 1830s, and 1840s, and again in 1857. Between 1800 and the Civil War, the number of evangelical churches grew twice as fast as the population; membership in the Methodist and Baptist denominations shot far ahead of the more moderate Anglicans (called Episcopalians after the Revolutionary War) and the Congregationalists (originally the Puritans), the leading churches of the colonial era. Since evangelical Protestants controlled most of the pulpits, voluntary societies, newspapers and magazines, and public school rooms, their influence extended everywhere—into small towns, the countryside, the cities, and even into the traditionally more relaxed South.

Whether driven mainly by religious convictions, the quest for wealth, fears of social unrest, or a combination of these motives, the middle class frowned on impulsive behavior. Philip Schaff, a visiting theologian from Europe, explained that the ideal American "holds his passion in check; is master of his sensual nature; obeys natural laws, not under pressure from without, but from inward impulse, cheerfully and joyfully."[6] Victorian moralists tried to instill in each individual an internal set of values. Ideally, an interior moral gyroscope would guide each person through the bewildering changes that were transforming American society.

A particular lifestyle and a reputation for personal character furnished a rationale for the accumulation of wealth and set one apart from the less reputable classes. Thus the growing middle class carefully cultivated good personal manners, dressed conservatively, and reined in impulses to talk loudly or laugh uproariously. Self-control included sex. While sharpening gender differences, Victorians prescribed an ideology of sexual restraint and repression in which men were asked to curb their natural passions while proper women were assumed to lack sexual desire. Although a gap existed between official ideology and actual sexual behavior, the middle class succeeded in limiting family size. In particular, during the nineteenth century the birth rate of Northern middle-class urban families fell sharply.

Adherents of the new moral discipline assigned special responsibilities to women.[7] Increasingly relieved by the Industrial Revolution from tasks associated with the older household economy, Victorians urged women to retreat to a special, separate sphere—the home. Presumed to be more delicate and sensitive than men, women were expected to cultivate compassion, gentleness, piety, and benevolence. Serving as models of propriety and acting in quiet ways, women were asked to exercise a large but unobtrusive influence over the community. Women assumed the main responsibility for the moral nurture of children and for restraining the impulsive tendencies of men. Men, on the other hand, occupied the public sphere; they worked outside the home and were supposed to be the visible leaders of the community. Until late in the nineteenth century, proper manliness for Victorians entailed hard work, good moral character, and self-control rather than virility, toughness, or aggression.

"RATIONAL" RECREATION AND MUSCULAR CHRISTIANITY

Middle-class Victorians recognized that by and large organized sports in the nineteenth century represented an oppositional culture that potentially challenged their hegemony over much of American life. Sports typically encouraged impulsiveness; a group of drinking, wagering, and shouting men watching a battle of cocks or a prizefight hardly squared with middle-class notions of propriety and self-restraint. Furthermore, sport was virtually the antithesis of work. Victorians valued work while they loathed idleness and viewed the idler with utter contempt. Finally, some of the more religious were inclined to accept the ancient belief that the mortification of the flesh enhanced one's spirituality; that which produced pleasurable physical sensations, including participation in sports, should thus be viewed with suspicion if not avoided entirely.

To promote what they called "rational recreation," those leisure activities that refreshed the mind and body for more serious endeavors, the middle class retreated from the public to the more private sphere of family, close friends, and of solitary activity. There, they avoided the rowdiness so frequently associated with public forms of recreation while enjoying in the security of their homes the increasing availability of inexpensive books, newspapers, periodicals, sheet music, musical instruments, and more exotic foods. For intimate social gatherings, the ubiquitous parlor served as a bastion of middle-class propriety and respectability. Consistent with the idea of the home as a special refuge and moral training ground, women became the main providers of middle-class leisure. Outside the home, middle-class men and women created respectable semipublic or public arenas of spare time activities. These consisted of fraternal groups for men, church societies for women, and temperance organizations for both sexes.

Rational recreation included the possibility of a program of vigorous physical exercises (not including competitive sports).[8] Some even thought that exercise might offset the evil attractions of the day's growing commercial amusements. For example, Frederick W. Sawyer, in *A Plea for Amusements* (1847), proposed supervised gymnastics as a substitute for theaters, circuses, dance halls, saloons, brothels, and sports. Every town and city in the nation, Sawyer wrote, should establish "athletic institutes" which would be devoted to exercises. We should "see to it," added Sawyer, "that we have enough healthy sources of recreation to empty the gambling rooms, the tippling shops, and the brothels."[9] Like the Puritans, Victorians also argued that one needed recreation in order to strengthen one's body for serious duties such as work.

Several of New England's antebellum intellectuals even drew invidious comparisons between the alleged robustness of Englishmen and the frailty of their fellow Americans. "I am satisfied that such a set of . . . stiff-jointed, soft-muscled, paste-complexioned youth as we [Americans] can boast in our Atlantic cities never before sprang from the loins of Anglo-Saxon lineage," declared physician, Oliver Wendell Holmes Sr. in 1858.[10] By espousing a life of greater physical strenuosity, Holmes provided an implicit rationale for schoolboys who wanted to participate in such fast-growing sports as football and baseball.

In the 1850s the argument for physical robustness received reinforcement from a tiny but growing band of muscular Christians. Influenced by the English writers Thomas Hughes and Charles Kingsley, American physicians, clerics, and essayists, joined by many newspaper editors, launched a crusade to reverse the popular impression that physical vigor and spirituality were incompatible. The tireless American champion of muscular moralism, Thomas Wentworth Higginson, recalling the classical Greek ideal, asked for a symmetrical life that gave equal attention to physical and spiritual growth. "Physical health," Higginson said, was "a necessary condition of all permanent success."[11] In linking personal success to a strenuous boyhood, Higginson introduced what would become a major motif in advice-to-boys books after the Civil War.

While Victorian reformers endorsed physical exercises as consistent with proper spirituality and as an antidote to commercial amusements and frail bodies, in practical terms during the antebellum era they enjoyed modest success. An effort to introduce German gymnastics into New England schools in the 1820s and 1830s, for example, failed to take permanent root. Most educators believed that the schools should be concerned solely with the intellectual and moral development of their charges, though the students themselves frequently engaged in informal sports.

The advocacy of regular calisthenics for young women by such reformers as Catharine Beecher also won limited support. Constricted by an 18-inch corseted waist, "a sea of petticoats," and a floor-length dress, the ideal woman, according to mid-nineteenth century novels, magazines, and thousands of lithographs, was pale and fragile. Consistent with this ideal, American women, wrote an English visitor in 1855, regarded "anyone who proposed vigorous exercise as a madman." Even walking was "suited only to such females as are compelled by necessity to labor for their bodily sustenance," wrote another observer.[12]

After the Civil War, the situation slowly but perceptibly changed. Increasing numbers of middle-class Victorians shifted their stance from unmitigated hostility to nearly all forms of competitive sports to support of physical contests for boys and young men, but *only* when governed by the spirit of amateurism and played under controlled conditions. With a decline in religious intensity and a rising concern about the "effeminacy" of American males, the call for a "vigorous, robust, muscular Christianity . . . devoid of all the etcetera of creed" began to resonate more powerfully through middle-class life. Competitive athletics, especially the sport of football, might nurture among boys and men much-needed primitive, aggressive, indeed, even martial virtues; they might not only strengthen the body but also safeguard men against the allurements of luxury and vice. In short, by the end of the nineteenth century, previously suspicious Protestant, Victorian, middle-class Americans were beginning to attribute large potential moral benefits to athletics (including moderate sports for women) when guided and controlled by the ethos of amateurism.[13]

AN OPPOSITIONAL CULTURE

Victorian culture never achieved a complete dominance over American life. Indeed, from the outset of the nineteenth century, there were substantial numbers of Americans who continued to adhere to their traditional ways. They frequently placed a higher value on play, sensual gratification, gusto, spontaneity, and display than on hard work, self-control, and punctuality. They sought to gain greater personal satisfaction, excitement, and a sense of belonging from their leisure activities rather than from their work. As members of what may be called an oppositional culture or a Victorian counterculture, their amusements often consisted of talking, drinking, gambling, and commercial spectacles, activities tied directly to preindustrial, preurban patterns of life.[14]

Broadly speaking, two major social groups comprised this oppositional culture. They were what the Victorians called "the unproductive rabble" from below and "the dissolute aristocracy" from above. In the European sense, the United States had no aristocracy of inherited privileges, but it did have wealthy landholders and merchants who remained unconverted to the middle-class ethos of self-restraint. Although they were never quite as successful in resisting Victorian hegemony as their English counterparts, the Americans sought to imitate the English gentry by preserving earlier pastimes, especially in the field sports and horse racing. Hedonistic sons of the elite, like their English complements, also engaged in sports slumming—participation in the low sports of the common people.

In addition, in the latter half of the nineteenth century, a group of new enriched men, the parvenu, became especially conspicuous for their presence and involvement in various sorts of commercial leisure. Other wealthy men in the postbellum era restricted their sports to socially exclusive clubs; many of them had only passing if any association with the oppositional culture (see Chapter 5).

Apart from the simple desire to preserve traditional forms of leisure, new conditions of work encouraged opposition to Victorian culture by those at the bottom of the social order. At the beginning of the century, most goods had been made in the small shops of independent artisans. Customers simply asked an artisan to fashion a pair of shoes or a chair according to their special wishes. Using skills passed down through many generations, the typical artisan was in effect simultaneously both a small manufacturer and a tradesman. Completely responsible for the final product, artisans frequently took a fierce pride in the quality of their work.

Although the factory system did not suddenly or completely annihilate the handicraft mode of production, the long-term trend away from small shops was unmistakable. Master artisans with foresight and capital enlarged their work forces, employed more machinery, and broke down the work into simpler tasks. The resulting work required fewer skills. The roles of employer and employee were more sharply separated. Masters, journeymen, and apprentices no longer worked side-by-side nor were their relationships any longer governed by long-established customs of mutual obligations and rights. The factory substituted a rigid discipline for more casual work patterns of the past. No longer did young apprentices or journeymen live in the household of the master artisan; increasing numbers lived in boarding houses.

The work place of white-collar workers, especially clerks, likewise underwent radical changes. In the first quarter of the nineteenth century, working as a clerk was in effect a training period for those sons of the upper classes who aspired to become business or professional men. Employed in thousands of small offices, they acted in multiple capacities; for instance, they served as copyists of correspondence and business documents, bookkeepers, and collectors of invoices and receipts. The typical clerk had opportunities to learn all aspects of the business. With only two or three clerks per office, he had frequent and intense personal interactions with his employer.

By mid-century, this system of apprenticeship-clerking had begun to falter. The rapid growth of the economy resulted in the expansion of the size of business and manufacturing concerns, and consequently the need for thousands of additional clerks. To meet the demand, businesses recruited clerks from the ranks of the educated classes in both the countryside and the city. At the same time business firms began to reorganize their offices; they subdivided the work of clerks. Rather than serving as jacks-of-all trades, clerks were employed for specific tasks such as copyists, bookkeepers, or simply retail sales personnel. With little or no opportunity for advancement, clerking for the overwhelming majority of young men became a dead-end job. The division of labor into simpler tasks and the introduction of the typewriter in the 1880s eventually resulted in the replacement of many male clerks by young female office workers.

Substantial numbers, perhaps a majority, of the workers accepted the values of their Victorian employers. White-collar workers in particular sought to get ahead by working hard, restraining their emotions, and practicing frugality. "Bank clerks, young merchants, [and] mercantile aspirants," observed *Harper's Weekly* in 1859, "all seem to think [that] time devoted to any exercise wasted, and the model clerk him who drudges six days every week at his desk without an hour of physical labor."[15] Finding less satisfaction in work than in the past, other workers, especially blue-collar workingmen, turned to the pleasures and associations offered by the adversaries of Victorian culture. For them, leisure activities frequently provided more excitement, fulfillment, and a sense of belonging than their work did.

Bachelors, whether employed as manual workers, skilled artisans, clerks, or whether businessmen or industrialist, were more likely to spurn Victorian values than were married men. From both the countryside and Europe more men than women swarmed into the growing cities. At mid-century, nearly 40 percent of the men between the ages of 25 and 35 were unmarried, a figure much higher than today. Bachelors, along with many married, working-class males, spent most of their leisure time with other males. Members of this bachelor subculture sought sensual gratification, friendship, and a sense of community in saloons, brothels, gambling halls, billiard rooms, cockpits, boxing rings, and race tracks. If and when bachelors found wives and succeeded in entering the middle class, they frequently left behind them the leisure ways of the oppositional culture. They then became proper middle-class Victorians.

Abraham Lincoln's early life in frontier Illinois illuminates the complex interstices of bachelorhood, tradition, and sports. Unlike many bachelors, Lincoln did not drink; indeed, his abstemious personal habits suggest that even as a young man he was well on his way to becoming a middle-class Victorian. Nonetheless, as a young unmarried man, Lincoln relished, according to the reminiscences of one of his close friends, "out door recreations & sports, and excelled at them." Especially popular in Lincoln's Illinois were backcountry sports, sports brought there by the numerous southerners who had migrated to the state from Appalachia. As a newcomer to Salem, Illinois, Lincoln had to prove his mettle by defeating a local tough in a no-holds-barred wrestling match. According to a report of the match, "all the men of the village and quite a number from the surrounding country were assembled."[16] Famed as a rail splitter, the six-feet-four-inch (eight inches taller than the average of his contemporaries) Lincoln liked to exhibit his extraordinary strength by lifting two axes by the end of their handles and raising them, elbows locked, straight over his head. Lincoln's reputation among the men of frontier Illinois for manliness, fearlessness, and athleticism in time abetted his political aspirations.

Immigrants gave added support to the oppositional culture. Each newly arrived ethnic group from the peasant societies of Europe frequently brought with them attitudes toward time-thrift, self-control, and temperance at odds with Victorian America. The new ethnics, along with many old-stock workingmen, were slow to acquiesce to the regimen of the new economy; they tried to preserve traditional holidays, preindustrial work habits, and "grog" privileges, the right to drink light alcoholic beverages during the workday.

A high percentage of bachelors, delayed marriages, rigorous norms of premarital chastity, and traditions of segregation by sex made all-male groups particularly important to Irish Americans. Whether married or unmarried, a male's standing within the larger Irish community often rested on his active participation in the bachelor subculture. Thus many of the "bachelors" were actually married men who spent nearly all their leisure time with other males. Gathering in saloons to drink, gossip, tell stories, and engage in business or political transactions, adult bachelors conducted the rites of passage for countless Irish youths. They promoted a gay, carefree life; they placed a high value on success in fighting, physical prowess, and sports.

The oppositional culture also included a southern component. Many men in the South resisted the strictures imposed on them by the sweeping successes of evangelical Protestantism in the nineteenth century. Revolving around feminine-dominated homes and churches, the evangelicals sought to restrain such traditional Southern and backcountry masculine vices as drinking, fighting, gambling, and swearing. Men, on the other hand, continued to place a high value on self-assertiveness, personal honor, and physical competitiveness. As in the past, they hunted, drank, fought, gambled, raced horses, and fought cocks. In the last half of the nineteenth century they also took up baseball with alacrity. Sparks flew when the male and the evangelical cultures came into contact, creating, in the words of Ted Ownby, "guilt and inner conflict in many Southerners who tried to balance the two."[17]

ENCLAVES OF THE OPPOSITIONAL CULTURE

Within the cities, the oppositional culture developed special enclaves or meeting places. In terms of the Victorian outsiders' face-to-face relationships, perhaps no formal association equaled the importance of the volunteer fire departments. In the nineteenth century, ethnics (especially the Irish), artisans, clerks, and petty shopkeepers formed literally hundreds of volunteer companies. When a fire call went out, the men instantly dropped their work (sometimes to the chagrin of their employers), donned brightly hued shirts, and rushed to beat competing companies to the blaze. In fire companies, the lusty men found all-male companionship, a sense of personal worth, an arena for the expression of manliness, and the excitement of team competition.

Drinking and gambling were equally important pleasures of the working class, ethnics, and bachelors (many were, of course, all three of these at once). Although gambling was roundly condemned by Victorians and illegal in many places, coffee houses, billiard parlors, saloons, and livery stables frequently harbored gambling establishments. Many of the nineteenth-century sporting spectacles arose from spirited arguments over the merits of a horse, a prizefighter, or a wrestler. Spectators wagered on all the spectacles, including many of the earliest baseball matches.

Few experiences equaled the intensity of a bet. For spectator, promoter, and athlete alike, winning a bet might be far more important than the thrill of winning itself. In wagering, one risked not only money, but also one's self-esteem. By choosing to bet on a particular team or individual athlete, the bettor might make a statement of ethnic or occupational pride as well. Successful wagering offered an occasion to display skills for men who increasingly found such opportunities denied in their workplaces. Indeed, one might suddenly earn large amounts of money quickly with a minimum of physical exertion. Winning a bet might also signify a favorable dispensation from the fates.

Unlike proper Victorians who advocated moderation in all things, many of those in the oppositional culture found solace drinking alcoholic beverages. They drank to escape from the trials of daily living and to promote fraternal goodwill. The focal point of drinking was the saloon. Saloons varied in the richness of their decor and the wealth of their clientele, but in many, workingmen could communally enjoy some upper-class comforts. By mid-century, the more elegant saloons had brilliantly lighted windows flanked by wicker doors that swung open easily. Inside a patron might see variegated lampshades, frescoed ceilings, a gilded bar with a glittering mirror behind it, and paintings of famous race horses, prizefighters, and voluptuous, scantily clad women.

Saloons served as ideal retreats for sportsmen. An advertisement of William Clark summarized some of the social attractions of a major metropolitan saloon: "Ales, wines, liquors, segars, and refreshments. All the sporting news of the day to be learned here, where files of the *Clipper*, and other sporting papers are kept. Here also may be seen numberless portraits of English and American pugilists." In addition, Clark's saloon offered "a room of other facilities . . . at all times in readiness for giving lessons in sparring under the supervision of the proprietor. Drop in, and take a peep."[18] Saloonkeepers frequently arranged dog fights, ratbaitings, cockfights, and prizefights. Pugilists and their backers invariably worked out of saloons. Saloons served as pool rooms; keepers posted the odds on horse races and, after mid-century, on baseball matches. In the latter half of the century, saloons sometimes had telegraph hookups so they could post the latest sporting results instantly.

A WORKING-CLASS SALOON This working-class western saloon, located in Abie, Nebraska, sports Fourth of July decorations. Notice the absence of women. Until well into the twentieth century, saloons served as a major rendezvous for the sporting fraternity.
(Nebraska State Historical Society)

By the 1850s, in New York City and other larger cities, both workingmen and upper-class slummers could gather at special halls that featured a regular fare of low sports. Of several of these places in New York, the best-known in the 1860s was Kit Burns's Sportsman Hall. Shaped as an amphitheater, the hall could seat up to 400 spectators. Apart from watching and wagering on how long it would take a dog to kill a pit full of rats, the patron might pay a quarter to see "Jack the Rat" decapitate a rat or a dime to witness him bite off the head of a mouse. Frederick Van Wyck, of a distinguished Knickerbocker family, suggested that patronizing such events served as a "rite of passage" for certain youth of the upper social ranks. At Tommy Norris's livery stable, he reported seeing a ratting, a cockfight, a goatfight, and a sparring match between two women who were nude above the waist. "Certainly for a lad of 17, such as I," reported Van Wyck, "a night with Tommy Norris and his attraction was quite a night."[19]

As the women fighters witnessed by Van Wyck suggests, there was a tiny complement of women in the nineteenth century whose lives revolved within and on the margins of the Victorian counterculture. Frequently of working-class and/or recent ethnic origins, many of them were prostitutes. Others worked in the commercial amusement business as actresses, athletes, or circus acrobats. There were even a few women professional runners and ballplayers. By brazenly participating in physical competition and parading their bodies in public, such women violated every Victorian standard of feminine propriety.[20]

RATTING PIT The spectators of ratting normally wagered on how long it would take a dog to kill a pit full of rats. Ratting, along with cockfighting, ganderpulling, and bear- and bullbaiting, was an ancient blood sport that survived within the nineteenth-century Victorian counterculture.
(Library of Congress)

NINETEENTH-CENTURY SPORTING GROUPS

In terms of nineteenth-century sports, the "sporting fraternity," or "fancy," as they were hailed, was an especially important component of the larger oppositional or Victorian counterculture. Although never a formal organization, the term "fraternity" implied shared values and interests, a special solidarity, and a surrogate brotherhood. In the promotion and viewing of sports as well as in such associated activities as drinking, gambling, and talking, the fraternity consummated some of the same intensely shared experiences and sense of belonging that existed ideally among blood brothers. As within a family, the fraternity developed its own set of special understandings, its own argot, its own acceptable behaviors, and its own concept of honor. The fraternity drew its membership from within the larger Victorian demimonde—hedonists in the upper class, workingmen, ethnics, bachelors, and those, like saloonkeepers, who sought to profit from the Victorian underworld. What distinguished them from others within the oppositional culture was their special interest in sports.

The sporting fraternity extended to both sides of the Atlantic. The English contingent of the fraternity, having organized commercial sporting spectacles earlier than the Americans, exercised an especially large influence. Americans conducted their horse races in strict accordance with the rules of Newmarket, their prizefights by the London prize-ring rules, and copied the latest London modes of wagering on contests. England furnished much of the sporting equipment in the antebellum era; many of the sporting books, magazines, and prints came from England. All the American sporting sheets gave extensive coverage to the news from Great Britain. By the 1820s, a bevy of professional English and Irish athletes regularly visited the United States to demonstrate their skills and compete for stakes. Soon American athletes reciprocated by visting English shores. While Americans had declared their political independence in 1776, they continued long afterward to rely heavily upon Britain for cultural guidance.

Whether in Britain or the United States, the sporting fraternity acted within a network of associations opposed to mainstream middle-class Victorian culture. The early "base ball fraternity," on the other hand, sought to win the support of Victorian America. Comprised of young clerks, artisans, and petty businessmen, the ballplaying fraternity tried to reassure Victorians of their game's propriety. A ballplayer "must be sober and temperate," reported *Porter's Spirit of the Times* in 1857. "Patience, fortitude, self-denial, order, obedience, and good-humor, with an unruffled temper, are indispensable. . . . Such a game . . . teaches a love of order, discipline, and fair play."[21] No one could have coined a more satisfactory list of Victorian virtues.

Yet not until the twentieth century did ballplaying achieve complete success in winning middle-class support. Mostly young and living away from family influences, the early ballplayers frequently ignored the austerities of Victorian life. In 1858, *Porter's Spirit*, the same sporting sheet that a year earlier had identified baseball with Victorian values, noted that a marked feature of postgame celebrations was "the indulgence of a prurient taste for indecent anecdotes and songs—

a taste only to be gratified at the expense of true dignity and self-respect." After the Civil War, as the sport became more commercialized, wagering on ballgames became more common. Circus master P. T. Barnum went so far as to say that "Idleness, Base-Ball and Billiards" had caused the economic panic of 1873.[22]

A third world of sport, one separate from both the sporting and baseball fraternities, developed mainly after the Civil War (see Chapter 5). Central to this universe of sport were ethnic and elite subcommunities. As part of their efforts to construct such communities, both ethnic groups and wealthy Americans formed hundreds of clubs. In some of the clubs, sports were largely incidental to other activities while still others made sports their major focus.

CONCLUSION

The nineteenth century witnessed momentous changes in the nation's economy, society, and culture. It was a century of industrialization, rapid population growth, immigration, urbanization, geographic expansion, and the greatest armed conflict on American soil. It produced a new cultural system, a set of beliefs, attitudes, and techniques that can be summed up as middle-class Victorian. Likewise, it spawned an oppositional culture. It is within this context that the following four chapters examine the history of nineteenth-century American sports.

NOTES

1. Quoted in Harold Seymour, *Baseball*, 2 vols. (New York: Oxford University Press, 1960, 1971), I, 25.

2. An emphasis on "modernization" informs Allen Guttmann's global work, *From Ritual to Record: The Nature of Modern Sports* (New York: Columbia University Press, 1978), and his *A Whole New Ball Game: An Interpretation of American Sports* (Chapel Hill: University of North Carolina Press, 1988). Melvin L. Adelman's *A Sporting Time: New York City and the Rise of Modern Athletics, 1820–70* (Urbana: University of Illinois Press, 1986) is a premier study of the application of modernization theory to a specific city while Dale A. Somers, *The Rise of Sports in New Orleans, 1850–1900* (Baton Rouge: Louisiana State University Press, 1972); Stephen Hardy, *How Boston Played* (Boston: Northeastern University Press, 1982); Steven A. Riess, *City Games* (Urbana: University of Illinois Press, 1989); and Gerald R. Gems, *Windy City Wars: Labor, Leisure, and Sport in the Making of Chicago* (Lanham, MD: Scarecrow, 1997) stress the role of the city more generally in comprehending the rise of sports. For analyses that emphasize the rise of sport in

terms of a contested territory between social groups, see especially Elliott J. Gorn, *The Manly Art* (Ithaca, NY: Cornell University Press, 1986); Scott C. Martin, *Killing Time: Leisure and Culture in Southwestern Pennsylvania, 1800–1850* (Pittsburgh: University of Pittsburgh Press, 1995); and S. W. Pope, *Patriotic Games* (New York: Oxford University Press, 1997).

3. Apart from the works cited in note 2, see J.R. Betts, "The Technological Revolution and the Rise of Sports, 1850–1900," *Mississippi Valley Historical Review* 40 (1953), 231–56, and Betts, "Sporting Journalism in 19th Century America," *American Quarterly* 5 (1953), 39–56.

4. The literature relevant to middle-class Victorian culture is enormous, but one may begin with David W. Howe, ed., *Victorian America* (Philadelphia: University of Pennsylvania Press, 1976); William L. Barney, *The Passage of the Republic* (Lexington, MA: D.C. Heath, 1987); Benjamin G. Rader, *American Ways: A Brief History of American Cultures* (Fort Worth: Harcourt College Publishers, 2001), chaps. 4–6; and especially Burton J. Bledstein and Robert D. Johnston, *The Middling Sorts: Explorations in the History of the*

American Middle Class (New York: Routledge, 2001).

5. Alexis de Tocqueville, *Democracy in America*, 2 vols. (New York: Vintage Books, 1951), I, 51.

6. Quoted in Lewis Perry, *Intellectual Life in America* (Chicago: University of Chicago Press, 1989), 230.

7. See especially Linda K. Kerber, "Separate Spheres, Female Worlds, Women's Place: The Rhetoric of Women's History," *Journal of American History* 75 (1988), 9–39, and for the growing body of gender literature as it relates to sport, Patricia A. Vertinsky, "Gender Relations, Women's History and Sport History: A Decade of Changing Enquiry, 1983–1993," *Journal of Sport History* 21 (1994), 1–24.

8. See Adelman, *Sporting Time*, 269–89 for the development of an ideology of sport by the New York City press, and, 362n for citations of other works treating the Victorian quest for rational recreation. Apart from Adelman, see especially J.C. Whorton, *Crusaders for Fitness* (Princeton, NJ: Princeton University Press, 1982; Harvey Green, *Fit for America* (New York: Pantheon, 1986); Roberta J. Park, "A Decade of the Body: Researching and Writing about the History of Health, Fitness, Exercise and Sport, 1983–1993," *Journal of Sport History* 21 (1994), 59–82; and Martin, *Killing Time*, Chaps. 5–7.

9. Quoted in Hardy, *How Boston Played*, 50.

10. O.W. Holmes, "The Autocrat at the Breakfast Table," *Atlantic Monthly* 1 (1858), 881.

11. T.W. Higginson, "Saints and their Bodies," *Atlantic Monthly* 1 (1858), 585–86.

12. Quoted in Lois Banner, *American Beauty* (New York: Knopf, 1983), 54. On the other hand, within the oppositional culture there were examples of physically active women. See Allen Guttmann, *Women's Sports* (New York: Columbia University Press, 1991), 96–98. Guttmann argues that these women apparently appealed to many Victorian men as well.

13. For quote, see E. Anthony Rotundo, *American Manhood* (New York: Basic Books, 1993), 86. 224. See also Clifford Putney, *Muscular Christianity: Manhood and Sports in Protestant America, 1880–1920* (Cambridge, MA: Harvard University Press, 2001); Mark Dyreson, "The Emergence of Consumer Culture and the Transformation of Physical Culture: American Sport in the 1920s," *Journal of Sport History* 16 (1989), 261–81; and Pope, *Patriotic Games*, chaps. 2–3.

14. See especially Morse Pecham, "Victorian Counterculture," *Victorian Studies* 18 (1975), 257–76; Gorn, *The Manly Art*; and R. B. Stott, *Workers in the Metropolis: Class, Ethnicity, and Youth in Antebellum New York City* (Ithaca, NY: Cornell University Press, 1990), chaps. 8–9.

15. *Harper's Weekly* 3 (October 15, 1859), 658.

16. Quotations from Kenneth J. Winkle, *The Young Eagle: The Rise of Abraham Lincoln* (Dallas: Taylor Trade Publishing, 2001), 64.

17. Ted Ownby, *Subduing Satan: Religion, Recreation, and Manhood in the Rural South, 1865–1920* (Chapel Hill: University of North Carolina Press, 1990), 68. See also Scott C. Martin, "Don Quixote and Leatherstocking: Hunting, Class and Masculinity in the American South, 1800–40," *International Journal of the History of Sport* 12 (1995), 61–79, and Patrick Miller, ed., *The Sporting World of the Modern South* (Urbana: University of Illinois Press, 2002), intro.

18. Quoted in John R. Betts, *America's Sporting Heritage* (Reading, MA: Addison-Wesley, 1974), 162.

19. Quoted in Adelman, *Sporting Time*, 242.

20. See especially Guttmann, *Women's Sports*, 96–105.

21. *Porter's Spirit of the Times* 2 (May 30, 1857), 10.

22. Quotations from *Porter's Spirit of the Times* 5 (October 9, 1858), 84; and Bryan D. Palmer, *A Culture of Conflict* (Montreal: Queens University Press, 1979), 26.

3
THE SPORTING FRATERNITY AND ITS SPECTACLES

What no one could have foreseen a few decades earlier was the remarkably sudden growth in American sports in the 1840s and 1850s.[1] While rural people continued to pursue traditional pastimes, the sudden takeoff of sports was mostly an urban phenomenon. Thousands of spectators gathered at tracks in virtually every state of the union to watch pedestrian (foot) races; equal numbers thronged the nation's harbor, lake, and river banks to see boat races. Although a championship prizefight (being illegal everywhere and hastily scheduled at unpredetermined sites) attracted at most 2,000 spectators, literally tens of thousands heard oral accounts or read about them in newspapers. While prior to 1845 no record exists of an organized baseball club in the nation, within 15 years several hundred clubs had been formed, and more than 10,000 boys and young men played in club matches.

Two cultural groupings, each described by contemporaries as "fraternities," were of critical importance to the sporting takeoff of the 1840s and 1850s. One was popularly known as the sporting fraternity and the other as the ballplaying fraternity. Members of the informal ballplaying fraternity organized voluntary associations, or clubs, for the playing of baseball and cricket. The baseball club members wrote and revised the rules of play, appointed officials, scheduled matches, and in 1858 formed a national association.

The second group was the sporting fraternity (or "the fancy"). The sporting fraternity scheduled and promoted sporting spectacles, those events that attracted crowds and public attention. From the spectacles, the fraternity frequently sought monetary gain; money might be made by winning wagers, selling liquor at events, or charging gate fees. By winning side bets and competing for stakes—a sum set aside for the winner by the promoters—athletes could also receive financial rewards for their feats. But sporting spectacles could mean far more than money to nineteenth-century men. The fraternity and its spectacles also offered opportunities for male comradery and shared excitement, as well as a refuge from femininity, domesticity, and the demanding routines of the new economy.

JOHN COX STEVENS: WEALTHY PATRON OF ANTEBELLUM SPORTING SPECTACLES

No single individual illuminates more fully the complex relationship between upper-class sportsmen, the sporting fraternity, and antebellum sporting spectacles than John Cox Stevens (1785–1857).[2] Heir to a steamboat fortune, Stevens at one time or another patronized, promoted, and wagered on horse, pedestrian (foot), and yacht racing; he also opened a large amusement park and furnished the playing grounds for some of the nation's first baseball matches. Like a substantial number of the landed and mercantile wealthy, Stevens cultivated an aristocratic lifestyle that was far more extravagant and expressive than the simplicity demanded by the republicans of the Revolutionary era but not as colossally ostentatious as that of the post-Civil War parvenus. Typical of many antebellum sports patrons, Stevens maintained a certain social distance between himself and the more ordinary sporting fancy. He never patronized prizefighting, for example, and, though he loved the theater, he did not associate with theater people.

JOHN COX STEVENS A wealthy New Yorker with a passion for horse racing and yachting, Stevens was probably the nation's premier antebellum patron of sports.
(Library of Congress)

Stevens's first passion was horse racing. During the Revolutionary era, horse racing had suffered a setback; indeed, fired by republican zeal, most of the states had banned the sport. But, in the 1820s and the 1830s wealthy landed and mercantile sportsmen led a nationwide turf revival. Regular racing circuits developed; the sheer number of thoroughbred races grew from 56 in 1830 to 130 in 1839. New sporting journals, in particular John Stuart Skinner's *American Turf Register and Sporting Magazine* (1829) and William T. Porter's *Spirit of the Times* (1831), helped plan the annual racing schedule, arrange for the payment of bets, fix rules of entry, and standardize handicaps. In a bid for respectability and to offset charges of corruption and chicanery, turf enthusiasts sometimes sought to discourage attendance at the track by ruffians and professional gamblers. They also argued speciously that the breeding and racing of thoroughbred horses improved the quality of horses for other kinds of work.[3]

In the 1820s Stevens established himself as the North's premier horseman. From his stables in Hoboken, Stevens raced horses frequently in New Jersey and New York and for 22 consecutive years he served as either the president or vice-president of the New York Jockey Club. In the "race of the century" held at the Union Course on Long Island in 1823, Stevens and one of his brothers were so certain of victory that, according to a likely apocryphal legend, "after their purses were exhausted, they took their watches from their pockets and diamond breastpins from their bosoms, and bet them on the result."[4] Fortunately for Stevens, American Eclipse, a northern horse, bested Sir Henry from the South in two of three four-mile heats. From 50 to 100,000 fans watched the exciting race. In partnership with his in-laws from the "aristocratic" Livingston family, Stevens purchased American Eclipse for $10,000 and Sir Henry for $3,000 and put them out for stud at his Hoboken stables. In the 1830s Stevens sold his stable. The sale was timely, for in 1837 a severe economic downturn nearly destroyed the turf.

In 1831 Stevens added to the family's reputation as patrons of amusements. Along with his brother, he set up a large park, the Elysian Fields, on the family's waterfront estate in Hoboken. According to diarist Philip Hone, two hundred "gentlemen" including New York's mayor and aldermen and members of the New York and Jersey City boat clubs, who were outfitted "in white jackets and trousers, round ship's hats, and checked shirts," attended the grand opening. They shared gourmet food and "abundant champagne."[5] Conveniently located across the river from New York City, the Elysian Fields (a place of perfect happiness in classical mythology) at one time or another served as the home of the New York Yacht Club, the St. George Cricket Club, the playing area of the New York Athletic club, and grounds for some of the nation's first organized baseball matches.

In establishing the Elysian Fields, nurturing the turf, and sponsoring pedestrianism, John Cox Stevens displayed a typical range of interests for a wealthy antebellum sportsman. These pastimes tied Stevens to the larger sporting fraternity. But his involvement in yachting was another matter. That he became New York's leading yachtsman clearly separated him from the more popular pastimes of the larger Victorian counterculture. Indeed, the New York Yacht Club, a creation of Stevens in 1844, served to sharply separate the city's upper strata from the more ordinary people.

Membership in the New York Yacht Club signified one's acceptance in the highest rungs of New York society. "A succession of gentlemen ranking high in the social and financial circles" of the city soon joined the club, wrote Charles Peverelly in 1866.[6] Stevens erected a handsome gothic clubhouse at the Elysian Fields; there the club held resplendent balls and festive dinners (with turtle as the favorite dish). The club took regular social cruises to Bar Harbor, Maine, Cape Hattaras, North Carolina, and other idyllic spots. In the postbellum era, the club's annual regatta at Newport became *the* social event of the summer season.

Yachting strengthened the bonds between upper-class American and British sportsmen. In 1851, Stevens organized a syndicate to build a special boat for the express purpose of challenging British yachtsmen to a race. Stevens' yacht, *America,* easily defeated 18 British yachts in a race around the Isle of Wight to win a coveted cup donated by the Royal Yacht Squadron. Queen Victoria visited the *America,* and congratulated the Yankees on their sterling performance. *America's* success encouraged the formation of other socially exclusive yachting clubs in cities along the Eastern seaboard. In 1857 the syndicate that owned *America* presented the cup to the New York Yacht Club on the condition that it should be contested for by yachtsmen from abroad. Since its inception, American yachts have won all but two of the matches for the coveted cup.

PEDESTRIANISM, ROWING, AND BILLIARDS

Ranking far below yachting in respectability was professional footracing, or pedestrianism. As early as the 1820s, a few sportsmen, taking their cues from England, had advanced small purses for both long-distance runners and walkers. John Cox Stevens shocked the sporting fancy in 1835 by offering a $1,000 purse to any pedestrian who could run ten miles in less than one hour; if only one ped accomplished the feat he would receive an additional $300.

Stevens's "Great Race" generated almost as much excitement as earlier horse races. At least 20,000 fans watched an international field of peds compete at the Union Race track. Patrick Mahoney, a butcher from County Kerry, Ireland, who was dressed in a green shirt with black slippers, set a torrid pace for the first five miles; five of the nine peds reached the halfway mark in less than a half-hour. But, to the delight of the spectators, Henry Stannard, a farmer from Connecticut who wore black pantaloons, pulled away from the others to finish in 59 minutes and 48 seconds. Stannard promptly mounted a horse, rode around the track to the cheers of the spectators, and made a short victory speech.[7]

The interest aroused by the Great Race of 1835, nationalistic rivalries with Britain, and the opportunities offered for wagering all catapulted footracing into one of the most popular sporting spectacles of the antebellum era. In 1844 a series of spectacular long-distance races at the Beacon Course in Hoboken attracted attention throughout the English-speaking world. Thirty-seven famed peds competed in the second race, including three from England, three from Ireland, and John Steeprock, a Seneca Indian. The victory by John Gildersleeve, a

New York chairbuilder, stoked the fires of white American ethnocentrism. "It was a trial of the Indian against the white man, on the point in which the red man boasts his superiority," reported an American newspaper. "It was a trial of the peculiar American *physique* against the long held supremacy of the English endurance."[8] Unfortunately for this interpretation, English peds proceeded to win the next three races at Hoboken.

"During the next ten to fifteen years," noted a contemporary observer, "there were more athletes competing and more races than ever before. People in virtually every state in the union attended professional footraces."[9] Promoters devised an ingenious variety of races. Peds ran sprints, hurdles, long distances, against times, and even against horses (with the human given a head start). Betting, drinking, and cursing, as well as occasional violence, accompanied the ped races. It was little wonder that proper Victorians loathed the sport.

Pedestrianism continued to enjoy some popularity after the Civil War. The 26-day walk of Edward P. Weston from Portland, Maine, to Chicago in 1867 for a purse of $1,000 spawned a short revival of long-distance walking races. In the

DEERFOOT, A FAMED SENECA PEDESTRIAN, 1835 The commercial spectacle of pedestrianism attracted Native Americans, African Americans, and assorted ethnic groups. A sport carried on outside the perimeters of Victorian respectability, the peds ran for prize money and the spectators wagered on the outcome.
(Library of Congress)

1870s, long-distance races, known as "go-as-you-please" races, drew large crowds, especially in New York City. In the go-as-you-please races, the peds attempted to cover as many miles as they could on an indoor track within a set time, usually six days. In six days they sometimes walked more than 500 miles.

As early as the colonial era, workers in rivers and harbors along the Eastern seaboard sometimes competed in rowing. A race on the Hudson River in 1824 pitting rowers from a British frigate against the Whitehall boatmen from New York City for a stake of $1,000 attracted between 20,000 and 50,000 spectators. In the 1830s a boating mania virtually swept the country. "The beauty and fashion of the city were there," according to a newspaper account of a regatta in Louisville on July 4, 1839, "ladies and gentlemen, loafers and laborers, white folks and 'niggers' . . . and all the paraphernalia of city life . . . formed the constituent parts of the heterogeneous mass that stood jammed and crowded upon the levee."[10]

Rowing developed along both professional and amateur lines. In 1834 New York City amateur clubs, composed of wealthy "young men of fashion," formed the Castle Garden Amateur Boat Club Association. The association expressly forbade "any club to row for money, or take part in a Regatta or Races with any club or clubs independent of those belonging to the Association." The association's annual regatta, "attended by the city's elites," Melvin Adelman has concluded, "was as much a display of fashion as it was a display of skill. Each club appeared with its distinct colors and uniforms, and every year the Wave Club, the best crew and quite possibly the wealthiest, came with a new boat constructed by Clarkson Crotus, the leading builder of the day."[11] Yet, enthusiasm for rowing among the city's upper class was short-lived. In 1842 the Castle Garden Association scheduled its last regatta.

In the mid-1850s professional oarsmen led a rowing revival. Beginning in 1854 Boston held annual regattas that featured challenge matches between the Irish longshoremen and the "Beacon Street swells." In the late 1850s in New York City, throngs estimated at 10,000 and more witnessed the annual professional regattas. In the East an informal professional racing circuit of sorts developed. The rowing fever spread to inland cities—to Pittsburgh, Chicago, Milwaukee, St. Louis, and Louisville. Like the pedestrians, professional scullers often published challenges in the newspapers. After the Civil War, amateur rowing, anchored this time in both private clubs and the nation's colleges, eventually supplanted professional rowing in popularity.

In the antebellum era, billiards developed a dual character. One form sprang from the "rich and the well-born," the other from the Victorian counterculture.[12] Only "gentlemen" of means played the polite version found in private residences or in exclusive men's clubs. Unattached males, workingmen, ethnics, and slummers, on the other hand, frequented the public parlors as well as saloons that had installed billiard tables. Inexpensive to play and proffering opportunities for gambling, male companionship, and displays of skill, billiards was an integral part of sporting fraternity life.

In the 1850s, Michael Phelan, billiards's "dominant personality and promoter in America," attempted to popularize and improve the image of the sport.

Nationwide attention focused on the first billiard "championship" of the United States held in 1859 at Fireman's Hall in Detroit. The two contestants, Michael Phelan and John Seereiter, allegedly played before a "genteel audience," which included several ladies. The terms of the match involved unusually large sums of money, a $5,000 side bet plus $5,000 to the winner from the promoters plus a portion of the gate receipts. Play began at 7:30 P.M. and lasted until five o'clock the next morning. Seereiter had the longest run, but Phelan won the match and walked away with a reported sum of $15,000. Author of several books on billiards, Phelan remained the sport's premier promoter until his death in 1871.

THE EARLY HISTORY OF AMERICAN PRIZEFIGHTING

As with all the other popular antebellum spectacles, American bare-knuckle prizefighting had close ties to Great Britain. In the late eighteenth century, Americans began to hear and read about the feats of English champions, but they inspired little immediate enthusiasm for fighting in the new republic. At the turn of the century, according to prize-ring lore, Tom Molineaux, a Maryland- or Virginia-born slave, won his freedom by defeating a fellow slave. Upon release from bondage, Molineaux eventually surfaced in New York City where he apparently fought a few surreptitious bouts for money. American newspapers gave Molineaux only passing mention in 1811 when he was bested in London (in a rematch) by the reigning English champion, Tom Crib.

In the 1820s and 1830s a small pugilistic fraternity began to emerge in the United States. Comprised mostly of gamblers, saloon operators, and hustlers, the fraternity welcomed both English and Irish boxers to American shores. As would be the case later, these earliest fight promoters capitalized upon ethnic rivalries. In the same era, English and Irish "professors of pugilism" offered (without many takers) sparring lessons to the nation's upper classes.

During the 1840s and 1850s, prizefighting may have been the nation's "single most important spectator sport."[13] By the mid-1850s, reports of scores of fights appeared in the newspapers; in New York City, the capital of pugilism, the papers carried accounts of three or four local sparring matches each week. A series of sensational championship bouts—Tom Hyer vs. Yankee Sullivan (1849), Yankee Sullivan vs. John Morrissey (1853), John Morrissey vs. John C. Heenan (1857), and John C. Heenan vs. Tom Sayers (1860)—captivated millions. Consequently the 1850s became known in ring history as the "Age of Heroes."

No antebellum fighter exceeded the popularity of John "Old Smoke" Morrissey. Born in Ireland, he had come to America as a three-year-old lad with his impoverished family. Morrissey combined fighting, gambling, and politics to ascend to fame and fortune. He first acquired a reputation as a brutal street brawler. In 1853 he defeated Yankee Sullivan for the unofficial American championship and four years later bested John C. Heenan, another Irishman.

Morrissey then retired from the ring and devoted his enormous energies to gambling and politics. Out of the earnings of his first fight he established a gaming house in New York that by 1860 had become city's most celebrated parlor. Within five years he had acquired an interest in at least five other gambling halls and was the largest single shareholder in a million-dollar annual lottery business. He also built the first horse race track (in 1864) and in 1867 established a lavish gambling parlor and restaurant in Saratoga, New York. Morrissey helped to transform Saratoga from a fashionable spa into America's version of Monte Carlo. He hobnobbed with some of New York's parvenu, but it was his popularity among workingmen that led to his triumphs in politics. Before his death in 1878, he had served two terms in the U.S. House of Representatives. Morrissey's feats like Benjamin Franklin's (though Franklin's were of a strikingly different sort) confirmed the American gospel of success.

After Morrissey's retirement from fighting, John C. Heenan assumed the championship mantle. In 1860, Heenan met Tom Sayers, the English champion, in a bout outside London. On both sides of the Atlantic, the Heenan-Sayers bout excited far more interest than had any prior fight. It attracted people of all sorts; members of the English aristocracy joined the riffraff in watching the two-hour bloodbath. In the seventh round, Sayers pulled a muscle in his right arm but continued to stage a masterful defense. Finally, with both fighters bloody and exhausted, the crowd out of control, and the constables about to stop the bout, the referee called the match a draw. In the United States, interest in the fight overshadowed news about the sectional conflict that would soon culminate in the Civil War. For the moment, the fight may even have deflected the nation's deep internal divisions. Even respectable Victorians saw the bout as an opportunity to once again twist the British lion's tail, and citizens in both nations identified their respective fighters with national virility.

MEANINGS OF PRIZEFIGHTING

As exemplified by the career of Morrissey and the Heenan-Sayers fight, pugilism mirrored larger nineteenth-century cultural conflicts. In particular, prizefighting reflected ethnic divisions. For example, in the 1850s American-born and Irish-born workers clashed on many fronts. The Irish were mostly Roman Catholics; the native-born Americans were mostly Protestant. Experiencing a decline in their status and a loss of autonomy in their work, native workers saw in foreigners scapegoats for their plight. Competition for jobs and political power further kindled ethnic hostilities. Prizefights dramatized these rivalries. The Irish, English, and old-stock American-born fighters represented their respective ethno-religious groups in symbolic contests for supremacy and honor.

Second, pugilism manifestly mocked Victorian values, especially the cardinal virtue of self-restraint. The prevailing rules permitted a battle just short of unregulated combat. Under the Broughton (1743) and London (1838) prize-ring rules, fighters fought with their bare fists; wrestling skills and brute strength were more important than finesse in boxing. A round ended only when a man was struck down by an opponent's fists, thrown to the turf with a wrestling hold, or deliberately fell to the ground to avoid further punishment. Once downed, a fighter had 30 seconds to recover before "toeing the mark," or "coming to scratch," terms that referred to a line drawn through the center of the ring. A fight ended only when a fighter was unable to come to scratch or conceded defeat. Under these rules fights could be savagely brutal, even fatal. In 1842, Thomas McCoy and Chistopher Lilly pummeled one another for 2 hours and 40 minutes before McCoy, drowning in his own blood, fell dead.

Unrestrained behavior often accompanied fights. Since fights in the antebellum era were illegal everywhere, the fancy scheduled them in remote places—backrooms of saloons, on barges, or in remote rural spots. They had to be ever watchful for the legal authorities. The fights attracted the roughest elements in American society—pickpockets, hustlers of various sorts, drunks, and bullies. Traditional ethnic animosities and abundant liquor added to the volatile mix. Those who sensed that their bets were in jeopardy or those who felt that their favorite had been treated unfairly sometimes joined the fray, not only swinging their fists or trying to wrestle their foes to the ground but also by flashing Bowie knives or brandishing pistols.

The ring inverted Victorian ideals about money and success. For Victorians, the accumulation of money validated years of hard work and self-sacrifice by its possessor. The gambler and the prizefighter, on the other hand, might earn hundreds of dollars by simply winning a single bet or bout; such a solitary stroke of success openly mocked such Victorian virtues as frugality and persistence. Rather than as evidence of good character, the pugilistic fraternity valued money as a means for enjoying the moment and the conviviality of their fellows. To some prizefighting, saloonkeeping, and gambling, among other pursuits, were also highly valued alternative avenues to success. To succeed in the world of commercial entertainment carried as much—indeed, sometimes more—esteem within the sporting fraternity than success achieved in other sectors of the economy.

The entrepreneurial opportunities offered by the ring as well as other forms of nineteenth-century commercial entertainment especially attracted those Americans of Irish descent. Enjoying English as their native tongue, less encumbered by Victorian inhibitions, and finding opportunities frequently blocked in the more "respectable" occupations, many Irish naturally turned to careers that satisfied the urban hunger for gambling, drink, and sport. Such pursuits required little education and could produce quick rewards in a society that placed a high value on material success.

Working-class Irish males held fighting ability in the highest esteem. Indeed, survival in the slums for a boy could depend as much on his skills in using his fists as on his intelligence. Fighting was a common means of settling disputes and maintaining one's standing among fellow juveniles. Street fighting prepared youths for careers as pugilists, criminals, policemen, or even politicians. (In antebellum New York City, local political factions employed "shoulder hitters" to intimidate rivals on election day. Prizefighters were among the ranks of the shoulder hitters.) When a youth became a successful prizefighter, he served as a role model for others. Throughout the nineteenth and into the early twentieth century, Irish boxers dominated the ring but were replaced by Jews in the 1920s, Italians in the 1930s, and blacks and Latin Americans in the 1940s. The prize ring perfectly reflected the order of ascent for ethnic groups from the urban ghettos.[14]

Likewise, ring supporters valued a conception of manliness at odds with the Victorians. To Victorians, the ideal man labored diligently, kept a tight rein on his impulses, and supported family life. But the changing role of the home from a productive economic unit (the household economy) to a domestic-feminine enclave and the radical changes in the nineteenth-century work places undermined traditional opportunities for proving manhood. Workingmen might demonstrate their heterosexual virility by patronizing prostitutes, but they more often confirmed their manliness in the company of other men. In gender-segregated leisure activities, they exhibited toughness, physical prowess, and generosity. To these men, the prizefighter, with his immense strength, muscular body, and swift, decisive answers, represented an appealing alternative to the effeminate, self-effacing Victorian ideal of manhood.

PRIZEFIGHTING IN THE POSTBELLUM ERA

Although the Civil War (1861–1865) brought to a close the Age of Heroes—the era that produced Yankee Sullivan, John Morrissey, and John C. Heenan—it may have increased public interest in the ring as well as in other sports. By bringing together massive numbers of young men in military units, the war replicated conditions similar to those that existed among the young workingmen and clerks in the cities. Seeking to escape boredom and establish an identity in an all-male milieu, the soldiers frequently turned to baseball, running, wrestling, shooting matches, and boxing. They eagerly subscribed to the purses needed to stage in-camp matches between boxers-turned-soldiers. At least two reported instances of troops temporarily laying down their weapons to enjoy pugilistic encounters between their Union and Confederate comrades suggested the possibility of substituting nonlethal, individual combat for the carnage of actual warfare.

Yet the popularity of boxing among soldiers failed to arrest a general decline in the ring during the 1860s and 1870s. Externally, the prizefight game suffered from the increased vigilance of legal authorities. In New York City, the center of postbellum boxing, the fancy could no longer take it for granted that they would be shielded from the law by local politicians. Internally, charges of fixes and failures of boxers to fight aggressively shattered the sporting fraternity's confidence in the integrity of the ring. Even so-called championships sometimes turned into farces. For example, in 1871, before the bout was interrupted by authorities, Jem Mace and Joe Coburn "fought" for an hour and 17 minutes without landing a single blow.

In the 1880s several circumstances joined to usher in a new era of prizefighting. One was Richard Kyle Fox, publisher and editor of the *National Police Gazette*. Printed on shockingly pink paper and distributed at discount rates to such all-male sanctuaries as barbershops, livery stables, private men's clubs, and volunteer fire departments, the notorious weekly *Gazette* exploited to the fullest the nation's racial bigotry, secret sexual lusts, and thirst for the sensational. "If not workplace democracy," concludes Elliott Gorn, "the ethos of the *Police Gazette* offered white working males a democracy of pleasure denied by Victorian culture."[15] Fox featured engravings of show girls in tights, printed stories of scandals and atrocities, ran advertisements for contraceptives, and promoted bizarre contests. The *Gazette* awarded belts and other prizes for winners of championships in (among others) prizefighting, weight lifting, and one-legged clog dancing.

Fox's favorite sport was pugilism. With little success, he plead for the legalization of prizefighting. By launching a campaign to unseat John L. Sullivan as heavyweight king and by randomly awarding belts and naming champions in different weight divisions, Fox attracted national attention to boxing and even brought a modicum of order to the intrinsically chaotic sport.

Key metropolitan saloons supplemented Fox's efforts to promote prizefighting. In the 1870s and 1880s one of the most important was Harry Hill's saloon, located on notorious Bleeker Street in New York City. Described by a reformer as "the last resort of a low class of prostitutes, and the ruffians and idlers who support the prize ring," politicians, wealthy slummers, gamblers, show people, and pugilists all made Hill's their headquarters. "If you were anybody at all in New York night life in the seventies and eighties," wrote a contemporary, "you got into Harry Hill's as often as possible. Here boxing and wrestling were held and articles were signed for bigger matches elsewhere, shows were cast, [and] large bets were made."[16] In the early 1880s William Muldoon, the most renowned Greco-Roman wrestler of the day, and John L. Sullivan, the prizefighting champion, both worked out of Hill's saloon. Harry Hill himself was the best-known and most-esteemed stakeholder and boxing referee in the country. Though usually less lavish, saloons in other cities served the sporting fraternity in a similar fashion.

Athletic clubs, whether comprised of the wealthy or composed specifically of fight promoters, also contributed to the new era of the ring. A growing interest in boxing among the membership of the elite athletic clubs, especially in New York, New Orleans, and San Francisco, improved the image of the fight game. Within the confines of the exclusive athletic clubs, young men of high social standing took sparring lessons from "professors of pugilism." The New York Athletic Club, for example, hired Mike Donovan, the middleweight champion, to teach "gentlemen eminent in science, literature, art, social and commercial life" the finer principles of the "manly art."[17] The New York club also scheduled the first national amateur boxing championships. Sometimes the wealthy slummers from the athletic clubs joined in an uneasy alliance with ethnic political leaders in campaigns to modify state laws or city ordinances that banned prizefighting.[18]

The entrance of athletic clubs into boxing also altered the nature of the sport. The clubs encouraged fighting for a specified number of rounds, though round limitations did not become a universal practice until the 1920s. The clubs joined Richard Kyle Fox in promoting weight divisions; by the mid-1880s, Fox was naming national champions, often with shadowy claims, for six distinct weight divisions. Finally, by bringing the matches indoors, charging admission, and offering specific purses to the winners, the clubs altered the traditional mode of fight promotion.

The clubs prompted the growing acceptance of the Marquis of Queensberry rules. Drafted under the patronage of the English marquis in 1865, the rules required the use of gloves, limited rounds to three minutes, provided for ten-second knockouts, and prohibited wrestling holds. The use of gloves gave boxing the appearance of curbing brutality, thereby making the sport more acceptable. Yet the new rules may, as Elliott Gorn has argued, have made the sport even more brutal, since gloves protected the bones in the hands from breaking (thus permitting the fighter to hit harder with impunity) and added weight to each punch. The banning of wrestling holds, the ten-second knockout rule, and the imposition of round limitations encouraged a faster-paced, more commercially appealing spectacle. A major breakthrough in the use of the Queensberry rules came in 1890 when New Orleans legalized gloved fights when sponsored by athletic clubs. The new ordinance paved the way for the first gloved championship bout between John L. Sullivan and James J. Corbett in 1892.

ENTER JOHN L. SULLIVAN

Into the new era of prizefighting stepped a new champion heavyweight whose contribution to boxing may have exceeded that of Fox, the saloons, the athletic clubs, and the use of the Queensberry rules. Born in Boston to Irish immigrant parents, John L. Sullivan achieved a celebrity status perhaps unequaled by any other public figure of his time.[19] After trying his hand at the various manual jobs available to an Irish youth in the 1870s, he discovered his talent for boxing. In exhibition matches in Boston theaters and music halls he soon developed a reputation as a slugger, and, with a knockout in 1882, he won the championship.

The public adored Sullivan. Shortly after winning the title, he began the first of several nationwide tours in which he offered the astonishing sum (for that day) of $1,000 to anyone who could stand up to him for four rounds. Reportedly only one person performed the feat; scores of others succumbed to Sullivan's mighty blows. Sullivan used gloves in these exhibitions, thereby both saving his hands from damage and adhering to local ordinances against bare-knuckle fighting. When no local hero stepped forward for punishment (as frequently was the case), Sullivan sparred with a member of his own traveling troupe, which typically included other boxers as well as wrestlers, clowns, and jugglers. The tour, Sullivan's love of fighting, and his flamboyant lifestyle raised the "Boston Strong Boy" to the pinnacle of national popularity.

In the meantime, Sullivan continued to defend his title. Between 1884 and 1886 he added 14 official victories to his record, and Fox launched a worldwide search to find a worthy challenger. Sullivan avoided only the black boxers, one of whom (Peter Jackson) might have sent him to defeat. In the late 1880s Sullivan's fortunes turned sour; he suffered from alcoholism and poor health, and, while on a European sojourn in 1888, fought the English champion, Charlie Mitchell, to an

JOHN L. SULLIVAN Sullivan, perhaps the nation's first truly national sports hero, was the heavyweight champion prizefighter between 1882 and 1892. An Irish American, he was particularly a hero of immigrant working-class Americans. (Madison Square Garden, L.P.)

embarrassing draw. The next year Sullivan met Jake Kilrain in the last bout of the bare-knuckle era. Whipped into tip-top shape for the match by wrestler-trainer William Muldoon, Sullivan dueled Kilrain under the blazing sun in Richburg, Mississippi, for 75 rounds before Kilrain's seconds finally threw in the sponge. During the bout, Sullivan's backers reportedly fortified him with copious drafts of tea mixed with whiskey. In the forty-fifth round, Sullivan began to heave up the concoction, leading one wag to claim that the champion's stomach "rejected the tea but held the whiskey."

Public interest in the bout knew few bounds. "Never, during even a Presidential election, has there been so much excitement as there is here now," concluded the *New York Times*.[20] Exhilaration mounted even higher in 1892 when Sullivan defended his title against James J. Corbett in New Orleans. Having relapsed into his old ways of drinking and eating too much and handicapped by age, Sullivan put on a poor show. In the twenty-first round Corbett "shot his right across the jaw and Sullivan fell like an ox."[21]

The Sullivan-Corbett match marked a series of important "firsts" in the history of prizefighting. Locked in circulation wars with one another, major daily newspapers switched from their usual condemnation to open support of the ring. Rather than signing the articles for the fight in a saloon or in the offices of the *National Police Gazette,* representatives of the two boxers met in the offices of Joseph Pulitzer's *New York World.* As a heavyweight championship bout, the fight was the first to be held indoors under electric lights, to use gloves, to employ the Marquis of Queensberry rules, and to be sponsored by an athletic club. Corbett himself lent a new aura of respectability to the ring. Although of Irish extraction, Corbett had not fought his way up from the streets; he had attended college, held a white-collar job as a bank clerk, and learned his boxing skills in an elite athletic club; hence, the sobriquet "Gentleman Jim." These departures reflected boxing's transition away from its folk, countercultural origins to a form of mass, commercial entertainment.

Sullivan was probably the first truly national sports hero. His climb to fame fulfilled the mythology of rugged American individualism and the gospel of self-help. Without the advantages of superior birth or sponsorship, he fought his own way to the top of the savage world of boxing. Although he was a special hero of working-class, Irish American males, his success in a sport that was becoming the ultimate symbolic test of masculinity won the admiration of many Victorians. "In 1892 I was reading aloud the news to my father," William Lyon Phelps, a professor at Yale reported. "My father was an orthodox Baptist minister . . . I had never heard him mention a prizefight and did not suppose he knew anything on the subject, or cared anything about it. So when I came to the headline CORBETT DEFEATS SULLIVAN, I read that aloud and turned the page. My father leaned forward and said earnestly, 'Read it by rounds!' "[22] Sullivan remained a celebrity long after his loss to Corbett. He performed in numerous vaudeville acts and plays (including the role of Simon Legree in a traveling production of *Uncle Tom's Cabin*) and even gave temperance lectures.

Yet neither the popularity of Sullivan, the Queensberry rules, nor the reforms instituted by the athletic clubs completely erased the traditional stigma associated with the prize ring. Even "lace-curtain Irish," the more successful Irish Americans who sought acceptance into Victorian society, dissociated themselves from the ring. The sport remained illegal almost everywhere and respectable women did not attend prizefights until the 1920s. Without a national regulatory body or a rational system for determining champions, boxing was an unusually chaotic and disorderly sport. Champions invariably avoided challengers unless they could be assured of a large stake—"win or lose." Young fighters with dreams of reaching the top sought out "patsies" so they could leave their records unblemished. And the bottom line for any fight was the anticipated profits of promoters. "Carrying" an opponent, "taking a dive," and "fixing records"— these and other fraudulent tactics were endemic to the fight game. Thus, despite the growing popularity of boxing among all social groups, the ambience of boxing remained working class and ethnic, and shrouded by the shady world of bookies, thugs, and racketeers.

POSTBELLUM THOROUGHBRED HORSE RACING

No sport served the needs of New York City's parvenu sportsmen for conspicuous display more effectively than thoroughbred horse racing. Failing to obtain consistent patronage from the nation's wealthiest classes, wracked by the ricocheting business cycle, and confronted with persistent charges of gambling, chicanery, and commercialism, antebellum racing had never enjoyed sustained prosperity. But during the 1860s, a small group of newly made millionaires decided to place horse racing on a fresh footing. By building new tracks, providing large stakes, reducing corruption, substituting the dash for long-distance racing, and founding the New York Jockey Club as a central governing body, these men ushered horse racing into a new "golden age."

The main leader of the movement to transform the sport was New York City's Leonard W. Jerome, a man who had made a fortune selling short in the Panic of 1857. Blessed with enormous energy, Jerome was by day a calculating investor on Wall Street and by night a dashing man about town. The handsome financier engaged in scandalous love affairs, patronized the theater and the opera, and threw dazzling parties. At one of his parties, the fountains spouted champagne and eau de cologne. Infatuated by singer Jennie Lind, the Swedish Nightingale, he named a daughter after her—the daughter who would one day make Jerome the grandfather of Winston Churchill. But as much as he loved beautiful women, Jerome's special and life-long passion was the turf.

In 1866, Jerome and his friends William R. Travers and August Belmont founded the American Jockey Club. Modeled after the socially exclusive Newmarket in England, the club purchased over 200 acres of land in Westchester County where it built Jerome Park. The new park was by far the most lavish course in the nation. Located high on a bluff overlooking the backstretch, the luxurious clubhouse contained a spacious dining room, overnight sleeping quarters, and facilities for trap shooting, skating, and later, polo. Initially, only club members could sit in the grandstands. "From this sacred spot the respectable public are tabooed," noted the *New York Clipper* sarcastically, "and none but the sweet scented and kid glove subscribers can enter."[23] Led by the ostentatious display of the New Yorkers, men of new wealth across the nation took up horse racing. Other, less exclusive tracks—Monmouth Park (1870) in New Jersey, Pimlico (1870) in Baltimore, and Churchill Downs (1875) in Louisville—soon followed the construction of Jerome Park.

The golden age of horse racing entailed more than the opening of new tracks. To reverse the negative antebellum reputation of the turf, Jerome Park barred the sale of intoxicants, discouraged professional gamblers, and made a special effort to attract "the carriage trade." The wealth and social position of the club extended its influence far beyond the City. The New Yorkers led the movement to replace the old system of racing three- or four-mile heats with the modern dash system of racing; the dash placed more emphasis on speed rather than "bottom," or stamina, and permitted the running of several races the same day. Large, permanent stakes, such as the Travers and the Belmont, added excitement and lent greater stability to the turf. In 1894, 50 giants in industry and finance founded the Jockey Club; the club provided uniform national rules, appointed officials, licensed jockeys, and set national racing dates.

Despite its wealthy patronage, thoroughbred racing operated outside of, or at best, on the fringes of Victorian respectability. As in the past, the centrality of gambling to horse racing continued to send shudders through the ranks of proper Victorians. Indeed, the introduction of bookmaking in the last quarter of the nineteenth-century opened new opportunities for gambling; it allowed the small-time bettor to wager as little as two or three dollars on any horse she or he pleased at publicly posted odds. That the horse racing fraternity turned to machine politicians to obtain the repeal (or exemption from enforcement) of laws restricting racing and gambling added to the suspicions of those who condemned the track for its unsavory character. As Steven Riess has documented, nearly every prominent Tammanyite had links to the track; the same was true of political leaders in Chicago, New Orleans, and other major racing centers.[24]

CONCLUSION

Throughout most of the nineteenth-century, one large universe of sport, that found in the spectacles staged by the sporting fraternity, remained outside the perimeters of Victorian respectability. The fraternity adapted and transformed horse racing, pedestrian races, prizefighting, and other traditional pastimes to meet demands or needs arising from vast changes in nineteenth-century American life. Although not totally separable from the larger oppositional culture, baseball, the first great team sport to become a commercial spectacle and the subject of the next chapter, tried to create a universe of its own.

NOTES

1. See especially Melvin L. Adelman, *A Sporting Time: New York City and the Rise of Modern Athletics, 1820–70* (Urbana: University of Illinois Press, 1986). For relevant documents, see George B. Kirsch, ed., *Sports in North America: A Documentary History, 1840–1860* (Gulf Breeze, FL: Academic, 1991).

2. See John Dizikes, *Sportsmen and Gamesmen* (Boston: Houghton Mifflin, 1981), chap. 5.

3. See Adelman, *Sporting Time*, chap. 4, and Nancy L. Struna, "The North-South Races: American Thoroughbred Racing in Transition, 1823–1850," *Journal of Sport History* 8 (1981), 28–57.

4. A.D. Turnbull, *John Stevens* (New York: Century, 1928), 486.

5. Allan Nevins, ed., *The Diary of Philip Hone, 1828–1851*, 2 vols. (New York: Dodd, Mead, 1927), II, 861.

6. Charles Peverelly, *The Book of American Pastimes* (New York: author, 1866), 19.

7. See George Moss, "The Long-Distance Runner in Ante-Bellum America," *Journal of Popular Culture* 8 (1974), 370–82.

8. Quotations from Adelman, *Sporting Time*, 213, 214.

9. Quoted in Melvin Leonard Adelman, "The Development of Modern Athletics in New York City, 1820–1870," unpub. Ph.D. diss., University of Illinois, 1980, 535.

10. *Spirit of the Times*, July 10, 1839.

11. Adelman, "Development of Modern Athletics," 482.

12. See Adelman, *Sporting Time*; Ned Polsky, *Hustlers, Beats, and Others* (Chicago: Aldine, 1967); and E. A. Miles, "President Adams' Billiard Table," *New England Quarterly* 45 (1972), 29–46.

13. Elliott J. Gorn, *The Manly Art: Bare-Knuckle Prize Fighting in America* (Ithaca, NY: Cornell University Press, 1986), 83. My treatment relies heavily on this superb work.

14. In addition to ibid., see S. K. Weinberg and Henry Arond, "The Occupational Culture of the Boxer," *American Journal of Sociology* 57 (1952), 460–69.

15. Elliott J. Gorn, "The Wicked World: *The National Police Gazette* and Gilded Age Culture," *Media Studies Journal* 6 (Winter 1992), 14.

16. Quotations from Gorn, *Manly Art*, 183, and D.B. Chidsey, *John the Great* (Garden City, NY: Doubleday, 1942), 13.

17. Quoted in Gorn, *Manly Art*, 199.

18. See Steven A. Riess, "In the Ring and Out: Professional Boxing in New York, 1896–1920," in *Sport in America*, ed. Donald Spivey (Westport: CT: Greenwood, 1985), 95–128.

19. Apart from Gorn, *Manly Art*, see Michael T. Isenberg, *John L. Sullivan and His America* (Urbana: University of Illinois Press, 1988).

20. Quoted in Gorn, *Manly Art*, 235.

21. Quoted in Dale A. Somers, *The Rise of Sports in New Orleans, 1850–1900* (Baton Rouge: Louisiana State University Press, 1972), 184.

22. William Lyons Phelps, *Autobiography with Letters* (New York: Oxford University Press, 1939), 356.

23. Quoted in Allen Guttmann, *Sports Spectators* (New York: Columbia University Press, 1986), 99.

24. Steven A. Riess, *City Games* (Urbana: University of Illinois Press, 1989), 181–87.

4
THE RISE OF AMERICA'S NATIONAL GAME

Nineteenth-century baseball evolved through three main stages. First was the simple, largely informal bat-and-ball games played by boys. Scholars dismiss the story of baseball's creation by Abner Doubleday in 1839 at Cooperstown, New York, as apocryphal. (For the origins of the Doubleday myth, see Chapter 9.) Long before 1839 boys in both England and America played a variety of games that entailed the use of a stick, a ball, and one or more base(s).

During the 1840s and 1850s, these boys' games evolved into the second stage: the club-based, fraternal game that was eventually to evolve into the game we know today as baseball. Young men in several larger cities (beginning mainly in New York City) formalized the boys' games into a single version of a bat-and-ball game. They organized clubs, adopted written rules, and initially placed a higher priority on playing for personal pleasure than on playing for spectators. While remnants of the fraternal game lingered on, as early as the 1860s baseball began to enter its third stage. In the third era baseball became a commercial, spectator-centered sport. The formation of the National League in 1876 signified the sport's full arrival as a business enterprise.[1]

THE CLUB-BASED FRATERNAL GAME

The baseball fraternity had its origins in the shared boyhood experiences of playing bat-and-ball games and in the American penchant for forming voluntary associations. A historic turning point came in 1842 and 1843 when a group of young clerks, merchants, brokers, professional men, and assorted "gentlemen" in New York City began playing a bat-and-ball game at the corner of 27th Street and 4th Avenue in Manhattan. According to legend, in 1845 Alexander Cartwright, a bank clerk, convinced the men to organize themselves as the New York Knickerbockers Base Ball Club. They chose as a playing site a portion of the Elysian Fields in Hoboken, a most "picturesque and delightful" place that was easily accessible from Manhattan via the Barclay Street ferry. After a hard afternoon of play, the club members retreated nearby to McCarty's Hotel bar, where they regaled one another with manly talk and quenched their thirst with spirituous drink.

Today's fans would find the Knickerbockers game both familiar and strange. Just as today, the game was played on a diamond-shaped infield. Three strikes swung at and missed retired the "striker" (batter), but the practice of having umpires call balls and strikes was unknown. The umpires, who at first were dressed in tails and a tall black top hat and sat at a table along the first base line, only gradually acquired this responsibility. On other matters, umpires rendered decisions only when controversies arose between the team captains. The fielders wore no gloves, and hoping to catch the pitches on the first bounce, the catcher stood several feet behind the striker. From a running start the "feeder" (pitcher) literally pitched the ball underhanded with a straight arm from a distance of 45 feet. In the early days, the pitcher was obligated to toss the ball gently, so the hitter could have a pitch to his liking.

The Knickerbockers club represented the essential elements of what soon became known as the "base ball fraternity." Unlike the larger sporting fraternity, the one that promoted pedestrian races and blood sports, the baseball fraternity's existence revolved around organized clubs. Like other voluntary associations of the day, the clubs drew up bylaws, elected officers, and held regular meetings. The club was both an athletic *and* a social organization. Initially, the Knickerbockers tried to restrict their membership to "gentleman amateurs"; one became a member of Knickerbockers by invitation only. A common interest in baseball, colorful uniforms similar to those of the volunteer fire departments of the era, and a large array of social activities strengthened the fraternal bonds among the ballplayers.

The fraternity offered young men, in particular clerks and artisans, satisfactions missing in their work as well as in other parts of their lives. "We would forget business and everything else, on Tuesday afternoons, go out into the green fields, don our ball suits, and go at it with a perfect rush. At such times, we were boys again," recalled Frank Pidgeon, a former captain of the Eckford club in Brooklyn.[2] Often unmarried and living away from home in impersonal boarding houses, the young men found excitement in baseball as well as opportunities to display their individual physical skills, companionship, and a sense of belonging.

Pageantry, rituals, and off-season social gatherings enhanced player fraternization. In a postgame ceremony, the winning team received the game ball as a prize; the ball was then properly inscribed with the outcome and date of the contest and retired to the club's trophy case. After interclub games, the home club frequently provided the visitors with a gala dinner. In 1858, for example, "the Excelsior Club was escorted to the Odd Fellows Hall, Hoboken, by the Knickerbockers Club, and entertained in splendid style. . . . Dodsworth's band was in attendance to liven the scene."[3] Perhaps an extreme example of the effectiveness of postgame rituals in promoting amity within the fraternity occurred in 1860.

According to the *New York Clipper*, after having shared a keg of lager, the players were unable to recall the score of the game that they had played earlier in the day![4]

Clubs even scheduled formal dances; sometimes the players seemed to have been as busy and proficient on the dance floor as they were on the playing field. For example, in the winter of 1860–61, Brooklyn's Eckford club, comprised of shipbuilding artisans, scheduled an annual ball and eight "hops." A special treat at the ball was Captain Frank Pidgeon, who exhibited his special talents in the "Parisian style" of dancing.

Enthusiasm for baseball soon spread beyond the ranks of petty shopkeepers, clerks, and artisans. Any group of men who enjoyed a working schedule that left a few daylight hours free and had the wherewithal to rent playing space might take up the game. In the greater New York area, clubs frequently organized along occupational, ethnic, and/or neighborhood lines. Boys played informal games on empty lots or in the streets. Special games and tours excited widespread interest in what was sometimes called the "New York game." In 1858, an "all-star" series between the best players from Brooklyn and the New York stars captured the attention of the entire city. Two years later newspapers across the nation reported a tour by the Excelsiors of Brooklyn to upstate New York and then on to Philadelphia and Baltimore. The Civil War, far from impeding the growth of the sport, encouraged the introduction of baseball by veterans (especially the Union ones) to hamlets across the nation. Representation at the annual baseball convention of the National Association of Base Ball Players (founded in 1858) increased from 62 clubs in 1860 to 91 clubs in ten states at the war's conclusion in 1865.

The press encouraged baseball's growth. While the regular daily newspapers initially gave only cursory attention to the fraternity's activities, such sporting sheets as the *New York Clipper* and *Porter's Spirit of the Times* not only reported the results of matches and other baseball news but also provided direct aid to young men interested in forming clubs. No single journalist gave the sport greater assistance than Henry Chadwick, who, because of his contributions to baseball, later became known as "Father Chadwick." Chadwick edited baseball's first annual guidebook, which by the mid-1860s claimed to have a circulation of more than 65,000. Other guidebooks soon appeared; they enabled avid fans to keep abreast of the latest rules, clubs, and statistics, as well as other news of the diamond. Chadwick also invented the box score and batting averages, quantitative devices that enhanced baseball's appeal.

As early as the mid-1850s, the baseball fraternity began to promote their sport as "the national game." Such a strategy fitted perfectly the tense mood of the 1850s. In a decade that spawned bitter divisions that culminated in the Civil War, yearnings for national unity spilled over into sports. Few public events captured the public imagination more than American challenges to English supremacy in horse racing, boxing, and even yachting. Comprised of mainly old-stock Americans, many of the first baseball clubs openly avowed their nationalism by taking on such names as Young America, Columbia, Union, Eagle, American, or National. As the English have their cricket and the Germans their *Turnvereins* (exercise clubs), *Porter's Spirit* declared in 1857, Americans ought to have "a game that could be termed a 'Native American Sport.'"[5] Baseball, its supporters agreed, filled that need. Not only had it evolved as a distinctive American sport but it also embodied more completely than any other sport the fast-paced nature of American life. In time, along with such other icons as the national flag, the National Anthem, and the Constitution itself, baseball established itself as a significant constituent of the nation's identity.

Yet, such an eminent position awaited the twentieth century. In the nineteenth century, baseball remained for many Americans outside the boundaries of respectability. The baseball fraternity and its game never won the unqualified endorsement of middle-class Victorians. To Victorian America, manifest instances of rowdiness and a loss of self-control too often characterized baseball and its followers. While businesses in some places organized their workers into teams, others worried lest their employees neglect their work for the sake of the game. "The invariable question put to young men applying for situations in New York," according to the secretary of the Irvington, New Jersey, baseball club in 1867, "is, whether they are members of ball clubs. If they answer in the affirmative, they are told that their services will not be needed."[6]

Without complete success, the fraternity tried to counter such negative attitudes by insisting on the game's compatibility with Victorian values. Baseball encouraged manliness, or self-control, rather than boyishness, or impetuous behavior, its defenders argued. Play by boys, according to the *Brooklyn Eagle*, kept the youngsters "out of a great deal of mischief. . . . [Baseball] keeps them from hanging around [fire] engine houses, stables, and taverns."[7]

BASEBALL AS A COMMERCIAL ENTERPRISE

At the very height of its success, the baseball fraternity began to disintegrate. Although features of the club-based, fraternal game lingered on (even to this day), commercial considerations quickly entered the sport. In the 1850s clubs began to encourage spectators to attend games and in 1862 an ambitious Brooklynite, William H. Cammeyer, built a fence around some land that he owned and charged admission fees to spectators who watched games there. The "enclosure movement," as the drive to build fences around fields and charge a gate fee was called, introduced a new era of baseball history. It was, as Henry Chadwick wrote, "really the beginning of professional base ball playing."[8]

As fraternal bonds weakened and "nines" seized upon the opportunities presented by gate charges, the teams began to play more games, practice more, embark on long summer tours, recruit athletes on the basis of their playing skills rather than their sociability, and even extend sub rosa payments to outstanding players. By the mid-1860s the postgame rituals of awarding the game ball to the winning team and hosting a dinner for visitors disappeared from the sport. Baseball's culture increasingly accepted the use of cunning tactics; indeed, the game's aficionados came to admire those players and teams who could successfully trick

EARLY PROFESSIONAL BASEBALL GAME, CIRCA 1887 *Although located in a pastoral setting, this field included a players' bench, clearly marked base paths, and an outfield fence to keep out nonpaying spectators. Colorful uniforms and outfield flags were part of baseball's pageantry.*
(UPI/Corbis)

the umpire or their opponents. Unlike the earliest days of the game, the "cranks" or "kranks," as the more rabid fans were called, cheered wildly for their heroes, heckled umpires and opposing players, and sometimes rioted. In the larger cities, more and more blue-collar youth, often of Irish or German extraction, found opportunities for monetary gain in baseball.

Charges of gambling and game dumping tainted commercial baseball's quest for respectability. Gamblers quickly seized upon the opportunities presented by baseball games. Justifiably, fans suspected that some games were fixed. New York gamblers, for instance, apparently controlled the Troy, New York, Haymakers, a team that acquired a notorious reputation for game fixing. In California, just as a fielder was about to catch a fly ball, the gamblers who had placed bets on the side at bat would fire their six-shooters. On several occasions, bettors even mobbed playing fields to prevent the competition of games in which they stood to lose money. "So common has betting become at baseball matches," complained a *Harper's Weekly* editor in 1867, "that the most respectable clubs in the country indulge in it to a highly culpable degree."[9]

The Victorian press condemned player behavior on other grounds as well. The typical professional player, according to the *New York Times* in 1872, was a "worthless, dissipated gladiator; not much above the professional pugilist in morality and respectability." The players spent their off-seasons, according to the *Times*, "in those quiet retreats connected with bars, and rat pits, where sporting men of the metropolis meet for social improvement and unpremeditated pugilism."[10]

Yet criticism for impropriety and commercialization hardly slowed baseball's burgeoning popularity. Indeed, the passing of each decade saw more young men taking up the sport. With opportunities for exhibitions of physical manliness limited by the radical changes in nineteenth-century work places and the prevailing Victorian restraints on self-expression, baseball offered an exciting arena for the display of physical prowess and aggressiveness in a controlled setting. On the diamond, young men could achieve reputations for their skills and experience a sense of belonging to a common culture that revolved around ballplaying.

Intense rivalries among nineteenth-century cities encouraged the creation of professional baseball teams. Even in the East where older cities could to some degree take their eminence for granted, smaller cities might see in their representative baseball teams an opportunity to embarrass a larger neighbor. "If we are ahead of the big city in nothing else," crowed the *Brooklyn Eagle* in 1862, "we can beat her in baseball."[11] Interurban rivalry was even more acute among the upstart cities of the West. Boosters tried to bolster extravagant claims on behalf of their city's superiority by conjuring up suitable institutions, such as churches, hospitals, libraries, colleges, and representative baseball nines.

The astonishing success of Cincinnati's Red Stockings, the nation's first publicly announced, all-salaried team, in 1869 vividly illustrated the possibilities of using baseball to advertise one's city. By vigorously pushing stock sales among local businessmen and politicians, Aaron B. Champion, the club's young president, raised enough money to employ star players from the East. Led by player-manager, Harry Wright, a former professional cricket player, the Red Stockings swept through the 1869 season of 58 games without a loss and only one tie. Over 23,000 fans watched their six game series in New York, previously considered the citadel of the baseball world. In Washington, D.C., President Ulysses S. Grant welcomed the "Cinderella" team and complimented the members on the excellence of their play. In September, the club crossed the United States on the newly completed transcontinental railroad to play a series of games in California. "Glory, they've advertised the city—advertised us, sir, and helped our business," exulted a delighted Cincinnati businessman.[12]

Cincinnati's success jarred other cities, including its longtime adversary, Chicago, into action. Chicago "could not see her commercial rival on the Ohio bearing off the honors of the national game," declared the *Lakeside Monthly* in 1870. "So Chicago went to work." Among others, Joseph Medill, owner of the *Chicago Tribune*, and Potter Palmer, owner of the famed Palmer House hotel, rose to the occasion by organizing the White Stockings baseball club as a joint-stock company. They "raised $20,000 with which to employ a nine that should," in the words of a jealous Boston newspaper, "'sweep the board.'"[13]

During the last three decades of the nineteenth century, small-time entrepreneurs, politicians, city boosters, and traction (transit) magnates formed dozens of joint-stock baseball clubs. Fortunately for them, the investors were frequently as interested in publicity as profits, for the clubs experienced staggering rates of failure. Indeed, even Cincinnati's Red Stockings, after apparently failing to earn a profit, closed down at the end of their second season in 1870. Leagues of representative teams were equally fragile; franchises joined and dropped out of the leagues with startling frequency. At one time or the other during the nineteenth century, the National League (1876–present), the most successful of the circuits, had franchises located in no fewer than 21 different cities.

The National Association of Professional Base Ball Players (1871–1875), baseball's first professional league, was a loose confederation of clubs. Any team, no matter what the size of the city they represented, that mustered a mere $10.00 entry fee could contend for the championship pennant. Teams scheduled their own matches; a team could qualify for the pennant by playing all other clubs at least five times during the season. That players were free to move from one team to another at the end of each season was another indication of the league's unbusinesslike character.

Harry Wright's Boston team dominated the new loop. After the 1870 season, Wright brought most of the Cincinnati team with him to Boston. Although narrowly losing the pennant to the Athletics of Philadelphia in 1871, the Boston team then won the next four consecutive championships. George Wright, Harry's brother, was the club's superb fielding, hard-hitting shortstop. Young Albert Spalding was the most baffling pitcher in the league, and Roscoe Barnes was the perennial batting champion. In 1875 the Bostons had the four top hitters in the circuit and ran away with the league flag, winning 71 games while losing only 8.

THE NATIONAL LEAGUE

In 1876, William A. Hulbert, president of a Chicago club, and Albert Spalding, Hulbert's recently acquired star pitcher and manager, led a coup against the National Association. They founded a new professional baseball league, "The National League of Professional Base Ball Clubs." Significantly, the founders substituted the term "clubs" for "players." They refused to admit nines owned by the players; instead, they restricted their new league to "regular [joint-] stock companies" located in cities of 75,000 or more residents. For the inaugural season of 1876, clubs in Boston, Chicago, Cincinnati, Louisville, Hartford, St. Louis, Philadelphia, and New York fielded teams. Any new club wishing to join the circuit had to have the approval of the existing clubs. By banning Sunday games, prohibiting the sale of liquor at ball parks, and charging a 50¢ admission fee, the league also sought to obtain the patronage of Victorians.

Yet the National League, like most other business arrangements based upon gentlemen's agreements, often failed to function as an effective economic cartel. Major ownership and management decisions remained mostly with the individual franchises and restrictive agreements or decisions could not ultimately be enforced by the league or the courts. Consequently, each club owner usually placed his interest before that of the league cartel. As Albert Spalding, a shrewd and long-time observer of professional baseball once put it: "The [baseball] magnate must be a strong man among strong men, else other club owners in the league will combine in their own interest against him and his interests."[14]

For its first six years, William Hulbert offered the National League strong, albeit sometimes questionable, leadership. By dramatically expelling four Louisville players in 1877 for taking bribes, he cracked down on loose player behavior. His other decisions were more debatable. When both the Philadelphia and New York teams refused to take their final season road tours in 1876, he led the movement to expel them from the league, even though they represented the nation's two largest cities. When the Cincinnati club persisted in selling beer at its park and playing Sunday games, Hulbert hounded them out of the league as well.

The expulsion of Cincinnati led to direct challenge to the National League. In 1881 six clubs formed the American Association, or "Beer Ball League," as it was sneeringly called by its critics. Indeed, investors in four of the six clubs had investments in breweries. In an attempt to attract fans from the lower income ranks, the association authorized the sale of liquor at games, charged only 25¢ for admission, and permitted play on Sunday. The association also invited National League players to jump their contracts, and several did. The success of the association led the leaderless National League to call for a strategic retreat. In 1882, the presidents of the two leagues plus the head of the Northwestern League (a minor league) signed a triparte National Agreement.

With the booming prosperity of the 1880s, interest in professional baseball reached unprecedented heights. On the playing field, the American Association clubs proved fully equal to the senior loop. The powerful St. Louis Brown Stockings, managed by young Charles Comiskey (later owner of the Chicago White Stockings), won four consecutive association pennants and two informal "World Championship Series" against the National League flagbearers. In the meantime, the truce between the circuits remained an uneasy one; from time to time clubs in both leagues violated the spirit if not the letter of the National Agreement of 1882.

Just as Chicago men had formed the National League and furnished the loop with its leadership, the Chicago White Stockings, under the leadership of Adrian C. "Cap" Anson, initially dominated National League play. Anson, who standing at 6 feet and 2 inches and weighing more than 200 pounds was a veritable giant for his era, played first base, won four batting crowns, and in 22 seasons failed to hit .300 only twice. Under Anson's capable guidance, Chicago won five pennants between 1880 and 1886.

Mike "King" Kelly competed with Anson for the adoration of Chicago's fans. "As Celtic as Mrs. Murphy's pig," Kelly inspired a host of legends. On one occasion as the sun was setting in the last of the twelfth inning, with two outs, the bases full, and the score tied, Kelly was playing the outfield for the White Sox. He leapt into the twilight trying to catch a mighty drive. As he came down, he held his glove high in the air and jauntily jogged to the dugout. The umpire yelled, "Out number three! Game called on account of darkness!" "Nice catch, Kell," his teammates exclaimed. "Not at all, at all," the King responded. "Twent a mile above my head."[15]

THE PLAYERS' REVOLT

While the National League and the American Association locked in fierce combat with one another for profits and ultimately survival, an equally serious conflict raged between club management and the players.[16] In the first place, the players and owners collided over player behavior. Like the industrial magnates of the day, baseball's management sought a sober, well-rested, disciplined work force. But the professional ballplayers were an unruly lot. Many of them came from the ranks of the Irish and German working classes, in which (at least for the Irish) drinking, brawling, and display were fundamental parts of their male homosocial worlds. Young and usually unmarried and with large quantities of free time unoccupied by team practices or playing games, the players frequented billiard halls, loitered in saloons, and consorted with gamblers and show people.

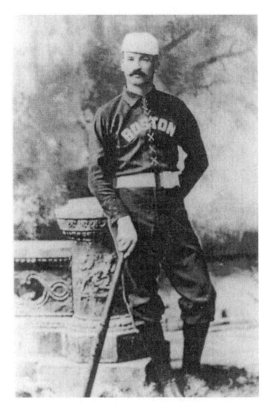

MICHAEL J. "KING" KELLY A colorful player both on and off the field, in the 1880s, Kelly was hailed by fans as the "King of Base Ball." In 16 major-league seasons, he compiled a .307 lifetime batting average, and in 1887 he was sold by the Chicago White Stockings for the then-astonishing sum of $10,000.
(Boston Public Library)

Player drinking was a special problem for the owners. Throughout the 1880s the National League campaigned against drinking, but reports frequently surfaced of players abusing alcohol. No one fought harder in principle against drinking than Albert Spalding, the president of the Chicago club. He once hired a Pinkerton detective to secretly follow his players. Seven of them, the detective reported, spent almost every night going "up and down Clark Street [in Chicago] all over the tenderloin districts, through the whole roster of saloons and 'speakeasy' resorts." After Spalding had the report read to the team, his star player, Michael "King" Kelly, finally broke the long silence. "I have to offer only one amendment. In that place where the detective reports me as taking a lemonade at 3 A.M. he's off. It was straight whiskey; I never drank a lemonade at that hour in my life."[17]

Apart from admonishment and fines, the National League deployed other weapons against the players. From the outset, the owners had agreed to "black-list"—refuse to negotiate with—any player who had been dismissed by another club or the league for any reason. In 1879 the owners discovered an even more ingenious weapon, the reserve clause. The reserve clause in effect gave a team that first signed a player a lifetime option on that player's services. Unable to offer his skills to any other franchise, the individual player bargained from a weak position. If a player believed that he should be paid more, for example, he had only two available responses: "hold out," refuse to play until promised a satisfactory salary, or quit baseball. Neither alternative was attractive. Holding out might mean the loss of income for the playing time that the player had cost the club and most players could not find jobs outside of baseball that paid equally well.

The owners quickly discovered another advantage in the reserve clause: They could "sell" players (strictly speaking they sold the player's contract rights) to other clubs. In 1887, Albert Spalding startled the baseball world by selling King Kelly to Boston for the then-spectacular sum of $10,000. The sale angered the players: Why should the owners receive compensation for skills possessed by the players, they asked? To the players, the sale smacked of human slavery and it dramatized their ultimate impotency when dealing with the owners.

The highly publicized sale of Kelly to Boston in 1887, clashes with the owners over drinking, rising salary expectations stemming from baseball's growing prosperity in the 1880s, a salary classification (salary cap) scheme of the owners, and the leadership of John Montgomery Ward triggered a full-scale players' revolt. Two years earlier, in 1885, Ward, a lawyer and a star player, had founded the Brotherhood of Professional Base Ball Players. Initially a secret organization, the brotherhood had been little more than a fraternal lodge that assisted players suffering temporary hardships. But when the league tried to impose a $2,500 ceiling on salaries in 1887, the angry players first considered a strike and then decided to form a competing big league in 1890.

An all-out war erupted between the newly created Players' League and the National League. The eight-team Players' League invaded seven of the senior circuit's cities and lured away its best players. In a novel departure from private enterprise, the players and investors assumed joint management of the new franchises. Albert Spalding, now a sporting goods entrepreneur and president of the

Chicago club, headed a war committee to suppress the player uprising. Capitalizing on the fears of the day, Spalding described the players as "hot-headed anarchists," who were bent on a "terrorism" that was characteristic of "revolutionary movements." While most of the newspapers happily printed Spalding's scorching denunciations, he had no success in prosecuting the defecting players for violating the reserve clause. Efforts to bribe star players to stay in the loop were also by and large unsuccessful. Reputedly, Spalding offered King Kelly a "blank check" to remain in the league, but Kelly refused, saying "I can't go back on the boys."[18]

Yet the Players' League lasted only one season. Competing on the same day in the same city for the same customers cost both leagues heavily. By opting for Victorian respectability—by refusing to permit Sunday games, barring beer at games, and charging a high gate fee (50¢)—rather than a direct appeal to ethnic, working-class fans, the players made a questionable decision. At the end of the 1890 season, by a combination of complex deals with its financial backers, Spalding brought down the Players League. In 1891 the American Association also folded, leaving only the National League as a major league circuit. The owners at once set about slashing player salaries. John Ward summed up the new position of the players. "Your inning is over, my boy," Ward explained to William Joyce, a player seeking a $200 advance on his salary.[19]

ETHNICS AND AFRICAN AMERICANS

For youth from the lower socioeconomic ranks, professional baseball offered a glamorous if, from a Victorian standpoint, suspect career opportunity. Most of the 240 big-league players of the 1880s advanced from the unstable minor leagues or came directly from the sandlots. Only a handful ever attended college, and only a few enjoyed professional careers outside of baseball. Most had short playing careers and when released became either blue-collar workers or workers employed in jobs provided by the Victorian underworld. An unusually large number of German and Irish names appeared on club rosters, suggesting that for these ethnic groups, major-league baseball may have been a means of social mobility. Nearly all big leaguers came from the cities, especially from the northeastern metropolitan areas.[20]

While Irish and German youth found career opportunities in professional baseball, prospects for blacks were far less certain. As early as 1867 the National Association of Base Ball Players specifically excluded black clubs from membership. Informally, from its founding in 1876, the National League enforced a "color ban" against both black players and black clubs. Nonetheless, a few blacks did play on professional teams in other leagues. The high point of integrated baseball in the nineteenth century came in the 1880s. In 1883, Moses Fleetwood Walker, a former Oberlin College student, signed with Toledo; the next year Toledo entered the American Association, then considered a major league.[21] Later in the season, Weldy Walker, Moses' younger brother, played six games with Toledo. Neither of the Walkers obtained a contract with Toledo in 1885, but Moses Walker and several other blacks continued to play on white minor-league teams.

The 1887 season marked a turning point for race relations in baseball. The biggest setback occurred in the International League, a top-flight minor league in which six of its ten teams fielded black players. "How far will the mania for engaging colored players go?" queried *Sporting Life*.[22] Confronted with protests from some of the white players, in July the league prohibited the admission of additional blacks into the circuit. Only a few days later Cap Anson refused to allow his Chicago White Stockings to take the field against Newark in an exhibition contest unless George Stovey, Newark's star black pitcher, was kept out of the game. Newark capitulated.

After 1887 conditions rapidly worsened, climaxing in the complete exclusion of blacks from white professional teams. The banning of blacks corresponded in time with a more general implementation of racial segregation in the United States. The "color ban" remained in the major leagues and its affiliates until 1946 when Jackie Robinson joined the Montreal Royals, a minor-league club owned by the Brooklyn Dodgers.

Excluded from racially integrated baseball, blacks had to carve out a separate sphere for themselves. Although the sources for the history of much of black baseball rest on oral legends, there is scattered evidence of blacks organizing clubs in the larger cities immediately after the Civil War. As early as 1867, for example, the Excelsoirs of Philadelphia and the Uniques of Brooklyn played a game hailed by the press as the "colored championship of the United States."

Although barnstorming black teams reached the apogee of their popularity in the twentieth century, in the late 1880s the powerful Cuban Giants, formed in 1885 by a group of ballplaying hotel waiters at a famed Long Island resort, took on all comers. Eventually they booked some 150 games a season, mostly against white clubs. In 1887, for example, they embarked on a long western tour on which they played major-league clubs in Cincinnati and Indianapolis as well as several minor-league teams. "The Cuban Giants . . . have defeated the New Yorks, 4 games out of 5, and are now virtually champions of the world," crowed the *Indianapolis Freedman* in 1888. But "the St. Louis Browns, Detroits and Chicagos, afflicted by Negrophobia and unable to bear the odium of being beaten by colored men, refused to accept their challenge."[23]

BETWEEN THE FOUL LINES AND IN THE STANDS

Most white fans probably cared little about the plight of blacks or about the business side of baseball. They were far more attentive to the action between the foul lines. There, in order to make the game more attractive to fans, professional baseball experimented with numerous rule changes. In the 1870s and 1880s the rule governing how high the pitcher could raise his arm above his waist while delivering the ball had been gradually relaxed until overhand pitching was fully legalized in 1884. In 1887 batters lost the privilege of calling for pitches above or below the waist and two years later the rulemakers set the number of pitches thrown outside the strike zone that entitled the runner to first base at four.

Managers gradually developed tactics familiar to modern fans. Infielders inched away from their respective bases and catchers moved closer to the plate. Fielders learned to back each other up in the event of wild throws or muffed balls. Unlike modern baseball, most of the fielders played several positions within a single season. In order to protect their hands from the sting of the ball rather than improve fielding, players began to don gloves in the mid-1880s. During the era of underhanded pitching, pitchers (like modern softball hurlers) typically worked a full nine-inning game and pitched day after day. Overhanded pitching and lengthening of the pitching distance to 60 feet and 6 inches in 1893 placed more stress on the pitcher's arm so that by the end of the 1890s most clubs rotated at least three hurlers.

Team captains and managers increasingly stressed offensive teamwork. Although the bunt was not yet widely used, clubs began to employ regularly the "hit-and-run" play during the 1890s. Base stealing and "stretching" hits into extra bases also became more commonplace. Teams developed psychological warfare into an art form. Players and managers verbally harangued opposing players and the umpire. Violence or the threat of violent acts included the use of spiked shoes to intimidate or inflict flesh wounds on defensive players, tripping or blocking runners, and outright fistfights. John Heydler, an umpire in the 1890s (and later National League president) described the leading offenders, the Baltimore Orioles, as "mean, vicious, ready at any time to maim a rival player or an umpire."[24] Such behavior stood in sharp contrast to that of the early baseball fraternity.

The ballparks of the day were inexpensive, jerry-built, wooden structures that were doomed to become early victims of decay, termites, fire, or even collapse from the excessive weight of fans. Wooden fences kept out nonpaying fans, though some of them avoided paying an admission by watching games through cracks or knotholes in the boards (hence the origins of the term *knothole gangs*). A roof sheltered some fans from the sun while others sat on unprotected sun-bleached boards (hence the term *bleachers*). At major games fans continued to congregate along the foul lines and in front of outfield fences. Scorecards and refreshments could be purchased at the park, but the lack of a public address system or numbers on players' uniforms challenged the fans' ability to recognize the players by name. Brass bands sometimes entertained fans between innings.

Professional baseball games attracted motley crowds. The *St. Louis Post-Dispatch* reported in 1883 that "a glance at the audience on any fine day at the ball park will reveal [among others] . . . telegraph operators, printers who work at night, travelling men [salesmen] . . . men of leisure . . . men of capital, bank clerks who get away at 3 P.M., real estate men . . . barkeepers . . . hotel clerks, actors and employees of the theater, policemen and firemen on their day off . . . butchers and bakers."[25] For the convenience of white-collar workers, clubs in several cities specifically arranged the starting time of their games in the afternoons. Steep ticket prices, the necessity of play during the daylight hours, and bans on Sunday games restricted potential attendance by unskilled workingmen. Women were far less likely than men to attend games; early photographs reveal the presence of an overwhelming preponderance of males. In sum, most of the fans probably came from the ranks of the larger sporting fraternity, show people, and middle-income groups who were uninhibited by Victorian attitudes.

While baseball grew to become the nation's most successful commercial sport in the nineteenth century, it continued to struggle for acceptance among proper Victorians. Baseball frequently drove a wedge between generations. Elders repeatedly warned their children about the moral perils arising from the game and discouraged them from pursuing baseball as a career. "You should never go to a ball game," lectured Pittsburgh Judge J.W.F. White in 1887 to a defendant in a larceny case. "Baseball is one of the evils of the day." Suspicion even extended into New York City's Jewish subculture. Future vaudevillian Eddie Cantor recalled hearing his grandmother shout at him as a child: "'Stop! You-you-you baseball player you!' . . . That was the worst name she could call me. To the pious people of the ghetto a baseball player was the king of the loafers."[26]

No group spurned professional baseball with more vigor than those upper-class sportsmen who were described by Henry Chadwick as a "shoddy class of Anglomaniacs." As the leading proponents of amateurism and gentlemanly traditions in sport, they looked upon the boisterous nature of the professional game with utter contempt. "Our professional baseball, with its . . . thousands of smoking, and sometimes umpire-mobbing spectators, is doing more harm than good," commented *Outing*, a magazine representing upper-class sportsmen. "The players are devoting their lives, instead of their spare time, to diversion instead of duty; and the spectators are wasting two or three hours of fresh air and sunshine looking at what they ought to be doing."[27]

Despite widespread misgivings, baseball successfully invaded the nation's popular culture. During the nineteenth century, the famed lithographers, Currier and Ives, released at least five baseball prints and as early as the 1880s fans could find a small card with a picture of a player on it with each package of cigarettes that they purchased. Ballplayers frequently appeared on the vaudeville stage—some merely to be seen, others to sing, and a few to even dance and say a few lines. Baseball and music quickly developed a close union; more than 50 baseball songs were published before 1900.

In a day far more given to popular poetry than ours, sportswriters loved to spoof the national game in verse. One poem, "Casey at the Bat," written in 1888 by San Francisco *Examiner*'s sportswriter Ernest L. Thayer, exceeded all others in popularity. In the late nineteenth and early twentieth centuries, actor DeWolf Hopper recited it countless times on the stage. No words more successfully captured the emotional power of the game than the final stanza of Casey:

> Oh! somewhere in this favored land the sun is shining bright;
> The band is playing somewhere, and somewhere children's hearts are light.
> And somewhere men are laughing, and somewhere children shout;
> But there is no joy in Mudville—mighty Casey has Struck Out.[28]

CONCLUSION

No nineteenth-century sport exceeded baseball in reaching such a large portion of the male population. Despite what many considered to be its tarnished associations, support for the game reached beyond the ranks of the urban sporting fraternity. During preadolescence, millions of boys—frequently against the wishes of their parents—learned the rudiments of the game and upon becoming teenagers many of them played on organized teams. By 1900, semiprofessional and professional nines comprised of young men representing towns or businesses could be found nearly everywhere and each summer millions of fans watched their games.

NOTES

1. A pioneering and still valuable book on nineteenth-century baseball is Albert Spalding's *America's National Game* (Lincoln: University of Nebraska Press, 1992). The standard multivolume histories are Harold Seymour, *Baseball*, 3 vols (New York: Oxford University Press, 1960, 1970, 1990); David Voigt, *American Baseball*, 3 vols (Norman: University of Oklahoma Press, vols. 1 and 2, 1966, and University Park: Penn State University Press, 1983); and Robert F. Burk, *Never Just a Game* and *Much More Than a Game* (Chapel Hill: University of North Carolina Press, 1994 and 2001). For an up-to-date one-volume treatment, see Benjamin G. Rader, *Baseball: A History of America's Game*, 2d ed. (Urbana: University of Illinois Press, 2002). For primary documents, consult Dean A. Sullivan, ed., *Early Innings: A Documentary History of Baseball, 1825–1908* (Lincoln: University of Nebraska Press, 1995), and for interpretive essays, John E. Dreifort, ed., *Baseball History from Outside the Lines* (Lincoln: University of Nebraska Press, 2001), and Jules Tygiel, *Past Time* (New York: Oxford University Press, 2000).

2. Quoted in George Kirsch, *The Creation of American Team Sports* (Urbana: University of Illinois Press, 1989), 116.

3. Quoted in Seymour, *Baseball*, I, 21.

4. Quoted in Warren Goldstein, "Playing for Keeps," unpub. Ph.D. diss, Yale University, 1983, 27. See also Goldstein, *Playing for Keeps* (Ithaca, NY: Cornell University Press, 1989) for a provocative interpretation of early baseball's history.

5. *Porter's Spirit of the Times*, 1 (January 31, 1857), 357.

6. Quoted in Melvin L. Adelman, *A Sporting Time* (Urbana: University of Illinois Press, 1986), 151.

7. Ibid., 173.

8. Quoted in Rader, *Baseball*, 21.

9. *Harper's Weekly*, October 26, 1867.

10. *New York Times*, March 8, 1872.

11. Quoted in Rader, *Baseball*, 32–33.

12. Ibid., 32.

13. Ibid., 33.

14. As quoted in Seymour, *Baseball* I, 270.

15. Tristram P. Coffin, *The Old Ballgame* (New York: Herder and Herder, 1971), 36–37.

16. See in addition to the books cited in note 1, Lee Lowenfish, *The Imperfect Diamond: A History of Baseball's Labor Wars*, rev. ed. (New York: De Capro, 1991), Part 1.

17. Quoted in Spalding, *America's National Game*, 184.

18. Ibid., 297.

19. Quoted in Seymour, *Baseball*, I, 270.

20. See Steven A. Riess, *Touching Base*, rev. ed. (Urbana: University of Illinois Press, 1999), chap. 5.

21. For an outstanding biography of Walker, see David W. Zang, *Fleet Walker* (Lincoln: University of Nebraska Press, 1995).

22. Quoted in Rader, *Baseball*, 59.

23. Ibid., 38.

24. Ibid., 76.

25. Ibid., 40.

26. Ibid., 50, 103.

27. Price Collier, "Sports' Place in the Nation's Well Being," *Outing* 32 (1898), 384–85.

28. For the full text, see Spalding, *America's National Game*, 540–41.

5
NINETEENTH-CENTURY SPORTING COMMUNITIES

*T*he first United States tennis championship tournament opened on August 31, 1881, at the posh Casino Club in Newport, Rhode Island. Fewer than 50 spectators, all wealthy vacationers who resided in their splendid stone "cottages" during the summer, milled around the court. The gentlemen, decked out in white flannels, striped jackets, and straw bowlers, stood while the ladies, who wore ankle-length petticoats and carried parasols to protect their delicate skin from the sun, sat on folding chairs or camp stools. The players themselves sported white flannels, long-sleeved shirts, and neckties, though they exchanged their bowlers for striped caps when playing. They played by the rules established by the All-England Croquet and Lawn Tennis Club, Wimbledon, England, in 1877. Richard D. "Dicky" Sears, a slight, bespectacled lad of 19 from a Boston Brahmin family, conquered a field of 22 players, all of whom came from wealthy families residing on the Eastern seaboard.

A deep chasm separated the sporting world of these Newport summer vacationers from the sporting universe of the lower, blue- and white-collar working classes. Only those in the highest social strata could watch or play in the tournament; the Casino Club was so exclusive that it had once turned away a president of the United States (Chester A. Arthur) for his inadequate social standing. The spectators paid no admission; they never cheered or gesticulated. Only polite, whispered conversation punctuated the progress of the match. To the Newport crowd, winning or losing was of no more importance than playing with proper grace, style, and etiquette. No one was paid to play. Following the match the players and spectators retired to the elegant Casino clubhouse where they could enjoy sumptuous food and drink. To most of the wealthy Newport residents, the tournament represented a pleasant interlude in their summer social season.

Yet the significance of tennis and other sports played by the rich extended far beyond the obvious. In a society characterized by an exceptionally fluid social structure, expensive sports provided a means by which the wealthy, especially the parvenu, could distinguish their numbers from the masses. The wealthy therefore tended to look upon sports requiring merely a field and a ball with contempt; these were the diversions of ordinary people. Instead, they lavished their attention on thoroughbred horse racing, yachting, polo, track and field, cricket, tennis, and golf, games that required large amounts of free time, costly facilities, elaborate equipment, and sometimes travel to far-away places. As we shall see in the next chapter, college football had similar origins; it was at first almost exclusively a sport of upper-class young men.

The wealthy were not the only social group to establish informal sporting communities in the nineteenth century.[1] African Americans and recently arrived immigrants founded their own sporting communities. With low or modest incomes and frequently victims of the prejudices of both the upper and middle classes, the sporting ways of these social "outsiders" were usually far less ostentatious than those of the wealthy. Yet they found in sport, along with neighborhoods, special theaters, music societies, restaurants, coffee houses, saloons, and

LAWN TENNIS, 1887 In the nineteenth century, only the nation's wealthiest citizens played lawn tennis. Notice that women wore bustles and full-length dresses.
(UPI/Corbis)

above all churches or synagogues, a means of preserving traditions and bolstering larger ethnic and racial communities.

ETHNIC (OR IMMIGRANT) SPORTING COMMUNITIES

To a remarkable degree, the history of ethnic (or immigrant) sporting communities reflects the complex processes of assimilation and retention of traditional ways. Because of their closer similarities in language and culture, immigrants from England, Scotland, and Wales experienced less pressure to maintain their old ways than did immigrants from other parts of Europe. The Scottish Caledonian and English cricket clubs, for example, functioned briefly as distinctive ethnic organizations. But as Scottish and English immigration declined and as these groups merged into the mainstream of American culture, their drive to preserve their ethnic traditions dissipated.

Extending far back in the mists of Scottish history, rural communities had held annual track and field games as a part of their larger festive culture. Scots brought these games with them to America, where they organized Caledonian clubs. Well over one hundred such clubs eventually formed; Scottish immigrants even founded Caledonian clubs in smaller cities. In 1887, for example, the *Scottish-American Journal* reported that "A Caledonian club has been organized at Great Falls, Montana, with a membership of 37 enthusiastic Scots." The clubs restricted membership to persons of Scottish birth or descent. The purpose of the clubs, as one of the founders of the Boston organization put it, was to perpetuate "the manners and customs, literature, the Highland costume and the athletic games of Scotland, as practiced by our forefathers."[2] Apart from sport, the Caledonian clubs sponsored extensive social activities, such as dinners, dancing, and bagpipe playing.

From the 1850s to the mid-1870s, the Caledonians occupied a special place in American track and field. In the 1870s, large crowds, as many as 20,000 in New York City, turned out to view competition in footracing, tug o'war, hurdling, jumping, pole vaulting, throwing the hammer, and putting the shot. In 1886 the New York Caledonian Club even added a 220-yard dash for women, which resulted in spectators breaking through the ropes in order to get a better view. The clubs seized upon the opportunities for financial gain. They opened competition to all athletes regardless of ethnicity or race, charged admission, and offered cash prizes to winners. The success of the Caledonians encouraged the formation of wealthy old-stock American athletic clubs as well. In the late nineteenth century, as Scottish immigration slackened, nearly all the Caledonian clubs folded.

For a brief time, cricket clubs functioned in a similar fashion for English immigrants. By the 1840s, when a new influx of immigrants arrived in the United States, England was already in the midst of a sporting revolution. Cricket was popular in both the southern downs and the industrial north of England. The skilled textile workers from the north brought cricket with them to the mills at Lawrence and Lowell, Massachusetts, and to the Manheim district of Philadelphia. Their version of cricket often included a rough-and-tumble style of play, male companionship, and hard drinking. After the matches, the immigrant work-ingmen gathered at favorite saloons to recount matches of the past and swap sto-ries of the homeland.[3]

In New York, Brooklyn, and Boston, English merchants and professional men organized formal cricket clubs. Their version of cricket was only somewhat more decorous than the workingmen's. They usually wagered for side bets and hired professional players if they could afford it, but they might also interrupt matches for a dinner, and the matches might continue over two or three days.

In the 1850s, cricket rivaled American baseball as a team sport spectacle. The St. George Cricket Club of New York, which employed a professional crick-eter from England as a trainer and was the premier club in the United States until the Civil War, attracted large crowds to its matches with clubs from Montreal, Toronto, and Boston. New York newspapers regularly gave its contests more cov-erage than the city's baseball games. In 1859, over 24,000 attended a cricket match at the Elysian Fields in Hoboken between an all-star American team and a touring professional "eleven." Extra ferries had to be engaged to handle the fans who crossed the river from Manhattan.

By 1860, there were ten clubs in New York and Brooklyn. Several pioneers of American baseball, such as Harry Wright and Henry Chadwick, came from the ranks of the English cricket clubs. For a decade or so after 1850, old-stock Ameri-can clubs sometimes played both cricket and baseball. But then came the Civil War. The war dealt cricket in New York and Brooklyn a blow from which it never fully recovered.

In the last half of the nineteenth century, teams from the British Isles, Aus-tralia, and Canada regularly toured the United States, playing both the English ethnic clubs and the powerful old-stock American clubs of Philadelphia. By 1887, there were at least 50 clubs scattered throughout the larger cities of the country. For a few years in the 1890s, clubs in Chicago, Detroit, Pittsburgh, New York, Philadelphia, Boston, and Baltimore played in the Inter-City Cricket League, an amateur circuit, and on the Pacific Coast clubs engaged in lively competition for the Harrison Championship Cup. But in the early twentieth century, as English immigration declined sharply and later generations assimilated into the host soci-ety, the English cricket clubs faded rapidly from the American sporting scene.

Being predominately Catholic and having a centuries' old animosity to-ward the English, Irish immigrants rarely adjusted as quickly or easily as the Eng-lish or the Scots to the dominant American culture. From the 1850s on, Irish Americans played a conspicuous role in the sporting fraternity, but after the Civil War they also formed their own clubs for both the perpetuation of Old World games and the playing of New World sports. A revival of Irish nationalism in the 1870s and 1880s stimulated a rebirth of such folk games as hurling and Gaelic football in both the Emerald Isle and the United States. Perhaps typical of cities containing substantial numbers of Irish was an announcement in the Boston *Pilot* in 1881: "A large number of the Irish people in Boston are becoming interested in the exhibitions of the games and pastimes of their ancestors."[4] In the 1880s and 1890s, at least five Irish athletic clubs in Boston regularly engaged in hurling, the national game of Ireland. With even more alacrity, Irish Americans formed associations for playing baseball, boxing, wrestling, and track and field.

TURNER SOCIETIES

Unlike the Scottish Caledonian and the English cricket clubs, the *Turnverein*, or the Turner societies, had first been organized in their native land of Germany. In reaction to the rule of Napoleon, the power of the German aristocracy, and the disunity of the German states, Frederick Ludwig Jahn formed the first *Turnverein* in Berlin in 1811. From the start, the Turners had a strong ideological cast. Urging universal education and a systematic program of gymnastics (the latter modeled after the ancient Greeks), Jahn hoped to create a united and democratic Germany. Young middle-class men—petty officials, intellectuals, journalists, and students—flocked to Jahn's new society. The Revolution of 1848 brought disaster for the Turners; many of them then emigrated to the United States.

The Turner immigrants faced a different challenge in America. Although the new republic had no hereditary aristocracy nor many of the other remnants of feudalism, American individualism ran counter to the deepest social instincts of the Turners. Utopian, free-thinking, and socialistic, they sought an organic community. They also arrived during the heyday of the Know-Nothing movement, a nativist crusade of the 1850s directed mainly against the Catholic Church and Irish immigrants. But, in several places, the Turners bore the brunt of mob action as well.

Perhaps even more crucial in driving the Turners together was the fierce antagonism they experienced from the "church" Germans. Their haughty anticlericalism and belief in their superior cultural achievements made it difficult for the Turners to find a refuge in the larger German ethnic communities of the United States. Hence, in many places, the Turner societies formed distinctive subcommunities, sharply separated from those Germans whose lives revolved around their churches.

Shortly after their arrival in the New World, the revolutionary émigrés of 1848 organized Turner societies. The Turner halls usually provided a complete social center with lectures, libraries, and a bar. Here, the Turners tried to preserve the speech, songs, and customs of the Fatherland. They often formed separate militia companies. In 1851 the Turners held a national gymnastics festival in Philadelphia. This competitive event became an annual affair, with gymnasts from over 150 societies eventually participating.

After the Civil War the Turners abandoned most of their radical political program but continued to sponsor an active social calendar that included gymnastics. In 1881, by competing in a gymnastics festival held at Frankfurt, a group of Turners from the Normal School of the *Turnerbund* located in Milwaukee initiated irregular competition between Turner teams from the United States and Germany, a competition that continued until World War I. One of the striking features of the Chicago World's Fair of 1893 was a mass exercise performed by 4,000 German American members of the national *Turnerbund*. In 1898, the United States commissioner of education declared that the introduction of school gymnastics in Chicago, Kansas City, Cleveland, Denver, Indianapolis, St. Louis, Milwaukee, Cincinnati, St. Paul, and San Francisco was due to the Turners and that "the directors of physical education [in these cities] are graduates of the Seminary or Normal School of the North American Turnerbund."[5]

Sports could both ease the transition of ethnic groups into American society and aid them in protecting and even enhancing their identity. Nineteenth-century baseball illustrated the twin processes. Since baseball could be played quickly, equipment costs were minimal, and any open space could serve as a playing area, it did not long remain an exclusive sport of old-stock Americans. Beginning in the 1850s, the Irish and the Germans took up the sport with enthusiasm. In New Orleans, for example, the Germans founded the Schneiders, Laners, and Lanwehrs, and the Irish, the Fenian Baseball Club. Baseball invariably accompanied the ethnic picnics of the Germans, Irish, French, and later, Italians. As late as the 1920s, a French-Canadian faction in Woonsocket, Rhode Island, resorted to baseball as a means of preserving their community from the forces of assimilation.[6] Sports not only provided immigrants with shared experiences but also the experience of playing and watching games could blur status, ideological, and personal differences within ethnic communities.

AFRICAN AMERICAN SPORTING COMMUNITIES

Inadequate evidence makes it difficult to reach more than tentative conclusions about the black experience in nineteenth-century sport. Newspapers and sporting journals rarely reported the sporting activities of African Americans. Until the Civil War, slavery obviously curtailed the athletic opportunities for blacks. In the antebellum era, planters sometimes promoted boxing bouts among their slaves and used them as crews for boating regattas. To the extent that they had equal leisure time and funds, free blacks in the urban areas were probably as active in sport as their white counterparts. In the New York City area, blacks sponsored occasional prizefights and scheduled a few professional pedestrian races.

In New Orleans, where the largest aggregation of free blacks resided in the antebellum era, African Americans formed two sport clubs—Bayou and LaVille—for the playing of raquette. Apparently borrowed from the Choctaw Indians, raquette was a team game resembling lacrosse. The Sunday matches between black clubs in the 1850s sometimes attracted as many as 4,000 spectators from all social ranks and both races. For a brief interval after the Civil War, a few interracial raquette contests were held, but interest in the game soon gave way to other sports.

With the abolition of slavery by the Civil War, opportunities for black participation in highly organized forms of sport became more common. Prizefighting was especially popular, a few black athletic clubs formed in larger cities, and literally dozens of black baseball teams took to the field. Baseball was by far the most popular team sport of urban blacks. In New Orleans, for example, several clubs scheduled a citywide "Negro championship" series in the 1880s. As in other parts of the country, it was not unusual for black and amateur or semiprofessional teams to play against one another. A newspaper account of a game played in 1887 at New Orleans, in which a black nine defeated a white club, noted: "The playing of the colored club was far above the average ball playing and elicited hearty and generous applause from the large crowd in attendance, which was about evenly divided between white and colored."[7]

THE WEALTHY NEW YORK SPORTING COMMUNITY

Of America's largest cities, New York continued its leadership among wealthy sportsmen. Since colonial times the city's high society had been more tolerant of play than its counterparts in Philadelphia or Boston. In all three cities a residue of the colonial elite joined with new men in the late eighteenth and nineteenth centuries to exploit the vast new opportunities presented in foreign trade, real estate, banking, law, and politics. But unlike New York, the Boston and Philadelphia mercantile-Federalist elites founded virtual dynasties. Their descendants, the Boston Brahmin and Philadelphia Main Line families, managed for the most part to perpetuate their inherited status; they continued to dominate the industrial, financial, and cultural activities of the respective cities—in many instances even to this day.

On the other hand, the rapid surge in population growth, commerce, railroad building, and the factory system in the latter half of the nineteenth century fractured the older New York elite. "Separate enclaves dominated trade, politics, culture, and fashion, although some common membership existed among these groups," concluded a historian of New York's upper class.[8] The absence of a clearcut dynasty or social arbitrator in New York gave rise to the "beautiful people" in the post-Civil War era. The nouveau riche frequently defied Victorian restraints. The "smart set," or "Four Hundred," as the press dubbed them, splurged their wealth on highly publicized activities available only to the superrich. Expensive sports promoted their consciousness as an elite social group and furnished them with a vehicle of self-advertisement.

A classic example was James Gordon Bennett Jr., the colorful and eccentric owner of the *New York Herald*.[9] Bennett's father, a recent Scottish immigrant who had built the *Herald* into the world's most profitable newspaper, had been a social outsider. The younger Bennett, however, used his father's vast fortune to lift himself into fashionable circles. In 1857, at the tender age of 16, he became a member of the New York Yacht Club. Nine years later, he captured the attention of the entire nation by winning the world's first transatlantic yacht race. The large purse of $60,000 won from side bets and the loss of six members of his crew who were swept overboard in a violent storm added to Bennett's reputation for bravado. In the meantime he sponsored Henry Stanley's exotic search for David Livingstone who had been missing for several years in the African jungles. Both Europeans and Americans avidly followed Stanley's reports from the heart of Africa. His eventual success in locating Livingstone became the stuff of a monumental legend.

Bennett had a direct influence on several sports. Beginning in 1873 he awarded cups and medals to collegiate track and field champions. After having witnessed polo played by English Army officers, he introduced the game into the United States in 1876. Bennett and his wealthy friends formed the Westchester Polo Club in New York and took the sport to the Newport summer colony. Acutely concerned with staying current with the latest English sporting fashions, American polo enthusiasts even extended upper-class comforts to their ponies; for example, they provided monogrammed linen sheets upon which their ponies could sleep. In 1886 Newport hosted the first international match with the Hurlingham Club of England.

Bennett's assistance to the sport of lawn tennis had more bizarre origins. According to legend, in 1878 he secured for a British army officer a guest card to Newport's most exclusive club, the Reading Room. He then dared his friend, who accepted the challenge, to ride a horse up the steps of the club's front hall. The Reading Room immediately revoked Bennett's guest privileges. Miffed, Bennett retaliated by building a lavish sports complex, called the Casino, a few blocks away. The Casino subsequently became the site for the first 34 national tennis championships.

By 1878 Bennett had left New York to live in Paris, an exile caused by a gross indiscretion. In mixed company he had relieved himself into a fireplace at his fiancée's New Year's Day party. His fiancée's family immediately broke the engagement; later her brother publicly attacked and humiliated Bennett, and eventually the two men fought a nonlethal duel. Bennett then left America, forever shunned by New York's Four Hundred. He seldom returned to the United States, but his *New York Herald* led the major dailies in reporting sporting news. Later in the century he contributed to the Olympic movement and promoted horse, auto, and air races.

SPORTS AND THE FORGING OF AN AMERICAN UPPER CLASS

In the nineteenth century, especially in its closing decades, sports frequently became an integral component of a nationwide quest to forge an American upper or ruling class. While there had always been Americans with aristocratic pretensions, the nation had never had a hereditary aristocracy in the European sense. But, fed by the spectacular transfusions of new wealth arising from the Industrial Revolution and the creation of giant corporations, by the 1880s and 1890s efforts to create what might be appropriately called an American aristocracy had, in the words of historian Robert Wiebe, "the look of a formidable enterprise."[10] Each city of any consequence had a fashionable residential area of the superrich. There, they built huge mansions. They sent their sons to the colleges that catered only to the nation's affluent. Edward H. Harriman, the railroad tycoon who went to work at the age of 14, dispatched his sons to Groton and Yale, H.J. Heinz, another self-made millionaire, sent his son to Yale, and John D. Rockefeller's children attended Brown and Vassar.

In the formation of a distinctive upper class, private clubs played a particularly significant role. Before the Civil War, men of old wealth, most of whom looked upon sport and conspicuous display with utter disdain, formed metropolitan men's clubs, such as the Philadelphia (founded in 1835), the Union in New York (1836), the Century in New York (1847), and the Somerset in Boston (1851).The clubs rarely tolerated any activity more vigorous than napping in easy chairs, smoking cigars, sipping brandy, reading newspapers, or quiet conversations.

After the Civil War, the number of clubs patronizing the wealthy ballooned. Union Leagues, centers of Republican respectability, and the University clubs, comprised of the graduates of the nation's most prestigious colleges, ranked slightly below the patrician metropolitan clubs. A variety of athletic, cricket (among old-stock Americans), and country clubs came next in the urban club hierarchy. Unlike the clubs above them, these clubs usually welcomed women as guests or as auxiliary members, and they promoted a spirited, physically active club life. The clubs and their activities (including sports) brought together old and new wealth. Experiences and values arising from the club nexus contributed to the formation of a distinctively American upper class.

Fascination with, and efforts to imitate, the European aristocracy, especially the English, were often marked characteristics of upper-class life in the United States. The nouveau riche frequently sent their children on European tours, married off their daughters to sons of the European nobility, and took up the latest European pastimes with alacrity. Prior to the 1850s, the English gentleman's leisure activities had consisted mostly of country weekend excursions, balls, riding to the hounds, perhaps a bit of cricket, horse racing, gambling, and hard drinking. But in the middle decades of the nineteenth century, many of the upper class became avid sportsmen—forming hundreds of clubs for cricket, yachting, track and field, rowing, cycling, lawn tennis, and eventually golf. In most instances, the English sportsmen preceded the Americans by a decade or more in organizing their sports.[11]

ATHLETIC CLUBS

For a dozen years or so, New York City's first athletic club seemed little concerned with social status. Inspired by the formation of the London Athletic Club in 1863, the first English amateur championship meet in 1866, and the athletic activities of the New York Caledonian Club, three well-to-do young athletes founded the New York Athletic Club (NYAC) in 1866. Apparently the founders simply wanted an opportunity to engage in track and field with men of similar social standing and congenial interests. (See Chapter 3 for the world of track and field of the Victorian counterculture.) All three of the founders belonged to local boating clubs, and they induced several of their fellow rowers to join the NYAC. During inclement weather the athletes worked out in the back parlor of a private residence. On fair days they went to the Elysian Fields or some other open space for running, vaulting, and shot-putting. In 1868 the club incorporated with 14 members and sponsored the first open amateur track and field meet. Having issued the New York Caledonian Club a special invitation, the meet was hailed as "an international match—America against Scotland."[12]

Soon other clubs—among them the Staten Island, American, Manhattan, Pastime, University, and Crescent clubs, all of New York—organized on the NYAC model. By 1879 wealthy sportsmen in Baltimore, Buffalo, Chicago, Detroit, and St. Louis had also established athletic clubs. In the 1870s the NYAC expanded its activities by building the first cinder track in the country at Mott Haven, introducing the use of spiked shoes and sponsoring the first national amateur championships in track and field (1876), swimming (1877), boxing (1878), and wrestling (1878). In addition to the individual sports, many of the clubs eventually sponsored football and basketball teams.

Beginning in 1882 the New York Athletic Club no longer functioned as an association devoted exclusively or perhaps even chiefly to athletics. In that year Alfred H. Curtis interested two of the city's wealthiest citizens, Herman Oelrichs and William R. Travers, in the club. Both Oelrichs and Travers were members of an exclusive upper-class social network that revolved around prestigious clubs; they were also prominent in the Four Hundred. Oelrichs, described by a contemporary as a "social leader" of the city, belonged to no fewer than 21 clubs, including the Union and New York Yacht clubs. Described as a leading patron of "gentleman's sports," he was himself a capable swimmer, boxer, and polo player. Travers, a stockbroker, bon vivant, and raconteur, was also a member of the Union Club and the Yacht Club as well as 24 other clubs. According to a contemporary, the decisions of Oelrichs and Travers to support the club drew into the "club's ranks the most prominent and successful men in New York City and vicinity."[13] By 1885 club membership had grown to 1,500.

The NYAC acted as a gatekeeper for those seeking admission to even more socially exclusive clubs. The NYAC carefully screened membership applicants and required a written application with pertinent personal information and the signatures of the members proposing and seconding the nominee for membership. With this information the membership committee could seek to locate the applicant's standing within the city's social hierarchy. The initiation fee of $100 and annual dues of $50 also helped weed out undesirables. Athletic clubs could impose other strictures. The University Athletic Club, for example, required that all applicants possess a college degree, preferably from an Ivy League school. In short, membership in the metropolitan athletic clubs became an important link in a web of exclusive, upper-class associations.

With Oelrichs and Travers at the helm, the NYAC rapidly expanded its social activities. In 1885 it completed construction of an elegant five-story, Venetian-style clubhouse at a cost of $150,000, which contained a gymnasium, swimming pool, dining rooms, club rooms, a bowling alley, rifle range, billiard room, a superb wine cellar, and sleeping rooms. In 1888 it acquired a country home at Travers Island where it built a track, clubhouse, boathouse, and clay tennis courts. Expanding the membership limit to 2,500 in 1892, the NYAC constructed an even more lavish facility at the corner of 59th Street and 6th Avenue. Other clubs, attempting to emulate the NYAC set up elaborate social calendars. "Wine, women, and song," according to the historians of the NYAC, "became more than a catch phrase—they were woven into the texture of NYAC activities."[14]

The 1880s and early 1890s marked the heyday of the athletic club. In 1887 an observer reported: "Athletic clubs are now springing into existence in the United States in such profusion as to baffle the effort to enumerate them. Scarce a city can be found having a population of more than 30,000 inhabitants, in which there is not at least one club of this class."[15] While the clubs in smaller cities enjoyed far less commodious facilities than the metropolitan clubs, they were usually made up of the community's wealthiest citizens. In most cases they also sponsored annual track and field competition, although their athletes rarely competed successfully with those of the larger clubs.

Clubs in Boston, New Orleans, Chicago, and San Francisco soon rivaled the New York clubs in terms of facilities and membership. In 1893 the Chicago Club, for example, built a nine-story clubhouse costing nearly $1 million, a structure more costly than any of New York's clubs. Sometimes the clubs sponsored exotic and extravagant shows. In 1895 the Olympic Club in San Francisco put together a detailed reconstruction of Greek and Roman games, complete with a Caesar, courtiers, senators, gladiators, and vestal virgins. Over 4,000 persons attended the event, which cost $2.50 per seat.[16] But the 1890s also brought severe financial problems to many of the clubs. Some had overbuilt and the economic depression of that decade brought about their collapse. After the 1890s the metropolitan athletic club movement never fully recovered, but the early twentieth century witnessed the formation of many less pretentious, smaller clubs whose energies were devoted primarily to sport rather than social exclusion.

NEW YORK ATHLETIC CLUB DINING ROOM, 1898 This photograph reveals the splendor of the socially exclusive New York Athletic Club.
(Library of Congress)

AMATEURISM AND ITS USES

Amateurism, which had its origins among upper-class English sportsmen, became a cardinal principle of American upper-class sporting ideology. In order to separate their pastimes from those of the ordinary people, the English amateur gentlemen insisted that play should not only be *without* pay, but also that playing should be done in a *special* way. Ideally, the amateur sportsmen always exhibited the principles of "fair play"; they never sought an advantage by unfair means or by seizing upon advantages that were unavailable to their opponents. In principle, amateurs needed no game officials to enforce the rules; they policed themselves. Gentlemen amateurs played with a distinct style. Those athletes who exhibited the greatest skills without apparent training and with the least physical exertion received the highest accolades. In quest of sanctions for their sporting ethos, the upper class also invented the myth of ancient Greek amateurism. While in fact the ancient Greeks never distinguished between professional and amateur athletes and did not have a concept of fair play, the myth of Greek amateurism has become a powerful idea in the world of modern sports.

Initially, the American athletic clubs raised no objections to pay for play. Members of the clubs sometimes even ran in matches alongside professional pedestrians for bets one week and then in the following week competed in their club's closed games for a medal. But, as the clubs became more concerned about social exclusion, they discovered the utility of British amateurism. As early as 1876, the New York Athletic Club restricted its fall games to "any person who has never competed . . . for public or admission money, or with professionals for a prize . . . nor has at any period in his life taught or assisted in the pursuit of athletic exercises as a means of livelihood."[17] In 1879, the National Association of Amateur Athletes of America, commonly known as the N4A and comprised of the most exclusive athletic clubs, essentially copied the NYAC definition of amateurism.

The effect of the N4A's and the NYAC's amateur rule was to reduce the likelihood of lower-middle and working-class athletes from participating in their games as well as in other parts of club life. "The youths who participate in the health-giving competitions, as a rule, cannot afford the expense of membership in the so-called Athletic Clubs," complained Frederick Janssen in 1885, "and they retire in favor of the wealthy young man whose sole claim to fame to athletic distinction is his connection with a 'high-toned' club." Prohibiting the less privileged from competition served the larger purpose of building distinctive upper-class communities. "There has grown up a system of clubs and associations whose best interests, pecuniary and social," explained Will B. "Father Bill" Curtis, a founder of the NYAC, "would partially or wholly lose their value were the amateur fence to be taken down or materially lowered."[18]

Yet, in practice, the clubs in one noticeable respect fell short of fulfilling amateur ideals. Without a set of established customs and the sponsorship of a powerful, landed aristocracy, upper-class sportsmen in the United States seemed to play their games with less restraint than their British counterparts. More often than not men of new wealth, the wealthy Americans, brought to sports the same winning-at-all-costs ethos that prevailed in the marketplace. Hence, defeating one's rivals by any means, including breaking the rules if one were not caught, was consistent with their experiences in the world of commerce and industry.

A winning-at-all costs ethos intruded into the relationships among the athletic clubs. In the 1880s the major metropolitan clubs embarked upon an era of intense rivalries with one another for athletic supremacy. In order to field the strongest bevy of athletes possible, the clubs extended thinly disguised subsidies to superior performers. A top athlete (unless he were black or too crude in social demeanor) might encounter few difficulties in finding a club that would grant him a free membership and sometimes other valuable perquisites as well.

The career of Lawrence E. "Lon" Myers, hailed as "the world's greatest runner," is a striking case in point.[19] Myers was of Jewish ancestry but nonetheless had no difficulty obtaining membership in prestigious athletic clubs. For most of his amateur career, which extended from 1878 to 1885, he ran for the Manhattan Athletic Club. Standing five feet seven and one-quarter inches tall and weighing a mere 114 pounds, Myers won 15 American amateur championships plus several English and Canadian titles. At one time or another, he held every American record in all distances from 50 yards to the mile run. When he died in 1899, he still held records in five distances.

In 1884 charges surfaced that Myers had violated the N4A amateur code. He had, according to a newspaper account, received pay for directing the construction of the Manhattan Club's new grounds, for serving as club secretary, and for editing a portion of a sporting weekly. In addition, Myers had allegedly sold some of his medals. Without disproving or denying the validity of these charges, the executive committee of the N4A formally upheld Myers's amateur standing. In the next year the Manhattan Club even scheduled a benefit on his behalf, which netted the athlete some $4,000. Shortly thereafter, Myers became an announced professional.

The passionate competition among the clubs (especially the NYAC and the Manhattan) and disputes over the eligibility of athletes resulted in the demise of the N4A. Amid bitter charges and countercharges, the New York Athletic Club withdrew from the association in 1886 and led a group of clubs in forming the Amateur Athletic Union (AAU) in 1888; the N4A collapsed the following year. Although the AAU eventually established a broad-based hegemony over amateur athletics in the United States, controversies revolving around the enforcement and meaning of amateurism continued unabated far into the twentieth century.[20] In the end, the promoters of the amateur ethos seized effective control of America's track and field athletics. "By the 1920s," concluded historian Steven Pope, "track and field ceased to be something working-class people dabbled in on holidays and weekends."[21]

CRICKET CLUBS AND COUNTRY CLUBS

In their quest to build and sustain upper-class communities, those aspiring for social exclusivity turned to sports other than track and field. In Philadelphia but not in other American cities, old-stock, upper-class Americans became enthusiastic cricketers.[22] The popularity of cricket among Philadelphia's elite sprang partly from chance. In the 1840s English textile workers employed at the Wakefield Mills introduced cricket to a group of young, native Philadelphians residing in the Manheim region. In the 1850s Manheim youngsters organized three clubs; one, the Young America Cricket Club, explicitly excluded from membership anyone who was foreign-born. By so doing, the club helped dissociate itself from the "steak and ale" style of cricket played among the English workingmen.

After the Civil War, men of old wealth built elaborate clubhouses and acquired spacious grounds. The top five clubs placed their grounds and built their clubhouses in the city's most prestigious neighborhoods. By the 1890s, within a ten-mile radius, Philadelphia had four beautifully kept, sumptuous grounds with lavish clubhouses; London, by comparison, had only two grounds of equal stature. Membership in the five "first-class" clubs ranged from 500 to 1,300 persons.

The clubs's cricketers even made a splash in international competition. In 1874 a team picked from the Philadelphia clubs accepted an invitation to play a series of matches at Halifax, Nova Scotia, with British and Canadian elevens for an international prize. After the Philadelphia eleven won the cup, it became the object of intense competition among the city's major clubs. By 1891, Philadelphia teams had played touring professional and amateur teams from the British Isles at least seven times, Australian clubs twice, and Canadian teams on numerous occasions. In both 1884 and 1889 the "Gentlemen of Philadelphia" visited England. They acquitted themselves well, winning four, losing three, and drawing five matches against top-flight English competition.

The cricket clubs were integral parts of Philadelphia's upper-class suburban life. Not only the expense of membership but also the time required to play cricket automatically excluded the ordinary workingman. As the "national game" of England, cricket also appealed to status-conscious Americans who sought to emulate the habits of English sportsmen. The clubs assumed a wide array of social functions similar to the metropolitan athletic clubs. The report of the Board of Governors of the Germantown Cricket Club in 1891 reveals the social character of the typical first-class club.

> That the grounds are socially a success is now an undisputed fact, and too much credit cannot be given to the Ladies' Committee. . . . Ladies' teas have been served every Tuesday; Thursday has been made music day, and Saturday match day, so that the entire week has been made attractive, and the attendance consequently large.[23]

The Germantown club enjoyed a new clubhouse, designed by the distinguished New York architectural firm of McKim, Mead, and White. Like the other clubs, it also sponsored an elaborate program of cricket for juniors. Club leaders believed that playing cricket inculcated the young with gentlemanly values.

While the Philadelphia cricket clubs continued to thrive in the twentieth century, cricket as a sport declined rapidly. As the clubs became agencies of social exclusion, cricket tended to be only a byproduct of the clubs' main function. Other diversions such as lawn tennis, golf, and swimming could serve the club membership equally well. Since tennis required less space and could be played much more quickly than cricket, it became, in time, the rage of the cricket clubs. Two members of the Merion club, William Jackson Clothier and Richard Norris Williams, were United States doubles champions in 1906, 1914, and 1916. And William "Big Bill" Tilden, the country's greatest player in the 1920s, learned his game on the courts of the Germantown Cricket Club. By the 1920s the cricket clubs could hardly be distinguished from any other superwealthy metropolitan country or golf club.

The metropolitan athletic and cricket clubs were forerunners of the great country club movement that first flourished in the 1920s. The country club was, in effect, a substitute for the English country home of the aristocracy or monied gentry. "It is a banding together for the purpose of making available to the group facilities which previously had been the privilege of the wealthy aristocrat," declared the official historians of the original Country Club at Brookline, Massachusetts.[24] While in England the aristocracy usually lived in the country and belonged to clubs located in the cities, rich Americans normally resided in the cities and sought outside their hurly-burly life an approximation of the English country home with its aristocratic privileges of servants and exclusive outdoor sports. The main activities of the early clubs centered on hunting, fishing, horseback riding, and other activities, which in England were reserved to those able to afford country estates.

The first "Country Club," founded in 1882, was far more socially exclusive than later imitators. "For many years after 1882 Boston had that of which it was very proud—its Society," wrote the country club historians. "Everybody was either in it or out of it; and those who were in it were proud of the fact and guarded its boundaries jealously. They played with each other, not with others; they competed with each other, not with others; above all, they married each other only, and so their children carried on the good(?) tradition."[25] The Brookline Country Club was one of the primary agencies for preserving the exclusivity of Boston "Society."

The country clubs and the summer resorts of the rich eased the process by which the wealthy shed lingering Victorian suspicions of play-for-play's-sake. At these private retreats, the rich could release inhibitions with far less fear of exposure than in public places. In sharp contrast to those middle-class Victorians who insisted that play could be justified only when it aided in doing one's proper work, the upper strata frankly favored play for its inutility, in short, simply for the pleasures it afforded the participants. The Grafton Country Club of Worcester, Massachusetts, for instance, even adopted as its motto, "Each to His Pleasure," a direct contradiction of the Victorian work ethic.[26] Club social life everywhere inclined toward greater personal freedom for the enjoyment of sensual pleasures. Attracting members of a new fast-growing middle class of white-collar workers, the country club movement mushroomed in the twentieth century (see Chapter 12).

CONCLUSION

Apart from the sporting fraternity and its spectacles, the nineteenth century also witnessed the growth of sporting communities based on class, race, and ethnicity. In particular, the Scotch, English, German, and Irish immigrants were important in forming ethnic sporting clubs. Their clubs and associated activities helped to preserve traditional cultural patterns as well as serve as agencies for the formation of larger ethnic communities. Wealthy Americans also constructed sporting communities; their athletic clubs and their sports fostered their separation from the masses. In the next chapter we will examine college football, a sport created mainly by the offspring of the nation's upper class.

NOTES

1. See B.G. Rader, "The Quest for Subcommunities and the Rise of American Sport," *American Quarterly* 29 (1977), 355–69. For both ethnic and elite sporting communities, see especially Stephen Hardy, *How Boston Played* (Boston: Northeastern University Press, 1982), and Steven A. Riess, *City Games* (Urbana: University of Illinois Press, 1989). For the sports of the upper class, see especially Donald J. Mrozek, *Sport and the American Mentality* (Knoxville: University of Tennessee Press, 1983).

2. Quotations in Gerald Redmond, *The Caledonian Games* (Rutherford, NJ: Fairleigh Dickinson University Press, 1971), 39, 45.

3. Melvin L. Adelman, *A Sporting Time* (Urbana: University of Illinois Press, 1986); J.A. Lester, ed., *A Century of Philadelphia Cricket* (Philadelphia: University of Pennsylvania Press, 1951); and George B. Kirsch, *The Creation of American Team Sports* (Urbana: University of Illinois Press, 1989).

4. Quoted in Hardy, *How Boston Played*, 138.

5. Quoted in A.E. Zucker, ed., *The Forty Eighters* (New York: Columbia University Press, 1950), 109.

6. Richard Sorrel, "Sports and the Franco-Americans in Woonsocket, 1870–1930," *Rhode Island History* 31 (1972), 112.

7. Quoted in Dale A. Somers, *The Rise of Sports in New Orleans* (Baton Rouge: Louisiana State University Press, 1972), 120.

8. F.C. Jaher, "Style and Status: High Society in the Late Nineteenth Century New York," in F. C. Jaher, ed., *The Rich, the Well Born, and the Powerful* (Urbana: University of Illinois Press, 1973), 259.

9. See Donald Seitz, *The James Gordon Bennetts* (Indianapolis, IN: Bobbs-Merrill, 1928), and Richard O'Connor, *The Scandalous Mr. Bennett* (Garden City, NY: Doubleday, 1962).

10. Robert H. Wiebe, *Self-Rule: A Cultural History of American Democracy* (Chicago: University of Chicago Press, 1995), 87. For the making of an American upper class, see especially E. Digby Baltzell, *Philadelphia Gentlemen* (New York: Free Press, 1958); E. Digby Baltzell, *The Protestant Establishment* (New York: Random House, 1964); Frederic Cople Jaher, *The Urban Establishment* (Urbana: University of Illinois Press, 1982); Ronald Story, *The Forging of an Aristocracy: Harvard & the Boston Upper Class, 1800–1870* (Middletown, CT: Wesleyan University Press, 1980); and Sven Beckert, *The Monied Metropolis: New York City and the Consolidation of the American Bourgeoisie, 1850–1896* (New York: Cambridge University Press, 2001). Beckert equates "bourgeoisie" with what I have here described as the upper class.

11. See esp. Richard Holt, *Sport and the British* (Oxford: Oxford University Press, 1989), and the discussion of S.W. Pope, *Patriotic Games: Sporting Traditions and the American Imagination, 1876–1920* (New York: Oxford University Press, 1997), chap. 2.

12. F. W. Janssen, *History of Amateur Athletics* (New York: Charles R. Bourne, 1885), 35. See also Bob Considine and F. R. Jarvis, *The First Hundred*

Years: A Portrait of NYAC (London: Macmillan, 1969); and J. D. Willis and R. G. Wettan, "Social Stratification in New York City Athletic Clubs, 1865–1915," *Journal of Sport History* 3 (1976), 45–63.

13. M. W. Ford, "The New York Athletic Club," *Outing* 33 (December 1898), 251.

14. Considine and Jarvis, *First Hundred Years*, 43.

15. Henry Hall, ed., *The Tribune Book of Open-Air Sports* (New York: Tribune, 1888), 332.

16. J. W. Hinwell, "The Chicago Athletic Club," *Outing* 33 (November 1898), 145–52, and Arthur Inkersely, "Graeco-Roman Games in California," *Outing* 25 (February 1895), 93–111.

17. *Spirit of the Times*, September 2, 1876.

18. Janssen, *History of Amateur Athletics*, 103, and *Outing* 6 (May 1885), 251.

19. See J.D. Willis and R. G. Wettan, "L.E. Myers: 'World's Greatest Runner,'" *Journal of Sport History* 1 (1975), 93–111.

20. See Richard Wettan and J.D. Willis, "Effect of New York Athletic Clubs on Amateur Athletic Governance, 1870–1915," *Research Quarterly* 47 (1976), 499–505, and Eric Danhoff, "The Struggle for Control of Amateur Track and Field in the United States," *Canadian Journal of History of Sport and Physical Education* 6 (1975), 43–85.

21. Pope, *Patriotic Games*, 24.

22. See Adelman, *Sporting Time*, chap. 5; Kirsch, *Creation of American Team Sports*; Lester, *Century of Philadelphia Cricket*; and J. T. Jable, "Cricket Clubs and Class in Philadelphia, 1850–1880," *Journal of Sport History* 18 (1991) 205–23.

23. Quoted in Lester, *Century of Philadelphia Cricket*, 31.

24. F.H. Curtis and John Heard, *The Country Club* (Brookline, MA: The Country Club, 1932), 4. See Richard J. Moss, *Golf and the American Country Club* (Urbana: University of Illinois Press, 2001), chap. 1.

25. Curtis and Heard, *Country Club*, 139. The question mark appears in the original quotation.

26. Quoted in Roy Rosensweig, *Eight Hours for What We Will* (New York: Cambridge University Press, 1983), 140.

6
THE RISE OF INTERCOLLEGIATE SPORTS

*P*acked full with students, a jerky little train steamed out of Princeton, New Jersey, early on the morning of November 6, 1869. Upon arrival at the sleepy town of New Brunswick, New Jersey, Princeton's young men, all white, Protestant, and from the upper class or at the least aspirants of upper-class status, received a warm welcome from their fellow students at the College of Rutgers. During the morning, the Princeton lads strolled about the town with their hosts; a few played billiards at a local parlor. That afternoon at 3 o'clock some two hundred students and assorted spectators gathered on the Rutgers Common. The milling fans paid nothing to watch the impending contest; there were no seats for comfort nor refreshments to satisfy hunger or thirst.

The students burst forth with a few college songs, and then the nation's first intercollegiate "football" contest got underway. Twenty-five young men lined up on each side. Rutgers soon demonstrated its superiority in "dribbling"—kicking the ball along the ground with short strokes—and won the game by six goals to four. (Though the students called it "football," the game resembled more closely what Americans today call "soccer.") That evening the Rutgers players treated their visitors to a festive supper and the guests joined their hosts in boisterous song and good humor.

Few if any of those present at this historic occasion dreamed that colleges would soon become, in the apt words of historian John Higham, major "theaters of organized physical combat."[1] Within three decades after 1869, as nowhere else in the Western world, sports—in particular football—emerged as a major enterprise on dozens of college campuses. College sports helped to foster a new social form, the college community, which was comprised of students, faculty, college presidents, the upper class, and the alumni. Members of the upper class also frequently saw special virtues in intercollegiate football; they believed that the sport nurtured personal character, manliness, and teamwork in their male children. (See also Chapters 7 and 8.) With its emphasis on planning, cooperation, and rationality, football seemed to its proponents especially suited to prepare young men for positions of leadership, in short to become members of the nation's ruling class.

In addition, involvement in football, as with track and field, golf, and tennis, served as a class marker. It let everyone know one's social position or, at the least, the position to which one aspired in the social hierarchy of the day. By playing and patronizing the game, the wealthy could distance themselves from the hoi poloi. Football "is a gentleman's game," as Walter Camp, the game's foremost champion bluntly put it, "as the 'Dandy' gentlemen regiments in the [Civil] [W]ar outmarched, out fought, and out plucked the 'bloody rebs,' so gentlemen teams and gentlemen players will always hold [dominate on] the foot ball field. Brutes haven't the pluck. . . . "[2] Of course by "gentleman" Camp meant upper-class collegians. Paradoxically, at the same time, football's defenders argued that the sport was a meritocracy, that unlike the class-ridden, inequitable British models of sports, one achieved success in American football solely on the basis of merit. Such a contention opened the door to a possible invasion of the nonwealthy. Nonetheless, until the twentieth century, college football remained a distinctively upper-class sport.

THE FIRST INTERCOLLEGIATE SPORT

Even before 1869, rowing, or crew, the first intercollegiate sport, revealed potential for evoking enthusiasm beyond that of the participating athletes.[3] Rowing probably owed its origins to the experiences of students in private clubs and to the publicity surrounding the intermittent English matches between Oxford and Cambridge that began at Henley in 1829. By 1844 students had formed small, informal clubs at both Harvard and Yale. Initially the Harvard club used its boats mostly to transport members from Cambridge across the inlet to Boston drinking establishments, but the club also on occasion competed for cash prizes against noncollegiate clubs in Boston regattas.

Although exciting and colorful, the first intercollegiate match in 1852 lacked the seriousness of later regattas. By offering to pay expenses, a small New England railroad persuaded Harvard and Yale crews to race on Lake Winnipesaukee as one of several festivities to promote the White Mountains area as a summer resort. An estimated 1,000 spectators witnessed the contest, including General Franklin Pierce, the soon-to-be elected president of the nation. Harvard won the race, but neither crew had hired a coach or trainer or otherwise prepared systematically for the contest. Indeed, the Harvard crew had "rowed only a few times for fear of blistering their hands." After the race, the crews and accompanying students "passed a very pleasant week at the lake, and returned together to Concord, New Hampshire, where amid much good feeling and many fraternal adieus, they finally separated."[4]

In the meantime, play in New England preparatory schools (expensive, elite private high schools) and the widely publicized exploits of aristocratic English schoolboys kindled a growing interest in sports among upper-class northeastern collegians. In particular, Thomas Hughes's phenomenally popular novel, *Tom Brown's School Days* (1857), which in the United States alone sold more than 225,000 copies in its first year of publication, excited American students. Hughes's muscular Christian views and vivid descriptions of sporting life at Rugby, according to a Harvard student in 1857, resulted in a "multitude from every class . . . playing at base[ball] or cricket, in a manner that would excite the admiration, even if it shocked the taste, of Tom Brown and his fellows at Rugby."[5]

Reports the next year from England of the Oxford-Cambridge crew race aroused American collegians to action. Correspondents covering the race lauded the English students for their physical prowess while expressing dismay at "the entire disregard for exercise among Americans." Angered by such reports, the editor of Harvard's student magazine wrote: "What say ye, Yale, Dartmouth, Brown, Columbia, Harvard, shall we introduce a new institution in America?"[6] Student representatives from four colleges responded to the challenge by forming the College Union Regatta Association in 1858. The association sponsored successful races in 1859 and 1860, each of which may have drawn as many as 20,000 spectators.

The race of Harvard against Oxford in 1869 on the Thames River in London, the race that "will be henceforth ever immortal in Anglo-American annals," as the London *Times* averred, indicated both the increasing public attention given to college rowing and the seriousness with which the students approached the contests. Unlike 1852, the Harvard crew practiced a full month before the race. Newspapers speculated that Harvard's defeat might have been due to their "soft diet" of too much milk and fruit rather than beef and ale, the hardy diet of the Oxford crew. The Harvard-Oxford race spawned the formation of a new rowing association in 1870. As many as 16 northeastern colleges competed in the regattas of the Rowing Association of America.

The "democratization" of college rowing eventually resulted in the withdrawal of Harvard and Yale from the association. In the mid-1870s both schools suffered humiliating defeats at the hands of smaller, less socially distinguished colleges. The victory of the "bucolics" over the "intellectuals," wrote a Harvard student after the Massachusetts Agricultural College defeated Harvard for the championship in 1871, "was a bitter pill for us to swallow."[7] After a smashing Cornell triumph in 1875, Harvard and Yale never again entered the association's regattas. For the balance of the century, they proceeded to row almost exclusively against one another.

During the 1870s and 1880s the stake that the students had in winning crew races escalated. The clubs went all out to win. They hired professional trainers and coaches (sometimes from England) to prepare them for the major regattas. Training was Spartan; crews maintained a strict diet (consisting mostly of meat) and rowed three to five miles before breakfast and about four miles in the afternoon. The crews gave up "their pleasure; they resigned their very will to the control of others," a contemporary wrote, all for "twenty thrilling minutes of the race."[8]

The regattas became an important date on the social calendars of the northeastern social elite. "The moneyed aristocracy which assembles yearly at Saratoga [which was the nineteenth-century's equivalent to Las Vegas]," *Outing* reported of the 1875 regatta, "gilded the grand stand and the shore of the lake, outshown in turn by the kaleidoscopic ribbons of the intent, excited, uproarious mob which represented the thirteen colleges."[9] Newspapers frequently carried more than a page of special dispatches plus extended discussion of the social leaders who graced the regattas with their presence. Even in the 1880s and 1890s, when football began to supplant rowing in popularity, intercollegiate rowing remained an important spectacle among the northeastern upper class.

EARLY INTERCOLLEGIATE BASEBALL, TRACK, AND FOOTBALL

From the outset, baseball also reflected the tendency of collegians to transform informal games into serious contests. In 1859, in the first recorded intercollegiate match, Amherst subdued Williams by the lopsided score of 73–32. Unlike Williams, Amherst had trained carefully for the game. According to a Williams professor, Amherst took "the game from the region of sport and carried it into the region of exact and laborious discipline."[10] When the Amherst lads learned of the victory, they rang the chapel bell, lit a bonfire, and set off fireworks. The Civil War temporarily set back baseball, but in the war's wake college clubs (unlike early crew and football clubs that were until the 1890s restricted mostly to the Northeast) formed in all parts of the country.

Until the 1880s the Harvard Base Ball Club, organized in 1862, fielded the strongest of the college nines. For a seven-year span, the Crimson did not lose a single intercollegiate game. In the summer of 1870, the nine took an extended, highly publicized road trip through the West, playing many of the major noncollege teams. They won 44 of 54 matches, and even frightened Harry Wright's powerful Cincinnati Red Stockings. In the words of a contemporary: "The game was remarkably close, the Harvards outplaying their opponents at bat and in the field; but at a critical moment in the last inning, professional training showed its superiority over amateur excitability, and the Red Stockings won 20 to 17."[11]

Throughout the nineteenth century, baseball remained the most widely played sport on college campuses. Better teams sometimes tested their talents with some success against major-league professionals. In 1879, in an effort to draw a sharp line between professional and amateur players, the northeastern clubs formed an association but provided neither a regular schedule of games nor for the naming of a champion team. The unstable association folded in 1887. College baseball had other problems. In the fall it had to contend with the growing popularity of football, in the spring with inclement weather, and in the summer frequently with the opposition of college authorities to team tours. During the summers, college players (usually playing under assumed names) joined professional nines. Without much success, college authorities tried to prevent students from playing for pay.

Intercollegiate track and field, destined to rival crew and baseball as a popular spring and summer sport, traced its origins to the commercialized versions of the sport. Influenced by the examples of the Caledonian games and the Oxford-Cambridge competition first scheduled in 1864, American students began in the 1860s to devote a special day to contests in running, jumping, and throwing. In 1874 Amherst even included a "fat man race" as part of its field day; later in the century Nebraska students awarded winners of the 100-yard dash a copy of Dante's *Inferno*.

Formal intercollegiate track and field began as a direct offshoot of crew. In 1873 James Gordon Bennett Jr., publisher of the *New York Herald*, offered a silver challenge cup valued at $500 for a two-mile race as part of the annual Saratoga regatta. Only three men, one each from Amherst, Cornell, and McGill of Montreal, competed in the first meet. The next year an expanded program included a 100-yard dash, 120-yard high hurdles, one- and three-mile runs, and a seven-mile walk. That most of the contestants had rowed for their varsity crews the previous day indicates the desultory character of the meet. By 1876, the collegians and their sponsors had become more serious; that year they organized the Intercollegiate Association of Amateur Athletics of America (IC4A). The IC4A decided to make the "costly prizes" awarded to the winner of each event of equal value and switched its annual games to the grounds of the New York Athletic Club at Mott Haven. The triumph in the college sports world of an amateur ethos hostile to cash prizes awaited the 1880s.

Until the 1880s, track and field training varied widely. In the northeastern colleges, an aspiring athlete might hire himself a professional trainer. As the trainers vied with one another for the services of athletes, unseemly disputes arose that, according to one critic, were not "in keeping with the spirit of gentleman's sport."[12] In 1882 Harvard hired J. G. Lathrop as a general trainer and supervisor of track and field and prohibited any association between the college's athletes and professional coaches, reforms that represented one of the earliest instances of college administrators assuming control of athletics.

College students used the first football games, the medieval-like interclass matches, as initiation rites for incoming freshmen. As with most other rites of passage, the game entailed the degradation of the initiates as a precondition for their acceptance into the group. Beginning in 1827 sophomores at Harvard subjected freshmen to a violent game on the first Monday of the school term. As early as 1840, Yale also took up the practice. These melees frequently resulted in black eyes, bloodied noses, sprained limbs, and shredded clothes. Postgame drinking, singing, and the cheering of the respective academic—not social—classes signified the acceptance of the freshmen by upperclassmen and the deepening of fraternal bonds among the participating students. Because of their disorderly character, university authorities periodically outlawed the rite.

During the 1860s and early 1870s two kinds of football began to achieve some prominence. One resembled association (soccer) football in Britain; it was a kicking game that prohibited picking up the ball with the hands. After the historic 1869 contest, Columbia, Yale, and Stevens joined Rutgers and Princeton in playing this version of football. In the meantime, a second kind of football, a hybrid of association football and rugby, one that permitted use of the hands, was growing in popularity in the Boston area. Familiar with this game, Harvard students refused to play the association game popular on other campuses. As the result of a series of games between McGill University and Harvard in 1874, the Harvard players became converts to rugby.

Given Harvard's esteemed position among the nation's colleges, within a few years the other elite northeastern schools followed suit. In 1876 student delegates from Princeton, Columbia, Yale, and Harvard founded the Intercollegiate Football Association; the rules of the new organization closely resembled those of the Rugby Union in England. Initially the association counted touchdowns as only one point and kicked goals as four. A modern observer would be especially surprised by the "drop kick," which entailed the kicker's dropping the ball and, as it bounced up, kicking it through the goal. As the ball became more oblong in shape (at first teams played with a large, almost round ball) and the points for touchdowns increased, the drop kick disappeared from football. The delegates to the 1876 convention also decided to hold a championship game at the end of the season, a decision that encouraged the teams to emphasize winning.

WALTER CAMP: FATHER OF AMERICAN FOOTBALL

No single person exceeded the importance of Walter C. Camp, appropriately hailed as the "Father of Football," in shaping the college game's early history. A member of the Yale squad from 1875 to 1882, Camp apparently compensated for his physical frailties as a youngster by becoming an all-around athlete; he played baseball, crew, track, lawn tennis, and football. After obtaining a bachelor's degree in 1880, he continued at Yale as a medical student and football player, eventually withdrawing from medicine because he could not tolerate the sight of blood. While employed as an executive with a local New Haven watch manufacturing firm, Camp continued an active involvement in football until his death in 1925.

During the 1880s, Camp was responsible for a radical set of rule changes, each of which contributed to the evolution of the modern game of American football. Camp liked the physical roughness of rugby, but not the importance that the game assigned to chance. Play in rugby started with a scrum; the ball was set down in the midst of a huddle of opposing players. Players then tried to drive the ball free with their feet so that a "back" could pick it up and run or kick it toward the opponent's goal line. Once a back had been downed with the ball, the players formed a new scrum. During the scrums, several minutes could transpire before the ball squirted out of a struggling mass of players.

In 1880 Camp persuaded the association rules committee to adopt a revolutionary way of putting the ball into play. The new rule provided for a line of scrimmage separating the offensive and defensive teams, and, unless fumbled or kicked to the opposing team, the offensive team could *retain possession* of the ball. Much to the disgust of fans and players alike, the Yale-Princeton game of 1881

YALE FOOTBALL TEAM, 1879   Walter Camp, shown here holding the ball, was the main architect of the uniquely American game and Yale's early dominance of the sport. (Yale University Library)

turned into a fiasco. Princeton repeatedly lost yardage while keeping possession of the ball in the first half and Yale employed the same strategy in the second half.

The next year, in 1881, Camp suggested an ingenious solution to this problem. If the offensive team failed to gain 5 yards in three attempts, it had to give up the ball. The down-yardage rule change led to the chalking of lines across the field at 5-yard intervals (hence, the origin of the term "gridiron").

The provisions for a down-yardage system, continuous possession by the offense, and a line of scrimmage initially spawned a wide open, offensive-oriented game. The offensive line and backs typically lined up far apart, forcing the defense to do likewise. While prohibited from throwing the ball across the line of scrimmage, the game featured sideline passes, open field running, and kicking.

In 1888, Camp came forward with another important departure from rugby—tackling below the waist. Legalization of the low tackle ended the wide open, improvisational style of play. Already officials had allowed offensive players to run "interference" (i.e., block) between the ball carrier and potential tacklers, a violation of rugby conventions. As early as 1884, Pennsylvania had started its offensive action with the "V trick," a formation in which players formed a V with their arms encircling the players ahead of them. Breaking this fearsome formation required defensive men without much if any protective gear to hurl themselves directly into the V or try to crash its flanks.

The new "mass momentum" style of offense encouraged by the legalization of the low tackle entailed massing players at a single point of attack. Fans were frequently treated to a spectacle of an incomprehensible mass of struggling bodies, shoving and pulling on one another in an effort to squeeze out 5 yards in three tries.[13] Far less improvisational than rugby or the older style of football, the new game was intrinsically less exciting and far more brutal.

In addition to the creativity of Camp, the evolution of American football rules arose from the prevalence of a winning-at-all-costs ethos among the collegians. Although American collegians of the late nineteenth century were nearly all from the upper social ranks, they were less inhibited by traditions of fair play than their upper-class English counterparts. Understood conventions rather than explicit rules governed much of the play of English "gentlemen." But when American students took up such games as rugby, they seized upon and exploited all the areas of the game not covered by explicit rules. Rules had to be written and rewritten to encompass every possible contingency or ambiguity. Often a new rule resulted in unforeseen possibilities for a team to gain a new advantage, so that yet

MASS MOMENTUM FOOTBALL This drawing illustrates the pushing and shoving characteristic of American football.
(UPI/Corbis)

another rule had to be formulated. Rulemaking then (as today) necessarily became a major preoccupation of American football authorities.[14]

Walter Camp also played an important role in undermining student control of football. In the earliest years, students themselves organized clubs, scheduled games, managed finances (such as they were), and wrote the rules. Student-elected team captains determined who would play, player deployment, and the team's training regimen. With so much authority in their hands, the football captains held esteemed positions on campuses. According to President Francis A. Walker of the Massachusetts Institute of Technology, the captains replaced those students renowned for "speech-making, debating, or fine writing" as campus heroes.

In their zeal to win, the students soon sought additional help. In the 1880s, they began to invite former players (called "graduate coaches") back to campus to assist them in preparing for key games. About 1885, Yale took this practice of informal coaching a step further. Walter Camp became the regular advisor to Yale captains and graduate coaches. Because of his full-time job, Camp could rarely attend practices, but his wife Alice observed practices and carefully noted player progress. Then in the evenings the team leaders met with Camp to consider tactics and strategies. "There is only one man in New Haven of more importance than Walter Camp," wrote Richard Harding Davis in 1893, "and I have forgotten his name. I think he is the president of the university."[15] The term "czar system" seemed so apt in describing Camp's dictatorial and centralized methods that it stuck. Indeed, in time, his system became something of a model for football programs across the nation.

Camp's influence extended far beyond New Haven. Football men everywhere recognized him as the game's preeminent authority and spokesman. He flooded the newspapers and periodicals with stories of games, inside knowledge, and trivia. Altogether, he wrote 20 books on sports—boys' novels, histories, and coaching manuals. In 1889 he devised an ingenious promotional gimmick—the creation of a fictional "All-America" football team. Each year until 1924 Camp personally determined the composition of a hypothetical team of the nation's best players. Camp devoted an enormous amount of energy to advising those involved in football programs elsewhere. His former players and captains spread out across the country as football missionaries, teaching their mentor's ideas and methods at other campuses.

By the turn of the century, colleges everywhere were trying to emulate the Yale system, but without equal success. Yale's record from 1872 through 1909 has never been equaled; the Elis recorded 324 wins, only 17 losses, and 18 ties. From the final game of the 1890 season to the ninth game of the 1893 season, the famed eleven scored 1,265 points to none for its opponents. Yale so dominated archrival Harvard that "Harvard felt a certain loss of manhood in not winning a single football game with Yale in the eighties and only two in the nineties," concluded a historian of the school.[16] Among the renowned Yale athletes were Amos Alonzo Stagg, the future longtime coach of the University of Chicago, W. W. "Pudge" Heffelfinger, who revolutionized line play, and Lee "Bum" McClung, who scored 500 points in four seasons. Perhaps Frederic W. Remington, who was to become a famed illustrator, best typified the spirit of Yale. In preparation for the Harvard game of 1878, he took his football jacket to a local slaughterhouse where he dipped it in blood to "make it look more businesslike."[17] Although Yale's dominance of college football ended in 1909, it was not until the 1920s that the supremacy of the elite northeastern men's colleges gave way to more powerful football teams from other regions.

Football was sometimes interpreted as a reflection of the fundamental character of the colleges. For example, Yale partisans claimed that the more democratic character of their institution accounted for their dominance over Harvard. Frank Merriwell, Yale's fictional hero, explained that at Harvard "a man's worth does not carry him so far as in Yale or Princeton. Here a man is accepted for just what he proves himself to be; there, he is accepted for what he has the reputation of being. Aristocracy cuts a mighty small figure at Yale, but in Harvard the bloods are the ones who play ball, row, and so forth."[18] While in fact students at both colleges were overwhelmingly from the upper social strata, fathers of Yale collegians were more likely to be men of new wealth than the fathers of Harvard's students. Until at least the 1890s, Harvard students also exhibited a certain disdain toward Yale's athletic "excesses." Commenting on the differences in spirit between the two colleges, philosopher George Santayana identified Harvard with ancient Athens and Yale with ancient Sparta.

FOOTBALL AND THE MAKING OF COLLEGE COMMUNITIES

Football, perhaps more than any other facet of higher education, became a major force in bonding diverse groups into larger college communities. Although most students were from families who were far better off than the national average, the fast-growing postbellum colleges attracted a heterogenous student population. Few of them came to college in order to enhance their spirituality, hone their intellectual skills, or acquire a larger body of knowledge—all goals more likely to be closer to the faculty's than the students' hearts. Instead, the sons and daughters of the new rich frequently sought degrees as a means of achieving a social position commensurate with their family's wealth. Unlike in the antebellum era, a college degree, particularly from an Ivy League school, was increasingly perceived as a passport to high society. Colleges, in this sense, contributed to the formation of a national upper class. Increasingly college training was also a prerequisite for becoming an engineer, accountant, doctor, or other professional person; hence, pursuant to career goals, families from the upper tier of the middle class began sending their children to college in ever larger numbers.

Regardless of motives, late nineteenth-century students made extracurricular activities the center of their college experience. The sheer number of literary societies, debate clubs, Greek letter societies, and college athletic associations burgeoned. The first sports clubs were usually composed of students who shared an interest in sports but were sometimes socially exclusive as well. Any freshman who wanted to join the Yale Navy in 1862, for example, had to be nominated for membership by an upper classmen. But as the rowing and football fevers mounted in the 1870s, the students began to organize collegewide athletic associations. Everyone was invited if not pressured to join; in the early years student subscriptions paid most of the expenses required to sustain intercollegiate sports.

Student involvement in athletics transformed the spirit of college campuses. Student newspapers became major boosters of sport, condemning "slackers," those who failed to attend games or display adequate enthusiasm. "School spirit," expressed in terms of zeal for the success of the football team, could be a precondition for acceptance among one's peers. The average man at the English universities of Oxford or Cambridge, Caspar Whitney reported in 1895, evinced only a "lukewarm" interest in the football team's prospects "compared with the spirit with which a Harvard, Yale, or Princeton undergraduate will discuss his eleven, and grow eloquent over the brilliant rushes of the half-back, or sorrowfully deprecate the slowness with which an end rusher gets down the field under a kick."[19]

College presidents and faculties quickly recognized football's power over undergraduates. Student riots, rebellions, and drunkenness declined with the advent of football at Yale, according to Professor Eugene L. Richards. The sport nurtured "a sense of friendship among the students—not fellowship in mischief, but fellowship in pluck and manliness, in generous admiration of their mates." Students might be divided by social background, personal values, and the lack of a common curriculum, but football, in the words of President Arthur Hadley of Yale, took "hold of the emotions of the student body in such a way as to make class distinctions relatively unimportant."[20] In effect, football promoted a college community of cheerleaders rather than scholars. College authorities usually welcomed the change, for football assisted them in making the peer group a major force in ensuring orderly student behavior.

These were not the only tangible benefits from football, college administrators concluded. They seized on the sport to draw attention to their colleges and to recruit students. Unlike England, where only Oxford and Cambridge competed for eminence, literally dozens of American colleges scrambled for public acclaim. Since what constituted preeminence in higher education was nebulous, Americans tended to equate success with size and public recognition. Administrators soon discovered that football was far more effective in attracting public attention than an institution's reputation for scholarship, religiosity, or inspired teaching.

Football assisted the nation's colleges in developing a new, more aggressively masculine image, one that was more consonant with the values of late Victorian culture. Through much of the nineteenth century, the popular media took delight in depicting the typical undergraduate male in effeminate terms—as a dyspeptic, shriveled up, and cowering scholar. The college men seemed interested only in gaining useless knowledge or cultivating an ineffectual spirituality. Football, on the other hand, projected the typical college man as rugged and fearless, as one who could hold his own in the world outside the walls of academe. In the face of a diminishing role of physical skill in the work place and the "feminization" of the larger culture, representing football as a hypermasculine sport by its enthusiasts may have helped relieve a growing anxiety among males about their manliness (see Chapters 7 and 8).

Above all, playing the sport built character, its supporters said. Its raw violence and intense competition promoted such inner traits as self-control, self-sacrifice, and pluck, traits that could also be useful for achieving success in the modern, industrial economy. Though football's defenders rarely if ever explained it, they seemed to believe that the character-building function of varsity football somehow spilled over into the lives of the nonplaying male undergraduates. Upon watching and cheering the football team, they too were believed to become more manly, cooperative, and self-disciplined. Neither did the game's enthusiasts recognize a supreme irony, that in fact the muscular ideal was becoming increasingly irrelevant to the achievement of success and power in the new economy. More often moving upward in that arena required specialized knowledge or personal charisma rather than physical prowess.

Playing and watching football games could also encourage behaviors and values exactly the opposite of what its proponents claimed would arise from the sport. There always lurked the danger that the games would swirl out of control, that instead of restraining themselves the collegians would violate the spirit if not the letter of the rules, that they would engage in unnecessary brutality, and that unseemly controversies would belie their claims for being "gentlemen." From the outset of the game's history, charges regularly surfaced that teams deliberately sought to physically intimidate and disable key players on opposing teams. With equal regularity, angry disputes arose over the rules and the eligibility of players. Drinking revelries also sometimes accompanied football contests. The manifest incongruity between the argument that football built character on the one hand and the actual behavior of the collegians on the other led to several efforts to either abolish or reform the sport. These campaigns reached a climax in 1905 and 1906. (See Chapter 11.)

Mirroring the larger culture's conception of proper gender roles for upper- and middle-class Americans, intercollegiate athletics took on different meanings for women students. As women's colleges and coeducational state universities grew in numbers and size, the defenders of female education were confronted with the argument that the rigors of intellectual activity damaged the health of young women, especially the proper growth of their reproduction systems. Educators responded that a carefully monitored exercise program could prevent such harm. Consequently, physical training became an integral part of the curriculum for women. Rather than vigorous sports, which educators believed were potentially dangerous, the programs entailed mostly mild exercises.

Although women rowed, hiked, rode horseback, ice skated, and on a few campuses even played baseball and field hockey prior to the 1890s, in most places they rarely engaged in competitive sports.[21] Instead, intercollegiate sports tended to reinforce prevailing gender stereotypes; women were relegated to the sidelines to cheer on the men.

While Victorian inhibitions prevented proper women from attending the more disreputable sporting spectacles of the nineteenth century, college football was different. The annual fall horse show and the Thanksgiving Day contest in New York City launched the city's winter upper-class social season; debutante balls and banquets soon followed. The antics, cheering, and enthusiasm of the younger ladies at football games led G. Stanley Hall, the president of Clark University in 1900, to conclude that "while the female does not as in the case of many animal species look on complacently and reward the victor with her favor, military prowess has a strange fascination for the weaker sex, perhaps ultimately and biologically because it demonstrates the power to protect and defend."[22] In short, football reinforced the prevailing gender distinctions of the day.

The colleges soon learned that football could aid them in recruiting students. Engaged in intense competition with other schools for students, college presidents extolled the strengths of their football teams. As early as 1878 President James McCosh of Princeton wrote an alumnus in Kentucky: "You will confer a great favor on us if you will get . . . the college noticed in the Louisville papers. . . . We must persevere in our efforts to get students from your region. . . . Mr. Brand Ballard has won us [a] great reputation as captain of the football team which has beaten both Harvard and Yale."[23] Football seemed an even more potent weapon in the battle for students among the land-grant institutions and numerous sectarian colleges of the West. Upon securing Princeton's Hector R. Cowan as a "coach" in 1895, University of Kansas president Frank Snow was ecstatic. "I repeat, this is an immense thing at U.K. and will tend to develop the green eyes rapidly of other Kansas institutions."[24] Faculty, students, and townspeople in Lawrence enthusiastically joined in raising the money necessary to pay Cowan's salary.

Upon assuming the presidency of John D. Rockefeller's newly endowed University of Chicago in 1892, William Rainey Harper set out to publicize the university by establishing a winning football team. Harper hired Amos Alonzo Stagg, a famed Yale player, as coach, making Stagg the first coach with professorial rank in the country. Harper gave Stagg unambiguous instructions: "I want you to develop teams which we can send around the country and knock out all the [other] colleges. We will give them [the players] a palace car and a vacation too."[25] Stagg responded with enthusiasm: "If Chicago university places a team in the field it must *be a winning team* or one which will bring honor to the University."[26] Fielding a successful football team might also generate private donations to a college. According to Stagg, during the halftime of a game in which Chicago trailed Wisconsin 12–0, Harper delivered an impassioned and blunt plea to the players. "Boys, Mr. Rockefeller has just announced a gift of $3,000,000 to the University. He believed that the university is to be great. The way you played in the first half leads me to wonder whether we really have the spirit of greatness. . . . I wish you would make up your minds to win the game and show that we have it."[27] Chicago's players responded accordingly; they won 22–12.

College authorities found that football nurtured an alumni loyalty that was far more profound than fond memories of chapels, classrooms, pranks, or professors. "You do not remember whether Thorpwright was valedictorian or not," wrote a young college alumnus in 1890, "but you can never forget that glorious run of his in the football game." The alumni continued to identify with the football team long after their official connection with the college had been severed. The lament of a Bowdoin alumnus in 1903 was echoed countless times by alumni elsewhere. Referring to a 16–0 defeat of Bowdoin by the University of Maine, he declared: "In my day the University of Maine was a standing joke. . . . We got licked to-day because we hadn't the stock—the stock sir . . . Old Bowdoin must fling open her gates and get some—some stock sir."[28]

Football fostered the formation of alumni subcultures. Alumni in cities far removed from their college campuses organized chapters, sponsored elaborate homecoming events, and printed bulletins listing the achievements of their classmates and the latest exploits of the football team. "The feeling of solidarity and loyalty in the student body that intercollegiate contests develop is a good thing," ex-President William Howard Taft explained in 1915; "It outlasts every contest and it continues in the heart and soul of every graduate as long as he lives."[29]

FOOTBALL BECOMES AN UPPER-CLASS SPORTING SPECTACLE

Initially, the general public all but ignored intercollegiate football games. Until the mid-1880s only a few students and alumni watched the contests; attendance rarely exceeded a few hundred fans. With few exceptions, the nation's wealthy paid no attention to the games. The students struggled to get the newspapers to publish even the shortest notices about their gridiron wars. But within a decade, all that changed. By the mid-1890s, the daily papers in New York, Philadelphia, and Boston were devoting a staggering amount of space to college football, and by then more than 40,000 fans attended major contests.

A revolution in the newspaper industry during the 1880s and 1890s, as Michael Oriard has detailed, contributed substantially into transforming college football into a major sporting spectacle, one that extended well beyond the exclusive patronage of the upper class.[30] Locked in circulation wars, the New York dailies, especially the *Herald*, the *World*, and the *Journal*, sought additional readers by expanding their coverage of sports. Football stories in October and November helped fill a void left in the sports calendar by the conclusion of the baseball and horse racing seasons. To grab the attention of readers, the papers employed banner headlines, exaggerated the heroics of individual players, filled their pages with lavish illustrations, and devoted as much space to the spectators and their behavior as they did to descriptions of the games themselves. Whereas in the 1890s only 30,000 to 40,000 attended the Thanksgiving Day games in New York City, nearly two million could read about the game in the metropolitan area's dailies.

The newspapers gave particular attention to the "Social Set," or those who aspired to become members of upper-class "Society." Woodcuts and line drawings in the newspapers and magazines of the 1880s and 1890s regularly featured well-dressed, fashionable, cheering spectators in the foreground while the players themselves were only dimly visible in the background. The *New York Herald*, referring to those present at the Yale-Princeton game of 1892, reported that "Mrs. William C. Whitney had a conspicuous box, trimmed profusely in Yale colors and beautifully decorated with a bevy of young girls." In another box, "His Luminous Magnificence the Sun patted pleasantly on the back by Mrs. Elliot Shepard when she stepped into the Shepard-Vanderbilt box and remarked, 'what a perfect day; what glorious sunshine.' And, indeed, the sun reciprocated thankfully to the compliment and smiled full and bright in her lovely face." Perhaps it was little wonder that Richard Harding Davis concluded in 1893 that the "sporting character of the event has been overwhelmed by the social interest . . . which . . . has made it more of a spectacle than an athletic contest."[31] Whether alumni or not, by becoming football devotees, social climbers could identify with a college and thereby with the nation's upper class.

To those seeking entry into exclusive upper-class communities, college connections became increasingly important. As early as the mid-1880s, the wealthy in New York City went to great lengths to display conspicuously their allegiance to a particular college. After Yale's defeat in 1889, the *Herald* reported that "Mr. Cornelius Vanderbilt [who had never attended a college] and his son William went back to the big house on Fifth Avenue and sadly removed the Yale flag that had floated so bravely all day."[32] Thereafter, at each of the Thanksgiving Day battles the Vanderbilts and Whitneys hung blue and white banners between their mansions across Fifth Avenue. Other wealthy families—the Sloanes, the Alexanders, and the Scribners—displayed the colors of Old Nassau (Princeton) with equal pride.

"Thanksgiving day is no longer a solemn festival to God for mercies given," declared the *Herald* in 1893. "It is a holiday granted by the State and the Nation to see a game of football."[33] By the mid-1890s, according to Ronald Smith's estimate, some 120,000 athletes, belonging to colleges, athletic clubs, and high schools, played in some 5,000 Thanksgiving Day football games. Until disbanded in the mid-1890s, few spectacles equaled the theatrics of the Thanksgiving Day contest held in New York City between the nation's two top college elevens. On Wednesday, an advance contingent of collegians arrived in the city to begin the festivities. The next morning a parade of horsedrawn coaches slowly made its way through the heart of the city to Manhattan Field. From atop their coaches, the rich fans ate their lunches and drank champagne. After the game, the fans boarded their coaches or the elevated trains for the return trip downtown. Happy parties crowded into restaurants for bacchanalian Thanksgiving Day feasts. During the evening celebrants attended the theaters where they sometimes interrupted the performances with raucous displays of school spirit.

By the 1890s many colleges were already playing what later became known as "The Big Game." No other game on a team's schedule was as significant as the Big Game with a traditional rival; the success of the entire season hinged on winning the contest. The Big Game sometimes entailed winning or losing a traditional trophy. Stanford and California struggled to win the Axe, Minnesota and Michigan for possession of the Little Brown Jug, and Purdue and Indiana for ownership of the Old Oaken Bucket. Enterprising undergraduates regularly devised schemes to steal such trophies from their rightful owners.

THANKSGIVING DAY GAME   Few occasions equaled the excitement and glamor of a Thanksgiving Day game between Yale and Princeton held in New York City in the 1890s.
(CORBIS BETTMANN)

The invention of colorful pageantry not only helped give colleges distinctive identities but also contributed to the success of intercollegiate football not just as a game but as a sporting spectacle as well. As had nineteenth-century militia units, volunteer fire departments, and baseball teams, the students adopted special colors to differentiate their enterprise from others. As early as 1854 Yale rowers donned blue flannel. Apparently crimson was first identified with Harvard when the crew purchased China red bandannas to distinguish themselves from the Irish green of other rowers participating in a Boston regatta. Georgetown's blue and grey arose from the divided loyalties of students during the Civil War. Rochester students rejected goldenrod yellow, the recommendation of an alumni committee, because of its association with the women's suffrage movement.

Mascots and nicknames offered even more room for the imagination. Sometimes students named their teams after their institution's founder. Thus Yale became the Elis and Williams College became the Ephs, an abbreviation of the first name of their founder Ephraim Williams. Nicknames sometimes evoked humorous images. For a time Washington College's team was known as the Shoo Flies and the University of Nebraska as the Bugeaters. After Yale students paid the princely sum of $300 for a prize English bulldog as a mascot, their team became known as both the Bulldogs and the Elis. When Texas students discovered that Bevo, their first longhorn mascot, had been branded with the score of the Texas A&M victory in 1915, they unceremoniously slaughtered and ate the steer.

College yells and songs frequently belittled opponents.[34] Illinois students chanted at their chief rival, Chicago:

> Tell all those Standard Oil Tanks
> Old Rockefeller's pride and joy
> Just how the boys in Old Chicago
> Got a jolt from Illinois

Dating from the 1890s, a Yale song (not printed in the college's official songbook) suggested an assault on "Fair Harvard":

> Though Harvard has blue stocking girls
> Yale has blue stocking men
> We've done Fair Harvard up before
> We'll do her up again.

Although it would not be until the 1920s that college football would emerge as a full-fledged national sporting spectacle, by the beginning of the twentieth century the sport was no longer limited to northeastern college campuses. In the 1890s, in a pattern similar to the Northeast, newspapers across the country seized upon football to boost circulation. In 1894, the *Nashville American*, for example, heralded the Big Game between the southern powers of Virginia and North Carolina, "as the social event of the year." Indeed, an enthusiasm for football became a means of rallying traditional southern honor and manhood against northern onslaughts. Imitating the collegians, high schools and athletic clubs across the nation also began to field football elevens. By 1905, a study found that 432 of 555 American cities hosted one or more football teams.[35]

CONCLUSION

Unlike anywhere else in the Western world, intercollegiate sports and the pageantry accompanying them became a major feature of the American educational system in the nineteenth century. Upper-class students from elite men's colleges of the Northeast provided the initial impetus for staging the games. In the United States, nothing was more important than intercollegiate sports in defining college identities and in giving them greater emotional depth. Sports helped to bind students, faculties, administrators, alumni, and social climbers into a single college community. Along with the social clubs described in the previous chapter, college life and intercollegiate sports also became important components of a much larger enterprise—the effort to create a national upper class.

NOTES

1. John Higham, "The Reorientation of American Culture in the 1890s," in John Higham, ed., *Writing American History* (Bloomington: Indiana University Press, 1970), 79. For all intercollegiate sports in this era, see especially Ronald A. Smith, *Sports and Freedom: The Rise of Big Time College Athletics* (New York: Oxford University Press, 1988), and Patrick B. Miller, "Athletes in Academe: College Sports and American Culture, 1850–1920," unpub. Ph.D. diss., University of California, Berkeley, 1987. For football, see also Parke H. Davis, *Football* (New York: Scribner's, 1912); Michael Oriard, *Reading Football: How the Popular Press Created an American Sporting Spectacle* (Chapel Hill: University of North Carolina Press, 1993); John Sayle Watterson, *College Football: History, Spectacle, Controversy* (Baltimore, MD: Johns Hopkins University Press, 2000); Gerald R. Gems, *For Pride, Profit, and Patriarchy: Football and the Incorporation of American Cultural Values* (Lanham, MD: Scarecrow, 2000); Mark F. Bernstein, *Football: The Ivy League Origins of an American Obsession* (Philadelphia: University of Pennsylvania Press, 2001); Guy M. Lewis, "The American Intercollegiate Football Spectacle, 1869–1917," unpub. Ph.D. diss., University of Maryland, 1965; and the provocative interpretation offered by A.S. Markovits in "The Other 'American Exceptionalism'; Why Is There No Soccer in the United States?" *International Journal of the History of Sport* 7 (1990), 230–64. Also see the review essay by John Nauright, "Writing and Reading American Football: Culture, Identities, and Sports Studies," *Sporting Traditions* 13 (November 1996), 109–27.

2. As quoted in Gems, *Pride, Profit, and Patriarchy*, 112.

3. See esp. Smith, *Sports and Freedom*, chaps. 3 and 4.

4. Quotations in J.A. Blanchard, *The H Book of Harvard Athletics* (Cambridge, MA, 1923), 26, 24.

5. "Mens Sana," *Harvard Magazine* 4 (1858), 201.

6. Ibid., 178.

7. Quoted in G.M. Lewis, "America's First Intercollegiate Sport: The Regattas from 1852 to 1875," *Research Quarterly* 38 (1967), 643.

8. J.R.W. Hitchcock, "The Harvard-Yale Races," *Outing* 6 (1885), 403.

9. Ibid., 393.

10. Quoted in Smith, *Sports and Freedom*, 55. See esp. chap. 5 for intercollegiate baseball in the nineteenth century.

11. J.M. Hallowell, "American College Athletics," *Outing* 13 (1889), 241.

12. Samuel Crowther and Arthur Ruhl, *Rowing and Track Athletics* (New York: Macmillan, 1905), 275–76.

13. It also led briefly to another interesting variation. See S.A. McQuilkin and R.A. Smith, "The Rise and Fall of the Flying Wedge, Football's Most Controversial Play," *Journal of Sport History* 20 (1993), 57–64.

14. See David Riesman and Reuel Denney, "Football in America: A Study in Cultural Diffusion," *American Quarterly* 3 (1951), 309–325.

15. Quoted in Oriard, *Reading Football*, 36.

16. S.E. Morison, *Three Centuries of Harvard* (Cambridge, MA: Harvard University Press, 1936), 410.

17. Quoted in Bernstein, *Football*, 12.

18. B.L. Standish, *Frank Merriwell's Loyalty* (New York: Street and Smith, 1904), 29. See also A.L. Sack, "Yale 29–Harvard 4: The Professionalization of College Football," *Quest* 19 (1973), 14–34, and George Santayana, *The Middle Span* (New York: Charles Scribner's Sons, 1945).

19. Caspar Whitney, *A Sporting Pilgrimage* (New York: Harper & Bros., 1895), 90.

20. E.L. Richards, "Athletic Sports at Yale," *Outing* 6 (1885), 453, and A.T. Hadley, "Wealth and Democracy in American Colleges," *Harper's Weekly* 93 (1906), 452.

21. See Cindy Hime, "The Female Athlete in American Society," unpub. Ph.D. diss., University of Pennsylvania, 1984, chap. 2.

22. Quoted in Frederick Rudolph, *The American College and University* (New York: Vintage Books, 1962), 393.

23. Quoted in ibid., 385.

24. Quoted in Lewis, "American Intercollegiate Football Spectacle," 158–59.

25. Quoted in ibid., 141.

26. As cited in Kooman Boycheff, "Intercollegiate Athletics and Physical Education at the University of Chicago, 1892–1952," unpub. Ph.D. diss., University of Michigan, 1954, 19. For football at the University of Chicago, see Robin Lester, *Stagg's University* (Urbana: University of Illinois Press, 1995).

27. A.A. Stagg and W.W. Sterit, *Touchdown!* (New York: Longmen's Green, 1927), 203.

28. Quotations in Rudolph, *American College*, 383.

29. W.H.Taft, "College Athletics," *Proceedings of the Tenth Annual Convention of the National Collegiate Athletic Association* (1915), 67.

30. See esp. Oriard, *Reading Football*, chap. 2.

31. Quotations in Lewis, "American Intercollegiate Football Spectacle," 92.

32. Ibid., 119–20.

33. As quoted in Smith, *Sports and Freedom*, 181. For the estimates that follow, see ibid.

34. For the following yells, see Miller, "Athletes in Academe," 198, 201.

35. S.W. Pope, *Patriotic Games* (New York: Oxford University Press, 1997), chap. 5; Andrew Doyle, "'Causes Won, Not Lost': College Football and the Modernization of the American South," *International Journal of the History of Sport* 11 (1994), 240–47; Oriard, *Reading Football*, 132.

7
THE RISE OF ORGANIZED YOUTH SPORTS, 1880–1920

*T*he 1880–1920 era witnessed the formation of a massive set of adult-managed youth sports programs. Well before 1890 youth had competed in sports, but usually on teams and in games that they themselves had organized or on teams composed largely of adults. After about 1890 the Young Men's Christian Association, private preparatory schools, churches, the Public Schools Athletic Leagues, the city playground associations, and the public high schools, nearly all of which reflected old-stock, Protestant, middle-class concerns, became major sponsors of boys' sports. Girls also participated in the organized youth sports boom, but on a far smaller scale and with far less adult support than the boys received (see Chapter 13).

The drive for adult-directed sports was an integral component of a larger movement to organize and manage the spare-time activities of the nation's youth.[1] In particular, the adult leaders concluded, boys' sports could build individual *character*. Sports could become a major character-building enterprise by filling the voids left by the disappearance of the household economy, the absence of early work experience, the weakened authority of religion, and the breakdown of the small geographic community.

Muscular Christianity furnished the initial rationale for the boys' sport movement. Later, professional "boy-workers" added a theory of play that was in turn grounded in evolutionary theory. The combined ideas of a virile Christianity and an evolutionary theory of play shaped the content and institutional structure of the adult-managed boys' sport movement.

THE SOCIAL CONTEXT

Those most concerned for the fate of youth believed that the new urban-industrialized society had dealt harshly with the old ways of child rearing. In particular, the new society had weakened the family as a nurturing institution. Earlier in the nineteenth century, children had lent assistance to their parents in spinning thread, weaving cloth, making garments, fabricating tools, constructing furniture, baking bread, or perhaps in helping their father pursue his trade. But by 1890, all save the most wretched families purchased many of their essential items in the marketplace. Father now toiled away from home, and the children were left at best with dull, routine chores, with "make-work" that in the view of reformers failed to exercise their "constructive impulses in a wholesome way."

Relieving the children of productive work in the home, most youth observers believed, had fatal consequences for healthy moral growth. Habits of good conduct could be nurtured best in a family jointly engaged in creative, essential work, not simply from proper moral instruction. "The transmission of morals is no longer safe in the family," Luther Gulick glumly concluded, "because the activities out of which morals arise have been taken away."[2]

Nor could numerous casual contacts with adults any longer shape a youth's character. Increasingly, the new society segregated teenagers from the general work force. In the early nineteenth century, children 14 or younger had been expected to leave the family and strike out on their own. Sometimes they became apprentices learning a skill, or they experimented with a variety of jobs and sporadically attended local academies. But the growing reliance on machinery in the nineteenth century gradually undermined the apprenticeship system. Countless youths were left with dead-end jobs that required few if any skills and offered even fewer opportunities for a better future. While the sons of workingmen had no choice but to continue taking jobs in industry at a tender age, middle- and upper-income parents began to encourage their sons to enter the growing white-collar sector of the economy. The key to becoming a lawyer, doctor, accountant, engineer, or business manager seemed to be an extended education, lasting until age 16 or even longer. Parents who could afford to do so began to withdraw their children from the job market and send them to school.

The push by middle- and upper-class parents for longer periods of formal education coincided with the passage of state laws that had the effect of barring younger adolescents from the work force. In the first two decades of the twentieth century, most of the states, as part of the "Progressive" reform impulse, increased the length of the school term from four months to nine months, extended compulsory school attendance to the age of 14 or older, and prohibited children from working at full-time jobs until they were 14 or even 16.

The separation of teenagers from the general work force undermined a traditional source of socialization. Instead of numerous casual contacts with adults through early work experience, youths now spent most of their time in school with other youngsters or in leisure activities that were unsupervised by adults. The school tended to restrict youth-adult interaction to the highly formal student-teacher relationship. The abundance of unmanaged spare time that younger adolescents increasingly enjoyed was a cause of deep concern for parents and youth observers alike.

Profound suspicions of the burgeoning cities shaped the attitudes and values of the boy-workers in the YMCA, the playgrounds, the Scouts, and the high schools. Urban children, declared one youth worker, "watch the drunken people, listen to the leader of the gang, hear the shady story, smoke cigarettes, and acquire those vicious habits, knowledge, and vocabulary which are characteristic" of the worst denizens of the city.[3] Furthermore, the city was the principal home of alien peoples who held strange beliefs and often violated the behavioral codes of old-stock Americans. Traditional social restraints seemed to evaporate in the cities. Boys were vulnerable to a host of perversions—"the mad rush for sudden wealth," emulation of the "reckless fashions set by gilded youth," membership in juvenile gangs, the "secret vice" (masturbation), and fornication.

While the city was an unmitigated college of vice for youth, the country was an academy of virtue. "The country boy roams the hills and has free access to 'God's first temples,' " waxed F. D. Bonyton, the superintendent of Ithaca schools in 1904. "What can we offer to the city boy in exchange for paradise lost? His only road to paradise regained is thru the gymnasium, the athletic field, and the playground."[4] Sports, many of the boy-workers came to believe, could serve as an effective substitute for the lost rural experience.

THE CULTURAL CONTEXT

To the advocates of the idea that sports could be employed as a powerful tool in building character, modern life had become too soft and effeminate (see Chapter 8). Frontiers and battlefields no longer existed to test manly courage and perseverance. Henry W. Williams observed that the "struggle for existence, though becoming harder and harder, is less and less a physical struggle, more and more a battle of minds." Apart from sports, men no longer had arenas for testing their manliness. Theodore Roosevelt worried lest prolonged periods of peace would encourage "effeminate tendencies in young men." Only aggressive sports, Roosevelt argued, could create the "brawn, the spirit, the self-confidence, and quickness of men" that was essential for the existence of a strong nation.[5]

In the post-Civil War era, manliness took on additional meanings. Traditionally, manliness meant the opposite of childlike; it signified adulthood, maturity, and self-control. But as the opportunities for the more overt expressions of manliness in the workplace declined and as male social dominance seemed less secure, manliness acquired tougher, more assertive qualities. It included the negation of all that was soft, feminine, or sentimental. Manly men purged longings for ease and comfort; they welcomed strife, strenuous exertion, and physical risks. Their fantasy heroes were daring hunters, cowboys, detectives, adventurers, and athletes rather than tepid businessmen, statesmen, clergymen, or literati.

Sport fiction furnished the most popular vehicle for the transmission of Christian manliness to boys. Thomas Hughes's classic, *Tom Brown's School Days*, published in 1857, inaugurated the new genre of boys' sport fiction. Immensely popular throughout the English-speaking world, *Tom Brown's School Days* spawned a few pale imitations over the next quarter century. And then in the 1890s came a virtual flood of boys' sport novels. Beginning in 1896, Gilbert Patten, writing under the nom de plume of Burt L. Standish, introduced the Merriwell series. Over the next 20 years Patten produced 208 Merriwell books, all of which revolved around boyhood manliness. Although a pious man, Patten refrained from preaching explicit Christian doctrines. Instead, he attempted to convince his youthful readers that vigorous participation in athletics would result in personal moral improvement and enhance one's probability of material success. Edward Stratemeyer, the inventor of the Rover Boys along with seven other series, was even more popular than Patten. Stratemeyer and his stable of hack writers stressed adventure, action, humor, and suspense at the expense of moral instruction. By 1920 most of the authors of boys' sport fiction had removed all overt moralizing from their novels, but the "manliness" of Thomas Hughes's original formula remained intact.[6]

In the last quarter of the nineteenth century, the popularity of Christian manliness began to extend beyond the eastern elite to middle-income Protestants, even to those of the evangelical temperament. The favorable response of these groups to muscular Christianity reflected a growing anxiety about the alleged "feminization" of American Protestantism as well as the excessive decorum of Victorian life. Church leaders had long been concerned with their inability to reach both adolescent boys and young men. Women and girls made up a large majority of most Protestant congregations. Furthermore, to those who advocated a virile Christianity, the churches overemphasized the feminine virtues of humility and submission. "There is not enough of effort, of struggle, in the typical church life of today . . . ," declared Josiah Strong, a popular exponent of a manly Christianity. "A flowery bed of ease does not appeal to a fellow who has any manhood in him. . . . Eliminate heroism from religion and it becomes weak, effeminate."[7]

By the 1890s, the Young Men's Christian Association (YMCA) had emerged as the outstanding institutional expression of muscular Christianity among evangelical Protestants. Founded by laymen in England in 1851 and subsequently transplanted to the United States before the Civil War, the original purpose of the YMCA had been to offer spiritual guidance and practical assistance to the young men who were flooding into the nineteenth-century cities. But after the Civil War, the local YMCAs began to broaden their programs. To attract young men and boys to their spiritual work they offered classes in "physical culture," largely in the form of gymnastics and calisthenics. Instead of young displaced males, the main clientele of the YMCAs became young men from the clerical classes (bookkeepers, stenographers, clerks, and salesmen), businessmen, a few skilled workingmen, and boys from the middle- and upper-income ranks.[8] By 1892 the YMCA membership had grown to nearly a quarter of a million, and the organization had 348 gymnasiums directed by 144 full-time physical leaders.

LUTHER HALSEY GULICK JR.

One man, Luther Halsey Gulick Jr., who began his career with the YMCA, played a preeminent role in all phases of the adult-directed boys' sport movement. Born of missionary parents, Gulick waged a "determined war" against the "subjective type of religion" fostered by pietistic Protestants. While he rejected the formal religious doctrines of his parents, he retained a zest for embarking on crusades. He discovered his equivalent of a spiritual calling by becoming in turn the champion of muscular Christianity within the YMCA, a major proponent of a new theory of play, the founder of the Public Schools Athletic League in New York City, an organizer and the first president of the Playground Association of America, a leader of the American Boy Scout movement, and the cofounder with his wife of the American Campfire Girls.

According to Gulick, he turned to the strenuous life partly as a way of compensating for his personal feelings of physical and psychical inadequacy. Throughout his life he suffered from severe migraine headaches, periods of dark depression, and a weak physical constitution, all of which he attributed to his father, who had been the victim of a nervous breakdown. Although Gulick obtained a medical degree, he found far more exciting work than medicine in 1887 as an instructor in the physical department of the International Young Men's Christian

LUTHER HALSEY GULICK JR. A pioneer in the Young Men's Christian Association, school sports, and the playground movement, Gulick helped develop a theory of play that exercised a vast influence over organized recreation for youth.
(Library of Congress)

Association Training School (later renamed Springfield College) in Springfield, Massachusetts. Since most of the general secretaries and physical directors of local YMCAs passed through the regular two-year curriculum or summer school of the training school, Gulick had found an ideal position for reaching a large national and even an international audience.

In journals he edited for the training school, in numerous articles and books, and in speeches delivered throughout the country, Gulick unrelentingly preached the same gospel: Spiritual life rests on the equal development of the mind and the body. Gulick invented the famous emblem of the YMCA, the inverted triangle which symbolized the spirit supported by the mind and the body. Unlike previous YMCA leaders, Gulick welcomed the introduction of sport into YMCA programs. "We can use the drawing power of athletics a great deal more than we are doing at present," he wrote in 1892, but he cautioned that ". . . we must work along our own lines and not ape the athletic organizations, whose object is the development of specialists and the breaking of records."[9]

Under Gulick's aegis, competitive sport, despite formidable opposition, began to supplant gymnastics in YMCA programs. The Springfield training school was a model of athletic activism. Throughout the 1890s the school fielded a baseball team. From time to time the college also sponsored competition with outside institutions in track and field, swimming, gymnastics, basketball, and volleyball. In 1890 Amos Alonzo Stagg, the famed Yale football player of the 1880s, enrolled at Springfield. He promptly gathered a team of faculty and students, about half of whom had never played football before, and challenged all the prominent Northeastern colleges to games. That fall, "Stagg's Stubby Christians" almost upset mighty Yale before succumbing 16 to 10 in the country's first indoor football game in Madison Square Garden. The vigorous sports program at Springfield and the experience of the students there inspired YMCAs everywhere to organize their own athletic teams.

While the physical curriculum of the training school continued to center on such subjects as anatomy and motor development, Gulick added a pioneering course in the psychology of play as well as training in specific sport skills. In his psychology of play course, he asked students to experiment with new games and sports that could be played in the confined space of gymnasiums and that would be appropriate to each level of maturity. The invention of both basketball and volleyball resulted from Gulick's inspiration and suggestions. In 1891, James Naismith, a young minister from Canada who was a student and part-time instructor at Springfield, put together the essentials of the game of basketball, and in 1895, William G. Morgan, while serving as physical director of the YMCA at Holyoke, Massachusetts, invented volleyball, a game especially for older men who found basketball too strenuous.

The unbridled enthusiasm of the young men and adolescent boys for basketball and other forms of athletic competition soon presented the YMCA leadership with a trying dilemma. On the one hand, the organized games obviously increased membership, interest, and the physical prowess of the participants. On the other hand, basketball threatened to convert the YMCAs into full-fledged athletic clubs. As early as 1892, Gulick had warned the association of the dangers of a spectator-centered orientation. Yet, by the mid-1890s, in one local YMCA after another, basketball threatened to drive all other forms of physical activity off the gymnasium floor. "In several places," Gulick reported in 1895, "the game was played with such fierceness last year, the crowds who looked on became so boisterous and rowdyish, and the bad feeling developed between teams so extreme that the game has been abolished in toto."[10] Yet most YMCAs took far less drastic steps. In 1895, the YMCA formed the Athletic League of North America with Gulick as secretary. To curtail excesses the league joined the Amateur Athletic Union, published a monthly newsletter, and developed an extensive body of rules and sanctions.

Ultimately, the league failed to ensure the "purity" of YMCA athletic programs. By 1905, YMCA teams regularly played over 2,000 games with outside competitors. In their contests with the collegians and athletic clubs, the Y athletes enjoyed remarkable success. For example, for more than a dozen years the Buffalo German YMCA team totally dominated championship basketball. They won the Buffalo Exposition tournament in 1901 and won the gold medal at the 1904 Olympic Games in St. Louis. Eventually, much to the relief of YMCA officials, the Buffalo "five" became an avowed professional team.

The spirit of rivalry, athletic specialization, and even professional tendencies of YMCA athletics equaled those of the athletic clubs and the colleges. Local Ys, despite the repeated admonitions of the Athletic League officials, were guilty of extending to star athletes special privileges such as free memberships, room and board, and generous traveling allowances to compete away from home. Many of the local secretaries and physical directors tried to resist "excessive" athleticism, but others capitulated to the demands of their membership.

In 1911, several years after Gulick had left the YMCA, the association changed the entire focus of its athletic programs. Henry F. Kallenberg, the new physical director at Springfield, recommended a radical break from past practices. The Y, Kallenberg argued, should promote a comprehensive sport program that would reach the "mass of young men and boys, [and] discourage prize winning and overtraining."[11] Competition should be restricted to males of a similar age and weight and be restricted to local teams. At Kallenberg's initiative, the league severed its relationship with the AAU and began to organize local amateur athletic federations composed of Ys, high schools, churches, Turners, and other groups. By 1920 the YMCA had essentially completed Kallenberg's reform agenda. Never again would the Ys attempt to compete at championship levels in athletics.

THE EVOLUTIONARY THEORY OF PLAY

In the 1890s, G. Stanley Hall, a pioneer in genetic psychology at Clark University, and Gulick, once a student of Hall's summer school, began to work out an evolutionary theory of play that exercised an immense influence on every phase of the early twentieth-century boys-work. Hall and Gulick believed that humans had acquired the fundamental impulse to play during the evolution of the "race." Each person, as he or she passed from birth to adulthood, recapitulated or rehearsed in an approximate way each epoch or stage of human evolution. The play activities of early childhood—spontaneous kicking and squirming in infancy and running and throwing when a bit older—corresponded to the play of primal ancestors. The track, field, and tag games common to children between the ages of 7 and 12 sprang from the hunting instinct acquired during the presavage stage of evolution. Games at this stage were individualistic. Finally, the complex group games of adolescent boys—baseball, basketball, football, and cricket—rested on a combination of the earlier hunting instinct and the new instinct of cooperation, the latter having emerged during the savage epoch of evolution, when savages hunted and fought in groups while subordinating themselves to the leadership of a chief.

That each person recapitulate the history of the race through sports was essential to proper physical, moral, and neural growth. Complex motor behavior became "reflexive" through repetition. Bountiful physical activity in childhood not only developed muscles but also spurred the growth of neural centers in spinal cord and brain. Directed motor behavior was also the primary agency in shaping what Gulick called moral "reflexes," or what might be viewed more popularly as the conscience. When the youth repeated the evolution of the race via games, he or she engaged in physical activities that embodied moral principles and encouraged their development. Too often, however, the instincts from which group games sprang could result in the ripening of wicked reflexes, such as the juvenile gang of the city, "the most perilous force in modern civilization," rather than team contests supervised by adults.[12]

Team sport, then, offered an unparalleled opportunity for adults to encourage the healthy growth of moral and religious reflexes in boys. Stemming from the instinct for cooperation, team sports required the highest moral principles—teamwork, self-sacrifice, obedience, self-control, and loyalty. "These qualities appear to me," Gulick wrote, "to be a great pulse of beginning altruism, of self-sacrifice, of that capacity upon which Christianity is based." The churches and the YMCA sought to de-emphasize the teaching of feminine traits to boys and present Jesus in terms of his "noble heroism . . . his magnificent manliness, his denunciation of wickedness in public places, [and] his life of Service to others. . . . " Gulick's conception of Christian manliness hardly squared with the injunction of Jesus to turn the other cheek when wronged. On one occasion, he advised that a boy should have the ability and the courage to "punch another boy's head or to stand having his own punched in a healthy and proper manner."[13] Gulick's advocacy of a hypermuscular Christianity implied a far more radical departure from orthodox Protestantism than he probably recognized. For his ideas not only made the religious and moral life almost exclusively a matter of vigorous activity— almost activity for activity's sake—but also suggested a naturalistic explanation for origins of human religious sentiments.

In one version or another, the evolutionary theory of play became part of the conventional wisdom of the boy-workers in the first two decades of the twentieth century. G. Stanley Hall repeated it almost verbatim in his classic two-volume work on adolescence published in 1905. Joseph Lee, a prolific writer on play, took as his major premise the notion that play arose from an earlier stage of man's evolution, from the "barbaric and predatory society to which the boy naturally belongs." Henry S. Curtis, a pioneer in both the playground and Boy Scout movements, wrote that athletics "are the activities of our ancestors conventionalized and adapted to present conditions. They are reminiscent of the physical age, of the struggle for survival, of the hunt, of the chase, and of war." William Forbush, an ardent disciple of Gulick and Hall, a Congregationalist minister, and a leader in the Boy Scout movement, may have reached the largest audience of all in his advice manual *The Boy Problem*, reprinted eight times between 1901 and 1912. Each boy, Forbush wrote, repeated the "history of his race-life from savagery unto civilization."[14]

The acceptance by the boy-workers of an evolutionary theory of play had important implications for the use of sport as a socializing agency. First, it seemed to require the creation of special institutions for boys that would be closely supervised by adults. Unregulated activity would fail to encourage desirable social traits. Second, the theory encouraged boy-workers to relinquish the extreme forms of piety associated with the evangelical temperament and emphasize activity at the expense of spirituality or intellectuality. The YMCA became increasingly secular in its programs. Many of the "institutional" or "social gospel" Protestant churches in the larger cities abandoned explicitly spiritual programs for boys in favor of organized activities ranging from dances to baseball matches. Beginning in Brooklyn in 1904, one city after another organized Sunday School athletic leagues. In 1916, through the creation of the Boys' Brigade, Catholics also joined the boys' sport movement.[15] Third, the play theory permitted boy-workers to subordinate ethnic, religious, and social class differences to a presumably universal experience of maturation. Thus the boy leaders saw no need to fashion special programs for boys with distinctive social or cultural characteristics.

Finally, evolutionary theory furnished a rationale for the sexual segregation of organized play, a rationale that would influence youth workers and physical educators until the middle of the twentieth century. They assumed that males and females had acquired distinct instincts or propensities over the course of human evolution. Of utmost importance to survival for males had been an adeptness in fighting, hunting, and running—activities recapitulated in the games of boys. Those females, on the other hand, who had become most adept in caring for the home, were more likely to survive and produce offspring. "So it is clear," wrote Gulick in 1920, "that athletics have never been either a test or a large factor in the survival of women; athletics do not test womanliness as they test manliness." Another Darwinist, psychologist G. Stanley Hall, opined that a woman "performs her best service in her true role of sympathetic spectator rather than as a fellow player."[16]

THE PUBLIC SCHOOLS ATHLETIC LEAGUE

In the first two decades of the twentieth century, Gulick, Hall, and their followers found ample opportunities to put their theory of play into practice. After leaving the YMCA training school in 1900 and serving for three years as principal of Pratt Institute High School in Brooklyn, Gulick, became the director of physical training of the public schools of Greater New York City in 1903. Rather than relying exclusively on traditional gymnastics and calisthenics to nurture physical and moral growth, Gulick quickly determined that *"all* the boys in the city needed the physical benefits and moral and social lessons afforded by properly conducted games and sport."[17] Consequently, he formed the Public Schools Athletic League (PSAL) in 1903. Although the PSAL was financially independent of the school system, it depended upon the city's 630 schools for implementing its program. It won the immediate plaudits of the city's press and the endorsement of such czars of industry and finance as Andrew Carnegie, John D. Rockefeller, J. Pierpont Morgan, S. R. Guggenheim, and Henry Payne Whitney, who contributed generously to the league's finances.

Underlying the enthusiastic reception of the league was a manifest fear of the city's foreign-born population. The founders were not only concerned with the absence of play experience by immigrant youths, recalled General George W. Wingate, the long-time president of the league, but they "also found the morals of the boys were deteriorating even more than their bodies."[18] The school boys often joined street gangs and defied the authority of their teachers. Above all, the ethnic youngsters exhibited a lack of understanding of American values and institutions. A carefully managed sport program, the founders believed, would reduce juvenile delinquency and "Americanize" the ethnic youth of the ghettos. By 1910, the PSAL, which was hailed as the "world's greatest athletic organization," had at least 17 imitators in other large American cities. In 1905, the league added a Girls' Branch, but unlike the boys' division, it did not permit public interschool competition.[19]

The league's comprehensive athletic program embodied the latest wisdom of the play theorists. To ensure maximum participation of the school boys, the league included three separate forms of competition. By reaching a minimum level of performance in several physical feats, every boy could win the Athletic Badge. A widely heralded means of encouraging overall physical development, the badge test served as a model for a similar program implemented by the Playground Association of America in 1913 and by President Eisenhower's physical fitness drive which began in the 1950s. The second form of competition, class athletics, pitted the average performance of one school class in certain track and field events against the average of another. Finally, the league sponsored district and city championships in more than a dozen sports. Baseball was especially popular. In 1907, 106 teams competed, and over 15,000 fans attended the championship game held in the Polo Grounds.

The introduction of rifle-shooting competition among the high school boys by the PSAL suggested the special fondness that most of the boy-workers had for martial virtues. By 1908, over 7,000 boys competed for marksmanship badges. Each year, President Theodore Roosevelt wrote a letter of commendation to the boy receiving the highest marks, and the E. I. du Pont de Nemours Powder Company awarded prizes to the school team having the highest scores. General Wingate declared that none of the sports conducted by the league "was likely to have as important an influence on the country at large as the system of instruction in military rifle shooting."[20]

"Duty," "Thoroughness," "Patriotism," "Honor," and "Obedience"— these were the official watchwords of the Public Schools Athletic League. To inculcate such values, the league consciously exploited the athletic interests of the students. Each year General Wingate wrote an open letter to the boys warning them of a host of dangers that might adversely affect their athletic performances. Above all, "you must keep out of bad influences of the street if you want to be strong," he wrote. While it may be doubted that Wingate's advice had much influence on the behavior of the boys while they were away from school, the teachers quickly recognized that the PSAL could be used effectively to promote discipline in the classroom. "All of the little imps in my class have become saints," wrote one teacher, "not because they want to be saints, but because they want to compete in your games." No student could compete without a certification from his teachers that his deportment and class performance had been satisfactory. Peer group pressure also encouraged student conformity. "Many a big, vigorous boy out of sympathy with his school work," reported another source, "is driven to his lessons by his mates so that he can be eligible to represent his school."[21]

Perhaps it was little wonder that the city's teachers volunteered to spend long hours after school and on weekends in planning and supervising every aspect of the league's program. The improvement by the student "on the side of ethics, school discipline, and *esprit de corps* is even greater," concluded a report in 1910, than in athletic proficiency.[22] Nonetheless, the PSAL failed to alter the lives over two-thirds of the city's adolescent boy population, for these older boys did not attend school and in most cases had already entered the labor market.

THE PLAYGROUND MOVEMENT

The early twentieth-century movement for city playgrounds furnished Gulick and his followers with even broader opportunities for implementing their evolutionary theory of play.[23] Before 1900, a few private citizens and charity groups had organized playgrounds—usually consisting of sandpiles and simple play equipment—for preadolescent children in the slums of the larger cities. A turning point came in 1903 when the voters of the Chicago South Park district approved a $5 million bond issue for the construction of ten parks. Unlike previous efforts, the Chicago system included field houses at each park with a gymnasium for both boys and girls.

The Chicago authorities hired a professional physical educator, Edward B. de Groot, as director and furnished each park with two year-round instructors to supervise play activities. The managers of the new system sponsored a host of activities ranging from organized athletic leagues to community folk dances. Inspired by the Chicago example and driven by anxieties arising from modern cities, middle- and upper-income taxpayers exhibited a remarkable enthusiasm for supervised recreation programs. Between 1906 and 1917 the number of cities with managed playgrounds grew from 41 to 504.

The same concerns and values that shaped the PSAL also guided the work of playground leaders. The evolutionary theory of play furnished them with ready-made formulas for supervising playgrounds. For example, among the questions on the standard examination administered to all candidates for employment with the New York playgrounds was: "What is meant by the 'club or gregarious instinct'? How can it be developed and utilized with beneficial results on the playground? What athletic events are appropriate for boys aged 10–14? . . . for boys aged 14 to 16?"[24] Not only were prospective playground leaders expected to master the principles and practical implications of play theory, they also had to be able to exercise the subtle psychological techniques essential for managing youth without resorting to harsh repression. The playground leaders abhorred the unsupervised, unstructured play that arose from the spontaneous impulses of children. Henry S. Curtis, in the leading textbook for playground supervisors, wrote that "scrub play," that is, play that the children themselves initiated, "can never give that training either of body or conduct, which organized play should give; for in order to develop the body, it must be vigorous, to train the intellect, it must be exciting, to train the social conscience, it must be socially organized. None of these results come from scrub play."[25]

Despite the enthusiasm of municipal governments for organized recreation, the playgrounds usually failed to extend their control over spare-time activities to those who presumably needed it the most—the ethnic youth in the slums. According to the sweeping claims of the playground leaders, supervised recreation sharply reduced the incidence of juvenile delinquency, but even Henry Curtis admitted that less than 10 percent of the urban youngsters regularly used available playgrounds. The playgrounds appealed most to the children of old-stock families of the middle- and upper-income ranks, youngsters who had been shaped by the same values espoused by recreation leaders. The children of the slums tended to admire physical prowess—particularly as expressed in street fighting—spontaneity, and defiance of authority rather than the values of self-restraint and cooperation so dear to the playground leaders.

Conflicts between recreation supervisors and ghetto youths were inevitable. To attract such youths, the leaders had to make compromises with the values of the slum subculture and remove heavy-handed, detailed supervision. Yet the absence of direction not only ran counter to prevailing playground theory, it could also result in the transformation of the playground into an asphalt jungle in which the strongest and most vicious boys ruled the grounds by intimidation. Even in 1920 there were clear harbingers of the typical inner-city playground of the mid-twentieth century, which, except for a few of the toughest adolescent boys in the neighborhood, often stood empty.[26]

PRIVATE ACADEMY AND PUBLIC HIGH SCHOOL SPORTS

Public high schools and private academies (sometimes called prep or boarding schools) also became major centers of adult-supervised sports. Competing with the public high schools for students, many of the Northeastern boarding schools made a special pitch to the rich. By emulating the living conditions and programs of the English public schools (which were in reality private), the American school leaders promised to instill in spoiled and pampered boys what St. Paul rector Henry Coit called "high-bred manliness." This, they did well, according to no less an authority than Theodore Roosevelt. "Nowadays," wrote Roosevelt in 1900, "whatever other faults the son of rich parents may tend to develop, [in the academies] he is forced by the opinion of all his associates of his own age to bear himself well in manly exercises and to develop his body—and therefore, to a certain extent, his character—in the rough sports which call for pluck, endurance, and physical address."[27]

No academy leader was more enthusiastic in the promotion of sports than Endicott Peabody, who founded the socially exclusive Groton School in 1884 and ran it for the next 56 years. From an old, distinguished family, educated mainly in England at Cheltenham where he had become familiar with the writings of Thomas Hughes and Charles Kingsley, Peabody determined to come to the aid of parents from his own social class, who, he observed, had "a tendency to overindulge their children . . . a natural result of which is that the children sometimes lack intellectual and moral and physical fibre."[28] To rebuild the fiber of the spoiled boys, Peabody subjected them to a regimen of daily cold showers, sports, chapel services, and Bible readings. While boys who were more intellectually or artistically inclined or disliked sports frequently hated Groton, it and similar boarding schools did tend to make good on their promises. They transformed rich boys into athletes and frequently gave them contacts that served them well in later life.

Unlike sports in the private boarding schools, the first public interscholastic sports were usually initiated by the students themselves. Students formed the first athletic organizations, scheduled the first games, managed the finances, and hired seasonal coaches. By the 1890s, in some places, the rage for football in larger public high schools in some places equaled or surpassed that of the colleges. At this point, high school authorities could no longer ignore interscholastic sports, for sports imposed on the academic functions of the school. High school sports not only absorbed student interest at the expense of their study, they were also guilty of all the same "abuses" as college sport—a winning-at-all-costs ethos, use of "ineligible" players, and financial mismanagement. "Athletic contests between different high schools," declared one irate principal in 1905, "cause a reduction in the class standing of the students participating, teach boys to smoke cigarettes, loaf in the streets during school hours, and use unfair methods in order to win, and make liars out of many teachers and students."[29]

To curtail such evils, high school educators across the country tried to increase their authority over interscholastic sport. By 1902, when the Fifteenth Educational Conference of Academies and High Schools met, the faculties had already gained basic control of interscholastic sport in Wisconsin, Illinois, and at several of the boarding schools of the Northeast. That year, the conference recommended strict faculty supervision, the limitation of interscholastic athletics to bona fide students, and the formation of associations to regulate competition. In 1920 educators founded the National Federation of State High School Athletic Associations and by 1923 only three states were without statewide interscholastic athletic organizations. By the latter year, according to one survey, 91 percent of the nation's high schools fielded football teams.[30]

The emergence of the "comprehensive" high school in the twentieth century encouraged both the extension of adult control and the growth of school sport. In the three decades before 1920 the comprehensive high school gradually supplanted the academic-oriented high school. In 1893, the Committee of Ten, chaired by President Charles W. Eliot of Harvard, had called for a continuation with only slight modifications of the classical curriculum, a course of study that featured Greek, Latin, mathematics, oratory, and writing. The committee visualized the high school as an academic institution designed to prepare students for entrance into colleges. In the years following, the committee's position came under heavy attack, especially from middle-class parents who wanted their sons to develop the social poise required of white-collar occupations and from "social" educators who believed the school ought to be a major agency for the preparation of youth for adulthood. By 1917, when a special committee of the National Education Association published *The Cardinal Principles of Secondary Education*, the social educators and middle-class parents had routed the defenders of the classical curriculum.[31]

The proponents of the comprehensive high school shared many of the perceptions and ideas of the boy-workers. They believed that modern industrial life had eroded the traditional socializing institutions. According to *The Cardinal Principles*: "In connection with the home and family life have frequently come lessened responsibility on the part of the children; the withdrawal of the father and sometimes the mother from home occupations to the factory or store; and increased urbanization resulting in less unified family life. Similarly, many important changes have taken place in community life, in the church, in the State, and in other institutions. These changes in American life call for extensive modifications in secondary education."[32]

To meet these changes, the committee recommended two goals for the high school: prepare the students for vocations and teach them the social values essential for coping with modern life. By social values the committee meant "those common ideas, common ideals, and common modes of thought, feeling, and action that make for cooperation, social cohesion, and social solidarity." Vocational preparation required that the school offer a wide range of subjects, expert guidance, and a differentiated curriculum. Inculcating the social values necessary for establishing a genuine community was a much more difficult task, for the students lacked a common curriculum, represented different "racial stocks," and had "differing religious beliefs." Like Gulick, the social educators believed that activity rather than the teaching of moral precepts was the key to developing good character. Thus they advocated that the high school give special attention to the "participation of pupils in common activities ... such as athletic games, social activities, and the government of the school."[33]

Underlying the attention that social educators gave to the extracurricular activities of their students was an acute awareness of adolescent sexuality, a subject approached with excruciating obliqueness. For example, a report of the

National Education Association of 1911 argued that moral training in high school had to differ from that in grammar school because the teenage years were a "time of life when [sexual] passion is born [and] which must be restrained and guided aright or it consumes the soul and body." Formal classroom work was not enough. Only athletics, Henry S. Curtis wrote, could "use the sex energy directly and so ease the strain"; they could "use the time that is often devoted to obscene gossip or experiences" by promoting "a healthful fatigue and sound sleep"; in short, they could "strengthen the will to resist" sexual urges.[34]

Educational leaders also recognized that interscholastic athletics could be used to solve the problem of controlling the behavior of a heterogeneous mass of potentially rebellious students. Apart from interscholastic athletics, the public high schools had no common goals that could inspire the allegiance of the student body as a whole. Many of the students attended school only because of parental or legal compulsion. Few students found in grades alone an adequate motive for a positive identification with the high school. Grades tended to encourage individual achievement and student competition rather than cooperation. But varsity sport could rally the student body in a common cause; it could create an *esprit de corps*, "a mass spirit in which each individual surrenders himself" to a common goal.[35] Such a communal spirit encouraged a positive attitude toward the high school and a peaceful acquiescence of the students to adult direction.

Moreover, high school sports helped give an identity and common purpose to many neighborhoods, towns, and cities which were otherwise divided by class, race, ethnicity, or religion. Geographic entities, like the schools without interscholastic games, might lack collective goals. Varsity sport could coalesce them into a united front. High school sport could become a community enterprise; the entire community might celebrate victories or mourn losses in concert.

The result of this identification of the community with school sport was evident in teachers' salaries, for school boards typically paid the coach more than any other teacher. "You know that, if a principal is looking for a teacher, one of the first questions he asks frequently is: 'Can this man be of use in connection with athletics?' " reported Edwin H. Hall as early as 1905, "and the man who can be of use in connection with athletics gets more money, gets the place sooner than another man."[36] Likewise, school boards invariably placed a higher priority on the construction of a gymnasium or a football field than they did a laboratory or library. In the 1920s, high schools, both small and large, built expensive athletic facilities. In Indiana, a hotbed of high school basketball, the seating capacity of a school's gymnasium sometimes exceeded that of the town's population.

The large stake of the community in interscholastic sport frequently subverted the ideals of the comprehensive high school. The actual participation of the student body at large in athletics, according to the principles of the social educators, was essential to the growth of desirable social habits. But school boards, reflecting the will of the community, placed a far higher priority on fielding a strong varsity team. They were reluctant to furnish the coaches and facilities required for mass student participation, particularly since, unlike interscholastic sport, financing would have to come largely from additional taxes. While intramural sports

STATE HIGH SCHOOL BASKETBALL TOURNAMENT, CIRCA 1921 This photograph of the Nebraska State High School Basketball Tournament at the University of Nebraska reflected the growing popularity of high school varsity sports. Interscholastic sports helped bind together neighborhoods, towns, and cities.
(Nebraska State Historical Society)

did experience a minor boom in the late 1910s and physical education instructors increasingly substituted athletics for gymnastics and calisthenics, the results were pitifully small in terms of social educators' goals.

Within the high school, varsity sport tended to glorify athletic success at the expense of other forms of possible achievement. James Naismith unwittingly suggested this point while praising the democratizing function of varsity sport. The athlete "who will perfect himself physically for the good of the institution is respected, regardless of his ancestry or his financial standing," wrote Naismith. "Mere manhood is recognized, while lack of it is sufficient to bar a student from the honors of his fellows."[37] In the high school status structure, the athlete almost always dwelt in the upper ranks, usually higher than the most outstanding academic students.

The identification of the community with interscholastic sport presented yet another problem to the conscientious social educator. The pressures to win resulted in varsity athletics developing a code of ethics independent of the social educators' values. Cooperation and fair play might extend to teammates but rarely extended to the opposing team. "Like the unscrupulous lawyer," wrote Alfred E. Stearns, a former private academy football coach, "the football player has seemingly come to believe that his business is to circumvent the laws of the game, not to obey them." Football coaches, hired above all to win games, frequently subordinated ethics to fielding a strong team. Often the football coach "is vulgar and profane," declared Stearns. "Sometimes he is brutal. Seldom does he exhibit, on the football field at least, those qualities demanded of a gentleman."[38] Stearns turned on its head the argument that sports built good character. Instead of sport developing men of integrity and self-control, Stearns feared that the high school athlete would carry with him into adulthood the unethical habits developed on the football field. While Stearns represented the sporting ideals of the English gentry, the requirements of winning rarely permitted the high school coach the freedom to employ varsity athletics as a training ground for the values of the social educators.

CONCLUSION

The adult-directed youth sports movement of the 1880–1920 era reflected rising concerns about the effects of economic and social change on traditional child-rearing practices. For both theory and practical direction, they turned to ideas offered by muscular Christianity and experts on youth. Proponents of a more manly Christianity and youth experts frequently joined hands in founding and directing special institutions, many of which provided youth with organized sports. While strenuous Christianity did not end with World War I (1914–1918), it no longer continued to resonate through middle-class life as powerfully as it had earlier in the century. Instead, what became preeminent, as historian David Macleod has observed, was a "mindless strenuosity" tied not to social reform nor evangelical Protestantism but to what cereal king John H. Kellogg aptly called the "new religion . . . *of being good to yourself*."[39] This therapeutic defense of sports stressed more its contribution to psychic and physical health rather than its alleged character-building benefits.

NOTES

1. For the larger movement to organize and manage the spare-time activities of youth, see Joseph F. Kett, *Rites of Passage: Adolescence in America, 1790 to the Present* (New York: Basic Books, 1979); and for historiography, Stephen Hardy and A.G. Ingham, "Games, Structures and Agencies: Historians and the American Play Movement," *Journal of Social History* 17 (1983), 285–301.

2. L.H. Gulick, *A Philosophy of Play* (New York: Scribner's, 1920), 219.

3. H.S. Curtis, *The Play Movement and Its Significance* (New York: Macmillan, 1917), 119–20.

4. F.D. Bonyton, "Athletics and Collateral Activities of Secondary Schools," *Proceedings and Addresses of the National Education Association* (1904), 210.

5. Quotations from H.W. Williams, "The Educational and Health Giving Value of Athletics," *Harper's Weekly* (February 16, 1895), 166, and J.L. Dubbert, *A Man's Place* (Englewood Cliffs, NJ: Prentice Hall, 1979), 116, 117.

6. See J.L. Cutler, *Gilbert Patten and His Frank Merriwell Saga* (Orono: University of Maine Studies, 1934); C.K. Messenger, *Sport and the Spirit of Play in American Fiction* (New York: Columbia University Press, 1981); and Michael Oriard, *Dreaming of Heroes: American Sports Fiction 1860–1980* (Chicago: Nelson-Hall, 1982).

7. Josiah Strong, *The Times and Young Men* (New York: Macmillan, 1901), 179–80. See Clifford Putney, *Muscular Christianity: Manhood and Sports in Protestant America, 1880–1920* (Cambridge, MA: Harvard University Press, 2001), and Tony Ladd

and James A. Mathisen, *Muscular Christianity: Evangelical Protestants and the Development of American Sport* (Grand Rapids, MI: Baker Books, 1999).

8. L.H. Gulick, "Young Men in the Cities, II," *Athletic League Letters* (February 1899); Paul Boyer, *Urban Masses and Moral Order in America 1820–1920* (Cambridge, MA: Harvard University Press, 1978), 115–16; L.W. Fielding and C.F. Wood, "The Social Control of Indolence and Irreligion: Louisville's First YMCA Movement, 1853–1871," *Folsom Club Historical Quarterly* 58 (1984), 219–36.

9. L.H. Gulick, "State Committees on Athletics," *Young Men's Era* 18 (1892), 1365.

10. L.H. Gulick, "Basket Ball," *Physical Education* 4 (1895), 1200. See also H. L. Gulick, "Abolish Basket Ball," *Men* 5 (1897), 687.

11. *Athletic League Letters* (June 1911), 1. In addition to *Athletic League Letters* (1896–1911), see W.H. Ball, "The Administration of Athletics in the Young Men's Christian Association," *American Physical Education Review* 16 (1911), 12–22.

12. L.H. Gulick, "Psychological, Pedagogical, and Religious Aspects of Group Games," *Pedagogical Seminary* 6 (1899); L.H. Gulick, "Psychical Aspects of Muscular Exercise," *Popular Science Monthly* 53 (1898), 793–805; and L.H. Gulick "The Psychology of Play," *Association Outlook* 8 (1899), 112–16.

13. Quotations in Gulick, "Psychological," 142; *Athletic League Letters* (June 1901), 65; and L.H. Gulick, "The Alleged Effeminization of Our American Boys," *American Physical Education Review* 10 (1905), 217.

14. G.S. Hall, *Adolescence*, 2 vols. (New York: D. Appleton, 1905), I, 202-03; Joseph Lee, *Play and Education* (New York: Macmillan, 1915), 234; Henry S. Curtis, "The Proper Relation of Organized Sports on Public Playgrounds and in Public Spaces," *Playground* 3 (1909), 14; W. B. Forbush, *The Boy Problem* (Boston: Pilgrim, 1901), 9.

15. See G.D. Pratt, "The Sunday School Athletic League," *Work with Boys* 4 (1905), 131–37, and "Recreation in the Church," *Literary Digest* 53 (1916), 256.

16. Gulick, *Philosophy of Play*, 92; Hall, *Adolescence*, I, 207.

17. L.H. Gulick, "Athletics for School Children," *Lippincott's Monthly Magazine*, 99 (1911), 201.

18. G.W. Wingate, "The Public Schools-Athletic League," *Outing* 52 (1908), 166.

19. A.B. Reeve, "The World's Greatest Athletic Organization," *Outing* 57 (1910), 107–14. See also J.T. Jable, "The Public Schools Athletic League of New York City: Organized Athletics for City Schoolchildren, 1903–1914," in S.A. Riess, ed., *The American Sporting Experience* (West Point, NY: Leisure, 1984), 219–38.

20. Wingate, "Public Schools," 174.

21. Quotations from ibid., 169; Reeve, "World's Greatest," 110; and C.A. Perry, *Wider Use of the School Plant* (New York: Charities Pub. Com., 1910), 308.

22. Reeve, "World's Greatest," 108.

23. See the literature cited in Hardy and Ingham, "Games, Structures and Agencies."

24. "Questions for Teachers to Answer," *Gymnasia* 2 (1906), 149.

25. Curtis, *Play Movement*, 81.

26. See ibid., 31, 83; H.R. Knight, *Play and Recreation in a Town of 6000* (New York: Russel Sage Foundation, n.d.), 25; L.H. Wier, "Playgrounds and Juvenile Delinquency," *Playground* 4 (1910), 37–40; Gulick, *Philosophy of Play*, 223–45.

27. Quotations in Putney, *Muscular Christianity*, 106

28. Quotation in ibid., 107.

29. "Public School Notes," *American Gymnasia* 1 (1905), 215.

30. L.H. Wagenhorst, *The Administration and Cost of High School Interscholastic Athletics* (New York: Teacher's College, Columbia University, 1926), 9, 21–23, 72, 81. "The Question of School and College Athletics," *School Review* 10 (1902), 4–8; Jeffrey Mirel, "From Student Control to Institutional Control of High School Athletics," *Journal of Social History* 16 (1983), 82–99; T.P. O'Hanlon, "School Sports as Social Training: The Case of Athletics and the Crisis of World War I," *Journal of Sport History* 9 (1982), 5–29.

31. See Kett, *Rites of Passage*, 235–36, and Joel H. Spring, *Education and the Corporate State* (Boston: Beacon, 1972), esp. chap. 6.

32. *Cardinal Principles of Secondary Education Bul.*, no. 35 (Washington, DC: GPO, 1918), 7–8.

33. Quotations in ibid., 21, 23.

34. "Tentative Report on the Committee on a System of Teaching Morals in the Public Schools," *National Education Association Proceedings* (1911), 360; H.S. Curtis, *Education Through Play* (New York: Macmillan, 1915), 225–26.

35. Webster Cook, "Deportment in the High School," *School Review* 10 (1902), 629. See also L.H. Gulick, "Amateurism," *American Physical Education Review* 13 (1908), 103. On occasion social educators and boy-workers advocated an explicitly repressive school atmosphere. Luther Gulick once asserted, for example, that the modern school required the "complete obliteration of individual differences." See Gulick, "Alleged Effeminization," 28.

36. E.B. Hall, "Athletic Professionalization and Its Remedies," *School Review* 13 (1905), 761.

37. James Naismith, "High School Athletics and Gymnastics as an Expression of the Corporate Life of the High School," in C.H. Johnston, ed. *The Modern High School* (New York: Macmillan, 1914), 434–35.

38. A.E. Stearns, "Athletics and the School," *Atlantic Monthly* 113 (1914), 148–52.

39. See David Macleod, *Building Character in the American Boy* (Madison: University of Wisconsin Press, 1983), 45, and J. H. Kellogg, "The Decay of American Manhood," *Association Men* 43 (October 1917), 115.

8
THE SETTING FOR ORGANIZED SPORTS, 1890-1950

*I*n the annual Thanksgiving Day championship football game of 1893, Princeton defeated mighty Yale 6–0. In the jubilant dressing room after the game, a Princeton coach held up his arm for silence. "Boys, I want you to sing the doxology," the coach solemnly said. Outside, fellow students yelled and cheered. Imploring their heroes to emerge so they could be acclaimed, the students banged their fists on the doors and windows. Inside, the men, their naked bodies matted with blood, sweat, and mud, sang the doxology "as sincerely as they ever did in their lives." In the meantime, not far away in the Yale dressing room, the losing men sobbed "like hysterical schoolgirls."[1]

Such scenes suggest the growing importance of sports. Indeed, in the 1890–1950 era organized sports were no longer peripheral spectacles, occasional oddities, or activities freighted with meaning for only certain workingmen, ethnics, blacks, or members of the nation's upper strata. "Ball matches, football-games, tennis tournaments, bicycle races, [and] regattas, have become part of our national life," concluded a writer in *Harper's Weekly* in 1895, "and are watched with eagerness and discussed with enthusiasm and understanding by all manner of people, from the day-laborer to the millionaire."[2] In the new era, organized sports achieved an institutional permanency and prominence in American life in some ways equal to those of business, politics, ethnicity, and religion. More than ever before, the proponents of sports saw the playing fields as special training grounds for the building of personal *character*, especially for developing the kind of traits essential for success in a highly competitive society. This chapter explores the external conditions that undergirded the ascendancy of organized sports in the 1890 to 1950 era. Chapters 9 through 13 will treat more specific topics for this era.

THE MEDIA AND SPORTS

New technology, such as radio, movies, television, automobiles, and eventually air travel, joined steady improvements in newspapers, special sporting sheets, telegraph, the telephone, steamships, and railways to continue the conquest of time and space begun in the nineteenth century. The sports page of the daily newspaper, mass-circulation periodicals, movie newsreels, and the broadcasting of sports on radio especially encouraged public interest in sports. Equally or more importantly, the media helped shape how the American public understood sports. In nearly all instances, the media presented sports in overwhelmingly benign terms. To have done otherwise would have risked offending advertisers and sports fans alike.

The modern sports page began to take shape in the 1880s and 90s but did not become a standard feature in all major daily newspapers until the 1920s. In 1887 Joseph Pulitzer's New York *World* created a separate sports section; then the other leading New York dailies—the *Times*, the *Herald*, the *Journal*—quickly followed suit. The sports page typically included both national wire service stories and stories written by local reporters; wire service stories tended to be less passionate while manifest partisanship frequently characterized locally written stories. Local writers also presumed an intimate, personal relationship with both the fans and the local teams and players.

By the 1920s the percentage of total newspaper space allocated to sports was more than double what it had been three decades earlier. Even the *New York Times* gave front-page coverage to major prizefights and the World Series. With the exception of two columns on page one, the *Times* devoted the entire first 13 pages of its issue of July 3, 1921, to the Dempsey-Carpentier heavyweight championship fight. Rather than having to confront the turmoil and unpredictability of front-page news, many Americans (especially men) turned first to the sports page where they found clear-cut triumphs and defeats, continuity, and orderliness. Regardless of natural disasters, revolutions, or economic crises, the games went on. "You pulled off the double play the same way for the Richmond County Juniors, the Auks or the White Sox," wrote Tom Wicker, a *New York Times* columnist, about baseball. "Baseball was a common denominator . . . it was the same one day as the next, in one town as another."[3]

The twentieth century brought to the fore a new generation of writers specializing in sports. Some converted the sporting experience into poetry; only poetry, they believed, could reduce the wonder of sports to human comprehension. Grantland Rice, the dean of early twentieth-century sportswriters, had a gift for writing verse a cut above the popular commercial jingles of the day. Youngsters memorized his lines and coaches used them to inspire their teams. His most famous: "When the one Great Scorer comes to write against your name, he marks—not whether you won or lost—but how you played the game." After Knute Rockne's 1924 Notre Dame team defeated powerful Army, Rice composed the best known opening lines in sportswriting history: "Outlined against a blue-grey

October sky, the Four Horsemen rode again. In dramatic lore they are known as Famine, Pestilence, Destruction, and Death. These are only aliases. Their real names are Stuhldreher, Miller, Crowley, and Layden."[4] Sportswriters frequently dispensed on-the-spot immortality to athletes. Even the racehorse Man O'War was immortal; he was dubbed the "horse of eternity."

Despite Rice's continuing popularity, by the 1920s his form of sportswriting had begun to wane. Rather than writing poetry or stringing together quotations from participants (often a characteristic of sports reporting in the age of television), Paul Gallico, Frank Graham, Damon Runyan, Ring Lardner, Westbrook Pegler, Heywood Broun, and Arch Ward (among others) tried to construct an interesting, lively, interpretive, and not infrequently exaggerated story of what had happened or was likely to happen. The best of them could weave a story as terse and tight as the strands of a steel cable. Apart from presenting a coherent narrative, they employed powerful, often onomatopoeic verbs, colorful figures of speech, and alliterative nicknames. Nicknames came in a virtual flood: the Galloping Ghost (Red Grange), the Fordham Flash (Frankie Frisch), the Sultan of Swat (Babe Ruth). They also delighted in using all three names of people involved in sports, such as Grover Cleveland Alexander, Kenesaw Mountain Landis, or George Herman Ruth, thereby conferring upon them a kind of tongue-in-cheek grandeur.

As in earlier times, newspapers continued to promote sports. For example, the Golden Gloves boxing program got underway in the mid-1920s with the aid of Captain Joseph Medill Patterson, co-publisher of the *Chicago Tribune* and later publisher of the New York tabloid, the *Daily News*. In 1928, led by Patterson and the sports staff of the two newspapers, the Golden Gloves became a national tournament. By 1955 some 25,000 youngsters tried to fight their way through the regionals to become one of eight finalists. Arch Ward, longtime sports editor of the *Chicago Tribune*, was especially important as a promoter; he invented both the annual All-Star Baseball Game (1933) and the College All-Star Football Game (1934). At the local level, newspapers sponsored countless athletic teams and a wide variety of sporting events.

Radio began to have an impact on sport in the 1920s but did not reach the apogee of its influence until the 1940s and 1950s. Initially, radio aired only the more spectacular events rather than regularly scheduled contests. As early as 1923 an estimated two million fans listened to the broadcast of the Louis Firpo-Jess Willard heavyweight fight. The *New York Times* deemed the 23-station network established to carry the 1926 World Series to be such a pioneering venture that it printed the entire narrative of the broadcasts in its sports section. Until upstaged by television in the 1950s, the radio broadcasts of the World Series were an annual rite. As early as 1934, the three major networks of the day paid $100,000 for the privilege of carrying the series. Broadcasts of regular season big-league games did not become universal, however, until the 1940s. When the number of local AM radio stations doubled between 1945 and 1950, the quantity of big-league games aired on radio ballooned astronomically. Apart from the sometimes far-flung regional networks associated with each club, nearly 500 stations scattered across the nation carried Mutual Broadcasting Company's "Game of the Day."

Radio executives soon discovered that sports fans liked announcers who were something more than disembodied voices objectively and dispassionately describing the action. The fans wanted announcers capable of becoming celebrities in their own right. Graham McNamee emerged as the new medium's first star. As the chief announcer of the National Broadcasting Company in the 1920s, McNamee enjoyed a remarkable capacity for using his voice to convey the gamut of emotions. Hailed as the "world's most popular announcer," McNamee covered the World Series, prizefights, major college footballgames, national political conventions, and important live news developments.

For many decades, millions of Americans found in the radio coverage of sports both an escape from the humdrum of everyday life and an entry into the wonderland of the imagination. "Radio—mysterious, disembodied, vivid as a dream—screamed for a fantasy response," wrote Bil Gilbert about his experiences listening to the games of the Detroit Tigers while a youngster in the 1930s. Even when not listening to the games, Gilbert imitated the Detroit broadcaster's voice as he described to himself his own tossing of a ball on the roof or throwing stones at a target. In his private world, where Gilbert always had his beloved Tigers crush rivals, he never suffered from the humiliation of defeat. To Gilbert and millions like him, the introduction of television in the 1940s and 1950s, destroyed the magic. "Thereafter baseball was never again serious," Gilbert concluded.[5]

THE NEW MIDDLE CLASS, MODERN CONSUMER CULTURE, AND THE QUEST FOR EXCITEMENT

In the 1890–1950 era evidence of a general retreat from the all-important middle-class concern with self-control was unmistakable. Even before this, from the standpoint of the middle class, the more expressive cultures of the working class, the immigrants, and African Americans placed too little emphasis on self-control. So did the families of the new rich, who frequently took their behavioral cues from the freer ways of the European aristocracy. But most significant for the development of sports in the first half of the twentieth century was a fast-growing, new middle class. Less evangelical, more impatient with demands for self-control, and increasingly dissatisfied with the tepidity of their day-to-day lives, a new generation of the middle class hungered for more personal freedom, for additional excitement, and for greater self-fulfilment.

With the rapid growth of corporate capitalism in the late nineteenth and twentieth centuries, virtually a new middle class came into existence.[6] Alongside the older middle class comprised of shopkeepers, skilled craftsmen, professional men, and the owners and operators of small factories came an explosive growth in the professions, middle managers, salespeople, and secretaries. Between 1870 and 1930 their numbers grew twice as fast as the work force as a whole. Often possessing specialized skills acquired through formal education, they shared an enthusiasm for rationality and what they frequently called "science." Rather than emphasizing so much personal character, a major concern of the older middle-class

Victorians, the new middle class took pride in their specialized knowledge. Personality was also more important to the new middle class. Especially away from their workplaces, members of the new class relaxed the traditional middle-class concern for self-control. There, they embraced new, more expressive forms of behavior. In their leisure activities, their lives revolved more around consumption, commercial amusements, informality, spontaneity, and intense feelings than the older middle class.

The new middle class became a major patron of the fast-growing, modern consumer culture. By the 1890s the nation's economy had begun to shift from one organized around production to one organized around mass consumption and leisure. In the Industrial Revolution's first phase, the main catalyst for rapid economic expansion had been the growing demand for "producer goods," those made for other producers rather than for individual consumers. A classic example in the nineteenth century was the steel industry, which had grown up primarily to meet the demands of the nation's burgeoning railway network. Although producer goods remained important to the nation's prosperity in the twentieth century, by the 1920s the manufacture for, and sales of goods to, millions of individuals had become the hallmark of a new phase of the Industrial Revolution.

By then, industrial technology had transformed the United States into a consumers' paradise. The automobile, the most prized of all the new consumer goods, emancipated millions of Americans from a network restricted to home, neighborhood, and workplace. Electricity revolutionized the home; by 1940, four out of five Americans could, if they had the financial means, plug in electric lamps, washing machines, vacuum cleaners, refrigerators, toasters, and radios. The Great Depression of the 1930s and World War II temporarily set back the national buying spree, but in the postwar era, plastics, aluminum, and transistors became the staples of a new round of consumption. The consumer cornucopia extended to commercial leisure. As early as 1909, the A.G. Spalding and Brothers catalog contained more than 200 pages of advertisements for sporting goods and exercise devices. Overall, the first half of the twentieth century witnessed a twelvefold increase in recreation expenditures.

The changing nature of work, rising real incomes (adjusted for changes in prices), a shorter work week, and paid vacations abetted the development of consumer culture. Although workers were subject to cycles of unemployment, wage earnings in manufacturing nearly quadrupled between the Civil War and 1929. The Great Depression of the 1930s set back worker gains, but earnings rebounded in the 1940s. At the same time, the average work week for those engaged in manufacturing followed a descending curve from 60 hours in 1890 to 47 in 1920 and 40 at mid-twentieth century. A week's paid vacation first became the norm for white-collar workers in the 1920s and then for blue-collar laborers in the 1940s. As income and leisure time both increased and the factories and bureaucracies gnawed away at job satisfaction, consumption became the centerpiece of more and more lives.

Newspapers, mass circulation magazines, movies, and radio encouraged Americans to seek fulfillment in consumption. The media bombarded the public with new models of "the good life" that had been only furtively glimpsed by earlier generations. To encourage buying, salesmen and advertisers unrelentingly assaulted the older Victorian virtues of thrift and prudence. They urged consumers to "buy now, pay later," to "live for the moment." "Life is meant to live and enjoy as you go along. . . . ," insisted Bruce Barton, a leading apostle of the consumer culture in the 1920s. "If self-denial is necessary I'll practice some of it when I'm old and not try to do all of it now."[7] The suggestions or implications of advertisers and the media that consumption aided in the solution to such personal problems as loneliness, weariness, absence of sexual gratification, and meaninglessness in the workplace won increasing favor.

Although the consumer culture by no means obliterated traditional Victorian values or behaviors, it spawned an alternative set of powerful dreams and expectations. Growing numbers of Americans were no longer so concerned with work, thrift, or self-restraint; they were more interested with obtaining the immediate pleasures arising from devotion to fun, play, sensual experiences, and less inhibited behavior generally. Consistent with the new attitudes, states and municipalities across the nation relaxed legal restrictions on amusements. Many states repealed or neglected to enforce their Sabbatarian laws. New York City, for example, finally obtained legal approval of Sunday baseball in 1919, though Philadelphia and Pittsburgh did not succumb until 1934. In the 1920s several states dropped their bans on such low sports as prizefighting, but conflicts accompanied these. Many tried to preserve traditional virtues, and even those who embraced consumption values experienced agonizing doubts. In their personal lives, they often tried the difficult, if not impossible, task of accommodating the older values conducive to production with the newer ones that encouraged consumption.

ISLANDS OF PLEASURE

Islands of pleasure flourished in the consumer culture. Some were holdovers from the nineteenth century. Blue-collar voluntary associations declined in importance and workingmen's theaters disappeared altogether, but urban workers continued in the twentieth century to gather on street corners and in saloons, billiard halls, bowling alleys, and other "low" spots of entertainment. In the first two decades of the twentieth century, the ethnic saloon reached its heyday in popularity. In Chicago, for example, a survey revealed that on an average day the number of saloon customers equaled over half of the city's population. But Prohibition in the 1920s, a depressed economy in the 1930s, and the growing privatization of leisure in the post-World War II era all contributed to a decline in the importance of the saloon as a special workingmen's oasis.

As in the past, saloonkeepers offered patrons opportunities for direct participation in sport and a place to discuss and wager on sports. In 1909, for example, over half of Chicago's 7,600 saloons contained at least one billiard table.

Despite persistent criticism by "respectable" people and competition from multifarious rivals in entertainment, even in the post-World War II era saloons continued to furnish countless men with opportunities for sport and places to nurture a male subculture.[8]

At the other end of the social spectrum, the wealthy continued to enjoy their own islands of pleasure. In the last half of the nineteenth century, the rich had established posh yacht, athletic, cricket, and country clubs as well as special compounds in cool summer places like Newport, Rhode Island, or in warm winter spots like Pinehurst, North Carolina. The summer and winter playgrounds of the superrich often displayed private mansions, golf courses, tennis courts, and handsome clubhouses, all manned by an army of servants. Each of the larger cities also had clubs restricted to only the wealthiest residents.

A notch or two below the superwealthy, more prosperous members of the middle class in cities and towns across the nation formed and joined country clubs. In the 1920s the country club came of age in the United States. Membership in a country club became a salient badge of distinction, obligatory for families seeking higher status in large and small communities. Entire families usually participated in club life. Wealthier clubs erected large, Mediterranean-style clubhouses, sometimes valued at more than a million dollars, while at the other extreme, avid golfers in small towns sometimes built clubhouses of unadorned pine at a cost of only a few hundred dollars. Regardless of the cost of their clubs, in their isolated playgrounds the nation's Protestant upper strata partook of hedonistic pleasures that had earlier been frowned upon. The lifestyle of the materially successful eased the transition of many Americans from a production to a consumption ethic.[9]

Although traditional places of pleasure of both the upper and lower classes persisted into the twentieth century, new islands of commercial leisure in which all classes and both sexes mingled grew in popularity. Beginning in the last quarter of the nineteenth century and continuing into the twentieth century, dance halls, amusement parks, vaudeville, and, above all, movie houses furnished millions of urbanites with intense experiences not found in the workplace or the home. Around the turn of the century, amusement parks proliferated; every large city had one or more parks, which usually included bathing facilities, vaudeville theaters, dance halls, band pavilions, circus acts, and mechanical contrivances such as Ferris wheels, all located in exotic settings. "Coney Island has a code of conduct which is all her own," Guy Carryl wrote in 1901.[10] Indeed, while at the amusement parks patrons suspended Victorian proprieties. Unlike the prevalent gender-segregated leisure of the nineteenth century, the younger members of both sexes and all classes came together at the amusement parks where they laughed merrily, talked loudly, embraced one another openly, and cavorted. The itinerant carnivals and circuses furnished similar entertainment to the millions in the smaller towns and in the countryside.

The popularity of amusement parks, carnivals, and circuses paled beside that of the movies. By the 1920s over 50 million people a week went to the movies, a figure equivalent to half of the nation's population. Even the hardships of the

1930s failed to curb moviegoing; movie attendance continued to climb until the nation entered the age of television in the 1950s. Awe-inspiring classical architecture and uniformed ushers lent the movie houses an aura of respectability, but, as in the amusement parks, the classes and sexes came together indiscriminately. The films presented models of consumption rather than production. They treated moviegoers to vivid displays of a leisured class who enjoyed sumptuous homes, lovely clothes, sleek cars, and personal servants.[11]

In the meantime, reformers sought to construct completely respectable islands of leisure. This process included the use of public school buildings and playgrounds, church and Young Men's Christian Association gymnasiums, municipal auditoriums and playing fields, and especially city parks. As early as the 1840s, reformers visualized parks as retreats in which urban residents could escape the ills of the cities and be rejuvenated by the powers of nature. In 1856 New York City acquired land in Manhattan that, under the direction of Frederick Law Olmstead, became Central Park; other larger cities soon followed the lead of New York. In the 1890s a new, more successful movement called for the creation of a system of smaller parks in neighborhoods rather than one large, centrally located park. By 1920 nearly every city in the nation had a network of parks and a parks commission. Municipal expenditures on parks continued to mount in the 1920s; in the depressed 1930s the federal government became a major funding agency for city parks.

Although reformers provided the initiative for the city parks movement, the history of parks invariably reflected struggles between groups with conflicting interests and values. In the nineteenth century, Protestant upper-class reformers sought to construct romantic parks that were in sharp contrast to life in the streets while ethnics and workingmen sought to open parks to vigorous games and even commercial amusements. In the twentieth century, reformers insisted that parks should be carefully managed by professionals. "The mere presence of open spaces is not enough, leisure itself is not enough," concluded a study of the municipal park movement.[12] Park administrators should nurture the social and cultural development of the parkgoers by organizing dramatic and musical performances providing nature classes, and supervising recreational activities. Actual park use usually resulted from delicate compromises worked out between park reformers and park users. By mid-twentieth century, parks reflected efforts to maintain sylvan oases along side busy ballfields, basketball courts, and swimming pools.

Business and industrial concerns established more recreation programs for workers. In the nineteenth century, most businessmen had either paid little attention to the spare-time activities of their employees or condemned them when they interfered with worker efficiency. George M. Pullman, the manufacturer of luxury railroad cars, was something of an exception.[13] Beginning in the 1880s, he tried to encourage worker loyalty and productivity by building a model town on the outskirts of Chicago. The town included worker housing, shops, a theater, a library, schools, parks, and a recreation program. The failure of the Pullman experiment to avoid a violent strike in 1894 led many industrialists to conclude that "welfare capitalism" was useless in preventing labor conflict.

Nevertheless, efforts by management in the 1920s to reverse union gains of the World War I era gave new life to welfare capitalism. Apart from such traditional union-busting techniques as blacklists, yellow dog contracts, injunctions, espionage, and violence, employers sought to prevent unionization by forming company unions, distributing chatty newspapers, inviting employees to make suggestions for improvements in the firm's operation, and forming company recreation programs. Industrial sports would not only improve worker efficiency, explained Carnegie Steel's welfare director, A. H. Wyman, sports also fostered "a stronger feeling of loyalty to their bosses" and the company.[14] Often companies, YMCAs, YWCAs, and city governments cooperated closely in providing facilities and supervision for organized sports programs for both men and women. (For women's industry-sponsored sports, see Chapter 13.)

As Pamela Grundy has demonstrated, sports could mean something quite different to employees.[15] In southern textile communities, baseball teams developed devoted followers and nurtured a remarkable group of professional players, many of whom eventually made it all the way to the big leagues. Frequently subjected to taunts and referred to as "poor white trash" and "lintheads," success on the diamond provided textile workers with a recognition, respect, and degree of autonomy that they could not otherwise have commanded. Industrial sports could help build confidence and communal ties; they could strengthen worker consciousness and the formation of labor unions. But, paradoxically, at the same time, industrial sports could, by encouraging good feelings among workers and more positive attitudes toward employers, blunt efforts at unionization

THE STRENUOUS LIFE

In the last two decades of the nineteenth century and the first two decades of the twentieth century, "progressive" reformers expressed a growing enthusiasm for a more strenuous life. In the antebellum era, only a small band of muscular Christians had had the temerity to suggest that individual and national character and strength required as much attention to physical fitness as it did to work or to the cultivation of spirituality. But by the 1890s calls for the strenuous life had become a virtual chorus; by then certain members of the old Eastern elite and a rising corps of experts on the human body were insisting that properly regulated sports conducted in the spirit of amateurism were vital to the nation's well-being. In the early twentieth century, more and more Americans, including those of both the old and the new middle class, agreed; they attributed to sports a potential utility equal to, or sometimes even larger than, that which had traditionally been assigned to religion, the home, or the school. Sports then became for many Americans an ideology, a kind of faith worth fighting for. To its ideological defenders, vigorous sports were even essential to the republic's health and survival.[16]

A belief that the nation was suffering from a massive malaise of the spirit helped to spawn the growing interest in physical strenuosity. Frequently allied with other social reforms, the apostles of the sporting ideology concluded that the vitality of the nation depended upon the generation of higher purposes than merely making or spending money. "No amount of commercial prosperity can supply the lack of the heroic virtues" found in modern life, wrote Theodore Roosevelt.[17] Likewise, too many of the nation's old elite had withdrawn from an active involvement in the world to a "cloistered life" of ease and sloth; there, they had become overly effeminate. Ancient Rome had fallen, declared Alfred T. Mahan, "when the strong masculine impulse which first created it had degenerated into . . . worship of comfort, wealth, and general softness."[18] In short, modern man was "overcivilized." Intrigued by Darwinian analogies depicting human society as a jungle in which only the fittest (often conceived unconsciously as the physically fittest) survived, the elite worried that human races possessing greater animal virility would crush the "Anglo-Saxon race."

Without a Civil War or a frontier to provide opportunities for the expression of heroism or nobility of character, the elite manifested its activism in an aggressive nationalism, an intense interest in untamed nature, and an enthusiasm for organized sports. No one expressed the principles of "dangerous sport" more fully than Francis A. Walker, a Civil War veteran who had become the president of Yale. In an address to the Phi Beta Kappa at Harvard in 1893, he declared that the Civil War had fortunately produced "a vast change in popular sentiments and ideals," showing that the "strength of will, firmness of purpose, resolution to endure, and capacity for action" expressed in the war were far nobler than the soft intellectuality and sentimentalism prevalent in the antebellum era. He went on to say that "the competitive contests of our colleges" offered the best hope of preserving "something akin to patriotism and public spirit," which counteracted "the selfish, individualistic tendencies of the age." Sports not only instilled idealism in the youth, Walker added, but they toughened the "cultivated classes" for leadership roles.[19]

No one exemplified the strenuous life in practice more fully than Theodore Roosevelt, the American president who had coined the phrase. From a family of old wealth, something of an intellectual, and unable to participate with enthusiasm in the sordid business of making money, Roosevelt rejected a life of ease for one of political and physical combat. He sought to embody the heroic virtues found in the soldier, the cowboy, and the prizefighter. Perhaps compensating for his puniness as a youth, he began at the age of 14 to take boxing lessons (even in his forties, while occupying the White House, he occasionally sparred), and he worked out regularly with dumbbells and horizontal bars. In his twenties, he left the safe confines of the East for the hazardous life of a cowboy in the Dakotas where he relished the opportunity to help in the capture of a band of cattle rustlers. Upon the outbreak of the Spanish-American War in 1898, he created and led a cavalry unit of cowboys and college students who won national acclaim for their bravery. Succeeding to the presidency upon the assassination of William McKinley in 1901, Roosevelt enthralled the nation with his vigor. He preached to and bullied opponents both at home and abroad. "In life, as in a football game," he once advised the nation's boys, "the principle to follow is: Hit the line hard, don't foul, and don't shirk, but hit the line hard!"[20] Revelatory of the close connection

Vol. XII *   SEPTEMBER, 1904   * No. 3

PHYSICAL CULTURE

What Shall
We Stand
For in
Politics?

PHYSICAL CULTURE PUBLISHING CO.

THEODORE "TEDDY" ROOSEVELT This picture of Teddy Roosevelt on the front cover of the September 1904 issue of Physical Culture *illustrated the compatibility between the president's promotion of the strenuous life and that of huckster and muscleman Benarr Macfadden, the publisher of* Physical Culture.
(Library of Congress)

between muscular Christianity and the strenuous life, Roosevelt recommended *Tom Brown's School Days* as one of two books that every boy should read.

Experts on the human body gave added support to the turn-of-the century campaign for the strenuous life. In fact, patricians probably drew some of their ideas from the professional physical educators as well as the muscular Christians. Roosevelt, Walker, and dozens of others passed through Dudley A. Sargent's famous physical fitness program (1879–1919) at Harvard. Sargent agreed that violent sports allowed young men to replicate the courage and hardiness that their fathers had experienced in Civil War combat. But, unlike the old elite, Sargent advocated exercises and the playing of sports primarily as a means of achieving general fitness rather than more esoteric social goals. Indeed, not all young men should play football; each person should engage in those sports and exercises that contributed to his all-around fitness.

World War I (1914–1918) intensified the enthusiasm for sports. Before America joined the allied war effort in 1917, sports became an important component of a national preparedness campaign. Shortly after American entry, General John J. Pershing asked the YMCA to manage Army cantonments; the YMCA, employing 300 trained physical directors, also took charge of the athletics of the American Expeditionary Forces in France. The YMCA established comprehensive sporting programs everywhere. The campaign to tie sports to the military reached a dramatic climax in 1919 with the scheduling of the Inter-Allied Games in Paris. The Army invited 29 of the victorious nations to participate in "keen rivalry, a free field, and fair play."[21]

Anxieties arising from the "roaring" 1920s brought additional support to the ideology of sports. Sports might help to check the behavior of the nation's youth, who, according to the popular media, were drinking from hip flasks, engaging in erotically suggestive forms of dancing, and taking wild automobiles rides. Rather than encouraging a capitulation to the baser impulses of the day, sports, its defenders averred, taught discipline, restraint, respect for authority, and the importance of following the rules. Sports ideologues praised what they called "sportsmanship," doubtlessly in part because good behavior by the athletes could not be assumed. The pursuit of victory, which was an integral part of every contest, could and sometimes did encourage behavior completely at odds with the ideal of sportsmanship.

In short, during the first half of the twentieth century, the ideology of sports penetrated deeply into very fabric of American life. It shaped the contents of a large body of juvenile literature and was a core ingredient in programs designed to manage the spare-time activities of adolescent boys (see Chapter 7). The rising profession of physical education employed it effectively to convince reluctant school boards and state legislatures across the nation to require physical training in the schools. To nearly the entire nation, the idea that organized sports conducted in the spirit of amateurism was an unusually powerful tool in building personal character became virtually a truism. Even evangelicals now began openly to use sports to recruit converts. And businessmen increasingly saw in sports a training ground for success in the marketplace. Furthermore, for many Americans, acceptance of the sporting ideology eased guilt feelings arising from their abandonment of the work ethic. After all, disciples of the strenuous life worked hard, even if only at their play.

Yet, while many Americans enthusiastically endorsed organized sports without any reservation, a small but growing band of literary and artistic rebels registered a loud dissent. By giving precedence to the physical over the mental, sports, to these "modernist" intellectuals, represented a misplaced value. Historians Charles and Mary Beard added another concern: At best, they said, sports provided only a momentary respite from the oppressions of modern society; at worst, sports were an opiate that promoted acquiescence to the status quo. Even a few sportswriters poked fun at the ballyhoo of sports promoters; others, like John R. Tunis, rued the capitulation of the joy of sports to commercial considerations. To Tunis, the new consumer society, of which sport was now an integral part, was destroying the pure spirit of play that he imagined had once prevailed. Unlike the opening decades of the twentieth century, an era in which Theodore Roosevelt led intellectuals in their enthusiasm for sports, throughout the remainder of the twentieth century, these and similar refrains reverberated forcefully through the nation's major intellectual and artistic circles.[22]

CHANGING IDEALS OF PHYSICAL BEAUTY

Prevalent assumptions about the proper role of females and their basic nature worked against the acceptance of a strenuous life ideology for women. Even though millions of women performed backbreaking chores such as farm labor, factory work, cleaning, and child rearing, most Americans accepted the age-old notion that women were by nature more delicate than men. This premise was reinforced by the changes in nineteenth-century economy. The rapid decline of the household as an economic unit contributed to the popularity of a "separate women's sphere." Success in the separate sphere required women to cultivate restraint, compassion, and delicacy rather than aggressiveness, competitiveness, and robustness. To the extent that this ideal of success for women was accepted, it deprived women of one of the most important popular arguments used by men to rationalize participation in sports.[23]

Many physicians and health authorities added practical objections to strenuous play. Characterizing women as the weaker sex, the experts worried that robust games would damage or inhibit the maturation of female reproductive organs. They therefore urged young women to shepherd their energies and, at most, engage in only mild, carefully regulated exercises. Believing that the menstrual period was an illness, they concluded that vigorous sport during menstruation could lead to a displaced uterus and a reduction in childbearing capacities. Even as late as 1953, the Amateur Athletic Union, in a study of the effects of athletics upon women, quoted a woman physician as saying that competition during menstruation might adversely affect the capacity of the athlete to be a "normal mother."[24]

Nonetheless, the persistence of these powerful strictures failed to curb a general trend after 1890 toward a greater freedom of physical expression for women. Rural, working-class, recently arrived ethnic, and wealthy women had never been as circumscribed in their roles as middle-class Victorian women. By the late nineteenth century, women in the middle-income ranks also began to break out of the confines of a rigidly defined special sphere. The widely heralded "new woman" of the 1890–1930 era sought an advanced education, often remained single, sometimes entered a profession or engaged in full-time social work, and supported women's suffrage. Partisans of the strenuous life did not always exclude women. Moderate athleticism could, some of the reformers concluded, aid women in playing their proper roles in society (see Chapter 13).[25]

Changing ideals of physical beauty affected the sporting experiences of both sexes, albeit in distinct ways. Male ideals tended to encourage strenuous play and exercises. The renowned weightlifter Eugen Sandow, who was introduced to the American public at the Chicago World's Fair in 1893 by Florenz Ziegfeld, popularized bodybuilding and the Greco-Roman muscular form among men.[26] Rudolph Aaronson, the producer of the burlesque shows of the voluptuous Lillian Russell, humorously noted that one could quickly calm the sexual aggressiveness of college men by merely telling them that they looked like Sandow. Although by no means the only model of male beauty, the Greco-Roman form enjoyed wide popularity among men in the twentieth century. In the 1920s and 1930s Johnny Weismuller, an Olympic swimming medalist, displayed his seminude muscular body dozens of times as Tarzan in the movies, and for three decades (beginning in the 1930s), Charles Atlas, a man of enormous muscles, sold countless mail-order courses to men and boys who wanted to achieve a similar body shape.

The Gibson girl, who dominated standards of female beauty between 1895 and World War I, provided a more ambiguous model for would-be sportswomen. Although she escaped some of the physical confinement of the Victorian era, she always engaged in sports with moderation. Nor did the flappers, the prevailing model of female beauty from about 1915 until the 1930s, usher in a

EUGEN SANDOW *Even at 52 years of age in 1909, Sandow, a pioneer in the history of bodybuilding, personified an emerging ideal of male beauty.*
(UPI/Corbis)

BICYCLING FEMALE *This advertisement for Crawford bicycles in the 1890s suggested greater physical freedom for women and opportunities for the sexes to mingle without chaperones, both which were daring departures from Victorian restraints.*
(Library of Congress)

women's revolution in sports. The flapper broke far more sharply than the Gibson girl with Victorian notions of proper dress and behavior. She bobbed her hair short, smoked and drank in public, mingled freely with men, danced the fast steps of the Charleston, abandoned corsets, shortened skirts, and wore fewer clothes. The quantity of cloth in a typical woman's outfit shrank from $19\frac{1}{2}$ yards in 1913 to 7 yards in 1925. And the popular Kellerman bathing suit of the 1920s completely bared legs and arms while clinging closely to the natural shape of the body.

Yet the energy, bravado, and physical freedom of the flapper signaled more precisely the advent of the modern beauty culture than a completely new era of women's sports. While Helen Wills, the queen of women's tennis, and Gertrude Ederle, the first woman to swim the English Channel, became celebrities in the 1920s, the typical American woman reserved her greatest admiration for Hollywood actresses. Most women devoted far more energy to competition in the beauty arena than on the playing fields. Actresses, beauty contestants, and fashion models established beauty standards for all women. Although in the 1930s and 40s the flapper gave way to new models of female beauty in the more sophisticated and imperious movie queens, the beauty culture continued to influence profoundly the behavior of American women. Not only did it circumscribe the potential of women as athletes, but it also publicly measured those women who did venture onto the playing field against the prevailing standards of feminine beauty and behavior.

AN AGE OF RACIAL SEGREGATION

Race, like sex, also limited the sporting opportunities of many Americans. Blacks soon discovered that the end of slavery and the new amendments added to the Constitution during Reconstruction failed to end racial prejudice or discrimination. In due time blacks in the South even lost the effective right to vote and hold public office. Disfranchisement, terror, and segregation laws all worked to keep blacks "in their places." By the 1890s in many localities "Jim Crow" policies, the common expression for the systematic segregation of African Americans, legally separated whites and blacks in ballparks, beaches, churches, trains, rest rooms, schools, and even water fountains. A series of decisions by the United States Supreme Court gave official sanction to segregation; in *Plessy v. Ferguson* (1896) the Court ruled that "separate but equal" public facilities were consistent with the Fourteenth Amendment. This opinion held sway for the next 58 years.

Legal segregation was only one of the manifestations of deeply embedded racism in the 1890–1950 era. Vicious racial stereotyping in the popular media depicted blacks as irresponsible and dangerous savages. For example, D.W. Griffith's epic film *Birth of a Nation* (1915) explicitly played upon white sexual fears; white audiences everywhere cheered the conclusion of an exciting scene depicting the Ku Klux Klan as the savior of white womanhood from the ravages of black sexual lust. The application of Darwinian ideas to the evolution of races added a supposedly scientific note to white belief in racial superiority. Racists argued that peoples with the highest material cultures, namely whites, had succeeded best in the racial "struggle for survival." Such views remained part of the conventional wisdom of white social scientists as late as the 1940s and 1950s.

Racial segregation and racism extended to sport as well, albeit not uniformly or consistently.[27] In the mid-1880s, whites rejected a short-lived experiment in racially integrated professional baseball. Although black and white professional teams played one another in exhibition matches, racially integrated professional baseball did not return until 1946 when Jackie Robinson joined the Montreal farm club of the Brooklyn Dodgers. Throughout the 1890–1950 era a small number of blacks (probably less than one percent of the total players) played on racially integrated college football teams in the North; likewise a somewhat larger number engaged in track and field competitions on behalf of northern colleges. During the 1920s a few blacks played in the National Football League before being unofficially banned in the 1930s. Blacks and whites rarely competed against one another in the elite sports of tennis and golf.

The bicycling rage of the 1890s reflected the typical problems confronted by blacks in sport. In the 1890s manufacturers perfected an inexpensive "drop frame," or "safety" bicycle, which led to the sport of bicycle racing. To protest black membership in the League of American Wheelmen, southern white affiliates in the early 1890s began to withdraw from the league. In response, in 1894 the bicycling league's convention adopted a "whites only" membership policy. "There is no question of our accepting the [N]egro in preference to the white wheelman of the south," wrote a league official. "If it should be narrowed down to a question such as that, we should undoubtedly decide that we want our southern brothers in the league in preference to the [N]egroes of the country."[28]

Only Marshall W. "Major" Taylor, a black man from Indianapolis, succeeded in breaking the racial barrier in professional bicycle racing.[29] Hailed as the "fastest bicycle racer in the world," Taylor, who won the national sprint championships in 1898, 1899, and 1900, broke many national and world records before retiring in 1910. From the beginning of his career as a "scorcher," Taylor was the victim of frequent racial slurs, white riders colluded in throwing him from his cycle or "boxing" him in, and in at least one instance he was physically attacked by a white rider after the completion of a race. Promoters prohibited Taylor from racing on all southern and several northern tracks. In 1897, fellow riders tried to exclude him from all-white tracks, but the conspiracy collapsed, attributable largely to the influence of bicycle manufacturers and racing promoters who recognized that Taylor attracted large crowds. Apart from Taylor, however, few other blacks were allowed to compete in "white" cycling. Most of them could race only in an all-negro circuit.

Of the major sports, blacks achieved something approaching equal opportunity only in the individual, unregulated, and countercultural sport of prizefighting. In the late nineteenth century, the sporting fraternity had not been adverse to pitting a black against a white when it promised to be profitable. From 1908 to 1915 it was a black, Jack Johnson, who held the world heavyweight crown, but the succeeding white heavyweight champions avoided black fighters until 1937 when Joe Louis won the title. On the other hand, below the championship levels black-versus-white fights were not uncommon. In fact, promoters frequently played on racial and ethnic antagonisms to generate interest in matches. Yet fears that too many blacks in boxing or that blacks with unpopular personalities might endanger potential profits limited black opportunities in the sport.

In addition to discrimination and prejudice, the failure of blacks to share fully in the fruits of the consumer society in the 1890–1950 era sharply reduced the potentialities of black sports. By and large, blacks simply had far less income than whites. Before World War I, nearly nine out of ten blacks toiled as farm laborers or tenant farmers in the southern countryside. Although the number of blacks employed in northern manufacturing had doubled by 1930, they received lower wages than white counterparts. The vast majority of blacks occupied the lower rungs of the occupational ladder; in Chicago in 1920, for example, only a tenth of the black males worked at skilled jobs compared to over one-quarter of the whites. Even as late as 1950 the median family income for blacks was about half of that for whites.

Yet, despite these limitations, blacks managed to fashion broad and varied community structures, of which sport was sometimes a vital component. Between 1910 and 1960, Northern cities, in what is sometimes labeled as the "great migration," received a huge influx of migrants from the South. Usually excluded by income and color from living where they pleased, the migrants crowded into all-black neighborhoods. Despite high rates of poverty, disease, crime, and marital discord, a sense of community arose in part from the services provided by black professionals, newspapers, small businesses, and even racketeers. Black voluntary associations, such as churches, lodges, and athletic clubs and teams, also lent stability to the ghetto communities. (For the role of baseball in black communities in the 1890–1950 era, see Chapter 10.)

In the South, racially segregated schools offered a special arena, one largely apart from the repressions and restrictions of Jim Crow, for the development of African American sports.[30] Within this space, sports frequently became a powerful means of self-discovery and individual expression. For both male and female students participation in athletics offered some assistance in girding African American students both emotionally and intellectually for the indignities of segregation; sports could and sometimes did provide them with large transfusions of self-confidence. By bridging and transcending the more expressive folk culture of lower-class African Americans and the more repressive culture of the middle-class black educators, sports brought socially diverse black people together, strengthened pan-racial consciousness, and helped forge stronger black communities.

CONCLUSION

In the 1890–1950 era sport achieved an entrenched prominence in American life similar to other important institutions. As it had in the past, sport continued to provide certain groups with satisfactions missing in other parts of their lives. It also continued to offer a special sense of community and identity to groups and places. Moreover, in the new era, the growing popularity of consumer values along with the ideology of the strenuous life swept away much of the traditional suspicion of sport. But not all groups shared equally in the fruits of the new era. In particular, those with inadequate incomes as well as women and blacks found their opportunities both to participate in sport and to consume commercial sport sharply circumscribed or nonexistent.

NOTES

1. R.H. Davis, "The Thanksgiving-Day Game," *Harper's Weekly* 37 (December 9, 1893), 1171.

2. H.S. Williams, "The Educational Value and Health-Giving Value of Athletics," *Harper's Weekly* 39 (February 16, 1895), 165. For a similar conclusion, see Charles D. Lanier, "The World's Sporting Impulse," *Review of Reviews* 14 (July 1896), 58. For overviews of several of the subjects covered in this chapter, see Steven A. Riess, *City Games: The Evolution of American Urban Society and the Rise of Sports* (Urbana: University of Illinois Press, 1989), and Gerald M. Gems, *Windy*

City Wars: Labor, Leisure, and Sport in the Making of Chicago (Lanham, MD: Scarecrow, 1997).

3. Quoted in Benjamin G. Rader, *In Its Own Image* (New York: Free Press, 1984), 13. For a superb overview of sports and the media between the 1920s and 1960s, see Michael Oriard, *King Football: Sport and Spectacle in the Golden Age of Radio and Newsreels, Movies and Magazines, the Weekly & the Daily Press* (Chapel Hill: University of North Carolina Press, 2001), chap. 1. For content analysis of sport coverage in the 1890s and 1920s, see R.S. Lynd and H.M. Lynd, *Middletown* (New York: Columbia University Press, 1929), 473, and H.J. Savage et al., *American College Athletics* (New York: Carnegie Foundation, 1929), 267–72. For the predominance of male readership, see J.H. Slusser, "The Sports Page in American Life in the Nineteen-Twenties," unpub. M.A. thesis, Univ. of California, Berkeley, 1952, 4; James L. Baughman, *The Republic of Mass Culture* (Baltimore, MD: Johns Hopkins University Press, 1992), 11; and Oriard, *King Football*, 28.

4. *New York Herald Tribune*, October 19, 1924.

5. Quoted in Rader, *In Its Own Image*, 28. On radio sports, see esp. Curt Smith, *Voices of the Game* (South Bend, IN: Diamond Communications, 1987).

6. See Benjamin G. Rader, *American Ways* (Dallas: Harcourt Publishers, 2001), 190–92.

7. Quoted in R.W. Fox and T.J.J. Lears, eds., *The Culture of Consumption* (New York: Pantheon, 1983), 32.

8. See Riess, *City Games*, 72–81, and J.M. Kingsdale, "The Poor Man's Club: Social Functions of the Urban Working-Class Saloon," *American Quarterly* 25 (1973), 472–88. For the persistence of the saloon into the 1960s and 1970s, see E.E. LeMasters, "Social Life in a Working Class Tavern," *Urban Life and Culture* 2 (1973), 27–52. For the persistence of ethnicity in sports, see Riess, *City Games*, chap. 3, and G.R. Mormino, "The Playing Fields of St. Louis Italian Immigrants and Sports, 1925–1941," *Journal of Sport History* 9 (1982), 5–19.

9. Richard J. Moss, *Golf and the Country Club* (Urbana: University of Illinois Press, 2001), and J.F. Steiner, *Americans at Play* (New York: Arno, 1933). For a study of upper-class life in Westchester, New York, in the 1930s, see G.S. Lundberg et al., *Leisure* (New York: Macmillan, 1934).

10. Quoted in John F. Kasson, *Amusing the Millions* (New York: Hill and Wang, 1978), 41.

11. See esp. Lary May, *Screening Out the Past* (New York: Oxford University Press, 1980).

12. Quoted in Paul Boyer, *Urban Masses and Moral Order in America, 1820–1920* (Cambridge, MA: Harvard University Press, 1978), 240.

13. See W.J. Pesavento, "Sport and Recreation in the Pullman Experiment, 1880–1900," *Journal of Sport History* 9 (1982), 38–62.

14. "Industrial Recreation," *Playground* 17 (June 1923), 178. See also U.S. Bureau of Labor Statistics, "Outdoor Recreation for Industrial Employees," *Monthly Labor Review* 24 (1927), and J.D. Hall et al., *Like a Family* (Chapel Hill: University of North Carolina Press, 1987), 135–39.

15. Pamela Grundy, *Learning to Win: Sports, Education, and Social Change in Twentieth-Century North Carolina* (Chapel Hill: University of North Carolina Press, 2001), 118–25.

16. See T.J.J. Lears, *No Place of Grace* (New York: Pantheon, 1981), chap. 3; Donald J. Mrozek, *Sport and the American Mentality, 1880–1920* (Knoxville: University of Tennessee Press, 1983); J.C. Whorton, *Crusaders for Fitness* (Princeton, NJ: Princeton University Press, 1982); Elliott J. Gorn, *The Manly Art* (Ithaca, NY: Cornell University Press, 1986), 185–206; G.M. Frederickson, *The Inner Civil War* (New York: Harper & Row, 1965), chap. 11; Harvey Green, *Fit for America* (New York: Pantheon, 1988), chap. 9; G.F. Roberts, "The Strenuous Life: The Cult of Manliness in the Era of Theodore Roosevelt," unpub. Ph.D. diss., Michigan State Univ., 1970; Mark Dyreson, "The Emergence of Consumer Culture and the Transformation of Physical Culture: American Sport in the 1920s," *Journal of Sport History* 16 (1989), 261–81; Mark Dyreson, *Making the American Team: Sport, Culture, and the Olympic Experience* (Urbana: University of Illinois Press, 1998); S.W. Pope, *Patriotic Games* (New York: Oxford University Press, 1997); and Gerald R. Gems, *For Pride, Profit, and Patriarchy: Football and the Incorporation of American Cultural Values* (Lanham, MD: Scarecrow, 2000), especially chap. 3.

17. Theodore Roosevelt, *American Ideals and Other Essays* (New York: Review of Reviews, 1897), 11.

18. Alfred Mahan, *The Interest of America in Sea Power* (Boston: Little, Brown, 1903), 121.

19. Quoted in Frederickson, *Inner Civil War*, 223–24.

20. Roosevelt, "What We Can Expect of the American Boy," *St. Nicholas* 27 (1900), 574. The

other book recommended by Roosevelt was Nelson Aldrich's *Story of a Bad Boy*.

21. See esp. Pope, *Patriotic Games*, chaps. 7 and 8, and Wanda Ellen Wakefield, *Playing to Win: Sports and the American Military, 1898–1945* (Albany: State University of New York Press, 1997), chaps. 1 and 2.

22. See Dyreson, "Emergence of Consumer Culture," 268–81.

23. For flat rejections of the strenuous life for women, see Henry Van Dyke, "The Strenuous Life for Girls," *Harper's Bazaar* 36 (1902), 575–78, and Arabella Kenealy, "Woman as Athlete," reprinted in S.L. Twin, ed., *Out of the Bleachers* (New York: Feminist Press, 1979), 35–51. See also Nancy L. Struna, "Beyond Mapping Experience: The Need for Understanding in the History of American Sporting Women," *Journal of Sport History* 11 (1980), 120–33.

24. *A.A.U. Study of Athletic Competition on Girls and Women* (New York: Amateur Athletic Union, 1953), 8. See also Helen Lenskyz, *Out of Bounds* (Toronto: University of Toronto Press, 1986), chaps. 1 and 2; J.A. Mangan and R.J. Park, eds., *From "Fair Sex" to Feminism* (London: F. Cass, 1987); and Patricia Vertinsky, "Exercise, Physical Capacity, and Eternally Wounded Woman in Late Nineteenth-Century North America," *Journal of Sport History* 14 (1987), 7–27.

25. See for example Susan K. Cahn, *Coming on Strong* (New York: Free Press, 1994), chap. 1; Anne O'Hagen, "The Athletic Girl," *Munsey's* 25 (1901), 728–38; Christine Harrick, "Women in Athletics," *Outing* 40 (1902), 713–21; and Dudley Sargent, "Are Athletics Making Girls Masculine?" *Ladies Home Journal* 29 (1912), 11.

26. See Lois W. Banner, *American Beauty* (New York: Knopf, 1983), and David L. Chapman, *Sandow the Magnificent* (Urbana; University of Illinois Press, 1994).

27. See David K. Wiggins, *Glory Bound: Black Athletes in White America* (Syracuse, NY: Syracuse University Press, 1997), especially its bibliography.

28. Quoted in Dale A. Somers, *The Rise of Sports in New Orleans, 1850–1900* (Baton Rouge: Louisiana State University Press, 1972), 223.

29. See M.W. "Major" Taylor, *The Fastest Bicycle Rider in the World* (Brattleboro, VT: Green-Stephen, 1972).

30. See especially Grundy, *Learning to Win*, chap. 6, and Patrick Miller, ed., *The Sporting World of the Modern South* (Urbana: University of Illinois Press, 2002), chaps. 5 and 6.

9
THE AGE OF SPORTS HEROES

The 1890–1950 era, especially the decade of the 1920s, teemed with sports heroes. "Never before, or since, have so many transcendent performers arisen contemporaneously in almost every field of competitive athletics as graced the 1920s," concluded veterans sports reporters Allison Danzig and Peter Brandwein in 1948.[1] Each sport had its magic name: George Herman "Babe" Ruth in baseball; William Harrison "Jack" Dempsey in boxing; Harold "Red" Grange in football; Robert T. "Bobby" Jones in golf; William T. "Big Bill" Tilden in tennis. And many others (including such female athletes as Suzanne Lenglen, Helen Wills, and Gertrude Ederle) stood close to the magic circle.

Why sports idols? The public acclaim accorded star athletes sprang from something more than performance, though indeed their athletic feats were often phenomenal. The same skill and shrewd promotion that successfully hawked automobiles, breakfast foods, and lipstick also sold athletes to the public. Behind the sport heroes stood professional pitchmen: George "Tex" Rickard, Jack "Doc" Kearns, Charles C. "Cash and Carry" Pyle, and Christy Walsh, to name a few. Then there were the journalists and radio broadcasters prone to hyperbole such as Grantland Rice and Graham McNamee. They created images of athletes which often overshadowed the athlete's actual achievements.

Yet the public idolization of athletes went even deeper than the skillful ballyhooing of the promoters and journalistic flights of fancy. Ultimately, the emergence of a dazzling galaxy of sport idols was a creation of the American public itself. Athletes as public heroes served a *compensatory* cultural function. They assisted the public in compensating for the passing of the traditional formula of success, the erosion of Victorian values, and feelings of individual powerlessness. As the society became more complicated and systematized and as success had to be won increasingly in bureaucracies, the need for heroes who leaped to fame and fortune outside the rules of the system grew. No longer were the heroes lone businessmen or statesmen, but the "stars" of movies, television, and sports.

In the new age of mass consumption and burgeoning bureaucracies, a popular culture of compensation flourished. The media helped create defense mechanisms for the helpless individual that rested upon a complex set of images, fantasies, and myths. Some were comic: Charlie Chaplin in the movies was the carefree little tramp who eluded cops, bullies, and pompous officials; even the machine could not bring him to heel. Some were dashing and romantic: Douglas Fairbanks slashed his way through hordes of swift-sworded villains. Some were tough: The classic Western hero, brave and handsome, killed bad men and Indians, thus dramatically serving the forces of "good" while saving white Americans from the "savages."

The popular culture of compensation also projected images of heroes vaulting to the top. In nineteenth-century drama and fiction, the hero won the hand of the rich man's daughter through his virtuous character; Rudolph Valentino won her through his irresistible physical charm. Even the kings of organized crime themselves enjoyed something of a celebrity status in the 1920s, furnishing forceful images of power and success.

Above all, fantasies and images of power and instant success flourished in the world of sport. In sport—or so it seemed—one could still catapult to fame and fortune without the benefits of years of arduous training or acquiescence to the demanding requirements of bureaucracies. Unlike most vocations, sheer natural ability coupled with a firm commitment to sport for its own sake could propel the athlete to the top. Determining the level of success of a doctor, lawyer, or business manager might be difficult, but achievement in the world of sport was unambiguous. It could be measured precisely in home runs, knockouts, touchdowns, victories, and even in salaries. Those standing on the assembly lines and those sitting at their desks in the bureaucracies found the most satisfaction in the athletic hero who presented an image of all-conquering power. Thus they preferred the towering home runs of Babe Ruth to the "scientific" style of base hits, base stealing, sacrifices, and hit-and-run plays personified by Ty Cobb; they preferred the smashing knockout blows of Jack Dempsey to the "scientific" boxing skills displayed by Gene Tunney. Perhaps it was little wonder that boys now dreamed of becoming athletic heroes rather that captains of industry, and girls dreamed of Hollywood stardom rather than the hearth.

BABE RUTH

No modern athletic hero exceeded Babe Ruth's capacity to project multiple images of brute power, the natural, uninhibited man, and the fulfillment of the American success dream.[2] Ruth was living proof that the lone individual could still rise from mean, vulgar beginnings to fame and fortune, to a position of public recognition equaled by few men in American history. With nothing but his bat, Ruth revolutionized the national game of baseball. His mighty home runs represented a dramatic fi-

GEORGE HERMAN "BABE" RUTH The peerless compensatory hero of the 1920s, Ruth may have been the most celebrated athlete in American history. This photograph reveals a somber, younger Ruth, before he became conspicuously corpulent.
(National Archives and Records Administration)

nality, a total clearing of the bases with one mighty swat. Everything about Ruth was extraordinary—his size, strength, coordination, his appetite for the things of the flesh, and even his salary. He transcended the world of ordinary mortals, and yet he was the most mortal of men. He loved playing baseball, swearing, playing practical jokes, eating, drinking, and having sex. Despite his gross crudities, wrote Billy Evans, a big-league umpire, "Ruth is a big, likeable kid. He has been well named, Babe. Ruth has never grown up and probably never will. Success on the ball field has in no way changed him. Everybody likes him. You just can't help it."[3]

Ruth saw himself as a prime example of the classic American success story. "The greatest thing about this country," he said in his ghostwritten autobiography, "is the wonderful fact that it doesn't matter which side of the tracks you were born on, or whether you're homeless or homely or friendless. The chance is still there. I know."[4] Ruth encouraged the legend that he had been an orphaned child. While the story had no basis in fact, his early years were indeed grim. His saloonkeeping father and sickly mother had no time for the boy; he received little or no parental affection. By his own admission, he became a "bad kid," who smoked, chewed tobacco, and engaged in petty thievery. At the age of seven, his parents sent him to the St. Mary's Industrial Home for Boys, an institution in Baltimore run by the

Xaverian Order for orphans, young indigents, and delinquents. Except for brief interludes at home, Ruth spent the next 12 years at St. Mary's. There, as a teenager, he won a reputation for his baseball prowess and in 1914 signed a professional contract with the Baltimore Orioles of the International League. In the same year the Boston Red Sox purchased him as a left-handed pitcher.

Ruth never struggled for success in baseball. For him, both pitching and hitting were natural talents rather than acquired skills. Converted from a top pitching star to an outfielder, Ruth surprised the world of baseball in 1919 by hitting 29 home runs, two more than the existing major-league record that had been set in a crackerbox ball park in 1884. He followed in 1920 as a member of the New York Yankees with a stunning total of 54 four baggers, which was a larger number than any entire team (except the Yankees) in the major leagues had compiled. For Ruth, this was only the beginning. From 1918 through 1934 he led the American League in homers 12 times with an average of more than 40 a season; from 1926 through 1931 he averaged slightly more than 50 home runs per season. For every 11.7 times at bat he hit a round tripper, an individual record that stood until the great hitting barrage of the 1990s. In addition, Ruth hit for an exceptionally high average. His lifetime mark of .342 has been equaled by few players in baseball history.

The public responded to Ruth's feats with overwhelming enthusiasm. Before Ruth, the Yankees' best annual attendance had been 600,000, but with him, the team drew more than a million each year. Everywhere in the league, the fans poured out to the ballparks to see the Yankees play, apparently caring little whether the home team won or lost, only hoping to witness the Babe hammer a pitch out of the park. Even Ruth's mighty swings that failed to connect brought forth a chorus of awed "Ooooooohs," as the audience realized the enormous power that had gone to waste and the narrow escape that the pitcher had temporarily enjoyed. Each day, millions of Americans turned to the sports page of the newspaper to see if Ruth had hit another homer. Indeed, the response may have been unique in the annals of American sport. "In times past," Paul Gallico, a sportswriter, reflected, "we had been interested in and excited by prizefighters and baseball players, but we had never been so individually involved or joined in such a mass outpouring of affection as we did for Ruth." To players and fans alike, Ruth was a pioneer exploring "the uncharted wilderness of sport. There was something almost of the supernatural and the miraculous connected with him too," continued Gallico. "I am not so certain now that Ruth is human," added Cleveland catcher, Chet Thomas. "At least he does things you couldn't expect a mere batter with two arms and legs to do. I can't explain him. Nobody can explain him. He just exists."[5]

The Ruthian image of home-run blasts ran counter to the increasingly dominant world of bureaucracies, scientific management, and "organization men." Ruth was the antithesis of science and rationality. Whereas Ty Cobb relied upon "brains rather than brawn," upon, as he put it, the "hit-and-run, the steal and double-steal, the bunt in all its varieties, the squeeze, the ball hit to the opposite field and the ball punched through openings in the defense for a single," Ruth, on the other hand, swung for the fences. Ruth, according to sportswriter F.C. Lane in 1921, "throws science itself to the wind and hews out a rough path for himself by the sheer weight of his own unequaled talents." Ruth seemed to embody the public preference for a compensatory hero with mere brute strength rather than one who exercised intelligence. Ruth played baseball instinctively; he seemed to need no practice or special training. He loved the game for its own sake. "With him the game *is* the thing. He loves baseball; loves just to play it," asserted a sportswriter.[6] No ulterior motives seemed to tarnish his pure love of the game.

The Ruthian image also ran counter to Victorian rules. Ruth's appetite for the things of the flesh was legendary. He drank heroic quantities of bootleg liquor; his hotel suite was always well stocked with beer and whiskey. People watched him eat with awe; he sometimes ate as many as 18 eggs for breakfast and washed them down with seven or eight bottles of soda pop. Ruth was not only the "Sultan of Swat," he was also a sultan of the bedroom. In each town on the spring training tours and in each big-league city, Ruth always found a bevy of willing female followers. His escapades were so well known that a sportswriter wrote a parody of them. "I wonder where my Babe Ruth is tonight? He grabbed his hat and coat and ducked from sight. I wonder where he will be at half past three? . . . I know he's with a dame. I wonder what's her name?"[7] Ruth probably did not know her name, for he had a notorious reputation for being unable to remember the names of even his closest friends. In the 1920s, to those many Americans who were rejecting what they called "Puritanism," Ruth could be identified as a fellow rebel. Marshall Smelser has written that Ruth "met an elemental need of the crowd. Every hero must have his human flaw which he shares with his followers. In Ruth it was hedonism, as exaggerated in folklore and fable."[8]

Ruth's propensity for immediate gratification had its more endearing side. He won a deserved reputation for loving children. Everywhere he went, children flocked to him, simply to see the great Bambino and perhaps to touch his uniform and obtain his autograph. Ruth enthusiastically welcomed their attention. He regularly visited children in hospitals. A legend that has some basis in fact added immeasurably to Ruth's popularity. In its simplest version, Ruth visited a young boy who was dying in a hospital. He promised the lad that he would hit a home run for him that afternoon. He did, which so inspired the boy with the will to live that he miraculously recovered.

The public also adored Ruth for his crude egalitarianism. He deferred to no one. Introduced, for instance, to President Calvin Coolidge, he responded: "Hi, Pres. How are you?" According to one story, possibly apocryphal, while Ruth was holding out for a higher salary in 1930, someone pointed out to him that a depression existed and that he was asking for more money than President Herbert Hoover earned. "What the hell has Hoover got to do with it?" Ruth demanded. "Besides, I had a better year than he did."[9]

Ruth's huge earnings added to his heroic stature. From the time Ruth set his first home run record in 1919, he was besieged by commercial opportunities outside of baseball. Since the early days of the game, star players had supplemented their salaries by product endorsements, vaudeville acts, and personal appearances, but no player had the opportunities that became available to Ruth. In the winter of 1921, Christy Walsh, a sports cartoonist turned business agent, convinced Ruth to permit him to handle the demand by newspapers for Ruth's "personal analysis" of each home run that he hit. For 15 years Walsh employed a stable of ghostwriters, among them Ford Frick, future commissioner of baseball, to write pieces allegedly by Ruth for newspapers and magazines. Ruth "covered" every World Series from 1921 through 1936. Eventually Walsh's syndicate provided ghostwriting services for a large number of athletes and public celebrities, including Knute Rockne, the famed Notre Dame football coach.

Walsh became the first modern athletic business agent. Beginning in 1921, he handled nearly all of Ruth's nonbaseball commercial ventures. In 1921 he signed Ruth to a vaudeville tour, the first of several, which called for Ruth to receive $3,000 per week for 20 weeks, a record-shattering sum for a vaudeville performer. He also managed Ruth's many barnstorming baseball tours in the off-season. He assembled a list of all the commercial products with which his client could be associated and set out to convince the manufacturers of the benefits to be gained by Ruth's endorsements. In time, Ruth promoted, among other products, hunting and fishing equipment, modish men's wear, alligator shoes, baseball gear, and sporty automobiles. In Boston he might trumpet the virtues of Packards, in New York, Cadillacs, and in St. Louis, Reos. He received pay to appear at banquets, grand openings, smokers, boxing and wrestling matches, and celebrity golf tournaments. When the purchasing power and the low income tax of that era are taken into account, Ruth's earnings were phenomenal. His total baseball income ranged between $1.25 million and $1.5 million, his nonbaseball earnings between $1 million and $2 million, for a total in the neighborhood of $3 million. Although Ruth was a hopeless spendthrift, Christy Walsh convinced him to put some of his income into untouchable annuities. Thus he survived the stock market crash in 1929 with enough money to retire comfortably in 1935.

Of America's legendary heroes, Ruth is the country's preeminent athletic hero. Even in an age that takes special delight in smashing false idols, Ruth remains the demigod of sports. His astonishing success reassured those who feared that America had become a society in which traditional conditions conducive to success no longer existed. He transcended the world of sport to establish an undefinable benchmark for outstanding performances in all fields of human endeavor.

Americans resented anyone who threatened to tarnish Ruth's heroic stature. When Henry Aaron approached Ruth's career record of 714 home runs, he said, "I can't recall a day this year or last when I did not hear the name of Babe Ruth."[10] Roger Maris, when he broke Ruth's mark of 60 home runs in one season in 1961, found himself the victim of a steady stream of abuse from fans, sportswriters, and people in the streets. They repeatedly noted that Ruth had compiled 60 home runs in a 154-game season while Maris had only 59 after 154-games. (Maris hit 61 homers in a 163-game season.) After the 1961 season, Maris quickly sank into obscurity, but the legend of Babe Ruth lived on. Long after the 1920s, Ruth has remained peerless among compensatory heroes.

EARL "RED" GRANGE *This publicity photograph of the nation's best-known football player of the 1920s suggests how heroes might satisfy conflicting needs. On the one hand, part of the Grange legend arose from publicizing his hard-working life as a youth delivering ice to residents in Wheaton, Illinois, which fit perfectly the formula of the self-made man. On the other hand, that Grange is accompanied by beautiful, admiring women suggests that he embodied the new consumer ethic as well.* (UPI/Corbis)

RED GRANGE

Pitchmen and journalists also found in the football player Red Grange an almost perfect subject of elevation to the status of a compensatory hero. Like Ruth, Grange projected an image of swift, decisive, all-conquering power. Rather than methodically grinding down the opposition with power plays, Grange's forté was the sudden and total breakthrough—the punt return, the kickoff return, or the long run from scrimmage that climaxed in a touchdown. By exhibiting his phenomenal talent for open field running in a game against Michigan in 1924, Grange stunned the football world. Before the game, Fielding H. Yost, the veteran mentor of many powerful Michigan elevens, assured everyone that the Illinois redhead could be stopped. With 67,000 fans present at the opening of the new Illinois stadium, Grange responded by scoring four touchdowns in the first 12 minutes of the game. He took the opening kickoff for a 95-yard touchdown run; he then had touchdown runs of 67, 56, and 45 yards from the line of scrimmage.

Modern technology accentuated the drama of Grange's feats. While few Americans were able to see Grange perform in the flesh, millions saw him in the newsreels in thousands of theaters. The image of Grange, speeded up on the flickering screen, was almost eerie, as it darted, slashed, cut away from would-be tacklers, and crossed the goal line one, two, three, or even five times within a few seconds. Little wonder that Grantland Rice hailed Grange as the "Galloping Ghost of the Gridiron."

Grange's career seemed to confirm traditional virtues and the survival of the dream of the self-made man. Like Ruth, he began life under adverse circumstances. One of five children, he was born in the small rustic town of Forksville, Pennsylvania, where his father supported the family by working in local lumber camps. His mother died when Grange was but five years old. Yet as a youth, he, unlike Babe Ruth, practiced all the Victorian virtues that seemed to be fast disappearing in the United States of the twentieth century. He neither drank nor smoked. He was modest and softspoken. He worked hard. During the summers while in high school and college he toted ice to Wheaton, Illinois, residents.

These character traits, according to Grange in his ghostwritten autobiography, paid dividends. Athletics "was my whole life and I put everything I had into it," he wrote. "The future took care of itself. When the breaks came I was ready for them." Confirming the legendary dream of American success, he wrote: "Any boy can realize his dreams if he's willing to work and make sacrifices along the way."[11]

Grange, of course, exaggerated. He owed his success to more than hard work and impeccable personal habits. He enjoyed marvelous natural talents for quickness afoot and the ability to change directions while carrying a football. In high school he was the Illinois sprints and hurdles champion. As a high school football player at Wheaton he created something of a sensation by scoring 72 touchdowns in three seasons of play.

Contacted by the alumni of several Midwestern colleges who wanted to bring his talents to their campuses, Grange finally resolved to attend the University of Illinois. Robert Zuppke, the Illinois head coach, recognized in Grange a potential football immortal. In the spring practice of 1923, he designed a powerful single-wing formation with Grange running at tailback. "I got a great break at Illinois," Grange later confessed. ". . . I ended up making most of the team's touchdowns and getting all the publicity, because Coach Bob Zuppke let me carry the ball 90 percent of the time. In most of the games I carried the ball thirty or forty times."[12]

Grange, like other athletic heroes of the 1920s, capitalized financially upon his fame. Shortly before he began his final season at Illinois, he was approached by Charles C. "Cash and Carry" (or "Cold Cash") Pyle, a small-time theater operator who was soon to become a sports impresario with few peers. According to Grange's recollection, Pyle simply said: "How would you like to make one hundred dollars, or maybe even a million?"[13] Grange promptly replied in the affirmative. Pyle then negotiated a secret deal with George Halas and Ed Sternamen, the co-owners of the Chicago Bears, a professional football team in the fledgling National Football League. At the end of the college season, Grange was to play the remaining league games of the Bears and then he and the Bears would embark on a national exhibition tour to be staged by Pyle.

The decision of Grange to join the professional ranks touched off a national debate. By abandoning his studies in the middle of his senior year, Grange flaunted the myth of the college athlete as a gentleman-amateur who played merely for the fun of the game or the glory of his school. Furthermore, professional football in the 1920s was associated with the working class and ethnic groups; it was held in low esteem by the middle and upper classes. Initially, sympathetic newsmen depicted Grange as an "innocent, decent, trusting chap," who was the "victim of a kind of conspiracy of get-rich-quick promoters who did not care how far they went in prostituting him to their ends." But Grange was hardly an innocent victim. He acknowledged, "I'm out to get the money, and I don't care who knows it . . . my advice to everybody is to get to the gate while the getting's good."[14] He did promise his admirers that he would someday finish his senior year of college, a promise he never kept.

Pyle's plan succeeded beyond expectations. Five days after Grange's final game with Illinois, he played with the Bears at Wrigley Field in Chicago on Thanksgiving Day 1925. The publicity barrage accompanying Grange's departure from Illinois helped attract 35,000 fans, to that date the largest crowd ever to attend a professional game. With Grange obliged to play at least half of each game, the Bears then played a grueling schedule of 10 games in 17 days. Everywhere they went—St. Louis, Philadelphia, New York twice, Boston, Providence, Washington, and Pittsburgh—they broke professional football attendance records. After taking an eight-day rest in Chicago, Grange and the Bears embarked upon Pyle's 7,000-mile, 35-day, 14-game barnstorming tour of the South and West. In matches against "pick-up" teams of mostly former collegians, Pyle insisted upon a $25,000 guarantee from local promoters for each game. Newspapers and press syndicates assigned their most distinguished sportswriters to accompany Grange. Never had such a tour by an athletic team attracted so much publicity nor been so financially rewarding. Ironically, the Galloping Ghost's performance, perhaps because of a nagging injury, was far less spectacular than it had been as a collegian.

In the meantime, Pyle lined up commercial endorsements for Grange. Within the first ten days after Grange had signed a contract with Pyle, they reportedly received 187 phone calls, 60 telegrams, and 39 personal visits from advertising men. Grange endorsed sweaters, shoes, caps, a Red Grange football doll, and soft drinks. The "Red Grange Chocolates," according to Pyle, sold six million bars in 30 days. In New York, Grange signed a movie contract, and Pyle flashed a $300,000 check to amazed reporters. Although the press headlined the event, Grange later admitted that it was "one of Pyle's wild publicity stunts"; Grange was actually to receive $5,000 a week while working on the film. Pyle recognized that large sums of money were important in establishing the heroic status of his clients. Altogether in the first year of their partnership Pyle and Grange split about $250,000 as their share of gate receipts and income from endorsements and promotions.

Emboldened by his spectacular financial success with Grange in the winter of 1925–1926, Pyle expanded his promotional horizons. He first demanded that he and Grange be granted one-third ownership of the Bears. When Halas and Sternamen refused, he attempted to place a second NFL team in New York, only to be blocked by the New York Giants. He then formed a new professional loop, the American Football League, with Grange and himself as co-owners of the New York Yankees. Because of Grange, the Yankees drew large crowds, but the other teams in the league lost money. After the 1926 season, the new league collapsed. Pyle, with Grange and the financial losses suffered by NFL teams during the 1926 season as leverage, forced the NFL to admit the Yankees as a "road team" for the 1927 season. A permanent knee injury suffered by Grange in the third game of the 1927 season brought financial ruin to the Yankees.

Grange and Pyle amicably severed their partnership. Pyle went on to other forms of sport promotion—professional tennis tours and two long-distance walking contests from San Francisco to New York ("Bunion Derbies"). Grange returned to the Bears as a superb defensive back and above-average straight-ahead running back. He played his last game in 1935 and, in the 1940s and 1950s, became a successful radio and television sportscaster.

JACK JOHNSON

Prizefighting champions, perhaps more than heroes from any other sport, evoked intense feelings about gender, ethnicity, race, and social class. Amid the great changes in nineteenth-century life, many men had turned to boxers for behavioral cues that would clearly distinguish them from women. Prizefighters often served as heroes of the working class, recently arrived ethnic groups, and African Americans. Few if any blacks were as well known or had infused blacks with greater pride than Jack Johnson, the heavyweight champion between 1908 and 1915.[15]

Johnson got a shot at the championship under unusual circumstances. Earlier champions had drawn the "color line," refusing to meet black challengers. But Johnson persisted; he literally pursued Tommy Burns, the reigning champion, around the world, issuing challenges as he went. Money finally changed Burns's mind. Hugh McIntosh, a wealthy Australian businessman, guaranteed to Burns $30,000 win or lose, a purse far larger than for any previous prizefight, to fight the black challenger. Johnson was to receive only $5,000. John L. Sullivan probably expressed the typical response of American whites to Burns's decision. "Shame on the money-mad champion! Shame on the man who upsets good American precedents because there are Dollars, Dollars, Dollars in it."[16] In 1908, in far-off Sydney, Australia, Johnson easily battered Burns into submission.

Almost at once, ex-champions, fight promoters, and newspapermen launched a hunt for a "Great White Hope" to retake the crown from Johnson. As Johnson disposed of several second-rate white contenders, the demand grew for

James J. Jeffries, a popular former heavyweight champion, to come out of retirement and rid boxing of the "black menace." Finally, in 1910, Jeffries agreed to battle Johnson at Reno, Nevada. Jeffries himself interpreted the fight in racial terms. "That portion of the white race that has been looking for me to defend its athletic superiority may feel assured," he said, "that I am fit to do my very best."[17] Jeffries's very best was not enough, for Johnson knocked him out in the fifteenth round. Johnson's victory ignited black celebrations across the country, but so much happiness was premature. In violent racial confrontations at least eight persons lost their lives.

The victories of Jack Johnson stunned white America. To both white and black, Johnson's ascension to the heavyweight throne possessed incalculable symbolic significance. In the most primeval of American sports, the ultimate metaphor of masculine conflict, the best of the black men had defeated the best of the white men. Newspaper columnist Max Balthazer wrote of the prospective Jeffries–Johnson fight: "Can the huge white man [Jeffries] . . . beat down the wonderful black and restore to the Caucasians the crown of elemental greatness as measured by strength of blow, power of heart and being, and, withal, that cunning or keenness that denotes mental as well as physical superiority?"[18]

THE PURSE FOR THE JOHNSON–JEFFRIES BOUT, 1910 In this publicity photograph, Tex Rickard (far left) and Jack Johnson examine the purse for the heavyweight championship bout between Johnson and James J. Jeffries. Rickard, who was to become the nation's leading boxing impresario, acted as both promoter and referee for the bout. The public response to the fight reflected the tense race relations of the era.
(Library of Congress)

To both races the fight could signify or suggest racial equality or even black superiority; above all, to whites, it might suggest a potential threat to America's apartheid. While Johnson personally ignored organized efforts for greater racial justice in America, his feats might inspire blacks to mount formidable challenges to white supremacy. To many whites, Johnson represented an enormous threat to the entire superstructure of racial segregation.

Never had a heavyweight champion been more controversial than Johnson. In an age in which racial animosity had reached a fever pitch, he exacerbated deep-set white fears. In the ring, while smiling broadly, he badgered, taunted, and jeered his white opponents. He was a big spender who loved the high life—flashy dress, champagne, night clubs, fast cars, and willing women. To most whites and some blacks he was the embodiment of the "uppity Nigger." He defied age-old racial customs; he married three white women and had sexual liaisons with many others.

By openly flaunting this taboo, Johnson intensified white sexual anxieties. Deeply embedded in white mythology were beliefs in black sexual promiscuity and superiority. According to historian Eugene Genovese, even early in American history "Europeans and Americans were hearing lurid tales of giant penises, intercourse with apes, and assorted unspeakable (but much spoken of) transgressions [by blacks] against God and nature."[19] White men feared that white women fantasized about sexual relations with black men. Speaking at the annual governors' conference in 1912, the governor of South Carolina described Johnson as a "black brute." "If we can not protect our white women from black fiends, where is our vaunted civilization?" he asked rhetorically.[20]

Johnson's enemies struck back. Local and state governments barred the showing of the Johnson-Jeffries fight films in American theaters; in 1912 Congress cooperated by prohibiting the transportation in interstate commerce of all moving pictures of boxing matches. Johnson himself became the victim of legal attacks. In 1912, the mother of one of Johnson's consorts charged him with abducting her daughter across state lines for immoral purposes, which, if true, would have constituted a federal crime under the Mann Act of 1910. But the young woman in question refused to substantiate her mother's accusation, and Johnson was acquitted. In the meantime, a federal grand jury returned another charge against Johnson for violating the Mann Act. Belle Shreiber, formerly a prostitute at the fancy Everleigh Club (reputedly the nation's finest brothel) in Chicago, confessed that she had been paid by Johnson to engage in "immoral" and "unnatural" acts during the pair's travels about the country. In 1913 a Chicago jury found Johnson guilty, and the judge sentenced him to jail for one year and a day. During the stay of execution to appeal the decision, Johnson jumped bail and fled the country, first to Canada and then to Europe.

Johnson's flamboyant career then careened toward a climax. While the search continued in the United States for a "Great White Hope," in Europe the champion met a few nondescript challengers and performed in vaudeville while his financial sources dwindled away. Finally in 1915, a year after World War I erupted in Europe, Johnson met Jess Willard in Havana, Cuba. Willard knocked him out in the twenty-sixth round. Johnson was 37 years old and had inadequately trained for the bout; he later claimed that he threw the match in return for $50,000 and an exemption from his prison sentence. A photograph of Johnson on the canvas during the knockout lends some credence to his claim, for the champion appears to have raised his glove over his face to shield his eyes from the blinding Havana sun. However, boxing authorities present at the fight and Randy Roberts, Johnson's biographer, have concluded that Johnson was indeed the victim of a genuine knockout.[21]

In any case, American officials refused to rescind the sentence. In 1920, he returned to the United States and served his time at Fort Leavenworth prison. Afterwards, he performed in vaudeville, gave temperance lectures, appeared in a few fights, and engaged in sparring exhibitions until 1945, when he was 68 years old. The next year Johnson died from injuries suffered in an automobile accident, thus ending one of the most dramatic and symbolically significant athletic careers in the annals of American sport.

THE GOLDEN AGE OF BOXING

The need for compensatory heroes, the ballyhooing of Tex Rickard and Jack Kearns, and the ascension of Jack Dempsey to the heavyweight championship of the world helped make the 1920s the "Golden Age" of American boxing.[22] Never before or since has boxing achieved such a high plateau of popularity. In the prewar years gate receipts from a single bout never exceeded $300,000; in the 1920s, Rickard promoted five consecutive million-dollar gates. Fans paid over $2 million to see the second Dempsey-Tunney fight. In terms of purchasing power, these sums were far larger than any modern gates. Over 100,000 fans witnessed each of the Dempsey-Tunney fights—again, figures unequaled in the annals of the boxing history. Day after day the major newspapers placed boxing items on the front page. They detailed both the private and public lives of the pugilists.

World War I helped soften the traditional animosity toward prizefighting. During the war, the army used boxing as part of the training of doughboys. After the war, often at the instigation of the American Legion, state after state dropped legal barriers to prizefighting. Boxing acquired a new level of respectability. Clandestine fights on barges, in the backrooms of saloons, or in isolated rural spots gave way to fights held in glittering arenas and huge stadiums. No longer were fights patronized exclusively by the slummers, roughnecks, ethnics, workingmen, and the "sporting set"; even "high society," "proper" women, and middle-income groups went to see the fights. Celebrities from all fields of American life turned the heavyweight championship fights into big "social events." The ordinary people may have come as much to see the celebrities as the fight itself.

No one in the 1920s sensed the possibilities of exploiting the public hunger for heroes better than Tex Rickard.[23] Rickard was aptly dubbed variously as the "King of the Ballyhoo," "King of Sport Promoters," and "Phineas T. Barnum" of the twentieth century. Long before the 1920s, he revealed a propensity for taking high risks and a talent for promotion. As a youth in the 1890s he had left a dusty cowtown in Texas for the Yukon-Klondike gold fields. While in Alaska, he reputedly won and lost several fortunes as a professional gambler, gold specula-tor, saloon owner, and barroom fight promoter. Rickard catapulted to the national level when he staged the famous Johnson-Jeffries fight in Reno in 1910.

For the next five years, Rickard pursued multiple careers as a gambling house proprietor, rancher in Paraguay, and fight promoter. In 1916 his name resurfaced when he promoted a "no-decision" bout between the heavyweight champion Jess Willard, who had beaten Jack Johnson in 1915, and Frank Moran in New York. Earning a $30,000 stake from the fight, he promptly doubled it by betting on Woodrow Wilson to win the 1916 presidential election. Having estab-lished a tacit priority for the promotion of future Willard fights, he was in a posi-tion to launch the Golden Age of American boxing. He needed only a new boxing hero to replace the uncharismatic Willard. Jack Dempsey, an unknown western fighter, soon filled that need.

On the face of it, Dempsey was an unlikely prospect for a popular hero. True, his social origins were modest; he was born into a poor, itinerant Irish American family at Manassa, Colorado. But until Jack Kearns became his man-ager in 1917, Dempsey had been little more than a saloon brawler, fighting in Western tank towns for a hundred dollars or less per bout. Dempsey's reputation as a great slugger rested as much on myth as fact. He had been the victim of a knockout in 1917, and he had lost a decision in 1918. His career knockout per-centage of .613 was unexceptional, well below that of Floyd Patterson and Primo Carnera, for instance, and only slightly above that of Tommy Burns, who is con-sidered the worst of all heavyweight champions by ring historians. As champion, Dempsey defended his title only six times in seven years and met only two gen-uinely formidable foes.

As a potential hero, Dempsey suffered from an even more serious liability. Having not served in the armed forces in World War I, the federal government in 1920 charged him with being a "slacker." Although acquitted on the grounds that he had provided financial support to his wife and mother, the issue clouded Dempsey's heroic image.

Dempsey acquired the reputation of being "Jack the Giant-Killer" largely through the hokum of Jack Kearns and Tex Rickard. Dempsey had the good for-tune of meeting Jess Willard, the "Pottawatomie Giant," in a championship bout staged by Rickard at Toledo, Ohio, in 1919. Willard towered over Dempsey. He stood six feet and six inches tall and weighed 245 pounds, while Dempsey was six feet and one inch tall and weighed 191 pounds. Dempsey floored the massive Willard five times in the first round; at the end of the third round, Willard, his face swollen twice its normal size, bloody and bewildered, conceded defeat.

The image of Dempsey as giant killer caught on at once. Publicity stunts, such as having Dempsey's sparring partners wear inflated chest protectors and catcher's masks, reinforced the image. The public accepted the mistaken notion that Dempsey was a little man. As Dempsey told it: "Jack Kearns' ballyhoo that made me 'Jack the Giant-Killer' was partially responsible. Various pictures that were published of my different fights, too, added to the misconception. Repeatedly they showed me fighting against men who were inches taller than I and many pounds heavier."[24]

The Dempsey–Willard fight launched Rickard's career as the nation's premier sports impresario. In 1920 the New York legislature legalized prizefighting. Two weeks after the law was passed, Rickard, with the aid of John Ringling of circus fame as a silent partner, obtained the financial backing to lease Madison Square Garden. Under his astute management, the Garden, which had been something of a white elephant to previous managers, became a highly profitable enterprise. Rickard offered a variety of attractions unequaled by any other palace of entertainment in the world. Boxing, wrestling, circuses, horse shows, six-day bicycle races, rodeos, professional hockey—these and many other activities became regular fare on the Garden's schedule.

Rickard juggled conflicting interests with the same skill and daring that he had perfected as a professional gambler. He courted newspaper reporters with frequent "leaks," free cigars, liberal quantities of liquor, and special seating privileges. He always reserved a number of free seats for the minions of the Tammany Hall political machine. Simultaneously, he won the support of New York's superrich. In 1921 at the invitation of Anne Morgan, philanthropic sister of J. Pierpont Morgan, he held a benefit fight in the Garden to kick off a fund-raising drive for wartorn France. Such clever gestures assisted Rickard in marshaling the funds for the Carpentier-Dempsey fight in 1921 and for the construction of a new $5 million Madison Square Garden in 1926.

Rickard exhibited the full arsenal of his promotional skills in the Dempsey-Georges Carpentier fight of 1921. Because of political hostility at the state capital in Albany, Rickard transferred the fight to Jersey City, where he had a huge wooden stadium built. As Dempsey later confessed, Rickard "dug up" Carpentier, the light heavyweight champion of Europe, and set out to convince the public that the fragile Frenchman was a serious contender for the crown. Rickard explained to Dempsey and Kearns how he planned to ballyhoo the bout. It would be a "foreign foe" versus an American; a war hero—Carpentier had twice been decorated for valor in World War I—versus a "slacker"; the "rapier" of the skilled fencer versus the "broadsword" of the peasant; the civilized man versus the "abysmal brute." "That's you, Jack," the elated Rickard reputedly exclaimed.[25]

The contrast in images was almost perfect. Ike Dorgan, Rickard's assistant, nicknamed Carpentier the "Orchid Man," set up his training camp on Long Island amid the "social crowd," refused to allow reporters to watch Carpentier spar, and touted the Frenchman's attractiveness to women. According to Dorgan and the press, Carpentier was handsome, debonair, and a "boulevardier," who danced beautifully and sang French chansonnettes.

As Rickard had hoped, the nation took sides. The American Legion passed a resolution condemning Dempsey; the Veterans of Foreign Wars retaliated by siding with the champ. In general, the "lowbrows," workingmen and ethnics, favored Dempsey. The "highbrows," especially the nation's literati, supported Carpentier. Even George Bernard Shaw, the distinguished British playwright, enlisted his vast literary talents in Carpentier's behalf.

As a financial event, the fight was an unprecedented success. Over 80,000 fans paid nearly $2 million to see the fight. Present were the "Who's Who of the social, financial, and entertainment world."[26] As an athletic contest, the bout was a farce. Dempsey had little difficulty in knocking Carpentier out in the fourth round. Nonetheless, everyone seemed satisfied. Even the dignified *New York Times* announced the results of the fight in front-page headlines. Few Americans were left untouched by the spectacle at "Boyle's Thirty Acres."

Rickard used similar tactics in promoting his next bonanza—Dempsey's fight with Louis Angel Firpo at the Polo Grounds in New York in 1923. Firpo, formerly a bottle washer for a Buenos Aires pharmacy, had come to the United States looking for easy money. Rickard corralled for Firpo a "proper assortment of weak-chinned or canary-hearted boxers . . . to pole-ax into unconsciousness." Firpo, a big, awkward man, soon won appellations by the press as the "Argentine Giant" and the "Wild Bull of the Pampas." Rickard hoped to convince the public that the bout would be "two cave men fightin' with tooth and claw."[27]

The actual fight conformed to the ballyhoo much better than anyone expected. In less than four minutes of action, Firpo went down to the canvas ten times, Dempsey twice. After the seventh knockdown of Firpo in the first round, Firpo arose and shot a right to Dempsey's jaw that sent the champion sprawling through the ropes. (George Bellows memorialized the event with his renowned painting, *Dempsey–Firpo*.) Reporters hoisted Dempsey back into the ring and the champ finished the round on wobbly legs. But in the next round, Dempsey, swinging both fists wildly, crushed Firpo for a knockout. The exciting battle produced boxing's second million-dollar gate. Most Americans might be the victims of forces beyond their control, wrote Bruce Bliven in the *New Republic*, but within the confines of the boxing ring both Firpo and Dempsey had decided "their own fates."[28] No sport in the 1920s exceeded boxing's capacity to furnish Americans with compensatory heroes.

In the succeeding three years in which Dempsey failed to defend his title, Rickard often stated that a "million-dollar fight" could be staged only once every two years. Rickard himself was busy with the management of the new Garden. Perhaps more importantly, Dempsey enjoyed living the life of a celebrity. Earning perhaps as much as $500,000 annually from endorsements, movie contracts, and vaudeville performances, he was in no hurry to return to the ring. Personal problems also intruded. Dempsey broke with Jack Kearns, his long-time manager, and Kearns proceeded to harass the champion with legal suits. Finally, Dempsey's wife, Estelle, did not want him to fight.

But the primary reason for Dempsey's absence from the ring may have been Harry Wills, the "Brown Panther" from New Orleans, who was clamoring for a crack at the championship. In every respect except race, Wills was a qualified challenger. The story of his inability to get a match with Dempsey is obscured in intrigue. On several occasions the New York Athletic Commission ordered Dempsey to fight Wills. Apparently these actions were designed to please the black voters of New York City. But, according to Rickard, each time he agreed to give Wills a title shot, he received a word from high political figures in Albany that the match would be blocked. Rickard claimed that the politicians in New Jersey also opposed the match.

Yet, if there was a single culprit in the controversy, it seemed to be Rickard. He showed no interest in staging the fight outside of New York or New Jersey, and he was probably the only person who could have raised a purse adequate for the bout. Apart from possibly being racist himself, Rickard may have feared a loss by Dempsey, a consequent reduction in the gates of future fights, and violent racial incidents similar to the outbreaks that had accompanied Johnson's defeat of Jeffries in 1910.

At any rate, Rickard sidetracked Wills and eventually found a new challenger for Dempsey, Gene Tunney, who "was almost universally regarded as a second-rater" by boxing aficionados. The insistence of the New York Athletic Commission upon a Dempsey–Wills match forced Rickard to hold the bout elsewhere. He chose Philadelphia's Sesquicentennial Stadium and scheduled the fight for September 23, 1926. The buildup followed Rickard's familiar formula. In the "Battle of the Century" it was the dark, savage-visaged, mauling Dempsey versus the smooth, "scientific" boxer Tunney. To the surprise of nearly all the 120,757 fans present and several million radio listeners, Tunney defeated Dempsey in the ten-round match on points. While scoring repeatedly on solid but nonlethal blows, Tunney simply avoided Dempsey's famed rushes. The fight was reminiscent of James J. Corbett's upset of John L. Sullivan in 1892.

Rickard achieved the pinnacle of his promotional career with the second "Fight of the Century" between Tunney and Dempsey in 1927. Over 104,000 customers paid more than $2 million to witness the event at Soldier Field in Chicago. Spectators on the outer perimeter of the stadium sat as far as 200 yards from the ring, making the boxers almost undiscernible. An estimated 50 million Americans heard Graham McNamee's broadcast from one of 73 stations connected to the NBC radio network.

For the first six rounds, the fight seemed to be a replay of the Philadelphia bout. Then in the seventh round, Dempsey landed a series of blows that crumpled Tunney to the mat. As the referee began to count, he waved Dempsey to a neutral corner of the ring. Dempsey ignored the motion, an action that may have cost him the heavyweight crown. By the time the referee convinced Dempsey to retire to a neutral corner, several seconds had expired. The referee then began the count anew, reaching nine before Tunney came to his feet. Although the referee's action conformed to the Illinois boxing codes, the legendary "long count" furnished a source of endless debate among fight fans. Tunney survived the seventh round and outboxed Dempsey in the final three rounds to win a unanimous decision. In defeat, Dempsey's popularity soared higher than when he had held the championship.

The contrast in the popularity of Dempsey and Tunney reflects the type of hero sought by the American public. The image of Dempsey as the mauler who relied upon quick, physical solutions was far more satisfying to the public than Tunney's exhibition of complex, defensive finesse. Millions of Americans who worked in large corporations, bureaucracies, and on assembly lines dreamed of equally direct and decisive answers to their countless frustrations.

In addition, Dempsey seemed more like a typical American than Tunney. Tunney married a socialite, had lectured to a class at Yale on Shakespeare, and was a personal friend of the writer Thornton Wilder. Americans wanted their heroes to be "average" in all respects except their specialty. Leo Lowenthal has written: "It is some comfort for the little man who has become expelled from the Horatio Alger dream, who despairs of penetrating the thicket of grand strategy in politics and business, to see his heroes as a lot of guys who like or dislike highballs, cigarettes, tomato juice, golf, and social gatherings—just like himself."[29] The "little man" could find confirmation of his own pleasures and discomforts by participating in those of Dempsey.

Dempsey's defeat by Tunney signaled the end of the Golden Age of American boxing. The public did not respond to the new heavyweight king; in 1928 Rickard lost some $400,000 in promoting the Tunney–Tom Henney bout. After the fight, Tunney retired from the ring, leaving the heavyweight scene in chaos. Then, in 1929, Rickard, while launching an elimination series to determine a new champion, suddenly died from an attack of appendicitis. Rickard's funeral revealed that the promoter was in his own right a public celebrity. Over 15,000 persons filed past his ornate $15,000 bronze casket in the main arena of Madison Square Garden. The next day, 9,000 attended his funeral. No new impresario replaced Rickard.

CONCLUSION

New needs arising from twentieth-century life resulted in the creation of a compensatory culture. Celebrities who were in part the creation of the media moved ahead of traditional heroes from the world of business, politics, and philanthropy in public esteem. Movie stars and athletes in particular assisted Americans in making the transition from a producer to a consumer society. During the Great Depression, the age of athletic heroes seemed to be over. "After 1930 our stream of superchampions ran dry, replaced by a turgid brook," wrote John R. Tunis in 1934. "The champions were now just ordinary mortals, good players but nothing more."[30] But once prosperity returned with World War II, Americans again found a set of peerless heroes in sports.

NOTES

1. Allison Danzig and Peter Brandwein, eds., *Sport's Golden Age* (New York: Harper & Bros., 1948), xi. Most efforts to explain the American heroes in modern times see them as fulfilling cherished American ideals or myths. See, for example, Leo Lowenthal, *Literature, Popular Culture and Society* (Englewood Cliffs, NJ: Prentice Hall, 1961), 109–41; Leverett T. Smith Jr., *The American Dream and the American Game* (Bowling Green, OH: Bowling Green University Popular Culture Press, 1975); J.W. Ward, "The Meaning of Lindbergh's Flight," in Joseph Kwait and Mary Turpie, eds., *Studies in American Culture* (Minneapolis: University of Minnesota Press, 1960); R.W. Nash, *The Nervous Generation* (Chicago: Rand McNally, 1970), 126–37; C.L. Himes, "The Female Athlete in American Society, 1860–1940," unpub. Ph.D. diss., Univ. of Pennsylvania, 1984,

chap. 5; Michael Oriard, *Dreaming of Heroes:* (Chicago: Nelson-Hall, 1982); B.G. Rader, "Compensatory Sport Heroes: Ruth, Grange, and Dempsey," *Journal of Popular Culture* 16 (1983), 11–22; E.J. Gorn, "The Manassa Mauler and the Fighting Marine: An Interpretation of the Dempsey-Tunney Fights," *Journal of American Studies* 19 (1983), 27–47.

2. Tom Meany, Martin Weldon, Claire Ruth with Bill Slocum, Lee Allen, Dan Daniel, and Waite Hoyt wrote early biographies. More recent books by Ken Sobel, Kal Wagenheim, Robert Creamer, and Marshall Smelser are in most respects superior, but see also esp. Smith, *American Dream*, and Harold Seymour, *Baseball: The Golden Age* (New York: Oxford University Press, 1971).

3. As quoted in Smith, *American Dream*, 207.

4. Babe Ruth and Bob Considine, *The Babe Ruth Story* (New York: Scholastic Books, 1969), 9.

5. Paul Gallico, *The Golden People* (Garden City, NY: Doubleday, 1965), pp. 36–37; and Smith, *American Dream*, 198.

6. Quotations from Ty Cobb with Al Stump, *My Life in Baseball* (Garden City, NY: Doubleday, 1961), 280, and Smith, *American Dream*, 190, 205.

7. Quoted in Seymour, *Baseball*, 431.

8. Marshall Smelser, "The Babe on Balance," *American Scholar* 44 (1975), 299.

9. Quoted in Seymour, *Baseball*, 428.

10. Quoted in Robert Creamer, *Babe* (New York: Simon & Schuster, 1974), 16.

11. Red Grange as told to Ira Morton, *The Red Grange Story* (New York: G.P. Putnam's Sons, 1953), 178. See also John M. Carroll, *Red Grange and the Rise of Modern Football* (Urbana: University of Illinois Press, 1999).

12. Grange, *Red Grange Story*, 174–75.

13. Quoted in ibid., 91. On the remarkable Pyle, see also Myron Cope, "The Game That Was," *Sports Illustrated* 31 (October 13, 1969), 93–96, 102–03.

14. Quotations in "Football History as Made by the Illinois Ice Man," *Literary Digest* 87 (December 26, 1925), 30, and J.B. Kennedy, "The Saddest Young Man in America," *Collier's* 77 (January 16, 1926), 15.

15. See esp. Randy Roberts, *Papa Jack* (New York: Free Press, 1983).

16. Quoted in Al-Tony Gilmore, *Bad Nigger!* (Port Washington, NY: Kennikat, 1975), 27.

17. Quoted in Finis Farr, *Black Champion* (New York: Charles Scribner's Sons, 1964), 107.

18. Quoted in Randy Roberts, "Jack Dempsey: An American Hero in the 1920s," *Journal of Popular Culture* 8 (1974), 412.

19. Eugene D. Genovese, *Roll, Jordan, Roll: The World the Slaves Made* (New York: Vintage Books, 1976), 458.

20. Quoted in Gilmore, *Bad Nigger!*, 107.

21. See esp. Roberts, *Papa Jack*, 12.

22. See esp. Danzig and Brandwein, *Sports Golden Age*, 38–85; Randy Roberts, *Jack Dempsey* (Baton Rouge: Louisiana State University Press, 1979); Gorn, "Manassa Mauler"; and Jeffrey T. Sammons, *Beyond the Ring: The Role of Boxing in American Society* (Urbana: University of Illinois Press, 1988), chaps. 3 and 4.

23. See Charles Samuels, *The Magnificent Rube* (New York: McGraw-Hill, 1957) and Mrs. "Tex" Rickard, *Everything Happened to Him* (New York: Frederick A. Stokes, 1936).

24. Jack Dempsey, *Round by Round* (New York: McGraw-Hill, 1940), 176.

25. Jack Dempsey with C.J. McGurik, "The Golden Gates," *Saturday Evening Post* 207 (October 20, 1934), 11.

26. Jack "Doc" Kearns with Oscar Fraley, *The Million Dollar Gate* (New York: Macmillan, 1966), 147–48.

27. Quotations in Jack Koefoed, "The Master of the Ballyhoo," *North American Review* 227 (1929), 295; Dempsey, "Golden Gates," 75.

28. Quoted in Roberts, *Jack Dempsey*, 181.

29. Lowenthal, *Literature*, 135.

30. J.R. Tunis, "Changing Trends in Sports," *Harper's Monthly* 170 (December 1934), 78.

10
BASEBALL'S
GOLDEN AGE

*U*ntil the 1950s no other team or individual sport seriously challenged baseball's supremacy as the "national pastime." Wars and economic downturns only temporarily set back steady gains in attendance at all levels of the game. Despite the often rowdy behavior of the players (and sometimes managers and owners as well), the sport gained in acceptability among all social groups. Even the president of the nation extended his endorsement; in 1910 William Howard Taft established the precedent of the president opening each season by throwing out the first ball. Baseball stars were sometimes better known than the president of the United States; only Hollywood actors and actresses successfully competed with them for celebrity status. Minor-league professional baseball also grew, from 13 leagues in 1903 to 51 circuits at mid-century. Every city, town, and village of any consequence had one or more amateur, semiprofessional, or professional team(s). Boys everywhere grew up reading baseball fiction, learning the rudiments of the game, and dreaming of one day becoming diamond heroes themselves.[1]

BASEBALL'S COMING OF AGE

During the first two decades of the twentieth century, professional baseball "came of age"; it became America's most entrenched and mature professional sport. This era witnessed the beginning of the modern World Series, the construction of great ballparks of concrete and steel, and the creation of the legend that baseball had uniquely American origins. As never before, the game bound communities and neighborhoods together. No other sport, it seemed to contemporaries, quite captured the essence of the nation's character as much as baseball. Such a contention was beyond argument, declared Albert Spalding, former player and sporting goods entrepreneur in 1911. It was like saying that "two plus two equal four."[2]

Appropriate to its embodiment of the nation's character, the custodians of the national game nurtured a creation myth. The legend that Abner Doubleday invented baseball at Cooperstown, New York, in the summer of 1839 took official form in 1907 with the report of a special commission of men of "high repute and undoubted knowledge of the Base Ball." The commission, appointed by Albert Spalding, engaged in no first-hand research but did send out letters of inquiry to old-timers who had been associated with organized teams in the antebellum era. (Later scholars discredited the work of the commission. See Chapter 4.)

The commission's conclusions, as Spalding so effectively put it, helped free baseball "from the trammels of English traditions, customs, conventionalities."[3] In 1939 the major leagues celebrated the "centennial" of baseball with impressive

ALBERT GOODWILL SPALDING No person exercised more influence over the early history of professional baseball than Spalding. He was not only once a star player, but he also helped to found and guide the National League through its early history, founded a sporting goods empire, and appointed the special commission that propagated the Cooperstown-Doubleday myth of baseball's origins.
(National Baseball Hall of Fame and Museum)

ceremonies at Cooperstown. There they dedicated a Hall of Fame, presented a pageant showing Doubleday's alleged contribution to the sport, and staged an all-star game. The United States government joined the festivities by issuing a commemorative stamp, marking 1839 as the official date of the national game's birth.

The Doubleday-Cooperstown myth helped give baseball a quasi-religious status. As Muslims have their Mecca and Christians have their Jerusalem or Bethlehem, baseball followers have their Cooperstown. Each year, thousands of Americans make the "pilgrimage" to the "shrine" at Cooperstown, the site of the Hall of Fame and Museum. There they can see statues and pictures of their former heroes and observe the "relics" used by them—old, discolored bats, balls, and uniforms. They can visit the "hallowed ground" of Doubleday Field, where the young Doubleday "immaculately conceived" the game. Cooperstown is rich in religious terminology: "shrine," "pantheon," "sanctuary," and "relics." Each year, sportswriters dutifully select great players of the past for "enshrinement," after which they become "immortals."[4]

The pre-1950 ballparks reminded the fans of the nation's simpler agrarian past. For urban spectators, surrounded by noise, dirt, and squalor, entering a major-league ball field could be an exhilarating experience. Suddenly they were transported into another world, one characterized by vistas of green grass and clean, white boundaries. As Steven Riess has observed, the owners gave their edifices pastoral-invoking names: Ebbets Field, Sportsman Park, the Polo Grounds. Such nomenclature remained popular until 1923, when Yankee Stadium was built. Parks built since then have had more futuristic or urban names: Metrodome, Astrodome, Superdome.[5] Whatever they were called, the massive baseball parks, built of concrete and steel, bore mute testimony to the importance of baseball. To the fans, they were much more than simply a place for commercial amusement. Few if any other civic monuments equaled ballparks in their power to evoke collective memories.

Baseball was allegedly a vehicle for promoting social integration, for building social solidarity through support of local teams, and for the assimilation of new immigrants. As Morgan Bulkeley, one-time president of the National League put it, "There is nothing which will help quicker and better amalgamate the foreign born, and those born of foreign parents in this country, than to give them a little good bringing up in the good old-fashioned game of Base Ball." Baseball helped prevent revolutionary conspiracies. "They don't have things [like baseball] on the other side of the ocean," declared Bulkeley, "and many spend their hours fussing around in conspiring and hatching up plots when they should be out in the open improving their lungs."[6] Yet, for all its democratic claims, organized baseball excluded blacks, and the newer immigrants from southern and eastern Europe apparently found no greater opportunities for advancement in baseball than they did in other professions.

Among the most tangible signs of baseball's coming of age was the annual World Series. Beginning in 1903 the pennant winners of the American and National leagues agreed to play a nine-game "World Championship" series. No postseason games were played in 1904, but in 1905 the World Series became a permanent feature of big-league baseball. The series furnished an exciting conclusion to the regular season; the entire nation soon became absorbed in its outcome. Fans congregated in the city streets to watch the play-by-play progress of the series as reported on the boards posted in front of newspaper offices. Reportedly, the series sometimes even delayed the proceedings of the United States Supreme Court.

The sheer drama of baseball was yet another attraction. Baseball had a cast of well-defined heroes and villains, familiar plots, comedy, and the unexpected. Since most of the fans had played the sport as youths and watched many contests, they understood the intricacies of the plot—the purpose of bunting, the hit-and-run play, a deliberate base on balls, the removal of a struggling pitcher, and the appropriate place for the insertion of a pinch hitter. Baseball was a rational sport, one in which means were manifestly related to ends. Even though one could never predict when a ground ball might strike a pebble and bounce over a fielder's outstretched glove, "baseball, year by year, [has] grown more scientific, more of a thing of accepted rules [of tactics], or set routine," wrote F. C. Lane, a baseball reporter. "This slow evolution of the sport displayed itself in batting, in the form of the bunt, the place hit and various other manifestations of skill."[7]

Early twentieth-century baseball presented a marvelous set of stock characters. "You know, there were a lot of characters in baseball back then," recalled Samuel "Wahoo Sam" Crawford in the 1960s. "Real individualists. Not conformists, like most ball players—and most people—are today."[8] The fans noticed and adored the special physical traits and idiosyncratic behavior of the players. Their colorful nicknames—Bugs, Babe, Rube, Wahoo, Sam, Mugsy, Chief, Muddy, Kid, Hod, Dummy, Dutch, Stuffy, Gabby, and Hooks, to list only a few—suggested baseball's capacity to produce stock characters. And, of course, the umpire served as the chief villain.

The players seemed to take a special delight in spicing the game with comedy and the unexpected. Perhaps none equaled the feat of Herman "Germany" Schaefer. He stole first base! With the score tied in a late inning, Schaefer was on first base and Davy Jones on third. Schaefer gave the sign for a double steal and broke for second. The catcher, fearing that Jones would steal home if he threw the ball, simply held it. In the words of Jones:

> So now we had men on second and third. Well, on the next pitch Schaefer yelled, "Let's try it again!" And with a bloodcurdling shout he took off like a wild Indian *back to first base*, and dove in headfirst in a cloud of dust. . . .
>
> But nothing happened. Nothing at all. Everybody just stood there and watched Schaefer, with their mouths open, not knowing what the devil was going on. Me, too. Even if the catcher *had* thrown to first, I was too stunned to move. . . . But the catcher didn't throw. He just stared!. . .
>
> So there we were, back where we started, with Schaefer on first and me on third. And on the next pitch darned if he didn't let out another war whoop and take off *again* for second base. By this time the Cleveland catcher evidently had enough, because he finally threw to second to get Schaefer, and when he did I took off for home and *both* of us were safe.[9]

AN AGE OF THE PITCHER

Until recently, baseball historians have labeled the first two decades of the twentieth century as the "dead ball era." However, recent research suggests that this designation is inappropriate. There is no conclusive proof that changes in the ball affected offensive production. Although run production increased in the wake of the adoption of a cork-cushioned ball in 1910, the improvement proved to be only temporary. On the other hand, there is evidence pointing to other reasons for the extraordinarily low offensive output during the early twentieth century.[10]

Tinkering with rules that affected the delicate balance between offense and defense is the most obvious cause for the fall in hitting. In 1893, a rule change required that the pitcher deliver the ball with his back foot anchored on a rubber slab and lengthened the pitching distance to its present dimensions of 60 feet and 6 inches. As expected, the new rule initially touched off an offensive barrage, but run production slowly drifted downward as pitchers adjusted to the longer distance.

Then came a sudden plunge in hitting, a descent that coincided with two key rule changes. One was the decision in 1900 to change home plate from a 12-inch square to a five-sided figure 17 inches across. The new plate added some 200 square inches to the typical hitter's strike zone, thereby allowing the pitcher to work the peripheries of the zone much more effectively than in the past. Second, the National League in 1901 and the American League in 1903 decided to count the first two foul balls as strikes. Prior to this foul balls counted nothing.

Hitters voiced other complaints in the new century. They griped about the pitchers deliberately soiling the balls with tobacco juice, spit, and dirt. In particular, the spitball, which behaved in an unpredictable manner as it approached the plate, greatly improved the performance of several hurlers. Yet, the greatest pitchers of the era were big, strong-armed fastball and curveball specialists rather than spitballers. In the new century pitchers were on the average nearly ten pounds heavier and an inch-and-a-half taller than they had been a decade earlier. Both of the two most-heralded hurlers of the era, Walter Johnson of the lowly Washington Senators and Christy Mathewson of the highly successful New York Giants, were exceptionally big men for their day.

Managerial tactics may also have contributed to the low offensive output. Given the increasing effectiveness of the pitchers, managers turned more and more to the "scientific," or "inside," baseball made famous by the Boston Beaneaters and Baltimore Orioles of the 1890s. They instructed the hitters to reduce the arc of their swing, hoping that they could more consistently meet the ball squarely. Although such a tactic may have resulted in more base hits, it reduced the number of extra base hits. Home run totals plummeted. Home runs, which were nearly all of the inside-the-park variety in that era, became so rare that the entire 1908 Chicago White Sox team hit only three. The bunt, which was used to obtain hits, cause errors, or sacrifice runners into scoring positions, was another favorite weapon of inside baseball. Manager Joe McCloskey of the St. Louis Cardinals once required his hitters to bunt 17 consecutive times; the strategy produced the two runs needed to win the game.

John J. McGraw, the colorful, controversial, and longtime manager of the New York Giants, was a master of the nuances of one-run-at-a-time tactics.[11] After nine years of play with the famed Baltimore Orioles in the 1890s, McGraw came to New York to take the helm of the Giants in 1902, a post he held for the next 30 years. He led the Giants to ten National League pennants and four "world championships." Like most of the managers of the era, McGraw concentrated upon the acquisition of good pitchers. Other than such pitchers as Joe McGinnity, Christy Mathewson, and Rube Marquard, the Giants had no outstanding stars, but they always had speed, aggressiveness, and the peerless McGraw.

Perfectly suited to New York City—the nation's center of commerce, high finance, show business, and ethnic diversity—McGraw attracted headlines both on and off the field. The epitome of the day's martinet managers, he exercised a harsh discipline over his players. He drilled them in the game's fundamentals: covering bases, place hitting, bunting, sliding, and base running. He brawled with players, fans, umpires, and league officials. Fans in other National League cities liked nothing better than to see his hated Giants defeated. McGraw took advantage of the excitement offered by New York City away from the diamond. He liked the theater, horse racing, gambling, parties, and highballs. All of these things, plus his Irish charm, endeared him to New Yorkers.

TY COBB

Had it not been for Tyrus "Ty" Raymond Cobb, long-time star of the Detroit Tigers, the pre-1920 era would probably be remembered only for its pitching heroes. In a career that spanned 24 seasons (1905–1928), Cobb had the highest lifetime batting average (.367) and won the league batting championship the most seasons (12)—he won the title nine times in succession—of any player in baseball history. Statistics, of course, fail to do Cobb full justice. He had no peer as a master of inside baseball tactics. With his spread-handed grip he would bunt if the infield played deep; if the infield tightened up, he would slash the ball through the holes or over the fielders' heads. His dazzling speed and recklessness on the base paths terrorized opponents.

Ty Cobb personified, in an exaggerated way, the rugged individualism of the nineteenth century. Lacking the exceptional physical attributes of a Babe Ruth, Cobb relentlessly drove himself to excel. To Cobb, baseball was a form of warfare. "When I played ball," Cobb wrote in his autobiography in 1961, "I didn't play for fun. . . . It's no pink tea, and mollycoddles had better stay out. It's a contest and everything that implies, a struggle for supremacy, a survival of the fittest."[12] Given such a view, Cobb ignored the old amateur traditions of the sport. Since the 1880s, players had engaged in brawling but usually within a framework of understood conventions that involved mostly verbal warfare but rarely slugging. Cobb used every weapon at his disposal—his spikes, fists, bat, and his tongue—all in an effort to intimidate and defeat his opponents. The other players and the fans soon

EARLY TWENTIETH-CENTURY STARS During the first two decades of the twentieth century, Walter Johnson, a pitcher for the Washington Senators (on the left), and Ty Cobb, an outfielder for the Detroit Tigers, were two of the most outstanding players in baseball. Disliked by fellow players, in this publicity photograph Cobb appears uncharacteristically amiable.
(Detroit Public Library)

recognized that Cobb was serious, that he was a man driven by internal demons that left even his sanity in question.

Instances of Cobb's aggressive behavior off the field were equally legion. Throughout the league he verbally challenged and sometimes fought taunting fans—in one case leaped into the stands and struck a fan who happened to be physically handicapped. In 1914 Cobb's wife got into an argument with a butcher over 20¢ worth of spoiled fish. Believing that his wife had been insulted, Cobb went to the butcher's shop, pulled out the revolver that he always carried, and demanded that the butcher telephone his wife an apology. The butcher, naturally, complied, but the butcher's young assistant dared Cobb to resolve the issue without the pistol. Cobb, quite willing to accommodate, proceeded to beat the boy insensate. Cobb was particularly brutal to blacks; on at least two occasions he struck black women. At the Pontchartrain Hotel in Detroit he allegedly kicked a black chambermaid in the stomach and knocked her down the steps because she had objected to being called a "nigger." Repeated warnings, fines, and suspensions by Ban Johnson, president of the American League, failed to curb Cobb's violent temper.

Cobb never became a popular hero in the mold of a Babe Ruth or even a Cap Anson. Almost everybody thoroughly disliked him, including his own teammates. He evoked fear and respect, but never affection; he never had a close, personal friend among the big-league players or managers. He ate alone, roomed alone, and for years at a time did not speak to certain of his teammates.

The depth of the feeling against Cobb by fellow players was demonstrated clearly in 1910 when Cobb appeared to have won the American League batting championship. In the final doubleheader of the season Napoleon Lajoie, the leading contender for the title, made eight hits in eight times at bat. Six of the hits came from bunts toward third base, which the notoriously slow-footed Lajoie had somehow beaten out. It soon became clear that the St. Louis Browns had deliberately tried to deny Cobb the crown by "giving" Lajoie free access to first base. (Incidentally, the strategy failed, for Cobb was able to retain the title by a single percentage point.) Fans everywhere came out to see the rampaging Cobb, partly in awe of his ability, but also in hopes of seeing him stymied by the local club or of witnessing a brawl in which Cobb would be the principal victim.

Cobb's ugly behavior and intense drive apparently arose from a combination of circumstances. Born of a proud family in Georgia that had once owned slaves, Cobb was inordinately defensive of his origins and the South. Teammates soon discovered this sensitivity. As a rookie he became the natural butt of unmerciful hazing. Teammates broke his bats, nailed his uniform to the clubhouse wall, hid his clothes, locked him in bathrooms, and tried to get him into a fight with the biggest man on the club. Cobb responded violently, eventually intimidating the rest of the players. Likewise, fans enjoyed ragging the superstar. At every league park except Detroit fans threw a steady barrage of verbal insults at Cobb. Sometimes Cobb had to be escorted from the park by the police. Perhaps it is little wonder that Cobb believed he was the target of a conspiracy.

For Cobb, the bizarre circumstances of his father's death seemed to have evolved into an obsession. He explained in his autobiography that "I did it for my father, who was an exalted man. They killed him when he was still young. But I knew he was watching me and I never let him down." The mysterious "they" referred to by Cobb was his own mother. Cobb's father had suspected his wife of unfaithfulness and had gone to her bedroom window to investigate. Apparently mistaking him for an intruder, she had killed him with a shotgun. The tragic incident occurred just as Cobb was entering the big leagues. "I had to fight all my life to survive," Cobb later wrote. "They were all against me . . . but I beat the bastards and left them in the ditch."[13] As Cobb grew older, the symptoms of insanity grew more pronounced. He talked frequently of a vague conspiracy to take away his life. When he died in 1961, only three people from Organized Baseball attended his funeral. Never had a more successful, a more violent, and a more maladjusted personality passed through the annals of American sport.

ORGANIZED BASEBALL'S QUEST FOR ORDER

As in the past, the owners of professional baseball struggled to establish a modicum of order within their ranks. On the one hand, they were proponents of free enterprise; they wanted the freedom to operate their individual ball clubs as they saw fit. Yet, such freedom could be economically disastrous, especially for franchises located in the smaller cities. So the big leagues entered into collusive agreements or what is frequently described as an economic cartel. Specifically, they sought to devise a means of avoiding direct competition among franchises for players, preventing the formation of rival big leagues, restricting the total number of big-league teams, and bringing the minor leagues under their control. Their resulting entity that became known as Organized Baseball was a large, unwieldy cartel. It was only partly and sporadically effective.

Baseball's quest for order in the pre-1920 era began inauspiciously. Despite the collapse of the Players' League in 1890 and the American Association in 1891, the decade of the 1890s was a grim one for the National League. Burdened by the debts accumulated from the brotherhood war and the purchase costs of four association clubs, the league also faced a general economic depression and public disillusionment with the professional game due to the players' revolt. The new 12-team loop was a near disaster. Teams with poor records, such as the Louisville and St. Louis franchises, which between them occupied last place for five of the eight years that the circuit existed, attracted few fans, and the New York and Chicago clubs, franchises vital to the success of the league, failed to field strong teams. Finally, in 1899, the league returned to eight clubs. The new circuit, composed of Boston, Brooklyn, Chicago, Cincinnati, New York, Philadelphia, Pittsburgh, and St. Louis, would remain intact until 1953, when the Boston Braves moved to Milwaukee.

But the woes of the National League were not over. The return of prosperity at the turn of the century, the elimination of the four weak franchises, and the conflicts within the league's counsel encouraged a challenge by a formidable rival—the American League led by the indomitable Byron Bancroft "Ban" Johnson. When the National League returned to an eight-team loop, Johnson, as president of the Western League (a minor league), convinced his followers to claim major-league status, to rename his circuit the American League, and to raid National League player rosters. With Johnson in firm control of the American League franchises and the National League owners divided, the senior loop finally sued for peace.

The peace settlement, known as the National Agreement of 1903, became the centerpiece of professional baseball. The leagues agreed to recognize each other's reserve clauses and established a three-man National Commission. Composed of the presidents of the two leagues and a third member chosen by them, the National Commission served primarily as a judicial body to resolve disputes arising from within the cartel. In the National League, the owners retained nearly absolute power to manage their franchises as they saw fit; in the American League, Ban Johnson ruled with a firm hand until the 1920s. The 1903 agreement also recognized the territorial monopolies of minor-league teams, granted them reserve rights in players, and set up a system by which the major leagues could annually draft players from the minors for a set price.

In the pre-1920 era, the club owners confronted two major challenges: keeping salary costs under control and the appearance of another contender for big-league status (the Federal League). The reserve clause allowed the owners to limit salaries to less than the players would have received on the open market. As attendance and club profits rose rapidly in the early years of the century, player salaries slowly drifted upward. Star players sometimes effectively "held out"; they refused to play until they obtained higher pay. Probably as many as ten stars received salaries of $10,000 or more by 1910, but players with ordinary talents might earn as little as $1,900 annually. When a third major circuit, the Federal League, threatened the cartel between 1912 and 1915, the salaries of superior players jumped sharply. Ty Cobb's salary, for example, leaped from $9,000 in 1910 to $20,000 in 1915. With the demise of the Federal League at the end of the 1915 season, however, the owners were once again able to hold the line on salaries.

In 1914, James A. "Long Jim" Gilmore, a Chicago iron manufacturer, aligned wealthy men in Chicago, New York, and St. Louis to reorganize the old Federal League into a circuit claiming major-league status. The Federals offered established big-league stars high salaries to jump to the new circuit. The major-league owners responded as they had during the Players' League war of 1890; they blacklisted players who had abandoned the majors, obtained court injunctions, and raised the salaries of their players.

Even though high salaries and low attendance plagued the Federal League in both 1914 and 1915, the big-league owners settled for an expensive peace. In effect, they sabotaged the new loop by bribing the wealthiest Federal League owners. For example, Albert Sinclair, who later gained notoriety in the Teapot Dome scandal, received permission to buy a controlling interest in the Chicago Cubs at a bargain price. In addition, Sinclair received an annual payment of $10,000 for ten years from the major leagues. On the other hand, those owners of Federal League clubs that were not in direct competition with the majors received nothing except the revenues from player sales. The settlement may have cost the major leagues as much as $5 million, tarnished the owners' image, and brought disaster to many minor-league clubs.

THE BLACK SOX SCANDAL AND THE REIGN OF KENESAW MOUNTAIN LANDIS

In September 1920 a shocking revelation rocked the country: The 1919 World Series had been fixed. The worst team scandal in the history of American sport, soon labeled the "Black Sox Scandal," crowded the "Red Scare" and every other major story off the front pages of the nation's newspapers. Americans were incredulous. According to baseball legend, a small boy approached "Shoeless Joe" Jackson, one of the alleged conspirators and a star outfielder with the Chicago White Sox. "Say it ain't so, Joe," begged the lad as tears welled from his eyes. "I'm afraid it is, son," Jackson responded. The hurt cut deeply. Boston newsboys condemned the "murderous blow" to the national pastime by the "Benedict Arnolds of baseball." In Joliet, Illinois, an angry fan charged Buck Herzog with being "one of those crooked Chicago ball players." A fight erupted and Herzog was stabbed, even though he was a member of the Chicago Cubs rather than the White Sox. Sensitive

Nelson Algren, then a lad on Chicago's South Side, became disillusioned. "Everybody's out for The Buck," he later concluded "even the big leaguers." A character in F. Scott Fitzgerald's *The Great Gatsby* reflected: "It never occurred to me that one man could start to play with the faith of fifty million people."[14]

Although the dismay that accompanied the Black Sox Scandal of 1919 proved that baseball had finally won wide-scale public acceptability, in retrospect the scandal should not have been so surprising. Like those engaged in other forms of commercial entertainment, many of the players, managers, and owners had close links with the urban demimonde. They spent much of their spare time at the race tracks, theaters, hotel lobbies, and saloons, where they consorted with publicly known gamblers. Most big-league players, including even Ty Cobb who was of old-stock, Protestant origins, did not hesitate to wager upon themselves or their teams. Yet organized baseball, fearing adverse publicity and the loss of valuable property in the form of the players, attempted to cover up all reports connecting baseball with gambling and game fixing. Had it not been for an enterprising reporter, Hugh Fullerton, the 1919 Black Sox scandal might have remained a mere rumor.

Later evidence revealed that eight Chicago players had taken money from gamblers to dump the 1919 World Series. Seven of the eight alleged fixers admitted to a grand jury they had received sums varying from $5,000 to $10,000—figures that exceeded the annual salaries of most of the accused—to throw the series to Cincinnati. Somehow, however, the grand jury records disappeared before the trial. (Later at a trial in which Joe Jackson sued Charles Comiskey, owner of the White Sox for back pay, the player confessions "mysteriously" reappeared—in the possession of Comiskey's attorney!)

At the trial held in 1921, all of the players repudiated their earlier confessions, leaving the testimony of Bill Maharg, a professional gambler, as the only substantial evidence against them. After a few hours of deliberation, the jury acquitted all the players plus two gamblers. The spectators in the courtroom roared their approval, and the jurymen and players retired to the local restaurant to celebrate. But the joy of the players was short-lived, for Judge Kenesaw Mountain Landis, the newly appointed Commissioner of Baseball, banished them from Organized Baseball for life.

While the Black Sox scandal of 1919 provided a major impetus for the reorganization of major-league baseball, discontent with the National Commission and the power of Ban Johnson, imperious president of the American League, had been building for several years. Baseball attendance had failed to grow in the 1910s and rumors of fixed games were rife. The commission had become almost impotent, and Johnson had, over the years, incurred the wrath of several powerful owners.

The new National Agreement of 1921 gave sweeping powers to a single man to head all of Organized Baseball. The owners extended to the commissioner the power to investigate anything "suspected" of being "detrimental to the best interests of the national game." If he determined that leagues, club owners, or players had taken actions harmful to the sport, he was given the authority to suspend, fine, or banish guilty parties. In their eagerness to improve the image of baseball and bring a semblance of order to the game, the owners even agreed to waive their rights to take disputes between themselves or with the commissioner to the civil courts. The Agreement of 1921 established the model for the governmental structures of professional football and basketball in the post–World War II era as well. By establishing a "czar" to censor movies in 1922, the movie industry also followed the example of baseball.

In the wake of the Black Sox scandal, Landis brought to baseball what Calvin Coolidge would shortly bring to national politics after the revelation of the Teapot Dome scandal. Both men projected an image of staunch integrity, a "puritanism" in the midst of the excess of the 1920s. With a flair for the theatrical that he had revealed as a federal judge, Landis promised an "untiring effort" to rid baseball of gamblers and gambling. "If I catch any crook in baseball," Landis pledged, "the rest of his life is going to be a hot one."[15] His very appearance instilled confidence. Unlike the pudgy, well-fed owners, Landis was thin, almost emaciated. With a craggy face topped by long, shaggy, unkempt hair, he looked like Andrew Jackson, one of his heroes. Like Jackson, Landis had a gift for using his imposing appearance and his controlled temper to dominate those who confronted him.

JUDGE KENESAW MOUNTAIN LANDIS Landis was commissioner of baseball from 1921 to 1944. This photograph reflects Landis's reputation for rectitude and toughness. In the wake of the Black Sox scandal of 1919, Landis helped improve the national game's image of integrity. (Chicago Historical Society)

Landis wasted little time in trying to alter the image of organized baseball. He arbitrarily banished more than a dozen players from the game for life. Even the owners did not escape his vigilance. He ordered Charles A. Stoneham, owner of the New York Giants, and John J. McGraw, Giant manager, to divest themselves of their stock in race tracks located in Cuba and New York. Yet during a reign which lasted until 1944, Landis treated the questionable actions of the owners far more gingerly than those of the players. He rarely interfered with trades between clubs or in their internal affairs. Despite his personal opposition to the "farm system," he took only limited steps to curb its growth. His power over the owners was incomplete, for if he antagonized enough of them he jeopardized his position.

While Landis gave baseball a new image of integrity, the United States Supreme Court furnished its legal salvation. All of the Federal League clubs of the 1913–1915 era except Baltimore had dropped their antitrust suits against the major leagues. Having received no remuneration from the 1916 peace settlement, Baltimore continued its court action. Justice Oliver Wendell Holmes Jr., speaking for a unanimous court in 1922, declared that professional baseball games did not constitute a "trade or commerce in the commonly-accepted use of the words." In a rather tortuous definition of terms, Holmes reasoned that the "personal effort" of ballplayers was "not related to production" and therefore could not be involved in commerce. Nor was interstate movement essential to their activity, for the movement of ballplayers across state lines was simply "incidental" to their playing ball. Whatever the merits of the legal justification of professional baseball's exemption from the antitrust laws, the decision provided a legal umbrella for the agreements upon which the professional baseball cartel rested.

At the same time that baseball sought to establish a new reputation for moral purity and received a new legal foundation from the Supreme Court, the game experienced a hitting revolution. According to traditional baseball history, the sudden ascent in hitting in the 1920s resulted from (1) the introduction of a new, more resilient, "jack rabbit" baseball; (2) using more balls per game; (3) outlawing the spit ball; (4) and the growing popularity of "free swinging" by the hitters. All of these reasons may have some merit, but recent research points mainly in one direction—that the success of Babe Ruth was the single most important reason for the hitting revolution.[16] Not only did the hitters who copied Ruth's full swings smash out more home runs, but they also seemed to strike the ball more squarely than those who had earlier taken a shortened swing.

At any rate, during the 1920s batting averages, scoring, and home run totals soared. By 1925 the combined batting averages of the major leagues was 45 points higher than it had been in 1915. Only four hitters in the first two decades of the century had hit .400 or better; eight batters achieved this distinction in the twenties. By 1930, major-league teams averaged scoring three and a half more runs per game than in 1915. But the most remarkable development of all was the quantity of home runs. Major-league totals quadrupled from 384 homers in 1915 to 1,565 in 1930. Aficionados of the old style of play, which featured tight pitching duels, bunts, sacrifices, hit-and-run plays, and steals—"scientific" or "inside" baseball—regarded the hitting revolution as abominable.

AN AGE OF TEAM DYNASTIES

Presumably, equalizing the conditions of the competition among teams would increase fan interest. If more teams had a viable shot at winning the pennant, no single team would dominate the championships over the years and pennant races
would be closely fought. Overall attendance should also be higher. The major
leagues had long argued that the reserve clause in player contracts and the draft
prevented the domination of the pennant races by a few of the wealthier franchises. Without the right to reserve players, professional baseball argued, wealthier
clubs could offer higher salaries to players on other teams and eventually corner
the market on the best player talent. In theory, the draft of promising minor leaguers gave each club equal access to new player talent; it negated the potential
advantages of superior wealth. But the historical record of baseball made a mockery of both of these arguments.

From the beginning of the century, the clubs located in the largest cities
enjoyed better records than those in smaller cities (see Figures 10–1 and 10–2).
From 1900 to 1952 (when the Boston Braves moved to Milwaukee), the New York
Giants, Brooklyn Dodgers, and Chicago Cubs, representative of the two largest
metropolitan areas in the National League, won 30 of 52 pennants. After 1925 the

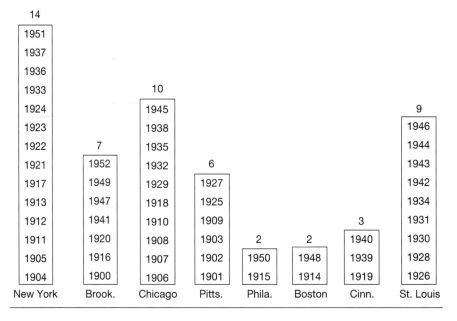

FIGURE 10–1   Disparity of competition as shown by pennants won in order of average population rank, National League, 1900–1952. Based on average population
during the period, adjusted for number of baseball teams in the metropolitan area
Source: Adapted from Roger G. Noll, ed., *Government and the Sports Business* (Washington,
DC: Brookings Institution, 1974), 46.

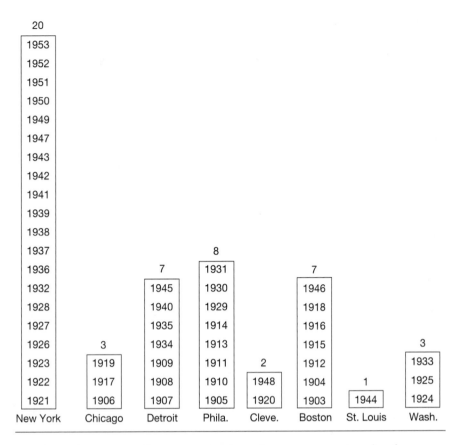

20							
1953							
1952							
1951							
1950							
1949							
1947							
1943							
1942							
1941							
1939							
1938							
1937			8				
1936		7	1931		7		
1932		1945	1930		1946		
1928		1940	1929		1918		
1927		1935	1914		1916		
1926	3	1934	1913		1915		3
1923	1919	1909	1911	2	1912		1933
1922	1917	1908	1910	1948	1904	1	1925
1921	1906	1907	1905	1920	1903	1944	1924
New York	Chicago	Detroit	Phila.	Cleve.	Boston	St. Louis	Wash.

FIGURE 10–2   Disparity of competition as shown by pennants won in order of average population rank, American League, 1903–1953. Based on average population during the period, adjusted for the number of baseball teams in the metropolitan area. *Source:* Adapted from Roger G. Noll, ed., *Government and the Sports Business* (Washington, DC: Brookings Institution, 1974), 46.

"Rickey effect" (Branch Rickey's farm system at St. Louis) reduced the close correlation between city size and playing strength. Yet Philadelphia, Boston, and Cincinnati, which ranked fifth, sixth, and seventh in average population when adjusted to the number of teams in the metropolitan area, won only seven pennants among them. Until the purchase of the New York Yankees by new owners in 1915, the size of the market area bore little relationship to team success in the American League. But after the Yankees acquired Babe Ruth in 1920, they proceeded to win 20 of the next 32 flags. Through 1980, the combined franchises in New York, Chicago, and Los Angeles won over half of the total flags of the two leagues.

The main cause for the success of the teams in the biggest cities was simple. The disparities in population between metropolitan areas produced substantial inequalities in attendance and therefore in incomes. Since the nineteenth century, the owners had tried to offset market size by giving 50 percent of the base admission price to visiting teams. But any revenues collected from seats that exceeded the base price, such as box and reserve seats, went to the home club. As more of the higher-priced seats were added to the stadiums in the twentieth century, the percentage of total gate receipts of the visiting teams declined. In 1892 the visiting teams received about 40 percent of the total revenue; by 1929 their share had declined to 21 percent, and by 1950 to only 14 percent. This disparity of incomes benefited those franchises located in large market areas, giving them additional bargaining strength within the big-league cartel and additional revenue for the purchase of superior players from other major- or minor-league clubs.

The history of the New York dynasty vividly reveals the importance of the market area served by the club and the advantages of wealthy, freespending owners. Before Jacob Ruppert Jr., a rich brewer, and Tillinghast Huston, a prosperous engineer, purchased the Yankees in 1915, the club had a mediocre record. The club's performance slowly improved as the owners purchased player talent from the minor-league clubs and other big-league clubs. The big Yankee breakthrough came between 1919 and 1923 when the Boston Red Sox virtually became their farm club. Harry Frazee, a Broadway producer and owner of the Red Sox, sought the money to finance his shows by dismantling his powerful baseball team. (The Red Sox had won pennants in 1915, 1916, and 1918.) In 1919, he sold star pitcher Carl Mays to the Yankees for $40,000, and the next year startled the baseball world by selling Babe Ruth to the Yankees for $125,000 (plus a $300,000 loan), a sum twice as high as had ever previously been paid for a player. By 1923, 11 of the 24-man Yankee roster had formerly played with Boston. The hapless Red Sox sank to the American League cellar in 1922, where they remained for eight of the next nine seasons.

Superior financial resources permitted the Yankees to dominate the American League. Over the next 45 years, the Yankees lost the flag only 14 times. A star player was worth more to the owners of the New York franchise than he was to an owner of a club in a smaller city; thus, franchises in low-drawing areas typically sold good players to the Yankees. The incentive for selling was often a matter of survival. The Washington Senators, Philadelphia Athletics, and St. Louis Browns repeatedly unloaded star players to the richer clubs. According to economist James Quirk, from 1920 to 1950, while the Yankees spent $1.6 million for talent, the St. Louis Browns sold a platoon of players for some $2.5 million. Had the Browns not sold these players, they would have lost $1.5 million in revenue.[17]

One franchise, the St. Louis Cardinals, under the direction of its brilliant general manager Branch Rickey, devised an ingenious method of avoiding expensive player purchases and offsetting some of the advantages enjoyed by the clubs in the larger market areas. Rickey's solution was the farm system. After joining the poverty-stricken franchise in 1917, Rickey slowly but methodically purchased direct ownership of minor-league clubs; by 1940 the Cardinal system contained 32 clubs and 700 players. The Rickey system produced remarkable results. The Cardinals won nine league championships between 1926 and 1946 and took second place six times. The Cardinals profited from player sales as well; in one year alone there were 65 players from their farm system on the rosters of other big-league clubs. Initially, owners of the other clubs resisted the ownership of minor-league clubs, but as the success of the Rickey system became evident, they too began to emulate St. Louis.

Despite the establishment of a commissioner's office and a revolution in hitting, evidence suggests that in the 1920s professional baseball declined in popularity in comparison to other forms of leisure activity. True, attendance moved upward, but not proportionate to the growth in population. In the eleven cities which hosted major-league teams, the population climbed 20.5 percent in the twenties while attendance at ball games grew by only 11.5 percent. The same trend appears to be valid for the minor leagues; the total number of professional leagues remained under the figures attained in the pre-World War I era. By contrast, attendance at motion picture theaters in the 1925–1930 era was 75 percent greater than during the preceding five-year period. While an estimated 20 million fans attended all professional baseball games in 1930, approximately 90 million patrons attended the movies each week.[18]

Professional baseball suffered heavily from the Great Depression and World War II. Attendance did not fully recover until 1946; it then enjoyed a temporary boom until 1949 when it entered another "famine era." There were great players aplenty in the thirties and forties—Hank Greenburg, Ted Williams, Joe DiMaggio, and Stan Musial, to name a few—but none had the magic of Babe Ruth. The introduction of night baseball—first by the black Kansas City Monarchs's portable lighting system in 1929, then in the minor leagues in 1930, and finally in the big leagues at Cincinnati in 1935—failed to restore attendance to pre-Depression levels. Only a few clubs prospered. The "have-not" franchises promoted a profit-sharing scheme, but it was voted down by the wealthier clubs. "I found out a long time ago that there is not charity in baseball," Jacob Ruppert, owner of the Yankees, explained, "and that every club owner must make his own fight for existence."[19] The owners did take effective action in reducing player salaries. Salaries had risen from an average of about $5,000 in 1923 to about $7,000 in 1933; by 1936 the average had fallen to $4,500. Wide disparities existed between franchises. The payroll of the Yankees, for instance, was almost five times that of the lowly St. Louis Browns.

In the face of the great economic crisis of the 1930s, professional baseball experimented with new ways to recoup lost fan support. Beginning in 1933 the major leagues scheduled an annual All-Star game between the best players of each league, and in 1936 baseball made its most important symbolic gesture to continuity with the founding of the Hall of Fame in Cooperstown, New York. Larry MacPhail, general manager of the Cincinnati Reds, daringly departed from some of the staid traditions of baseball. At Cincinnati, MacPhail introduced night baseball (1935), red uniforms, cigarette girls in satin pants, and usherettes. Such innovations led a sportswriter to predict that, when MacPhail arrived in Brooklyn in 1937, fans would be treated to the spectacle of a "merry-go-round in center field of Flatbush." MacPhail's promotional gimmicks, however, paled beside those of Bill Veeck, who, in the post-World War II era, once employed a midget as a pinch hitter.

MacPhail, more than any other single person, broke down the resistance to radio broadcasts of games. Although in the 1920s the Chicago Cubs had permitted all of the club's games to be broadcast and the club had experienced a sharp increase in attendance, most clubs feared that radio broadcasts would reduce attendance. In 1934 the Yankees, Giants, and Dodgers, all located in New York, even signed a formal ban on the broadcasts of their games. But as radio stations and networks discovered that they could sell commercials during the broadcasts (and thus pay clubs for broadcast privileges) resistance weakened. When MacPhail came to Brooklyn as general manager, he refused to renew the ban on baseball broadcasts in New York; he sold the rights to Dodger games for $70,000. Both the Yankees and Giants then succumbed to the new medium. By 1950 each club averaged $210,000 from broadcast rights.

Professional baseball continued to suffer through World War II before experiencing a sudden spurt in popularity in the late 1940s. The big leagues even considered closing down during the war, but President Franklin D. Roosevelt urged that play continue, though quality would invariably suffer because of the service of players in the armed forces. For opening day in 1944, the *Sporting News* reported that only 40 percent of those who had played in 1941 were still in the starting lineups. Clubs filled their rosters with physical rejects or players who were too old or too young for the military draft. In 1945, the St. Louis Browns even employed a one-armed (but able) outfielder. Wartime player shortages also led to the creation of a professional women's league (see Chapter 13).

BLACK BASEBALL

Given the abysmally low incomes of the vast majority of blacks, the ghettos supported a surprisingly rich sporting life. As in white neighborhoods prior to the 1950s, baseball was by far the most popular sport. Every ghetto featured several black semiprofessional or professional teams. Sometimes local industries sponsored teams, but often blacks themselves organized and managed the teams. At the higher levels of play, black gamblers, especially those in the numbers racket, formed clubs. In Pittsburgh during the 1930s Gus Greenlee, that city's numbers king, poured massive amounts of money into his professional baseball team. Likewise black gamblers bankrolled teams in (among other cities) Newark, New York, Philadelphia, Baltimore, and Nashville.[20]

Grounded in the patronage furnished by the ghettos of the larger cities, several black professional baseball leagues rose and fell. In 1920, Andrew "Rube" Foster, a star pitcher and manager of the Chicago American Giants, formed the Negro National League comprised of teams in Detroit, Indianapolis, Kansas City, St. Louis, and two teams in Chicago, but the Great Depression temporarily killed the league in 1931. In 1933, the league reformed, and four years later, became the Negro American League. The Negro leagues achieved their greatest prosperity in the 1940s when the annual all-star games held in Chicago filled major-league parks to capacity and teams frequently attracted as many as 5,000 (nearly all black) fans to regular season weekend contests. The success of the black teams in off-season exhibition games with white teams indicated that many of the players were of major-league caliber, but for most white fans, such black superstars as Leroy "Satchel" Paige and Josh Gibson toiled in total obscurity. The gradual integration of white baseball after 1945 eventually spelled the end of the black leagues.

The Negro leagues were never as central to black baseball as the major leagues were to white baseball. Of some 200 games played by each black team in a season, only a third were league games. Ghetto residents simply did not have enough discretionary income to support talented black leagues. Thus, to survive, the black teams had to engage in barnstorming. While traveling throughout the United States, Canada, and the Caribbean Basin republics, they played other professional black teams, local semipro teams (both black and white), and ad hoc major league barnstorming teams. The game played by barnstorming teams was skillful, but showmanship was also an essential ingredient of black baseball. Although successful in catching fans' interest, the stunts and comedy of the black teams reinforced the negative stereotypes of blacks held by white fans.

CONCLUSION

The 1890–1950 era might be described as the golden age of baseball history. The game enjoyed an uncontested supremacy among American sports fans; unlike today neither football nor basketball were even close rivals. The era produced larger-than-life heroes such as Walter Johnson, Ty Cobb, Babe Ruth, and Satchel Paige as well as supernally consistent dynasties such as the New York Yankees and the St. Louis Cardinals. The white professional game was organized into a hierarchy of leagues, governed first by a National Commission (1903–1921) and, beginning in 1921, by the Commissioner of Baseball. But, until 1946, when Jackie Robinson joined the Montreal farm team of the Brooklyn Dodgers, the game reflected the dogged persistence of the nation's racial segregation.

NOTES

1. The standard multivolume histories are Harold Seymour, *Baseball* 3 vols. (New York: Oxford University Press, 1960–1990); David Q. Voigt, *American Baseball* 3 vols. (Norman: University of Oklahoma Press and University Park: Penn State University Press, 1966–1983); and Robert F. Burk, *Never Just a Game* and *Much More Than a Game* (Chapel Hill: University of North Carolina Press, 1994 and 2001). For an up-to-date one-volume treatment, see Benjamin G. Rader, *Baseball: A History of America's Game*, 2d ed. (Urbana: University of Illinois Press, 2002). See also S.A. Riess, *Touching Base*, rev. ed (Urbana: University of Illinois Press, 1998); Leverett T. Smith Jr., *The American Dream and the National Game* (Bowling Green, OH: Bowling Green University Popular Culture Press, 1970); Richard Crepeau, *Baseball: America's Diamond Mind* (Lincoln, University of Nebraska Press, 2000); G. Edward White, *Creating the National Pastime: Baseball Transforms Itself, 1903–1953* (Princeton, NJ: Princeton University Press, 1996);

and Dean A. Sullivan, ed. *Middle Innings: A Documentary History of Baseball, 1900–1948* (Lincoln: University of Nebraska Press, 1998).

2. Albert Spalding, *America's National Game* (Lincoln: University of Nebraska Press, 1992), 4.

3. Ibid.

4. For these parallels, see Seymour, *Baseball*, I, 4.

5. See S.A. Riess, "Baseball Myths, Baseball Realities and the Social Functions of Baseball in the Progressive Era," *Stadion* 3 (1980), 273–311.

6. Quoted in Seymour, *Baseball*, II, 4.

7. Quoted in Smith, *The American Dream*, 190.

8. L.S. Ritter, *The Glory of Their Times* (New York: Macmillan, 1966), 49.

9. Ibid., 44–45.

10. See Rader, *Baseball*, 87–91.

11. See esp. Charles Alexander, *John McGraw* (New York: H. Holt, 1988).

12. Ty Cobb and Al Stump, *My Life in Baseball* (Garden City, NY: Doubleday, 1961), 280. See also Charles Alexander, *Ty Cobb* (New York: Oxford University Press, 1984).

13. Quotations in Seymour, *Baseball*, II, 111.

14. Quotations in ibid., 278.

15. Ibid., 323. See also Norman Rosenberg, "Here Comes the Judge! The Origins of Baseball's Commissioner System and American Legal Culture," *Journal of Popular Culture* 20 (1987), 129–46, and Clark Nardinelli, "Judge

Kenesaw Mountain Landis and the Art of Cartel Enforcement," in Peter Levine, ed., *Baseball History* (1989).

16. See Rader, *Baseball*, 113–16, and William Curran, *Big Sticks* (New York: Morrow, 1990).

17. Ray Kennedy and Nancy Williamson, "Money: The Monster Threatening Sports," *Sports Illustrated* 49 (July 1978), 80. See also L.E. Davis, "Self-regulation in Baseball, 1909–1971," in Roger Noll, ed., *Government and the Sports Business* (Washington, DC: Carnegie Foundation, 1974), 349–86.

18. See J.F. Steiner, *Americans at Play* (New York: Arno, 1933), 84, 86, 109–110; J.R. Tunis, "Changing Trends in Sports," *Harper's Monthly* 70 (December 1934); and A.J. Young Jr., "The Rejuvenation of Major League Baseball in the Twenties," *Canadian Journal of History of Sport and Physical Education* 3 (1972), 24.

19. Quoted in Voigt, *American Baseball* II, 251. See also Bill Rabinowitz, "Baseball in the Great Depression," in Levine, *Baseball*.

20. See esp. Robert Peterson, *Only the Ball Was White* (Englewood Cliffs, NJ: Prentice Hall, 1970); Donn Rogosin, *Invisible Men* (New York: Atheneum, 1973); Jules Tygiel, *Baseball's Great Experiment* (New York: Oxford University Press, 1983), chap. 2; Janet Bruce, *The Kansas City Monarchs* (Lawrence: University Press of Kansas, 1985); and Rob Ruck, *Sandlot Seasons* (Urbana: University of Illinois Press, 1987).

11

THE INTERCOLLEGIATE FOOTBALL SPECTACLE

*I*n 1939, a year in which the United States was still in the midst of the Great Depression and World War II had just commenced in Europe, the *New York Times Magazine* announced the arrival of a new football season. L. H. Robbins, the author of the piece, only casually acknowledged the game on the field; instead he sought to describe the total atmosphere that accompanied college football games. "The cheer leaders turning cartwheels on the turf. The mascot mules, lion cubs, bulldogs and what not." The coaches on the sidelines and on the benches the "blanketed reserves." "The bands and the banners. The scorecard scouts flashing their signal cards." In the stands, the "beauty and mink and chivalry and coonskin. . . . And below, on white-striped green, the half-dozen officials who risk their middle-aged lives and limbs to run the game, and twenty two-lusty lads who play it."[1] For nearly all the fans, it was not the game itself, but the total experience that brought them outdoors on crisp fall afternoons.

In describing the centrality of *spectacle* to college football, Robbins recognized an important fact. During the first half of the twentieth century, baseball was the national pastime, but it was football, especially the college game, that emerged as the nation's single greatest team sporting spectacle. In a society that celebrated few holidays, college football became a "time out" from normal routines, a time of pageantry and revelry in which millions let go of their emotions and had fun. With its player uniforms, school colors, card sections, bands, cheerleaders, cheering spectators, hip flasks, and homecoming queens, football was in a vital sense America's equivalent to Europe's great carnivals and festivals. Indeed, by the 1930s, journalists were calling the sport "King Football." In communities small and large across the nation, the sportive monarch offered millions a momentary release from their daily cares. King Football helped to tie them together and to provide them with a shared identity.

The principal aim of this chapter is to tell the story of how, during the first half of the twentieth century, college football became a major sporting spectacle. The story includes the great football crisis in the opening years of the new century, major rule changes in 1906, 1910, and 1912, and the formation of an organization in 1906 that subsequently became the National Collegiate Athletic Association (NCAA). It includes the enormous takeoff in the popularity of the sport in the 1920s and its enduring popularity in the 1930s and 1940s, the importance of football as a source of local pride and identity, the significance of the coach as hero, the partial democratization of the sport, and the continuing dilemmas that resulted from institutions of higher learning producing great commercial spectacles. The story ends in the 1950s, a decade that witnessed the beginnings of a new era of college football history.

THE AGE OF CRISIS, 1890–1913

The story of football's emergence as a great public spectacle began in an age of crisis. Between 1890 and 1913, bitter and heated conflicts threatened the game's very existence. Controversy flared up over the eligibility, recruitment, and subsidization (paying) of players. Above all, deaths and injuries suffered on the gridiron alarmed both critics and defenders of the game.

SATURDAY'S HERO, 1908 This illustration from a popular periodical represents the idealized hero of the day—well-proportioned, square-jawed, blue-eyed, and blonde. (Curtis Publishing Company)

Much of the controversy revolved around amateurism. Many, including many of the game's most articulate enthusiasts, were upper-class Anglophiles. They continued to believe that the game ought to be played in a manner similar to English upper-class sports. Football, they said, should be an athlete-centered affair, one that was played out of a deep love for one's college and for the sheer fun of it. Athletes should never play for pay. Neither should they play too seriously or strenuously. For "gentlemen," sport should always be an avocation rather than a vocation.

Apart from the lingering weight of custom, amateurism had its practical uses as well. Not only did amateurism encourage patrons of the sport to believe, or sense, that the spirit of the college game differed sharply from professional sports, but also that problems that might arise between the colleges as "employers" of athletes and the athletes as "employees" might be sidestepped or avoided more easily. Even to this day, at a time when scholarships for play are taken for granted, the ideal of amateurism, or at least its pretense, continues to occupy a significant place in college sports. Fans themselves sense, or delude themselves into believing, that the collegians are more committed to their teams and play with more team gusto than the professionals.

Nevertheless, from the outset, American collegians had never fully embraced the English version of amateurism. While powerful upper-class traditions of restraint and conventions governed English college sports, custom meant far less to American collegians. Indeed, though they too initially came from the upper social ranks, they and their supporters frequently accepted a winning-at-any costs ethos. The American students brought with them to the gridiron the values of the marketplace. "The spirit of the American youth, as of the American man, is to win, to 'get there,' by fair means or foul," observed a *Nation* writer in 1890, with some exaggeration, "and the lack of moral scruple which pervades the struggles of the business world meets with temptations equally irresistible in the miniature contests of the football field."[2]

One temptation was to recruit the best athletes available, regardless of their status as students. As early as the 1860s and 1870s, Northeastern colleges hired professional rowers to strengthen their crews. Before football became a serious campus enterprise, few objected to allowing anyone connected with the college to play on college elevens. As late as 1900, in some parts of the South and the West, townspeople and younger faculty members joined college squads. In a 1898 game, Virginia accused North Carolina of employing two professional stars but raised no objections to the eligibility of Professor Edward V. Howell, who scored the winning touchdown for the North Carolina eleven. The most controversial recruitment practice entailed the employment of "tramp athletes." Each fall in the 1890s and into the early years of the next century, these paid athletes made their way around the country playing college football. Caspar W. Whitney surely exaggerated when he claimed in 1895 that in the Midwest and Far West "men are bought and sold like cattle to play this autumn on 'strictly amateur' elevens."[3] But, at best, the tramp athletes maintained only the vaguest pretenses of being bona fide students; sometimes they played on one college team on Saturday, a pro team under an assumed name on Sunday, and on yet another college team on the following Saturday.

Play for pay was not exclusively a Midwestern and Far Western phenomenon. Upper-class colleges in the Northeast also subsidized athletes. In 1905, *McClure's* magazine reported that James J. Hogan, the renowned captain of the Yale team, lived in a style befitting a prince. He enjoyed free tuition, a free suite in swank Vanderbilt Hall, a $100 scholarship, a ten-day paid vacation in Cuba, and a monopoly on the sale American Tobacco Company products on Yale's campus. Apparently the students took Hogan's good fortunes in stride, for they affectionately spoke of smoking "Hogan's cigarettes."[4]

Apart from paying players to play and using nonstudents on their teams, college athletic associations also sought to enhance their prospects of winning by employing professional coaches. Early in the twentieth century, even Harvard, which had attempted more than most other schools to imitate the English system of athletics, turned to a full-time professional coach. Embarrassed by the team's abysmal record against Yale, in 1905 the Harvard Athletic Committee offered Bill Reid the then-astronomical sum of $7,000 annually to take charge of its football team's fortunes; this was nearly twice the salary of the typical Harvard professor. Reid carefully monitored the athletic performance of his charges, organized winter workouts using weights and wrestling to get his men into top-notch physical shape, kept a card file on all 4,000 Harvard students as potential recruits, and scheduled weaker teams early in the season so that the Crimson could "lick [its] opponents in increasing strength as the season progressed and as [the] team developed."[5] The stress of coaching nearly destroyed Reid; his weight fell, and, in order to obtain sleep, he turned to drink and drugs. Even though he lost only three games in two years, he viewed his coaching stint "as a failure." Two of his three losses had been to archrival Yale.

The arrival of the professional coach altered the experience of the players. "Players like to win," observed a former Yale player in 1904, "but head coaches and especially paid coaches, had to win."[6] To win, some coaches drove their players relentlessly; they subjected them to countless repetition of the same plays and to verbal harangues. "What has become of the natural, spontaneous joy of the contest?" asked Owen Johnson through a fictional character early in the century. "Instead, you have the most perfectly organized business systems for achieving the required result—success. Football is slavish work."[7] The players usually hated the practices but loved playing the games and having adoration heaped on them on Saturday afternoons. Yale athletes at least could also savor a bountiful training table, which featured choice beefsteak or mutton for dinner that could be washed down with ample quantities of milk, ale, or sherry.

THE ISSUE OF BRUTALITY AND MAJOR RULE CHANGES

The eligibility of players, paying players for play, and the professional coach—these were only three of the major issues in college football that fomented concern both on and off college campuses. Another even more emotionally charged issue was brutality. Although flying wedge formations had been banned in 1894, teams

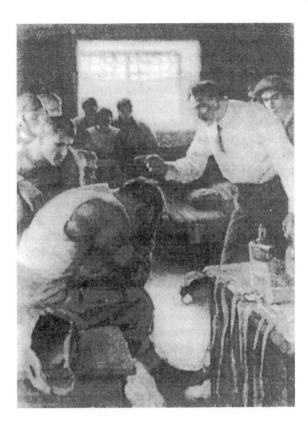

THE COACH, 1910 This drawing in a popular periodical represents the growing influence of the professional coach in the college game.
(Century Magazine)

continued to use mass-momentum plays in which guards and tackles lined up in the backfield and, once the ball was snapped, they tried to push and pull the ball carrier forward through the defensive line. To many observers, this style of play seemed to be nothing more than a physical free-for-all; out of the melees fans might observe players with bloodied heads and broken limbs, some might be unconscious, and on occasion a player died from wounds sustained from playing the game. In 1897, after the death of a player in that state, the state legislature of Georgia even abolished football, but the governor vetoed the measure.

Criticism of football reached a crescendo in 1905 and 1906 when muckraking journals such as *McClure's*, *Collier's*, and *Outlook* published scathing exposés of the sport. The magazines told in shocking detail how American collegians ignored the conventions of gentlemanly behavior, the "insidious" role of money in the sport, and how teams devised tactics to "knock out" key opponents early in the contests. In 1905, the president of the United States, Theodore Roosevelt himself, decided to intervene. Roosevelt had long been obsessed with physical fitness; he feared above all else that boys born into luxury would become effeminate men. Football was a healthy antidote, teaching "pluck, endurance, and physical address." Roosevelt had a personal stake in the Harvard eleven; his son was a member of the squad. He often sent the team personal letters of encouragement, but it was the entreaties of Endicott Peabody, the headmaster of the elite Groton School and an ardent Anglophile, who prompted the president to act. Concerned that the boys in the elite prep schools along the East Coast were emulating the improper behavior of their older college counterparts, Peabody urged the president to "get the coaches of Harvard and Yale and Princeton together, and persuade them to undertake to teach men to play football honestly."[8]

Roosevelt agreed, though he had no intention of opening the meeting to a full-fledged debate on the merits of college football. He invited only selected coaches, faculty, and alumni of the Big Three—Harvard, Yale, and Princeton—to the White House conference. His expressed aim was "to get them to come to a gentleman's agreement not to have mucker play." In the end, the delegates presented the president with a mild statement promising to eliminate unnecessary "roughness, holding, and foul play." Roosevelt, satisfied with the resolution, urged its immediate release to the press. The White House conference neither stilled the critics nor stopped rough play. Columbia and the Massachusetts of Institute of Technology abolished football; Stanford and California decided to substitute rugby for football.

A major turning point in the debate over brutality came late in the 1905 season, when Harold P. Moore, a Union College player, died from injuries suffered in a game against New York University. Henry B. McCracken, the chancellor of New York University, called a conference of college presidents representing schools on his university's schedule. "I would not trust the reformation of the game to the present Rules Committee [headed by Walter Camp and dominated by the Big Three]," McCracken wrote.[9] Meeting in December 1905, the McCracken conference decided to convene a national college convention and to form a new rules committee.

Delegates from 62 colleges representing all sections of the country save the West Coast and the members of Walter Camp's rules committee met in New York on December 28, 1905. The convention quickly organized the Intercollegiate Athletic Association (IAA) and appointed its own rules committee. (In 1910, the IAA was renamed the National Collegiate Athletic Association.) The delegates gave no punitive powers to the IAA but did allow it to formulate standards of conduct for member colleges. Until the post-World War II era, rather than the regulation of the recruitment, eligibility, and subsidization of players, the most important function of the NCAA was the creation of rules committees.

In 1906 the IAA's rules committee adopted a series of rule changes that it hoped would reduce brutality and give offenses more freedom of action. To provide an incentive for teams to abandon the mass-momentum plays designed to squeeze out short yardage gains, a first down could now only be obtained by gaining 10 yards (rather than 5) in three attempts. The committee also approved the forward pass but circumscribed its potential use by requiring that the ball be thrown 5 yards or more to the right or left from where it had been put into play. Furthermore, the offense was assessed a 15-yard penalty for an incomplete pass.

The "Revolution of 1906," as these rule changes have been described, neither opened the game up offensively nor ended football injuries. The 10 yards-to-gain-a-first-down rule actually encouraged an even more conservative style of play. Most teams did not bother to mount offensive drives on their half of the field; instead they frequently punted on first down, hoping to induce the opposition into mishandling the ball. Play in the 1909 season was as brutal as ever; reportedly 30 players (8 of them college men) lost their lives. So in 1910 the IAA rules committee took more drastic action: It abolished interlocking interference and required that there be at least seven men on the line of scrimmage when the ball was put in play. Over Walter Camp's objections, the 1910 rules liberalized the forward pass by allowing the ball to cross the line of scrimmage at any point. Two years later (in 1912), the committee gave the offense four downs to make 10 yards, and the value of a touchdown was increased from 5 to 6 points.

If not revolutionary, the cumulative rule changes in 1906, 1910, and 1912 did mark the beginning of the "modern" game of football. Slowly, the coaches, particularly in the West, began to exploit the potential of the forward pass. In 1913, when Notre Dame came east to play Army, passes from Gus Dorais to Knute Rockne resulted in a stunning upset for the tiny men's Catholic school. Later in the same season the cadets profited from their earlier disaster by using the "Western" passing game to defeat archrival Navy. Producing a more exciting game for spectators, these early twentieth-century rule changes helped to make college football the nation's premier sporting spectacle.[10]

THE FORMATION OF CONFERENCES

Neither changes in the way the game was played nor the formation of a national association addressed the issues of recruitment, eligibility, and subsidization of college athletes. In theory, by joining together, establishing a set of common rules, and imposing harsh penalties on one another's violations, the colleges could have established a level playing field. (This is, of course, essentially what the NCAA sought to do in the post–World War II era.) But, given their continuing allegiance to amateurism and their reluctance to admit that their football programs were commercial enterprises, college authorities never seriously contemplated the possibility of forming a national economic cartel. Instead, they ultimately allowed each school to govern its sports as it saw fit.

Yet, self-imposed controls frequently failed to ensure harmony among the colleges. Unseemly charges and countercharges revolving around the use of nonstudents as players, paid players, and unnecessary brutality in the late nineteenth and early twentieth centuries regularly soured intercollegiate relationships. To obtain greater order in intercollegiate sports, many of the colleges turned to regional associations or conferences. As early as 1858, students at Harvard, Yale, Brown, and Trinity organized the College Rowing Association. Eventually the students also formed associations in baseball, football, and track and field.

Beginning in 1895 with the organization of the Intercollegiate Conference of Faculty Representatives, later known as the Western Conference, and even later as the Big Ten, which was initially composed of the large Midwestern universities of Chicago, Illinois, Purdue, Michigan, Minnesota, and Northwestern, college presidents rather than student and alumni representatives took the initiative in attempting to bring more order to intercollegiate athletic relations. From its founding, the conference conceived of itself as the "anchor of amateur athletics in America." The conference pioneered in the establishment of rules of eligibility, prohibition of subsidies to student athletes, and the faculty supervision of athletes—measures subsequently copied by other conferences. The Conference of Faculty Representatives had one major weakness: It left enforcement in the hands of faculty committees of the member institutions.

Faculty athletic committees by no means guaranteed that a college's sports program would adhere to strictly amateur principles. Edward S. Jordan, after an examination of college football in 1905, flatly asserted that "faculty control is a myth."[11] In the first two decades of the twentieth century at the typical college, the faculty, regardless of its stated powers, shared the actual supervision of sports with coaches, presidents, trustees, and the alumni. Any of these groups might thwart faculty control. Moreover, for the most part, the faculties were just as interested in the success of the football team as any other group. Often they were handpicked by the college president. Finally, for a faculty representative to challenge prevailing athletic practices usually meant subjecting him- or herself to exceptionally hostile reactions from football fans both inside and outside of the college. While the establishment of conferences did not end controversies between colleges nor the subsidization of players, conferences did help reduce the use of "tramp athletes."

THE REIGN OF KING FOOTBALL

The reign of football as the king of American sporting spectacles began in the 1920s, a decade that has often been hailed as the "golden age of American sports." During the 1920s, attendance at college games doubled and gate receipts tripled. From Columbus, Ohio, to Los Angeles, California, colleges built colossal stadia of steel and concrete. Many colleges named their fields "Memorial Stadium," thereby explicitly linking football to patriotism and the casualties of World War I. In 1920, only one college field could seat 70,000 fans, but by 1930 seven enjoyed in excess of that capacity. By comparison, only two major-league baseball parks could hold 70,000 spectators in 1930.

College football also weathered the Great Depression more successfully than professional baseball. In the first years of the Depression, attendance fell and a few colleges dropped the sport, but estimates in 1937 placed total fandom at 20 million, a figure twice as high as that of 1930.[12] Apparently the college game attracted higher income groups who withstood the rigors of the Depression more

CONSTRUCTION OF A STADIUM OF STEEL AND CONCRETE, 1923 Both old and new technology were brought to the construction of this new stadium at the University of Nebraska. As monuments to the veterans of World War I, the new stadia of the 1920s—many of which were called "Memorial Stadium"—frequently identified football with patriotic sentiments.
(University of Nebraska Archives)

successfully than did baseball's fans. Attendance declined in the years that the United States was involved in World War II (1941–45) but shot up again in the postwar era.

Attendance was only one measure of "King Football's" success. College football became the darling of the media. During the 1920s, the sheer space devoted to football in the nation's press doubled. By the end of the decade, five different newsreel companies offered theatergoers moving pictures of the previous Saturday afternoon's action. In the 1930s, King Football strengthened his reign. In that decade, fans could hear dozens of games on radio, football was the subject of no fewer than 48 full-length movies, and the most popular mass-circulation magazines of the day, the *Saturday Evening Post* and *Colliers'*, published a total of 42 football stories.[13]

Much of the success of King Football's reign in the interwar years and afterward rested on the sport's growing capacity for evoking community pride and identity. As early as the 1890s, the game helped bind together local college communities of students, professors, alumni, and townspeople. It continued to do so throughout the twentieth century. "Through no design or deliberation on the part of any man or group of men," observed Ralph Cooper Hutchison in 1952, "football has become the emotionally integrating force of the American college." Through football "all elements of college society enjoy a common experience—athlete and nonathlete, student and professor, town and gown, men, women, and children."[14]

In the twentieth century, as Michael Oriard has persuasively argued, the forces of modernity increased the importance of football as a constituent of local identities. By the 1920s and 1930s, a national consumer culture, a nationalization of sights and sounds via the media, the growth of a new white-collar class that thought of itself in national rather than local terms, the shocking behavior of youth, the growing ethnic, racial, and religious pluralism of the big cities, and a growing secularization of American life—all seemed to threaten those who grounded their identities in their local communities. Peoples from the countryside and smaller cities and towns tended to see themselves under siege by the modern ways of the big cities. The older middle class of small businessmen, locally oriented professionals, prosperous farmers, and skilled workingmen continued to find their identities and their values in the ways handed down from the past and in their families, their churches, and in their local communities or neighborhoods rather than in their occupations or in what was currently fashionable. Locally based athletic teams joined extended families, local churches, local civic organizations, and gossipy local newspapers in bolstering a traditional way of life.[15]

Not unexpectedly, then, college football was especially popular in the smaller cities and towns that hosted major state universities. "Football commands much more than the average amount of interest in Nebraska," observed the *Saturday Evening Post* in 1951. "In this prairie state of great open stretches and small communities, where the average town is only 375 people, the university's football team is one of the strongest common bonds."[16] Citizens in states without a conspicuously significant history, great civic monuments, or remarkable physical scenery not only frequently formed powerful emotional bonds to their state university's football team but also found in the team an important source of personal identity.

College teams gained standing and local importance to the extent that they could obtain national recognition. In the 1920s and to a somewhat lesser extent in the 1930s the route to prestige led to the Northeast, where the Big Three— Harvard, Yale, and Princeton—continued to rule and where the most influential sportswriters covered games. Colleges everywhere sought to schedule and win games with the Big Three. If unsuccessful in scheduling such games, they sought foes from among lesser-known schools in other regions. That four special trains brought 750 Southern Methodist University fans to a game at West Point with Army in 1928 offers a glimpse of the degree to which fans were committed to winning intersectional recognition.

Allegedly each region possessed a distinctive style of play, yet in fact during the interwar years college offensive systems were highly portable. Either Knute Rockne's famed Notre Dame Box or Pop Warner's equally famous single- and double-wing formations prevailed nearly everywhere. Each of these formations featured "hikes" directly from the center to the ball carrier (or passer) who stood several yards behind the line of scrimmage. Unlike the earlier mass formations, the newer systems featured sweeps outside the tackles or ends. "There are no longer any distinctive systems in football," wrote Fielding H. Yost on the eve of the 1940 season. "Nobody sees a balanced line any more except at Notre Dame, and even some of the Rockne-trained coaches are getting away from it. There is only one formation that's any good and it's the single wing."[17] In that very year, however, Clark Shaughnessey at Stanford reintroduced the T formation which gradually replaced the single wing in popularity. All of the formations since then essentially represent variations on the T.

Nevertheless, in the minds of fans and the media, the playing style of the college teams mirrored the cultures of the regions from which they came. Reflecting the spirit and character of the Midwest, that region's college teams were said to feature a run-oriented, rock-'em, sock-'em style of power football; Jock Sutherland's University of Pittsburgh teams epitomized this kind of football. Reflecting the Wild West shootout spirit of the Southwest, teams from that region were said to rely more on a wide-open passing attack; Southern Methodist's "aerial circus" epitomized the wide-open style. (That these stereotypes possessed some validity was probably due more to differences in weather than regional cultural variations.) Teams from the Deep South emphasized defense and were said to play with the fervent spirit of the antebellum Old South.

The employment of football to express regional consciousness and identity was especially powerful in the South. For the South, at least in the minds of the media and many fans, every intersectional contest became a reenactment of the Civil War. The media from both sections, for example, identified Dixie running backs with DeForest's raiders or Pickett's cavalry at Gettysburg. Writers from both North and South embraced the "romance with the legendary Old South and Lost Cause," according to Michael Oriard, in order to feed a "longing for regional identities in the face of a rapidly expanding 'mass' culture" of the twentieth century.[18]

Not all of college football's popularity sprang from its capacity to arouse regional or local identities. Alums of the Northeastern elite schools, who were scattered across the country, avidly followed the football exploits of their alma maters. The world wars supplied ready-made cheering sections for the two service academies. Those who had worn khakis in the wars supported Army; bell-bottoms made one a Navy rooter. After World War II, when the Big Three de-emphasized football, the annual Army-Navy games attracted more national interest than the classic Yale-Princeton or Yale-Harvard matches.

No football team exceeded the "Fighting Irish" of Notre Dame in attaining a national following and fervent fan support. Beginning in the 1920s, Catholics everywhere, regardless of their ethnic origins, even those who had never been near a college (dubbed by sportswriters as "the subway alumni" if from the big cities or as the "coal field alums" if from the Catholic communities of western Pennsylvania, eastern Ohio, and West Virginia) became rabid Irish fans. When Notre Dame met Army in their annual tilt in New York, the passions of the city's large ethnic population reached a fever pitch. "New York was never before, or since, so sweetly gay and electric as when Rock [Knute Rockne, Notre Dame's coach] brought his boys to town," wrote Paul Gallico. "The city was wild with excitement."[19]

As a minority within a predominately Protestant culture, one that came under assault from the revived Ku Klux Klan in the 1920s, Roman Catholics found a powerful source of identity and pride in the successes of Notre Dame's football team. Regardless of any other connection with the college, Notre Dame for them became "our team." "In the 1930s," according to Mary Jo Weaver, a professor of religion at Indiana University, "the custom began in primary and secondary parochial schools, each Friday in the fall, to have students pray for a Notre Dame victory the following day. . . . It was an important part of our 'Holy War' against the Protestant majority in America."[20]

As in the instance of Notre Dame, football could be a means of college building. In a nation in which colleges and universities engaged in keen competition for students and public support, football victories, especially victories in intersectional games, could call local and national attention to hitherto obscure and little-known colleges. Indeed, tiny Centre College of Kentucky's victory over mighty Harvard in 1921 made anything seem possible. Attention gathered from such gridiron exploits, college authorities frequently believed, aided in the recruitment of students, increased support for the institution by local business and community leaders, deepened the bonds of alumni loyalty, and, if a public-supported institution, might increase appropriations from state legislatures. To the extent that college leaders accepted the idea that football could be a means of institution building, they were more likely to throw their support behind their college's football team and to acquiesce to violations of the amateur spirit or code.

THE FOOTBALL COACH AS HERO

Unlike baseball and other sports in which heroes sprang from the ranks of the players, in football the coaches rather than the players usually won public renown. There were of course exceptions; Red Grange in particular played a prominent role in bringing about the reign of King Football. But, while student athletes came and went, coaches such as Amos Alonzo Stagg (Chicago), Knute Rockne (Notre Dame), Glenn "Pop" Warner (Pittsburgh, Stanford, Carlisle, and Temple), and Dana X. Bible (Texas A & M, Nebraska, and Texas) became well-known public figures with enduring reputations. The heroic status of coaches flowed in large part from the belief that football coaches played a far more important role in determining the outcome of games than, say, their baseball manager counterparts. Good coaching spelled the difference between victory and defeat.

Given the stakes involved and the belief in the importance of the coach, perhaps it was little wonder that by the 1920s football coaches typically received higher salaries than the highest paid professors on campus.

Knute Rockne outdistanced all other rivals in capturing the public imagination. As with Babe Ruth, Red Grange, Jack Dempsey, and other sports-related heroes of the 1920s, his life seemed to be the very embodiment of the self-made man. Born in Norway, Rockne as a boy had immigrated with his family to Chicago. At the age of 22, according to legend, he "went down to South Bend [Indiana] with a suitcase and $1,000 feeling the strangeness of being a lone Norse-Protestant invader of a Catholic stronghold."[21] (Later, Rockne converted to Catholicism.) He played football there, and, after graduation, he stayed on as a chemistry assistant and assistant football coach. In 1918, at the age of 30, he landed the head coaching job at Notre Dame.

Rockne's fame sprang mostly from what Murray Sperber has described as *"Notre Dame's unique formula."* The formula included a rich athletic culture, "fan identification based on ethnicity and religion, an innovative and charismatic coach, a phenomenal won-lost record, powerful media allies [whom Rockne, like other successful coaches, diligently cultivated], and immense and increasing numbers of supporters throughout the nation, and most important of all, *the invention of the formula.*[22] Playing against the best teams with whom he could schedule games (Big Ten and Northeastern elite colleges refused to play the upstart Catholic school),

KNUTE "ROCK" ROCKNE *First as a player, then as a coach, Rockne made Notre Dame synonymous with success in college football. Catholic ethnics everywhere in the nation identified with Rockne's powerful teams of the 1920s.*
(Indiana Historical Society)

Rockne's teams recorded 105 victories, 12 defeats, and 5 ties. His teams enjoyed five unbeaten and untied seasons.

No coach was more charismatic than Rockne. Both the players and the press loved him for his quick wit. He could be caustically hilarious. "The only qualification for a lineman is to be big and dumb," he reputedly said. Then turning to the smirking backs, he said: "To be a back, you only need to be dumb."[23] According to the media hype of the day, Rockne was not only a teacher but also a father figure; he, along with fellow coaches at other colleges, guided the "boys" through the difficult rites of passage that transformed them into "men."

While trailing Army by a touchdown in 1928, Rockne allegedly made the most memorable half-time speech in football history. He told of George Gipp, famed Notre Dame halfback, who had tragically died from pneumonia at the end of the 1920 season. Gipp instructed Rockne on his deathbed: "When things are wrong and the breaks are beating the boys, tell them to go in there with all they've got and win one just for the Gipper."[24] In the second half, the Irish responded with two touchdowns, to win 12 to 6. In 1940, Warner Brothers retold the story in the popular film *Knute Rockne—All American*, in which Pat O'Brien played Rockne and Ronald Reagan played the Gipper. To answer his extensive mail and handle his endorsement opportunities, Rockne hired a personal agent (Christy Walsh). When Rockne died in a plane crash in 1931, he assured his own apotheosis.

THE INCOMPLETE DEMOCRATIZATION OF COLLEGE FOOTBALL

As the story of the rise of Notre Dame football to national prominence suggests, in the first half of the twentieth century the sport became less class-exclusive, ethnic-exclusive, and religiously exclusive than it had been in the past. True, until the 1940s, the "blue bloods" of the Big Three—Harvard, Yale, and Princeton—continued to occupy a disproportionate space in the minds of those who were involved in college football. Also true, the fans of games across the country continued to be upscale; in magazine illustrations and advertisements football fans dressed more formally than baseball crowds, thereby suggesting that they occupied a higher place in the nation's social hierarchy than baseball fans. Equally true, until the late 1940s, when substantial numbers of World War II veterans began to arrive on college campuses, an overwhelming majority of the students came from the ranks of the upper-middle and upper class. Not only was the working class almost completely absent from college campuses, but so also were all but a few African Americans.

Nonetheless, in two fundamental respects the sport became more democratic. In the first place, football spread geographically from the elite Northeastern schools to the lesser-known and less-distinguished state universities and private schools. Football helped "to put on the national map" isolated state universities such as Kansas and Nebraska and hitherto unknown Southern schools such as Alabama and Georgia Tech. But particularly noteworthy was Notre Dame, which became a great symbol of the American melting pot. That this small Catholic, ethnic college gained national renown suggested (but did not, of course, prove) the conclusion that Catholic ethnics had finally won acceptance by the dominant culture.

In the second place, the brawny stars who lured fans to the massive new stadiums in the 1920s increasingly came from farming and working-class, ethnic families. Lower-class youth who surmounted prejudice, or sometimes their own shame, to become college football heroes emerged as a favorite trope of the newspapers, periodicals, and movies in the interwar years. In 1929, Dan Parker, a writer for the New York tabloid the *Daily News*, offered a graphic description of how football could be an avenue of upward mobility for downtrodden youth. The college coaches who "go out into the highways and byways and rescue stout peasants from a career behind the plough and yank young huskies right out of the maws of the police force, and put them in way of acquiring a modicum of higher learning so that they may become successful bond salesmen in later life—these magnanimous coaches, I say, are performing a noble mission in life."[25]

Paradoxically, the ethnic invasion of college football came at the very time that the United States developed a policy of immigration exclusion. Following the conclusions of popular pseudo-science of the day that conceptualized ethnic and racial groups hierarchically, the Immigration Act of 1924 sharply reduced immigrants from Southern and Eastern Europe while totally excluding those from Asia. Yet, the media rarely if ever presented the appearance of the new ethnics in college football in negative terms; instead, during the 1920s the media for the most part simply ignored ethnicity. Apparently, the media believed that football was a powerful force in transforming immigrants into "100 percent" Americans. Insofar as the offspring of the immigrants themselves were concerned, they frequently saw in the playing of football and other sports a way of gaining acceptance by, and improving their lot in, the dominant culture.

In the face of Nazism in the 1930s and early 1940s and Communism in the late 1940s and 1950s, college football became part of a national ideology that called for the homogenization of American culture. In all aspects of the culture, the urge was to unite, to include, to blend, in short, to create a single, unitary "American way of life." In this tense atmosphere, college football became a model of social inclusiveness. According to this ideological posture, in the United States, unlike its Nazi and Communist foes, no ethnic or religious group was excluded from the American way of life. The conspicuous presence and successes of ethnics, Catholics, and Jews in college football probably increased feelings among members of these groups that they were for the first time fully Americans.

Such feelings were far less likely among Native Americans and African Americans. For a historic moment, Native Americans did occupy a special and renowned place in the world of college football. Early in the twentieth century, led by the legendary Jim Thorpe, tiny Carlisle, an Indian boarding school in Pennsylvania, captured national attention with its phenomenal football victories. Wracked by scandal, Carlisle closed its doors in 1918, but in the 1920s, another small Indian boarding school, Haskell Institute in Lawrence, Kansas, to some degree filled the void left by Carlisle's departure from the football scene. While expressing admiration for the sportsmanship and trickery of the Native American teams, the white media typically presented their games with white teams as encounters with the exotic and as allegories of the long struggle between the two peoples for the domination of the Americas. That Indians, who had as recently as 1890 offered armed resistance to the white invasion, were playing the white man's game of football not only provided evidence that Native Americans were now harmless but may also have affirmed for many whites the superiority of their own way of life. As for the Indians themselves, they may have seen football as not only an arena for having fun but also one in which they could contest the white world on its own terms and symbolically avenge the daily humiliations that they faced in the dominant society.

In the national white media, African Americans were all but invisible during the interwar years. The press rarely mentioned race when discussing the blacks who played on Northern white teams. Nonetheless, every African American player seemed to be a marked man; in 1921, in the most brutal of many incidents, Jack Trice, the first black athlete at Iowa State, died from injuries suffered in a game against Minnesota. In order to placate their opponents, when playing Southern

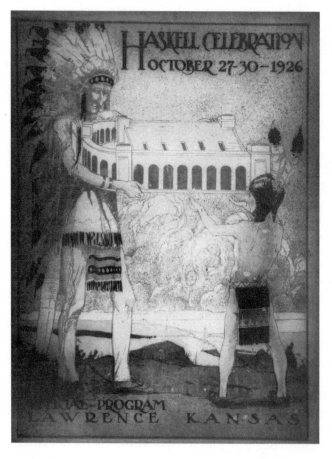

FROM "SAVAGERY" TO "CIVILIZA-TION" The cover of the 1926 program dedicating the construction of a new football stadium at the Haskell Institute, an Indian boarding school in Lawrence, Kansas, suggests that playing football contributed to the assimilation of Native Americans into the dominant culture. However, notice that both the chief presenting the stadium and the boy receiving the stadium are wearing traditional clothing.
(Haskell Institute)

foes, Northern teams frequently benched their black players. While the number of black players on Northern college teams began to increase in the 1930s, the full-scale racial integration of college football got underway only after World War II (see Chapter 18).

Many Americans continued to see college football as an especially effective testing ground for manliness and masculinity. According to most of the media as well as the commentary of coaches and players, football was *the* one sport in which a "sissy" could not survive. Football, concluded Grantland Rice in the 1920s, served as a barrier to the "striking tendency in many of our leading colleges to-day toward jazz music, tea dances and bootleg booze." At a time when "so much of the world [is] turning to softness or the comfortable ease money can buy," added Rice, football instilled "iron in the soul and steel in the heart."[26] Boys with the misfortune of having falsetto voices, "angel faces," pink cheeks, curly hair, or some other explicitly female trait could, according to a popular theme found in the mass-circulation periodicals of the day, prove their manliness on the gridiron. As the separate spheres of the sexes characteristic of the nineteenth century broke down, as work required less physical prowess, and as men and women engaged increasingly in shared activities, football became one of the few arenas in which traditional manliness could be affirmed. Simultaneously and perhaps paradoxically, it was also one in which open male bonding could be expressed without arousing suspicions.

CONTINUING CONTROVERSIES

While most football fans worried little or not at all about the commercial or semi-professional character of the college game, a small but loud set of critics continued to reiterate charges similar to those that had been leveled at the game during the opening years of the twentieth century. In particular, these critics, who were usually intellectuals, focused on a fundamental contradiction at the heart of big-time college athletics: How could the colleges maintain the illusion that their athletes were student amateurs while recruiting and frequently subsidizing athletes with little or no regard for their academic qualifications or performances?

This contradiction was at the bottom of a continuing set of "crises" as well as fitful attempts at reform. The first of these erupted in 1925 when Red Grange decided to turn professional before finishing his senior year of college (see Chapter 9). The next came in 1929 when the Carnegie Foundation issued a bombshell. Based on information gathered from 112 colleges and universities, the report's chief author, Howard J. Savage, concluded that only 28 colleges operated "ethical" athletic programs. Unethical practices ran the gamut from occasional contacts with potential recruits by coaches and friends of the team to "an intensely organized, sometimes subtle, system" of recruitment.[27] Savage also reported that the guilty colleges engaged in elaborate and ingenious systems of paying players to play. "Needy" athletes frequently received pay for nominal work such as pushing a broom, supervising intramural athletics, or dispensing towels. They might have well-paying jobs off campus; for example, in the 1930s, Ohio State University track star Jesse Owens had a job operating an elevator in the state capitol building in Columbus. Some colleges, especially those in the South and the Southwest, avoided hypocrisy simply by granting direct "athletic scholarships." Given its findings, the Carnegie report reached an obvious conclusion: "Apparently the ethical bearing of intercollegiate football contests and their scholastic aspects" were "of secondary importance to the winning of victories and financial success."[28]

After making a strong case for the importance to the colleges of having winning teams and generating money, the Carnegie report unrealistically called on college presidents and faculties to lead campaigns on behalf of institutional self-restraint. A tiny number of college presidents sought to do just that. They tried to reform their football programs by eliminating athletic scholarships, disallowing special treatment of athletes on campus, curtailing the recruitment of students solely on the basis of their athletic talents, and reducing the power of booster organizations. But, in doing so, many of the reform presidents, especially those at state universities, risked being fired. Hence, in most instances, the state university presidents retreated from reform. As Blair Cherry, the former head football coach at the University of Texas, bluntly put it: "In the final analysis the public, not the colleges, runs college football."[29]

The story of reform in private universities followed a somewhat different trajectory. Beginning in the mid-1930s and continuing into the postwar era, the once-powerful Ivy League schools of the Northeast (Harvard, Yale, Princeton, Brown, Penn, and Cornell) began a gradual process of de-emphasizing football. Like other intellectuals in the interwar years, Robert Maynard Hutchins, appointed president of the University of Chicago in 1929, openly rejected the time-honored argument that football was effective in building good character. In 1939 Hutchins persuaded the university's regents to abolish the sport. That the Chicago eleven failed to have a single winning season after 1924 made the decision more palatable to the university's alumni and patrons.[30] While Chicago's highly publicized step had little initial impact on the other colleges, in the immediate postwar era when colleges embarked on an unrestrained recruitment frenzy and the expenses of running competitive programs escalated to new heights, such one-time major Catholic powers as Fordham, St. Mary's, and Santa Clara dropped the sport. More than a dozen other schools followed their example.

CONCLUSION

While the colleges sought to reconcile the requirements of commercial entertainment with their educational objectives and the amateur sporting tradition, during the first half of the twentieth century, football, especially the college version of the sport, became the nation's premier team spectacle. By mid-century, the sport had enthusiastic followings in all regions of the country; in fact to many fans the sport seemed to reflect fundamental regional differences. The sport was no longer restricted to upper-class youth. Except for African Americans who were for the most part still limited to playing on black college teams, Catholics, the offspring of recently arrived European immigrants, farm boys, and working-class youth were amply represented on college elevens across the nation. Not only did the game seem to embody the ideal of a "melting pot," but in the face of Communist threats abroad and presumed threats at home it also became a vital ingredient in the post-World War II era of what was considered by many to be "the American way of life."

NOTES

1. Quoted in Michael Oriarid, *King Football: Sport and Spectacle in the Golden Age of Radio and Newsreels, Movies and Magazines, the Weekly and the Daily Press* (Chapel Hill: University of North Carolina Press, 2001), 199–200. I am deeply indebted to this book for its research and analysis of college football as spectacle. For other aspects of the chapter, see also Ronald A. Smith, *Sports and Freedom: The Rise of Big-Time College Athletics* (New York: Oxford University Press, 1988); Robin Lester, *Stagg's University: The Rise, Decline, and Fall of Big-Time Football at Chicago* (Urbana: University of Illinois Press, 1995); Murray Sperber, *Shake Down the Thunder: The Creation of Notre Dame Football* (New York: Henry Holt, 1993); John Sayle Watterson, *College Football: History, Spectacle, Controversy* (Baltimore, MD: Johns Hopkins University Press, 2000); Patrick B. Miller, "Athletes in Academe: College Sports and American Culture, 1850–1920," unpub. Ph.D. diss., University of California, Berkeley, 1987; and Guy M. Lewis, "American Intercollegiate Football Spectacle, 1869–1917," unpub. Ph.D. diss, University of Maryland, 1964.

2. *Nation* 51 (November 20, 1890), 395.

3. *Literary Digest* 12 (November 30, 1895), 128.

4. H.B. Needham, "The College Athlete," *McClure's Magazine* 25 (1905), 15–28, 160–73.

5. Quoted in Smith, *Sports and Freedom*, 160. See also Ronald A. Smith, ed., *Big-Time Football at Harvard, 1905: The Diary of Coach Bill Reid* (Urbana: University of Illinois Press, 1994).

6. Quoted in Smith, *Sports and Freedom*, 147.

7. Quoted in B.M. Kelley, *Yale: A History* (New Haven, CT: Yale University Press, 1974), 298.

8. For the issue of brutality, see Lewis, "American Intercollegiate Football Spectacle," 223–346; Smith, *Sports and Freedom*, chap. 14; and Watterson, *College Football*, Part 1. Watterson has found that

the press grossly exaggerated the number of deaths attributable to football.

9. Quoted in Lewis, "American Intercollegiate Football Spectacle," 234.

10. See Sperber, *Shake Down the Thunder*, 40.

11. E. S. Jordan, "Buying Football Victories," *Collier's* 36 (November 18, 1905), 23. For the 1920s, see Sperber, *Shake Down the Thunder*; Harold J. Savage et al., *American College Athletics* (New York: Carnegie Foundation, 1929), 100–101; and Watterson, *College Football* chaps 8 and 9.

12. See J. F. Steiner, *Americans at Play* (New York: Arno, 1933), 86–94, and *New York Times*, December 26, 1937.

13. Oriard, *King Football*, 11–17

14. Quoted in ibid., 14.

15. See Benjamin G. Rader, *American Ways* (Fort Worth, TX: Harcourt College Publishers, 2001), chaps 8 and 9.

16. Quoted in Oriard, *King Football*, 70.

17. Quoted in Ron Fimrite, "A Melding of Men All Suited to a T," *Sports Illustrated* 47 (September 5, 1977), 92.

18. Oriard, *King Football*, 89. See also the essays by Patrick B. Miller and Andrew Doyle in Patrick Miller, ed., *The Sporting World of the Modern South* (Urbana: University of Illinois Press, 2002). However, also note that Ted Ownby in the same book asserts (336) that, in the South, college football "did not dominate newspapers, normal conversation, and life on Saturdays on campuses and in campus towns until the post-World War II period."

19. Paul Gallico, *The Golden People* (New York: Doubleday, 1965), 142.

20. Quoted in Sperber, *Shake Down the Thunder*, 436–37.

21. Quoted in Edwin Pope, *Football's Greatest Coaches* (Atlanta: Tupper and Love, 1955), 195.

22. Sperber, *Shake Down the Thunder*, 185.

23. Quoted in Pope, *Football's Greatest Coaches*, 189. Sperber in *Shake Down the Thunder* subjects this legend along with others about Rockne to a systematic reexamination.

24. Quoted in Pope, *Football's Greatest Coaches*, 200.

25. Quoted in Oriard, *King Football*, 240.

26. Quoted in ibid., 332.

27. For the impact of the report, see ibid., 106–07; Watterson, *College Football*, 158–76; John R. Thelin, *Games People Play: Scandal and Reform in Intercollegiate Athletics* (Baltimore, MD: Johns Hopkins University Press, 1994), 15–37.

28. Savage, *American College Athletics*, 298.

29. Quoted in Harry Paxton, ed., *Sport U.S.A.: The Best from the Saturday Evening Post* (New York: Thomas Nelson and Sons, 1961), 405.

30. See esp. Lester, *Stagg's University*.

12
THE CLUB SPORTS GO PUBLIC

On September 16, 1926, William T. "Big Bill" Tilden's six-year reign over the tennis world finally ended. During the quarterfinal of the national championships at the West Side Tennis Club, Forest Hills, New York, Tilden fell to a Frenchman, Henri Cochet, in five sets. In the final set the spectators repeatedly broke into wild cheers. Trailing at 1–4, Tilden seemed to be on the verge of one of his patented comebacks. As he served with smashing force and volleyed crisply at the net, the crowd roared with applause at each of his winning shots. He pulled even at 4–4. "The champion, it was agreed, was still the champion of old, capable of lifting his game in an emergency to unassailable heights," waxed one reporter. Both men held service for three games, giving Tilden a 6–5 lead. Then the debacle came. Tilden won only four points in the last three games, conceding the final set 8–6. "Tilden, the invincible, whose magic with a racquet confounded the greatest players of the world and made America supreme in tennis, at last . . . relinquished his scepter."[1]

In the 45 years separating Richard Sears's victory at the Newport Casino Club in the first national championship tournament and Cochet's dramatic upset of Tilden, tennis experienced a remarkable transformation. In the first instance, a small company of summer vacationers had casually followed the action. In 1926, more than 7,000 fans gathered in the steel and concrete stadium of the West Side Tennis Club, and newspapers all over the world reported the upset in blazing headlines. The quality of play had improved sharply. The players at Newport had relied upon soft, looping shots; the serve had functioned merely to put the ball into play. Both Tilden and Cochet could hit smashing serves at over 90 miles an hour, and from either the forehand or backhand side, they could hit deep, hard drives or they might hit deft drop shots. For Sears, tennis had been an avocation, but for Tilden and Cochet (although both were technically amateurs) tennis was a full-time endeavor. They played or practiced nearly every day. Tennis was an international sport that featured both men's and women's competition. Top-flight players might travel to Italy, France, Germany, England, and Australia to play in tournaments. In short, tennis, like the other elite club sports of track and field and golf, "went public." The spectators rather than the clubs became the ultimate determinants of the character of the sport.

TENNIS GOES PUBLIC

Before the 1920s, tennis showed few signs of going public. From the outset of its history, the sport had been associated with the English upper classes and rich Americans who played on their estates or in their exclusive clubs. In 1873, Major John Wingfield, an avid player of the ancient game of court tennis, popularized a game of lawn tennis in England. Soon thereafter members of the Marylebone Cricket Club in England and the All England Croquet Club at Wimbledon took up the sport. Wimbledon held the first of its famous tournaments in 1877. Controversy surrounds the issue of when and who first introduced the game in the United States, but apparently two courts—in Staten Island, New York and Nahant, Massachusetts—were built in 1874. In 1881, the posh Newport Casino Club became the home of the United States Lawn Tennis Association (USLTA) and served as the site of the first national tennis championships.

Associations with upper-class clubs, women players, and the absence of brute physical strength in the game were both blessings and handicaps. At the turn of the century even the term "lawn tennis" evoked images of prissy dudes in white flannels, pitter-pattering a ball across a net at Newport, Bar Harbor, or Seabright with lady friends. When several Harvard men "deserted" rowing for tennis in 1878, a *Harvard Crimson* editorial writer heaped scorn upon them. "Is it not a pity that serious athletics should be set aside by able-bodied men for a game that is at best intended for a seaside pastime?" he asked. "The game is well enough for lazy or *weak* men, but men who have rowed or taken part in a nobler sport should blush to be seen playing Lawn Tennis."[2] Paul Gallico recalled that during his childhood in New York in the early twentieth century "it was worth your life to be caught anywhere east of Lexington Avenue carrying a tennis racquet under your arm." Invariably a player would be greeted by boys who hooted in falsetto voices: "Deuce, darling," or "Forty-love, dear."[3]

Despite such verbal abuse, a few brave men played the sport, perhaps partly because of its popularity among the upper classes of England. By 1895, 106 clubs belonged to the USLTA. Then, primarily because of the sudden popularity of golf in the elite clubs, membership in the association fell sharply, not returning to the 1895 level until a decade later.

Harbingers of a new era appeared in the early twentieth century. One was an increase in international competition. As early as the 1880s, Englishmen had invaded the Newport tournament and Americans had reciprocated by competing at Wimbledon; such visits became common in the first two decades of the twentieth century. In 1900, a wealthy Harvard player, Dwight F. Davis, encouraged national rivalries by establishing the International Lawn Tennis Challenge Cup (Davis Cup). In the pre-World War I era, teams from the United States and England (and later Australia and New Zealand) competed annually for the cup. Until the 1960s, the Davis Cup was one of the most coveted prizes in international competition.

Interest in the game increased when, in 1909, Maurice McLaughlin, a flashing redhead from San Francisco, introduced a new style of play to Newport. He brought to tennis raw power and speed which he had learned on the fast, hard-surfaced courts of California. The transfer of the national championships in 1915 from Newport to the West Side Tennis Club at Forest Hills, a section of Queens in New York City, reflected the determination of the USLTA to attract a larger audience. In 1923 the West Side Tennis Club built the country's first modern tennis facility suited for spectators.

A turning point for tennis as a public spectacle came in the 1920s with the appearance of two outstanding players: Big Bill Tilden and Suzanne Lenglen.[4] The victory of Lenglen in the women's singles at Wimbledon in 1919 and Tilden's triumph in men's singles at Forest Hills in 1920 marked the beginning of an age in which tennis players sometimes became public celebrities. Both Lenglen and Tilden combined superb athletic performances with colorful personalities. Between 1919 and 1926, Lenglen took six titles at Wimbledon, while Tilden won the same number at Forest Hills. Tilden, a tall, gaunt egotist, shared the limelight of men's tennis with no one. Lenglen, glamorous and equally controversial, held sway just as imperiously over women's tennis. (For Lenglen and Helen Wills as women sport heroes, see Chapter 13.)

Tilden was slow to develop into a championship player. From a once socially prominent Philadelphia family whose status had slipped downward, Tilden learned his tennis at the Germantown Cricket Club. Remarkably, even for his day, he did not become a master of the sport until he was 27 years old. After defeat in the finals of the national championships in 1919, he spent the next winter correcting a weak backhand. The next year he stormed back to win the first of seven national championships; he shared the doubles title five times at Forest Hills, won Wimbledon singles crowns three times, and won 17 Davis Cup matches while losing only five.

Like Babe Ruth, Tilden fitted perfectly into the ballyhoo of the 1920s. To Tilden, the tennis court was a dramatic stage and he was the leading actor; he loved the theater and performed the lead in several shows, including one Broadway production. If attention at a tournament wandered from him, he brought it back by subtly allowing himself to teeter on the brink of defeat. He then made what appeared to be an incredible comeback. On the court he could be arrogant and irritating. Linesmen who made "bad" calls received menacing glares, and Tilden might deliberately "throw" the next point to express his utter contempt. To the American public, Tilden was the colossal giant, who single-handedly held off the tennis invaders from Europe.

Tilden's feuds with American tennis authorities reflected the dilemmas confronting a once socially exclusive, amateur sport that was in the process of becoming a public spectacle.[5] While promoting tennis as a spectator sport, the United

States Lawn Tennis Association persisted in trying to preserve the amateur image of the game; it adamantly refused to permit players to profit directly from the sport. As early as 1924 the USLTA tried to prevent Tilden from earning money from his ventures into tennis journalism.

The controversy reached a climax in 1928 when the USLTA suspended Tilden from Davis Cup play. News of the banishment drove the 1928 presidential election, the assassination of Mexico's president-elect, and a search for aviators lost in the Arctic off the front pages of the nation's newspapers. Even the normally phlegmatic American president Calvin Coolidge demanded an explanation. With the decision threatening to destroy public interest in the Davis Cup challenge round scheduled in Paris, infuriated French officials complained through diplomatic channels to the U.S. government. The USLTA backed down.

The USLTA's rigid stance on amateurism in part reflected the function that tennis performed for upwardly mobile families of new wealth. By the 1920s, when tennis began to attract substantial public attention, the management of the association had fallen into the hands of those who sought to employ the game as a vehicle for lifting themselves into the upper echelons of elite social circles. To retain the image of tennis as a high-status sport, these social climbers were adamant in defending a rigorous definition of amateurism. Yet rigid adherence to amateurism created a dilemma. For tennis to be successful as a spectator sport, the players had to become full-time athletes. This meant that unless the players were wealthy, they were forced to circumvent the amateur rules.

That local clubs and their members could gain prestige by sponsoring the development of star players also encouraged violations of the amateur spirit. A promising boy or girl, even if from families of modest financial means, could find him- or herself sponsored by a club or a patron. The player's expenses for instruction and appearance in tournaments would be paid fully by someone else. Such a system, according to Sumner Hardy, president of the California Lawn Tennis Association, "made bums out of the boys."[6] At a tender age their lives centered around little else but tennis.

Blatant hypocrisy was an inevitable byproduct. While tournament authorities paid the traveling expenses of players (the more prominent the player, the higher the allowance granted), they refused to offer cash prizes or schedule open tournaments in which both amateurs and professionals could compete. To have done so would have jeopardized the social functions performed by the sport for the social climbers.

Since powerful amateur associations controlled the major tournaments of the world and the press generally took a dim view of professional tennis, only a few players could equal their earnings as amateurs. In 1926 Charles C. "Cash and Carry" Pyle, Red Grange's business manager, attempted to eliminate "shamateurism" in tennis by organizing a pro tour. He hoped to force the amateur associations to open their tournaments to pros and award cash prizes. He signed Suzanne Lenglen, Mary K. Browne, and Vincent Richards (but not Tilden) to a tour of the United States and Canada. Apparently Pyle profited from the venture, but when Lenglen demanded a larger share of future gates, he abandoned his venture into pro tennis.

In the early 1930s only Tilden, though in his forties and no longer the world's premier player, could command a large enough audience to make pro exhibitions profitable. To succeed, pro tours required continual infusions of new talent, in other words, recent winners of major amateur tournaments who had received large quantities of free publicity. Such a system meant that only a few professional players could earn a decent living from tennis. Before it became a success, pro tennis had to wait for the advent of television and open tournaments in the 1970s.

GOLF GOES PUBLIC

The history of golf's going public both paralleled and departed from that of tennis. Both sports had origins in socially exclusive clubs. Historians of golf credit Joseph M. Fox, a member of Philadelphia's Merion Cricket Club, and John Reid, a transplanted Scot and an executive of an iron works in Yonkers, New York, with introducing modern golf into the United States. In 1887 Reid organized the first modern golf club, the St. Andrews Club, named after the historic club in Scotland.

In the early 1890s, golf caught the fancy of superrich tycoons in New York, Boston, Philadelphia, and Chicago. In 1891, William K. Vanderbilt brought over the famed Scottish golfer Willie Dunn to build the first professionally designed links, the Shinnecock Hills course, in Southampton, Long Island, where many wealthy New Yorkers had summer homes. The Shinnecock Hills Golf Club hired Stanford White, the noted architect, to design an opulent clubhouse. The clubhouse and course became models for wealthy men interested in forming clubs elsewhere. By 1900 rich golfers could follow the seasons. When the winter winds began to blow, they left their courses at Newport, Brookline, Yonkers, Long Island, and Chicago for sumptuous resorts built for them in Florida, Georgia, and North Carolina. In 1894 both the St. Andrew's Club and the Newport Golf Club scheduled national tournaments. With but few exceptions, a reporter concluded in 1898, golf "is a sport restricted to the richer classes of the country."[7]

Social exclusivity and the time and money required to play led most Americans initially to ignore or scorn the sport. Popular hostility to golf in the first decade of the twentieth century impelled Theodore Roosevelt to warn William Howard Taft of the political dangers of playing the game. "It would seem incredible that anyone would care one way or the other about your playing golf, but I have received literally hundreds of letters from the West protesting it." He further cautioned: "I myself play tennis, but the game is a little more familiar; besides you never saw a photograph of me playing tennis. I am careful about that; photographs on horseback, yes; tennis, no. And golf is fatal."[8] Ignoring Roosevelt's warnings, Taft became the nation's first golf-playing president.

Like tennis, golf featured international competition. Long before 1920 golfers played on both sides of the Atlantic. In 1922 George H. Walker presented a cup for biennial competition between amateur teams representing the United States and Great Britain, and in 1927 Samuel Ryder did the same for professional teams. As in tennis, both sexes competed in golf, though the best-known women golfers, Alexa Stirling and Glenna Collett, never achieved the celebrity status of Suzanne Lenglen or Helen Wills nor the public recognition of such male golfers as Walter Hagen, Gene Sarazan, or Bobby Jones. Yet while the two sports had these important similarities, they evolved in significantly different ways.

Golf went public without the controversy that characterized the emergence of tennis as a public spectacle. Unlike tennis, which had developed almost simultaneously in both Great Britain and the United States in the late nineteenth century, golf was already a well-established sport in Scotland when it invaded American shores. Thus the American clubs tended to imitate Scottish customs. In the British Isles the unoccupied links of land (hence the term "links" to describe golf courses) that bordered or stretched into the sea furnished natural hazards. Having no equivalent physical features along the Atlantic seaboard, American clubs had to build inland courses. To approximate the hazards found in the British Isles, they constructed artificial bunkers, sandtraps, small lakes, and planted trees along the fairways. From the earliest days of the sport in the United States, the clubs hired professional Scottish or English golfers to teach the finer arts of the game and followed the British custom of holding open tournaments. Both amateur and professional golfers could compete in open tournaments. Finally, the absence of gate receipts at golf tournaments until the 1920s discouraged the adoption of the tennis practice of extending traveling expenses to "amateur" players.

Golf enjoyed a larger fan constituency than tennis. Abetted by the rapid growth of country clubs in the 1920s, golf spread (as one wag put it) from the upper "Four Hundred" to the upper "Four Million." Apart from being a conspicuous status mechanism, golf furnished an escape from the confinement and annoying details of downtown offices. On the course, according to the promoters of the sport, businessmen found a pastoral retreat in which they could soothe overwrought nerves. The golf course also became a substitute for the office and the conference room; there businessmen laid the groundwork for future transactions or confirmed old agreements. Sometimes golf seemed only a pretext for convivial gatherings at the "nineteenth hole," the clubhouse bar.

As early as 1913 golf exhibited potential as a public spectacle. Prior to that date a gallery of 200 was considered unusual for a national tournament, but in 1913 a crowd of more than 3,000 watched Francis Ouimet, a 20-year-old amateur golfer, upset Britain's two leading professional golfers in a playoff in the United States Open tournament. Earlier, whenever overseas stars had consented to play in American meets, they had nearly always emerged victorious. Only one American, Walter J. Travis, had ever won a major European championship. In 1913 Harry Vardon, winner of six British open titles and often hailed as the world's greatest golfer, and Edward "Ted" Ray, reigning British Open crown holder, embarked upon an exhibition tour of the United States. Attracting record crowds wherever they went, they interrupted their tour in mid-September to play in the American Open at the Country Club in Brookline, Massachusetts.

An almost unknown golfer, Francis Ouimet, a former caddie at the Country Club and the son of a French-Canadian father and an Irish-American mother, surprised everyone by tying the British aces at the end of regulation play. The next day, on a rain-soaked course, Ouimet won the playoffs, trouncing Vardon by five strokes and Ray by seven strokes. Newspapers across the country gave Ouimet's victory headline coverage. Overnight, Ouimet was an American hero. "Here was a person all of America, not just golfing America, could understand—the boy from 'the wrong side' of the street, the ex-caddie, the kind who worked during his summer vacations from high school—America's idea of the American hero," exclaimed Herbert Warren Wind.[9]

One participant in the Brookline tournament, Walter C. Hagen, was largely responsible for making professional golf respectable. The first golf pros, mostly transplanted Scotsmen and Englishmen, had been jacks-of-all-trades. They designed the early courses, kept the grounds, made and repaired the hickory-shafted golf clubs, trained and managed caddies, and gave instruction to novices. Little or none of their earnings came from tournament winnings, product endorsements, or paid exhibitions. While wealthy club members sometimes joined the club pro in friendly games, they viewed him as simply another employee and hence as a social inferior. In open tournaments the clubs barred the pros from the locker rooms and other clubhouse amenities. As late as 1930, the official programs of the United States Open prefixed the names of amateurs with "Mr." while deleting this distinction from the names of pros.

WALTER HAGEN Hagen, the first professional golf hero, sipped from one of the many cups that he won during his 30-year career. Hagen also seemed to embody the new consumer ethic that had become so conspicuous in the 1920s.
(National Archives and Records Administration)

Hagen helped "democratize" golf. Being a former caddie from a family of modest means did not deter the irrepressible Hagen. He treated kings, industrial tycoons, and caddies all alike. Because of his prowess as a golfer, his pleasing personality, his sartorial elegance, and his impeccable manners, he broke down social barriers in both the United States and Europe. Apparently Hagen unintentionally touched off the "Midlothian Incident" of 1914. Hagen, then a brash, young, but personable professional who feigned ignorance of clubhouse social conventions, simply made himself at home in the Midlothian Country Club locker room and clubhouse. While no one knows whether words were exchanged or threats were issued, the country club finally acquiesced, constituting what has been described as a "social revolution in American golf."

Before the late 1930s, the prize money available in tournaments was modest. In 1916 millionaire Rodman Wanamaker donated a prize of $2,500 to the winners of an annual Professional Golfer's Association (PGA) tournament. During World War I, the American Red Cross sponsored a benefit tour to which it charged admission to spectators. In 1921 the United States Open copied this practice and soon other golf meets followed suit. Swelling gate receipts permitted the major tournaments to increase their meager purses. In the early 1920s a professional tour of sorts developed in the South. Wealthy golf enthusiasts, often with real estate promotion as a primary motive, began to sponsor professional tournaments in resort areas. Yet no golfer could earn a decent living on tournament winnings alone.

Hagen relied upon tours and product endorsements rather than tournaments for his earnings. Hagen employed Robert "Bob" Harlow, a veteran Associated Press correspondent, as his business manager. (Harlow, hailed as the "founder of professional golf as it is today," later served many years as the tournament manager of the PGA.) Harlow capitalized upon Hagen's popularity by lining up endorsements for golf equipment and arranging tours that took Hagen from the largest cities to golf's remotest outposts. Except for tournament interruptions, from late spring to early fall Hagen gave exhibitions five days a week and during the winter months he played on the "winter circuit" from Florida to California. Harlow "ticketed" the galleries at one dollar a person for weekdays and two dollars for weekends. During the twenties Hagen probably earned between $30,000 and $50,000 annually.

THE EMPEROR, BOBBY JONES

While Hagen wooed thousands of golfers to his exhibitions, the amateur Bobby Jones had no equal as a truly national, even international, golfing celebrity.[10] Jones was born into a wealthy Atlanta, Georgia, family. In 1916, when he was only 14, Jones competed in the United States Amateur at the Merion Cricket Club in Philadelphia. He managed to qualify and swept through his first two challengers before succumbing to the defending champion in the third round. Despite defeat,

Jones was the sensation of the tournament, hailed by sportswriters as the "child prodigy" of golf. For several years, the high expectations generated at Merion went unfulfilled, but in 1923, when he was apparently on the verge of retiring from competitive golf, he won his first major tournament, the U.S. Open.

From 1923 to 1930, he was virtually the "emperor" of world golfers, both professional and amateur. He collected 13 national titles—5 United States Amateurs, 4 United States Opens, 3 British Opens, and 1 British Amateur. In the last nine years of his career he competed in 12 national championships and finished first or second in 11 of them, a feat Jones considered to be greater than his winning of the Grand Slam in 1930. He climaxed his short golfing career with the Grand Slam—the American Open and Amateur and the British Open and Amateur, a feat not duplicated since. After the Grand Slam in 1930, when he was at the very peak of his game at the age of 28, Jones announced his retirement.

The American public adored Bobby Jones. Every time he returned from victories in Europe, he received the welcome of a conquering hero—a ticker-tape parade down Broadway to New York's City Hall to receive the keys of the city from Mayor Jimmy Walker. Public excitement knew no bounds when Jones won the last leg of his Grand Slam, the American Amateur at the Merion Cricket Club in 1930. A vast throng, estimated at 18,000, made a great human fringe around the greens and packed the fairways, following Jones from hole to hole. "Today's match was far more of a spectacle than it was a contest," declared the *New York Times*. "It was merely an exhibition on Jones' part, a parade to victory."[11] Women reached out to touch him and little boys sat on their fathers' shoulders to catch a glimpse of their hero.

The conservative, "gentlemanly" Jones stood in sharp contrast to the more hedonistic Hagen. Rather than flamboyance, Jones cultivated an image of modesty. At the same time that he competed in golf tournaments, Jones attended college, obtained a law degree, was admitted to the bar, and began the practice of law. Above all, the public loved the fact that Jones was an amateur, had defeated the best of the professional golfers and taken the measure of the European champions. By a large strain on the imagination, weekend "duffers" could identify Jones as one of their own. He, like them, held down a regular job and presumably played the sport for the sheer fun of the game.

That the image of Jones sometimes failed to correspond with the facts did not bother his admirers. Upon retirement from tournament competition, Jones, like the pro golfers, attempted to capitalize upon his reputation. With his "Boswell" and longtime traveling companion, O.B. Keeler, Jones did a weekly half-hour radio show re-creating the highlights of his career. He made two series of instructional films for Warner Brothers, reputedly for a profit of $180,000, and lent his name to a Spalding line of golfing equipment. He furnished the initiative and much of the design for a magnificent new golf course at Augusta, Georgia, the Augusta National. In 1934 the Augusta course became the home of the Masters tournament, an invitation-only affair consisting of the world's top golfers. In due time, the Masters became one of four major recognized tournaments in the world.

As a leisure-time golfer, Jones occasionally played in the Masters (even as late as 1948) and other meets, but he never again won a major tournament.

The retirement of Jones, the Great Depression of the 1930s, and World War II set back the American enthusiasm for golf. Without Jones as a drawing card or the emergence of a new golfing celebrity of equal stature, major amateur tournaments were fortunate if gate receipts equaled expenses. Although almost a third of the country clubs folded, the Public Works Administration and the Works Progress Administration of the New Deal built about 200 courses. Of about 5,200 courses in 1941, some 2,000 were either municipal or privately owned, daily fee courses. In the 1930s, the "Age of the Amateur" also passed. After the victory of Jones in 1930, only one amateur (in 1933) ever again won the U.S. Open.

Finally, the 1930s introduced the "Age of Steel" and concerted assaults on pars. The average winning score for the U.S. Open in the 1930s dropped six strokes below that of the 1920s. Experts attributed the better scores to high-pressured balls, replacement of hickory shafts with steel, the use of more specialized and more perfectly matched clubs, and the "new look" of the nation's golf courses. In the 1930s, many clubs filled in traps, thinned the roughs, cropped the grass shorter on the fairways, and softened the greens by watering them more copiously. The 1940s brought forward a new breed of professional precisionists—Ben Hogan, Byron Nelson, and Sam Snead, for instance—but not until the advent of television and Arnold Palmer in the 1960s did golf again achieve the public attention it had received in 1930.

TRACK AND FIELD

Well before 1890 the fan had been a potent force in track and field. As early as the 1840s and 50s, professional pedestrianism, which was grounded in the Victorian counterculture, had gained a considerable following, and it continued to enjoy some support in the early years of the twentieth century. The Scottish Caledonian clubs had also welcomed fans to their meets; they had charged admission to spectators and awarded cash prizes to winning athletes. Initially, spectatorship was an issue that divided the sporting world of the social elites. The fashionable clubs had sought to use a sport as an agency for building status communities. Status ascription might be strengthened by restricting competition to amateur athletes and spectators to club members and invited guests. On the other hand, the clubs might enhance their reputations by holding outstanding meets and fielding superior athletes. Eventually the latter characteristic prevailed. Consequently many of the prominent clubs opened their gates to the public at large; they became the nation's premier promoters of track and field. In the twentieth century, the athletic clubs and their parent body, the Amateur Athletic Union (AAU'), continued to stage some of the most eminent meets in the nation.

The elite athletic clubs encountered increasing competition from other organizations in the nurture of superior athletes and the sponsorship of track and field meets. Foremost of these competitors were the high schools and colleges. Northeastern colleges organized the Intercollegiate Association of Amateur Athletes of America (commonly known as the IC4A) in 1876 to supervise running events that had been held at Saratoga, New York, since 1873. In 1876, the IC4A began to conduct annual, full-scale track meets. Until the NCAA staged its first championships in 1921, the IC4A was the nation's most prestigious collegiate track meet. After 1921 it remained an important event for Eastern schools.

The University of Pennsylvania (Penn) Relays, which began in 1895, introduced a colorful athletic carnival that combined intercollegiate and interscholastic track. At the Penn Relays of 1925 more than 3,000 athletes representing more than 500 colleges and secondary schools competed before 70,000 fans in the finals. The Penn Relays spawned imitators across the country, one of the more notable being the Drake University Relays at Des Moines, Iowa. Early in the twentieth century, several other groups joined the athletic clubs, the AAU, and the colleges in the promotion of track and field. In New York City the Millrose Games, the Knights of Columbus Games, and the Wanamaker Mile, among others, added to the opportunities available to spectator and athlete alike.

For more than half a century promotional groups and regulatory bodies competed for governance of track and field. The main power struggle involved the NCAA and the AAU. As the colleges furnished ever larger numbers of the nation's top-flight athletes, they increasingly resented the senior organization's (the AAU's) authority to determine the eligibility of amateur athletes, its collections of fees for meets that it did not sponsor, the control that it attempted to exercise over international competition, and the AAU's domination of the American Olympic Committee. Sometimes only ad hoc compromises allowed the United States to field a team at the Olympic Games. Only in 1978, and then only after an act of Congress—the Amateur Sports Act—did the warfare between the AAU and the NCAA finally end.

All too often the athletes were the victims of both the power struggle between the AAU and the NCAA and the amateur code. While in principle amateur athletes could receive no financial remuneration from their feats, promoters could win both glory and profits from staging meets. Anxious to attract star athletes to their meets, unscrupulous promoters secretly "overpaid" expense allowances and apparently sometimes made direct payments to the athletes. As in the case of tennis and golf, to be a champion in track and field required training and frequent competition. Unless the athlete was independently wealthy, he or she had to supplement his or her income in some fashion. The temptation to benefit financially from one's athletic skills was difficult to resist.

Furthermore, according to world champion sprinter Charles W. Paddock, who repeatedly warred with the AAU, the promoters often placed the athletes in an impossible position. On the one hand, they would extend to the young, inexperienced athletes "extra expenses." On the other, whenever the athlete protested any matter, he could then be threatened with exposure and suspension.[12] "Shamateurism" continued to plague the world of track and field after World War II.

THE REVIVED OLYMPIC GAMES

In due time, the revived Olympic Games became the world's premier track and field spectacle.[13] Pierre de Coubertin, the aristocratic French Anglophilic founder of the modern Games, sought to sanction their revival by calling upon the myth of Greek amateurism. He advocated athlete-centered ideals. The Games offered the young men of the world a forum for unification by peacefully competing in sports. Unofficially, Coubertin, who smarted deeply from the humiliating defeat that the Germans had administered to the French in 1870–71, also hoped the example of the Games would strengthen the national character of the French people. Moreover, responsibilities for the management of the Games and the national teams rested with committees of nonathletes. Finally, forces external to the Olympic movement (including national pride, commercial consideration, and boosterism) shaped much of the history of the Games.

Until 1908 the Olympic Games remained a minor event in American track and field competition. The Americans made no concerted effort to field a strong team at the first Games held at Athens in 1896. College athletes sponsored by the Boston Athletic Association reinforced by a few others who paid their own expenses comprised the total American squad. Harbingers of the use of the Games for nonathletic purposes were evident even at Athens. The Greek royal family blatantly exploited the Games to enhance their power, and the first Games initiated the practice of raising the national flags of the winning athletes at a victory ceremony. The next three Games were essentially sideshows to other more publicized attractions: the Paris Exposition of 1900, the World's Fair held in St. Louis in 1904, and the Franco-British Exposition of 1908 held in London. In addition, the Greeks scheduled what has been called a "rump" Olympics at Athens in 1906. Only 15 countries competed in the 1900 Games, and only 11 nations participated in the third Olympics held at St. Louis in 1904.

Rivalries between the large and patriotically motivated American and British teams marred the London Games in 1908. The British interpreted Ralph Rose's refusal to dip the flag as the American team passed the royal box as an insult. For the first time, Olympic officials required that all competitors perform as part of a national "team." By 1908 American track and field officials took the Games seriously. They had organized a national Olympic committee that selected teams of first-rate athletes and subsidized them for their trips abroad. In "the greatest ovation in the history of athletics," reported the *New York Times*, 250,000 people turned out for a parade in New York City to welcome the American athletes home from London. At each of these early Games, American athletes tended to dominate track and field but fared poorly in other forms of competition.

In the 1912 Olympic Games held at Stockholm, Sweden, the Games "arrived," at least as far as the Americans were concerned. The Americans went all-out to win the track and field events; the team included a Native American and several African Americans.

Jim Thorpe, the great athlete from the tiny Carlisle (Pennsylvania) Indian School, emerged as the hero of the Games.[14] Already well known for his football feats, Thorpe captured the pentathlon and decathlon. He won four of the five individual events in the pentathlon and scored a 700-point margin over his nearest competitor in the decathlon. Americans hailed Thorpe's victories as confirmation of the "melting-pot's" effectiveness. But only six months after his performance, bureaucrats in the AAU and the American Olympic Committee decided to make an example out of Thorpe by punishing him for a violation of the amateur code. When it was revealed that Thorpe had played on a minor-league baseball team in the summer of 1909, the AAU revoked his amateur status and the International Olympic Committee then took back his Olympic medals.

World War I was only a temporary setback for the Games. Although the Games scheduled for Berlin in 1916 were canceled, the postwar Games were far bigger and more extravagant than the prewar affairs. The 1920 Games, awarded to Antwerp in recognition of the horrendous sacrifices made by the Belgians during World War I, were modest. But each of the following Games—Paris in 1924, Amsterdam in 1928, Los Angeles in 1932, and Berlin in 1936—was more extravagant than its predecessor.

Despite a worldwide depression, the Los Angeles promoters determined to make the 1932 spectacle a showcase for their city as well as the state of California. To

JAMES "JIM" THORPE Native American, star college football player, and hero of the 1912 Olympic Games, Thorpe later played big-league baseball and professional football. In 1950 the Associated Press named him the "Athlete of the Half-Century." (Library of Congress)

finance the spectacle, the city floated a $1.5 million bond issue, and the California voters, in a special referendum, approved the expenditure of $1 million in state funds. At Los Angeles the athletes found magnificent facilities: a 105,000-seat stadium, an indoor auditorium with seats for 10,000, a swimming structure with a seating capacity of 12,000, and the first specially constructed Olympic Village.

Not to be outdone by the Los Angeles buccaneers, the Nazis put on an even bigger show at Berlin in 1936. They built a new 100,000-seat track and field stadium, six gymnasiums, and many smaller arenas. They installed a closed-circuit television system, a radio network that reached 41 nations, photofinish equipment, and electronic timing devices. The Nazis commissioned Leni Riefenstahl, a brilliant producer, to make a $7 million film of the event. Her film *Olympia* subsequently became a classic in cinematography.

The building of more elaborate facilities reflected the increased politicization of the Games. Politicization had begun well before the 1920s and 30s. From the outset, Coubertin had promoted the Games as a means of inspiring the youth of France to greater physical prowess and courage and at the same time as a means of encouraging international ideals. The decision to have the athletes compete as national teams rather than as individuals inevitably gave rise to international rivalries. On the eve of the 1908 Games, James E. Sullivan, leader of the American Olympic delegation, bluntly declared: "We have come here to win the championship in field sports, and we are going to do it."[15] For the 1908 Games the American press devised an unofficial point system so that national achievements could easily be compared. The national organizing committees soon found that by appealing to patriotic sentiments they could raise more money to send athletes to the Games.

Political animosities arising from World War I drove the International Olympic Committee to exclude the losers in the war (the Central Powers of Germany, Austria, Hungary, and Turkey) from the Games of 1920 and 1924. Neither did the IOC extend an invitation to the newly established communist regime in Russia to compete in the postwar Games. (Soviet Russia did not participate in the Games until 1952.) Such actions revealed clearly that the Olympic movement was not immune to the exigencies of international politics.

The politicization of the Olympics reached a climax with the 1936 Games. Nazi Germany's blatant anti-Semitism sparked a movement in the United States to boycott the 1936 Olympics. As early as 1933, shortly after Adolf Hitler had taken command in Germany, Americans serving on the International Olympic Committee protested Nazi discrimination against Jews and the AAU voted to boycott the games unless Germany's policy regarding Jewish athletes be "changed in fact as well as in theory."[16] While the German Olympic Committee took nominal steps to reassure the Americans, Hitler, in 1935, proclaimed the "Nuremberg Laws," which deprived German Jews of their citizenship and legalized social practices designed to preserve the integrity of the "Aryan race."

The issue of boycotting the Games divided American athletic officials into bitter camps. Avery Brundage, the self-made millionaire president of the American Olympic Committee (AOC), led the advocates of participation while the president of the AAU, Judge Jeremiah T. Mahoney, a Catholic who was disturbed by Nazi paganism and anti-Semitism, led the boycott movement. Both sides published pamphlets, issued press releases, and gave radio interviews. A Gallup poll revealed that 43 percent of the American people favored a boycott. Brundage, in a private letter to a Nazi friend, interpreted the boycott movement as a Jewish-Communist conspiracy. "Jews and Communists," he wrote, "threatened to spend a million dollars to keep the United States out of Germany . . . by use of bribery, corruption and political trickery, and other contemptible tactics."[17] A showdown came at the AAU convention in 1935 where Brundage, by a two-and-a-half vote margin, was able to obtain the defeat of a resolution that would have delayed the American decision to enter the Games pending further investigation of German behavior.

Controversy continued at the Games in Berlin. Although the German fans enthusiastically welcomed the American black athletes, a German newspaper contemptuously referred to them as the "Black auxiliary." When Cornelius Johnson, a black, won the high jump with a record leap, Hitler, who had personally congratulated the first two winners in track and field, suddenly left his stadium box. This action led to the potent myth that Hitler had refused to shake the hand of Jesse Owens, the American star of the games, although during the subsequent days, Hitler carefully avoided public congratulation of any winner.

Bitterness flared within the American ranks. At the last moment the American track and field coach, Dean Cromwell, dropped two Jewish athletes from the 400-meter relay team. Although Cromwell insisted that he substituted other athletes (including Owens) in order to prevent a surprise German victory, the argument was lame. Everyone else believed the Americans could easily have won without the substitutions, and one of the Jewish athletes had times equal to those of one of the substitutes.

The career of Jesse Owens provided striking evidence of America's persistent racism. The son of Alabama sharecroppers, Owens migrated with his family to Cleveland, Ohio. In both high school and college he won a wide reputation as a track star. (In most cases even Northern colleges excluded blacks from their team sports but sometimes welcomed them in the individual sports.) As a sophomore at Ohio State University in 1935 he broke four world records at the annual Big Ten meet. In the 1936 Olympics he competed in 12 events, including preliminary heats, and set or equaled world marks nine times. In 1950 the sports reporters selected him as the best track athlete of the first half of the twentieth century.

Yet in terms of American race relations, Owen's remarkable victories had their ironies. On the one hand, he gave the lie—at least in the case of sport—to the Nazi argument for "Aryan" supremacy and he was a hero to white and black Americans alike. Yet in 1935 and 1936, 26 blacks lost their lives in the United States from lynchings. In 1936 the walls of racial segregation in the United States seemed as unbreachable as ever; no blacks played in major-league baseball or professional football and few played on integrated college teams. After the 1936 Olympics, Owens himself was reduced to exhibitions such as running against a horse merely to sustain a living. After World War II, he became a more or less official spokesman of the United States in the Cold War conflict with the Soviet Union.

JAMES "JESSE" OWENS Hero of the Olympic Games of 1936, Owens received a warm welcome upon his return to the United States. However, most of his hopes for financial gain from his athletic gains never materialized. Later Owens became a leading black spokesman for the United States in the Cold War and a moderate on civil rights issues.
(Ohio State University Photo Archives)

Owens preferred the role of the symbol of what a black man could accomplish in sport rather than that of a crusader for black rights.

After 1936 many of the nations who had sent their athletes to the Nazi Games began to prepare for both war and the 1940 Olympics. Ironically the 1940 Games were scheduled for Tokyo just as the 1916 Games had been set for Berlin. In 1938 the Japanese withdrew their invitation to host the 1940 Games and World War II caused the cancellation of the 1944 Olympics.

CONCLUSION

In the twentieth century, individual sports such as golf, tennis, and track and field escaped some but not all of the strictures associated with their early histories. No longer located exclusively in a network of socially elite clubs, they increasingly became part of a larger public and commercial sporting world. Although in nearly all cases the champions of the individual sports remained technically amateurs, they more often than not received some form of pay for their play and had to train with the same rigor as their professional counterparts in team sports. Perhaps because they normally did not require as much social interaction, minorities and women found more (though by no means equal to white males) opportunities in the individual than in the team sports.

NOTES

1. Quotations from Allison Danzig and Peter Brandwein, eds., *The Greatest Sport Stories from the New York Times* (New York: A.S. Barnes, 1951), 255, 256.

2. United States Lawn Tennis Association, *Official Encylopedia of Tennis* (New York: Harper & Row, 1971), 10.

3. Paul Gallico, *The Golden People* (Garden City: Doubleday, NY, 1965), 64.

4. See Allison Danzig and Peter Brandwein, eds., *Sports Golden Age* (New York: Harper & Bros., 1948), 208–27; Frank Deford, *Big Bill Tilden* (New York: Simon & Schuster, 1975); Larry Englemann, *The Goddess and the American Girl: The Story of Suzanne Lenglen and Helen Wills* (New York: Oxford University Press, 1988).

5. See Gallico, *Golden People*, 124–27; Paul Gallico, *Farewell to Sport* (New York: Knopf, 1938), 149–50; and J.R. Tunis, *$port$* (New York: John Day, 1928), 47–75.

6. Quoted in Tunis, *$port$*, 165.

7. H.L. Fitz Patrick, "Golf and the American Girl," *Outing* 32 (December 1898), 294–95.

8. Quoted in Harold Seymour, *Baseball*, 2 vols. (New York: Oxford University Press, 1971), II, 45–46.

9. H.W. Wind, *The Story of American Golf*, 3d rev. ed. (New York: Knopf, 1975), 85. See also Stephen Hardy, *How Boston Played* (Boston: Northeastern University Press, 1982), 179–85.

10. See esp. Ron Fimrite, "The Emperor Jones," *Sports Illustrated* 80 (April 11, 1994), 104ff.

11. Danzig and Brandwein, *Greatest Sport Stories*, 342.

12. See C.W. Paddock, *"The Fastest Human"* (New York: Thomas Nelson, 1932), 48–49, 158.

13. See Mark Dyreson, *Making the American Team: Sport, Culture, and the Olympic Experience* (Urbana: University of Illinois Press, 1998); R.D. Mandell, *The First Modern Olympics* (Berkeley: University of California Press, 1976); John MacAloon, *The Great Symbol* (Chicago: University of Chicago Press, 1981); John Lucas, *The Modern Olympic Games* (New York: A.S. Barnes, 1980); Allen Guttmann, *The Games Must Go On: Avery Brundage and the Olympic Movement* (New York: Columbia University Press, 1984); Allen Guttmann, *The Olympics: A History of the Modern Games* 2d ed. (Urbana: University of Illinois Press, 2002); and S.W. Pope, *Patriotic Games* (New York: Oxford University Press, 1997), chap. 3.

14. See R.W. Wheeler, *Jim Thorpe*, rev. ed. (Norman: University of Oklahoma Press, 1979).

15. As quoted in P.J. Graham and Horst Ueberhorst, eds., *The Modern Olympics* (Cornwall, NY: Leisure, n.d.), 32.

16. Richard D. Mandell, *The Nazi Olympics* (New York: Macmillan, 1971; Urbana: University of Illinois Press, 1987), 71. In addition to the works cited in note 13, see William J. Baker, *Jesse Owens* (New York: Free Press, 1986); Arnd Kruger, "The 1936 Olympic Games—Berlin," in Graham and Ueberhorst, *Modern Olympics*, 168–82; George Eisen, "The Voices of Sanity: American Diplomatic Reports from the 1936 Berlin Olympiad," *Journal of Social History* 11 (1984), 56–78; and Duff Hart-Davis, *Hitler's Games* (London: Macmillan, 1986).

17. Quoted in Kruger, "1936 Olympics," 171.

13
THE RISE AND DECLINE OF ORGANIZED WOMEN'S SPORTS, 1890–1960

*F*or more than two decades, no female athlete was better known than Mildred "Babe" Didrikson. In 1950 the Associated Press chose her as the Woman Athlete of the Half-Century. Her phenomenal feats in women's basketball, in track and field, and finally in golf earned her this distinction. Yet, while Didrikson demonstrated that a woman could achieve excellence in sport and even earn money from it, she was, for much of her life, looked upon with suspicion if not hostility. This was mainly because Americans were unable to separate Didrikson's athletic exploits from issues of gender.

Both men and women tended to identify sports with men and manliness rather than as gender neutral. Hence, the playing of sports by women invariably elicited responses that extended far beyond the playing field. Female athletes playing baseball, basketball, or running around a track called attention not merely to the physical differences between the sexes but also to the cultural constructions of femininity and masculinity as well. Although definitions of womanliness and manliness have changed over time, the dissonance arising from what was understood by the culture as a whole to be "womanhood" on the one hand and "masculine sport" on the other is fundamental to understanding the history of women's sport in the 1890–1960 era.[1]

THE ATHLETIC GIRL

The arrival of a widely heralded "athletic girl" at the turn of the twentieth century brought into sharp relief the incongruities of manly sports and Victorian womanhood. The athletic girl's enthusiasm for walking, riding, motoring, cycling, and playing competitive games crossed over an invisible but nonetheless firm line separating gender stereotypes. By insisting on the right to enjoy sport, the athletic girl also joined the wider demands of the "new woman" of the day who was seeking access to politics and the traditionally male professions.

In challenging the entrenched ideas of manly sport and Victorian womanhood, the athletic girl could draw some strength and inspiration from her predecessors. As early as the 1830s a few educators, health reformers, and feminists had urged moderate exercises to counter evidence of female frailty. In the postbellum era, the burgeoning number of women entering colleges presented exercise advocates with additional opportunities to advance their cause. Intellectual activity, it was widely believed, depleted women of vital energy. Women physical educators countered that properly regulated exercise could restore energy, reduce nervousness common to women, and prevent traumas to the female's reproductive system.

The effectiveness of this argument helped to wedge open the door for women physical educators to enter the halls of academe and establish themselves as a distinct profession. The Sargent School (opened in 1881) and the Boston Normal School of Gymnastics (founded in 1889) led the way; within a decade dozens of their graduates fanned out across the country. They set up separate physical education departments in the colleges, granted degrees to majors, and put females students through a regimen of exercise routines.

Rather than from the physical educators who emphasized exercises, the athletic girl probably drew more direct strength from a growing community of nineteenth-century upper-class sportswomen. Apart from having more discretionary income than women in the lower classes, women in the families of the "idle rich" could escape some of the confinement implied in the popular Victorian notions of a separate women's sphere and the cult of domesticity. Personal servants relieved them of a vast range of duties associated with household management and child care. Wealthy women were thus freer to exhibit family affluence by cultivating lives of conspicuous leisure and consumption. They dressed according to the latest fashions, hosted and attended expensive parties, and spent at least a part of their summers in either American or European resorts. Although initially most women engaged only in the social life of athletic and country clubs, the privacy of the clubs helped shield would-be women athletes from charges of being unfeminine.

Even before 1890, a few wealthy women inched their way toward a more active sporting life. They took up archery, croquet, tennis, and golf, all of which were individual rather than team sports, less demanding in terms of strength, and conducive to graceful physical movements. As early as 1877 women in Staten Island, New York, formed their own athletic club under the umbrella of the men's Staten Island Cricket and Base Ball Club.

The new sport of lawn tennis was apparently responsible for the founding of the Ladies' Club. In 1875, Mary Outerbridge, who had watched English army officers play tennis in Bermuda, convinced her brother to lay out a court at the Staten Island club. Wives and daughters of the club members soon took up the game with enthusiasm; the club sponsored the earliest women's tournaments, although the first women's national tennis championship took place in 1887 at the

Philadelphia Cricket Club. Within a decade, the Ladies' Club had grown to more than 200 members. Similar circles of sporting women emerged in the other major northeastern cities.[2]

Yet, upper-class women played with far more restraint than their male counterparts. When at play, the women usually wore regular, full-length dresses, including tight-laced corsets that emphasized full bosoms and hips. Play entailed the utmost discretion; for example, a woman did not dare place the mallet between her legs to execute a more effective croquet shot, or if playing tennis, smash overheads or run swiftly about the court. In this sense, elite female sports subtly reinforced gender differences rather than challenged orthodox views of women.

Elite women's sports also bolstered class differences. "Archery, like tennis, is too refined a sport to offer any attractions to the more vulgar elements of society," wrote Alfred B. Stary in 1883. The same might be said for tennis and golf. "Refined" women played suitably "refined" games, as Susan K. Cahn has observed, hence protecting upper-class women "from violating the boundary between proper womanhood and 'vulgar' women of other classes."[3]

The bicycling rage of the 1890s afforded one of the first widely publicized tests of the limits of female physical expression for middle-class women. Welcoming the freedom of movement afforded by the cycle, thousands of women took to "the wheel." They boldly rode astride the vehicle and donned shorter, more comfortable skirts. Most physicians, both male and female, welcomed the potential of mild exercise and the more practical forms of dress introduced by the bicycle but worried that cycling might lure young women away from the home and its duties, lead them to remote spots alone with men where they might succumb to seduction, or stimulate the genitals resulting in equally unimaginable horrors. Although the cyclists conjured up images of autonomous women emancipated from Victorian inhibitions, freer forms of female dress seemed to be the most enduring legacy of the cycling fad.[4]

It was out of this milieu of middle- and upper-class women, then, that the athletic girl, who was sometimes indistinguishable from the turn-of-the century "Gibson girl," arrived. Although possessing an aristocratic air, her popularity cut across age, class, and regional lines. Witty, sophisticated, and at ease on the golf course, the tennis court, or on horseback, she expanded the acceptable boundaries of physical freedom for women. Indeed, advertisers, the popular press, and health and beauty authorities began to establish the modern linkage between physical activity and female beauty. Dudley Sargent, a prominent physical educator, even added that "good form in figure and good form in motion . . . tend to inspire admiration in the opposite sex and therefore play an important part in what is termed 'sexual selection.' "[5]

Eleanora Sears, the winner of four national women's doubles championships in tennis, a mixed doubles championship, and a national women's squash championship, was perhaps the best-known example of the athletic girl. Her women's "firsts" included swimming four and one-half miles between Bailey's Beach and First Beach at Newport, automobile racing, and airplane flying. When in 1912 she wore pants, rode astride her horse, and requested permission to participate in a polo practice with men, the men not only rebuffed her but the Burlingame Mother's Club also censured her behavior as "immodest and wholly unbecoming a woman."[6] In their sports, women did not have the same luxury of self-abandonment permitted to men.

The negative reaction to Sears in 1912 reflected the continuing limits imposed by prevailing association of athletics with manhood. Ideally, the athletic girl should possess "a wholesome athletic air that does not smack too much of athletics." The relationship between the female athlete and romance (ultimately including marriage) always lurked in the background. "Even today, when athletics are fast opening to women, when tennis and golf and the rest are possible to them," explained Charlotte Perkins Gilman in 1898, "the two sexes are far from even in chances to play." Unlike male sports, women in their sports were "forced to court 'attention' [from men], when not really desirous of anything but amusement."[7]

EARLY WOMEN'S BASKETBALL

In the meantime, physical education teachers discovered that their female charges frequently preferred competitive sports to exercises. No sport exceeded the importance of basketball in defining the special character of women's sport in the schools. Soon after Naismith invented the game in 1891, it became the most popular sport among college women; they loved the freedom of movement and the vigorous competition it offered. On the basketball floor, women could assert themselves physically, which could instill feelings of confidence denied to women elsewhere in their lives. The sport also allowed them to indulge in emotions that they normally kept under tight control. Consider the evocation of feelings expressed in this poem that referred to an annual interclass tournament at a North Carolina normal school (teacher's college) in 1911:

> Sing a song of tournament!
> A week full of care,
> Colors waving, rooters raving
> Balls in the air!
> When the game is over,
> The winning class goes wild!
> They yell and squall like savages.
> But the losers all are riled.[8]

In most cases women played on class teams or in physical education classes, but a substantial number of colleges (especially outside of the Northeast) at one time or another fielded varsity teams. Interscholastic basketball may have been even more popular. Prior to 1925 over half the states scheduled high school championships for girls. Enthusiasm for the sport ran high in many places. Upon returning home from winning the Michigan state championship in 1905, the town of Marshall welcomed its heroines with "bonfires, 10,000 Roman candles, crowds, noise, Supt. Garfield, ex-mayor Porter, and all red-corpuscled Marshall."[9]

Since the popularity of women's basketball posed a serious challenge to the traditional gender order, it quickly encountered criticism. Women's basketball, opponents said, encouraged the growth of large muscles and thereby reduced the differences in body shapes between men and women. Basketball might also endanger the female reproductive system. Finally, the critics charged that basketball frequently unleashed uncontrollable passions to which women were especially prone. Behind this criticism lurked implications of a loss of sexual control. That across the country reports surfaced of young men scaling fences, peeking through gym windows from ladders, and employing binoculars to catch forbidden glances of young women playing basketball did nothing to reassure those who suspected that the sport might be unleashing the traditional bonds of sexual control.

Because they conceived of colleges both as parents in absentia for female students and as training grounds for the development of social graces essential to fulfilling the ideal of womanhood, college trustees, administrators, and faculties often objected to the varsity game. Intercollegiate games might entail travel away from campus, inadequate supervision, male coaches, performances before sexually mixed audiences, sacrificing modesty to the excitement of the game, and exhibiting aggressive behavior "unsuitable" for women. A former University of Nebraska student recalled that it was "not an unheard of thing to meet at a promenade a proud coed blushing behind a black eye received in the afternoon's practice."[10]

Women physical educators played a key role in shaping the history of women's basketball. By insisting that only trained women could properly manage women's sports in the schools, they tried with some success to carve out for themselves a special occupational domain. The construction of a professional network revolving around shared experiences in teachers' training colleges, participation in physical education associations, and personal friendships enhanced the power of women physical educators.

Control of the rulemaking process assisted the educators in limiting the strenuosity of the women's game and reducing tendencies toward the spectator domination of the sport. In the 1890s, Senda Berenson, director of physical education at Smith College, developed a modified set of rules for women. The men's rules, she decided, encouraged too much roughness, too much physical and emotional exertion, and the domination of play by the better athletes. Thus she prohibited the players from snatching the ball out of an opponent's hands, and a player was not allowed to move out of her designated area. To prevent intentional fouling, the women's rules by 1914 awarded an automatic point to the offended team plus a free throw to the victim of the foul. In 1899 a committee of educators led by Berenson induced the A.G. Spalding Company to publish these rules as the "Official Rules" of women's basketball. Several other sets of rules competed with

SCHOOLYARD GIRLS' BASKETBALL GAME In this early twentieth-century photo-graph in Lincoln, Nebraska, the young women apparently played by men's rules. Notice however, that there are 11 players. The woman on the left is described by an inscription on the photo as the "director."
(Nebraska State Historical Society)

Berenson's, and probably as late as 1914 half the girls in the country still played by boys' rules. Nonetheless, despite the apparent opposition of many players and fans, the distinctive women's game eventually triumphed and prevailed in most educational institutions until the 1960s.

Women educators developed a stand in opposition to all intercollegiate and interscholastic competition for girls. Pressure came partly from the "evils" associated with men's athletics. "The spirit of athletics in this country . . . that one must win at any cost—that defeat is an unspeakable disgrace, must be avoided in women's sport," warned Berenson in 1901.[11] Sharing assumptions similar to those of the boy-workers in the early twentieth century, they also thought that sports, if properly managed by trained adult women, could nurture social traits desirable in girls. By teaching valuable lessons in cooperation, properly supervised team sports could help offset the extreme individualism characteristic of society at large. In offering a critique of individualism such a stance placed the women educators in opposition to the dominant values of the day.

THE ARRIVAL OF WOMEN SPORTS' HEROES

The 1920s witnessed an extraordinary growth in women's athletics. Across the nation large numbers of women for the first time began to play golf, tennis, basketball, swim, and engage in other sports. Skill levels improved. In 1924, Sybil Bauer, a 20-year-old backstroker from Chicago, broke the world (men's) record in the backstroke and two years later Gertrude Ederle became only the sixth person to swim the English Channel. The leading women performers in golf, tennis, and swimming joined male athletes in becoming national celebrities. Consequently, women's sport in the 1920s became an important arena for sorting out and assessing popular meanings of womanhood and manhood.

The public responded to the female athletic heroes with mixed feelings. As part of the larger revolt in the 1920s against the confines of Victorian America, many welcomed the greater freedom represented in both the women athletes and the flappers. Both flourished in an era when female fashions broke sharply with the past, when the notions of feminine beauty were changing, when more physically demanding dance styles were introduced, and when female sexuality was accepted with more ease. "The American woman who proves herself to be adept in cowboy sports is to be found at the Pendleton Round-Up," reported an Oregon newspaper in 1925. "She is an exponent of modernism and proves the Victorian world is quite in oblivion, and that the woman of today is a true athlete."[12] Yet the public also expressed concerns that, in their pursuit of victory, the female athletic champions were departing too far from the past, that they were taking on too much of the "male" qualities of strength, determination, and aggressiveness.

Tennis stars Suzanne Lenglen of France and Helen Wills of the United States vividly revealed the public's mixed responses to champion women athletes.[13] Lenglen, who dominated the women's tennis world from 1919 to 1927, was tennis's version of the flapper. While Victorians had linked female beauty to character traits such as reticence and purity, the public of the 1920s admired Lenglen for her body shape, of which she exposed more than any previously renowned women's athlete, and for her physical movements. With seeming effortlessness, she leapt and glided about the court. She flaunted her sexuality. No previous woman had been so uninhibited—both on and off the court. "I just throw dignity to the winds," she reportedly said, "and think of nothing but the game."[14]

Helen Wills, who replaced Lenglen as the dominant woman player in the mid-1920s and retained that position until the mid-1930s, represented a less daring departure from past conceptions of womanhood. With her pigtails, schoolgirl costume, and placid temperament, she reassured those worried about the excesses of the flapper. The media hailed her as "The American Girl," or simply as "our Helen." And although "Little Miss Poker Face" wore a "false, unnatural front . . . like a cold gray veil," or it can be inferred like a man, when she played, off the court, sportswriters typically reported, she was epitome of femininity—a "gay, sprightly, pleasing young girl who could enjoy herself and be gracious in the process."[15]

Though Gertrude Ederle was from a working-class, ethnic background, the press depicted her as one who kept in perfect suspension malelike athletic performances with traditional femininity. When in 1926 Ederle became the first fe-male to swim the English Channel, the newspapers immediately acclaimed her as "America's Best Girl." Upon her return to the United States, New York gave her a reception that dwarfed the greeting extended to Sergeant Alvin York upon his re-turn from World War I. Movie, stage, and commercial offers poured in. A pair of songwriters composed a quick tribute: "You're such a cutie. You're just as sweet as tutti-frutti. Trudy, who'll be the lucky fellow?"[16]

Ederle's swim represented multiple victories. She practiced the virtues of Victorian domesticity. According to her mother, Gertrude developed her strength from doing household chores; she was a " 'plain home girl,' who preferred sewing and cooking to smoking, drinking, and going out with young men." The press, Ederle's family, and the politicians turned the swim into a patriotic occasion; Ederle herself said that "It was for my flag that I swam." German Americans took a special pride in the feat of an offspring of an immigrant family; some saw in Ederle hope for a reduction in the wartime antagonisms that had been directed toward German Americans. And that Ederle had bested the male mark for swim-ming the Channel by more than two hours seemed to belie the assumption that women were the "weaker sex." For women (and many men as well), Ederle blend-ed perfectly such older feminine virtues as modesty and domesticity with such newer female traits as strength and independence.[17]

Though never soaring to the heights of public acclaim reached by Ederle in 1926, Babe Didrikson remained in the public limelight far longer. Between 1930 and 1932 Didrikson broke American, Olympic, or world records in five separate track and field events. In 1930, 1931, and 1932 she was an "All-American" girls' basketball player and led her team, the Golden Cyclones, to the Amateur Athletic Union (AAU) women's national championship in 1931. As a golfer, both profes-sional and amateur, she had no peer; she won 34 of the 88 tournaments she en-tered. Reportedly, she bowled a 170 average, could punt a football 75 yards, and for short distances could swim close to world record times.

Growing up in a working-class culture that held female strength and as-sertiveness in higher esteem than did the middle and upper classes, Didrikson had no hesitation about joining the local boys in their games. At Beaumont (Texas) High School, she participated in all sports available to girls—volleyball, tennis, golf, bas-ketball, and swimming. In 1930 the Employers Casualty Company of Dallas offered her a job (ostensibly as a stenographer) to play for its Golden Cyclones basketball team. The company also sponsored her as the only member of its squad at the women's AAU track and field championships in 1932. In the space of three hours in a single afternoon, she won six gold medals and broke four world records—in the baseball throw, javelin, 80-meter hurdles, and high jump. At the 1932 Olympics, she shattered world records in the javelin, the 80-meter hurdles, and the high jump, though the Olympic officials disqualified her high jump because she had "dived" over the bar. Had women been permitted to enter more than three events in the Olympics, Didrikson would undoubtedly have won even more gold medals.

After her success at the 1932 Olympics, Didrikson tried to capitalize financially on her athletic skills and celebrity status, but opportunities for women

MILDRED "BABE" DIDRIKSON Shown here at the 1932 games held at Los Angeles, Didrikson was perhaps the world's greatest woman athlete in the first half of the twentieth century. Although she won great fame from sports, her success did little to alter the popular association of athletics with masculinity and maleness.
(Natural History Museum of Los Angeles County/ Seaver Center)

to profit from sports were virtually nonexistent. One of her few recourses was to become essentially an exhibitionist, to display her athletic prowess on the road, often as a sideshow to the main attraction. In 1934, she formed a mixed-gender basketball team that played local men's teams in small tank towns across the nation. The next year she pitched a few innings in spring training games for several major-league teams and that summer toured with the bearded House of David baseball team. Although her earnings were substantial for the Depression years, she disliked the life of an itinerant athlete. In the late 1930s she turned to a career as a professional golfer.

Didrikson's larger significance to women's sports is difficult to assess. While she won the admiration of millions of Americans for her feats and her uninhibited candor, her successes and behavior aroused deep-seated fears among those concerned about departures from traditional femininity. Paul Gallico, perhaps her severest critic among sports reporters, described Didrikson in her early years as a "muscle moll," "who never wore make-up, who shingled her hair until it was as short as a boy's . . . and who despised silk underthings as being sissy."[18] Her speech was always candid and sometimes earthy. When touring with the be-whiskered House of David team, a female spectator once asked Didrikson where her beard was. "I'm sittin' on 'em, just like you are!" she quipped.[19]

Her biographers concluded that "she was used as a kind of bogeywoman by mothers who wished to prevent their budding tomboy daughters from pursuing sports."[20] Perhaps in part due to her marriage to a professional wrestler, George Zaharias, in 1938, and in part to gain greater acceptance as a professional golfer, Didrikson cultivated a more feminine image in her later years. In a long headline, *Life* magazine put her alleged transformation from a "tomboy" into a "lady" bluntly: "Babe Is a Lady Now: The World's Most Amazing Athlete Has Learned to Wear Nylons and Cook for Her Huge Husband."[21] Journalists then took a special delight in reporting her skills in cooking, decorating, gardening, and other "housewifery arts." Such a portrait apparently helped to calm public anxieties arising from Didrikson's departures from traditional gender expectations.

THE WAR OVER TURF AND PRINCIPLES

As Didrikson's career illustrated, a sporting universe revolving around women from families with modest social origins began to flourish between the 1930s and the 1950s. Working-class women discovered expanded opportunities for sports in community-based programs. The community-based programs included sports sponsored by churches, Ys, settlement houses, city recreation departments, commercial or industrial concerns, and private promoters.

Industrial sports attracted the most public attention.[22] During the 1920s and continuing through the depressed 1930s and through the war years of the 1940s, assorted industries offered sports to all interested female employees. In one of the more successful programs, that of the Hawthorne Works of the Western Electric Company in Chicago, in 1923 over 500 women participated in bowling, 127 in horseback riding, and 96 in rifle shooting. Each fall the Works also scheduled a major track meet for women employees. Yet probably a majority of working women did not seize the opportunities offered by industrial recreation programs; they preferred the pleasures proffered by the amusement parks, dance halls, and movie houses or, if married, might find their spare time occupied with housekeeping.

A second kind of company-sponsored women's program entailed sports for superior female athletes. In most cases, company teams consisted of the better athletes selected from among existing female employees. But other firms were determined to build top-flight teams as a means of advertising. Colonel Melvorne McCombs of the Employers' Casualty Company in Dallas, Texas, systematically recruited high school stars to play on the company's female basketball team; only incidentally were the girls employed in clerical positions. The team grabbed public attention both for its victories and its exploitation of female sexuality. For uniforms McCombs substituted "panties of bright orange satin" and jerseys for the far more conservative bloomers, long stockings, and middy blouses common to women's teams of the 1920s. According to McCombs, the controversy over the team's brief apparel raised average game attendance from 150 to 5,000.

The growth of community-based sports during the 1920s encouraged women's participation in national and international competition. The all-male Amateur Athletic Union (AAU) responded by inaugurating a national swim meet in 1916, a track championship in 1924, and a basketball tournament in 1926. A few women had participated in women's golf, tennis, and archery exhibitions at the 1900 and 1904 Olympic Games. The United States sent a team of skaters and swimmers to the 1920 Games; the American women won four of five gold medals in swimming and diving and continued to dominate these events at the 1924 and 1928 Games.

In the meantime pressures from Europe led to the inclusion of women's track and field competition in the Olympic Games. In 1921, Alice Milliat founded the Féderative Sportive Féminine Internationale (FSFI) which sponsored the first Women's Olympic Games in Paris in 1922. The competition furnished by the new Women's Olympic Games convinced the Olympic officials to adopt a five-event track and field program for the 1928 Olympics. As part of the compromise, the FSFI then changed the title of its meets to the International Ladies' Games, which continued to be held until 1934.

These developments alarmed women physical educators. Partly, they saw the growth of highly competitive, male-dominated sports as an infringement on their professional turf. Only professionally trained women had the rightful authority and knowledge to direct the physical and moral development of young females, they insisted. Partly their objections were philosophical. They rejected the men's elitist athletic model that gave priority in resources and training to top-flight athletes. They also repeated past concerns about highly competitive sports endangering the health of young women and causing them to develop "masculine" mannerisms. In particular, they questioned the effects on women of engaging in "games of strife," such as track and field and basketball.

To counter these dangers and assert their control over women's athletics, the women physical educators launched an all-out assault on the AAU, Olympic officials, and the leaders of the community-based programs. Within the profession they worked through the Committee on Women's Athletics, founded in 1917. Outside the profession they found an ally in the National Amateur Athletic Foundation, founded in 1922. The next year the foundation established a special Women's Division comprised of leaders in women's education, the Girl Scouts, YWCAs, and women's clubs. With interlocking directorships and overlapping memberships, the two groups presented a united front.

The 1923 platform of the Women's Division served as a guiding principle for women's athletics until the late 1960s. Taking as its premise the democratic motto "a sport for every girl, and every girl in a game," it stated that women's athletics should "be protected from exploitation for the enjoyment of the spectator, the athletic reputation, or the commercial advantage of any school or organization. . . . " Furthermore, "individual accomplishment and the winning of championships" should be subordinated to universal participation.[23] By challenging the values of extreme individualism, intense competition, commercialism, and passive spectatorship, the educators not only found themselves at sharp odds with the dominant trends of the day but at the same time also offering a powerful critique of those trends.

To embody their principles in practice, physical educators in the Women's Division invented alternatives to interscholastic and intercollegiate athletics. These took four principal forms: intramurals, telegraphic meets, play days, and sports days, all of which had a player-centered orientation. A survey of 77 colleges taken in 1936 indicated that 74 percent had been involved in a telegraphic meet, 70 percent in a play day, and 41 percent in a sports day.[24] Telegraphic meets curbed the competitive spirit between schools by replacing face-to-face competition with telegraphed reports of performances and excluding spectators. Frequently, the colleges competed in only one activity. Play days, which brought together all the girls from several schools to a single site, minimized competitiveness by arbitrarily selecting girls from several schools to form teams. The play days also featured a wide array of informal contests and placed a high emphasis on social interaction among the girls. Sport days, on the other hand, did permit teams representing the colleges to play, but to ensure a player-centered orientation, the educators altered the rules of such games as basketball and refused to announce winners.

The Women's Division enjoyed more success at the college than at the high school level. While winning sweeping victories in closing down intercollegiate sports, a survey in the mid-1920s found that more than half of the respondents approved of interscholastic basketball for girls. Assisted by the financial exigencies of the Great Depression, women educators claimed credit for the discontinuation between 1931 and 1939 of 14 statewide high school basketball tournaments for girls.[25]

Yet in many places interscholastic basketball remained, especially in the smaller rural school districts of the South and Midwest where physical educators had little or no power. A classic example may have been Iowa. In 1925, educators in the larger school systems induced the Iowa High School Athletic Association to abolish the statewide basketball tourney for girls. However, the smaller schools, led by their high school superintendents and principals, promptly formed a rival organization to sponsor the continuation of a state tournament. With men serving as most of the coaches, sponsors, and organizers, in time Iowa girls' basketball came to rival the boys' in popularity.[26]

The publicity and sense of identity that the girls' teams provided to smaller communities overrode reservations that administrators may have had about the desirability of varsity sports for girls. "We really want our town to be on the map," explained a small-town high school principal in 1928.[27] In addition, a few educators bluntly challenged the fundamental premises of the 1923 platform of the Women's Division. "Physical weakness, menstrual periods, menopauses, etc. is a lot of cheap talk and poppy cock," exclaimed an irate Wisconsin principal. He opposed all efforts to "discourage interschool competition among high school girls."[28]

Outside the schools, the women educators and recreation leaders encountered even more formidable opposition to their efforts to modify or eliminate highly competitive sports for women. Newspapers frequently backed community-based women's teams, leagues, and tournaments. Municipal and industrial league programs were even more common. In Chicago, a site of more activity than most, Susan Cahn has found that in the early 1930s there were 15 women's teams in a

YMCA league, 105 in a Catholic Youth Organization's program, 92 in the Chicago American League, and 30 teams under the aegis of the Women's Basketball Association. All but 42 of these teams played by men's rules.[29] In World War II, due mainly to sponsorship of defense plants, women's community-based basketball continued its expansion. Local industrial basketball furnished the foundation for the AAU to offer the more skilled women opportunities to compete in its national tournament held annually from 1926 to the present.

AAU women's basketball violated nearly every principle of the Women's Division. The players wore brightly colored satin uniforms, thereby challenging the physical educators' credo of modesty. By selecting beauty queens from among the players competing in local and national tourneys, the AAU added sex appeal and tried to counter mannish images of their mainly working-class athletes. Critics claimed that the players abandoned all self-control. According to John R. Tunis's lurid account of an industrial league game, the women "pulled hair, hit one another viciously in the ribs with sharp elbows, tripped one another, tore one another's clothing, in fact did everything but play basketball."[30]

A few itinerant women's professional basketball teams appeared as early as the 1920s. The most famous and enduring of these was the All-American Red Heads, organized in 1936. The Red Heads toured the country playing mostly local men's teams. Reportedly by 1947, despite a five-year break due to World War II, the Red Heads had played before two million fans in 46 states. With players sporting wigs or dyed red hair, the team combined basketball and showmanship in a fashion similar to the Harlem Globetrotters. Much of the humor they generated revolved around gender. As one magazine put it, the Red Heads set up "the age-old contest between male brawn and female guile."[31] A female player might distract her male antagonist by running her hands through his hair or she might coax a male opponent to put his arms around her, only to have the referee call a foul.

The war against industrial league basketball extended deeper than matters of turf and principle. Industrial basketball mirrored class and sexual styles that were an anathema to middle- and upper-class physical educators. A product of working-class culture, industrial basketball included not only the game itself but also the sale of erotic titillation. While industrial basketball exploited the sexual attractions of women and the dominance of male coaches limited the chances for women professionals in these fields, the female athletes themselves rarely objected. Products of the gender expectations of their culture, they did not feel like victims. They were simply grateful for the opportunity to play organized basketball.[32]

FEMALE CHEERLEADERS

During the the 1920s and 1930s, the same decades that witnessed the growing popularity of women's sports, female cheerleaders began to stake out their own claims on the athletic world. Before that, cheerleading at athletic events had been almost, if not exclusively, a male domain. At the nation's first intercollegiate "football" contest in 1869 between Princeton and Rutgers, according to a press report, "some Nassau Hall residents let fly with a throaty 'Siss, boom, Ahhh!' . . . rocket cheer."[33] At first, as in the Princeton-Rutgers game, little if any planning or organization went into the cheers. A male student along the sidelines or a player on the bench might suddenly stand up and urge the spectators to shout their support for his team. But, by the 1890s, along the sidelines of football games across the nation, solitary male "yell captains," "rooter kings," "yell leaders," or "yell masters" stood with their backs to the game while exhorting the fans to root for the home team. By the 1920s, colleges routinely featured two or three male cheerleaders, who wore uniforms consisting of slacks and sweaters in school colors, used megaphones, and led synchronized yells. In that decade, the yell leaders symbolized the carefree undergraduate who lived mainly for the campus's social rather than its academic life.

A few female cheerleaders joined male squads in the 1920s. While cheerleading, as in the instance of sports, frequently offered young women a source of physical confidence and the pleasures of self-expression, the cheerleaders faced criticisms similar to the pioneers in women's athletics. Critics questioned the propriety of women displaying themselves publicly and engaging in unseemly jumping and yelling. In addition, in performing the same acrobatic stunts as males, females might harm their reproductive capacities. Loud yelling might also damage their voices. However, unlike the case of women's sports, the defenders of female cheerleading were able to draw on the dominant culture's growing emphasis on female appearance. While young women might not be able to do the acrobatic feats of the men, a Midwestern advocate of female cheerleading confessed in 1938, "girls are more magnetic in appearance and will become the center of attention for the crowd and the leading of the cheers [by them] will, therefore, be easy."[34]

Those who selected cheerleaders frequently chose appearance before skill. "Take away the cheerleaders from the hundreds of high school basketball games in the state and what do you have?" queried a North Carolina newspaper. "Just a dull display of physical prowess."[35] In many places by the mid-1930s, high school and college cheerleaders appear to have held more esteemed positions on campuses than varsity women athletes. At any rate, the heroine of a 1934 young adult novel dreamed of being "eligible for the highest honor for girls in high school, the much coveted position of cheer leader."[36] Nonetheless, female cheerleaders did not become widely recognized sex symbols until after World War II. By then, the contrasts between the female cheerleaders and male players had become more vivid than ever before, and, hence, female cheerleading enhanced the "manliness" of male athletic contests.

In the post-World War II era, the growing celebration of cheerleading, majorettes, and beauty queens at male athletic contests meshed with a massive effort by the media and the fashion industry to "refeminize" the American woman. During the war the popular culture had blended the glamor of Hollywood stars with the man-sized jobs of Rosie the Riveters, but once the war ended the movies, magazines, radio, and television began to feature women in terms of marriage, full figures, billowing skirts, carefully coifed hair, and bountifully applied makeup. In

1950, *Preview*, a college basketball magazine, explained its choice of Norma Jean McMillan as "Queen of North Carolina Basketball: 'Miss McMillan is . . . a cheerleader, but she was chosen by *Preview* because we think she is a very pretty young woman. No other reason.'"[37] By the 1950s, the media frequently presented cheerleaders as a blend of the wholesome girl-next-door and as a voluptuous sex object.

Along with cheerleading, the growing popularity of tournament and homecoming beauty queens accentuated the postwar impulse to sharpen female-male distinctions. The selection and reign of queens could heighten the eroticism at sporting events. In 1950, the queen of the Dixie Classic, Tulane student Sarah French, presented Sammy Ranzino with the championship trophy. She then kissed him with such ardor that he dropped the trophy.

By mid-century, the growing polarization of what were considered appropriate "masculine" and "feminine" activities not only encouraged the feminization and erotization of cheerleading but also led to a decline in varsity women's sports. In the 1920s, the public seemed for the most part to take for granted the femininity of women student athletes; for example Elizabeth Newitt, a star basketball player at Charlotte, North Carolina's Central High School, was voted the school's most attractive student. But after the war, suspicions of "mannishness" and even lesbianism increasingly accompanied women's sports. Having already retreated from support for women's varsity sport, women's physical educators frequently accommodated the new emphasis on femininity by giving less attention to the physical fitness and more to the appearance of their charges. Perhaps illustrative of the switch in emphasis was the fact that earlier in the century members of a Charlotte Central High School team had called themselves the "Amazons." However, a postwar Charlotte annual dubbed a high school physical education class "Our Glamazons."[38]

THE RISE AND DECLINE OF WOMEN'S SOFTBALL AND BASEBALL

As a mass-participatory sport, softball took the nation by storm during the 1930s and 1940s. Versions of the game had been played indoors or in restricted outdoor spaces as early as the 1880s, but for reasons that remain unclear it failed to win much of a following until the 1930s. Requiring less space than baseball, relatively inexpensive, and the beneficiary of New Deal public works projects, softball satisfied the recreational needs of the Great Depression. The Amateur Softball Association, formed in 1934, offered championship play to both men and women. Play by defense workers during World War II and technical advances in outdoor lighting provided additional stimuli to softball's growth. By 1946, the *New York Times* estimated that 600,000 teams played before 150 million spectators.[39]

Girls and women took to the sport with enthusiasm. Because of the larger, "softer" ball and a smaller diamond, the game seemed particularly suitable to women, youngsters, and less brawny men. In Chicago and Los Angeles, the two major urban centers of softball during the 1930s, the game was especially popular among working-class women. Meeting a need for cheap entertainment during the

Depression and serving as an agency of community cohesion, small-town women's teams also prospered. Indeed, in such towns women softball players, like their counterparts on high school basketball teams, sometimes became local heroes.

Toward the end of the 1930s and in the 1940s, the women's game acquired a more masculine image. In particular women at the higher levels of play tended to play with the power, energy, and speed traditionally associated with men. The working-class origins of the top players also contributed to women's softball growing reputation as a tough, manly sport. According to the press, women players often acted and looked like male players. "Give 'em a cud of tobacco," wrote Robert Yoder in the *Saturday Evening Post* in 1943, "and these softball players would look just like their big-league brothers."[40]

Familiar with the popularity of women's softball in Chicago and worried that big-league baseball might be closed down during World War II, Philip K. Wrigley, chewing gum magnate and owner of the Chicago Cubs, came up with the idea of organizing a professional women's league. Initially employing a 12-inch ball, 65-feet base paths, and underhanded pitching, the All-American Girls Softball League (changed two years later to "Baseball") began play in 1943 with four teams. Its 108-game schedule attracted 176,000 fans, which, according to one

1947 ALL-AMERICAN GIRLS BASEBALL LEAGUE STARS This league tried to avoid a a "masculine" look by insisting upon a "feminine" appearance.
(State Historical Society of Wisconsin)

estimate, was "a higher percentage of the population [in the cities served by the league] than major league baseball ever [drew] in its greatest attendance years."[41] At the peak of its popularity, the league attracted nearly a million fans annually.

Arthur Meyerhoff, who was the league's longtime operator, consciously sold the women's game as a novel exhibition of feminine beauty and masculine playing skills. A league handbook put Meyerhoff's point bluntly: "The more feminine the appearance of the performer, the more dramatic the performance."[42] To ensure a more feminine look than that of typical softball players, short skirts were mandatory and the league required that the players attend a charm school conducted by Helena Rubenstein's famed Chicago-based beauty salon and finishing school. There they learned how to apply makeup, fix their hair, and display proper feminine social graces.

Although the finishing school program was abandoned after two years, the league's dress code was more stringent than ever. "MASCULINE HAIR STYLING? SHOES? COATS? SHIRTS? T-SHIRTS ARE BARRED AT ALL TIMES" read the code of 1951.[43] Whereas ejection from a game by the umpire could cost a player a $10 fine, a much stiffer penalty of $50 awaited the player who appeared "unkempt" in public. That the league recruited no black players reflected not only the racism of the day but the prevailing white stereotypes of female beauty as well.

While seeking to conform to traditional notions of femininity and beauty, the All-American Girls Baseball League entertained several million fans and offered nearly 500 women the opportunity to play professional baseball. Beginning in Kenosha and Racine, Wisconsin, South Bend, Indiana, and Rockford, Illinois, the league at its peak fielded clubs in ten medium-size Midwestern cities. In the 1950s financial woes arising mostly from declining attendance beset the league, and it folded in 1954.

The collapse of the All-American Girls Baseball League was part of a larger trend. With the huge exodus of inner-city residents to the suburbs and the growing popularity of television during the postwar era, Americans turned increasingly to at-home diversions (see Chapter 14). Not only did minor- and major-league baseball attendance suffer, but the proportionate number of men and women playing softball declined as well. The popularity of women's AAU basketball, which had reached an all-time high in the 1940s, also plummeted in the 1950s. Likewise, occasional "powder puffs," girls playing football on college campuses in the 1940s, disappeared.

The Girls Baseball League, as well as the women's softball and basketball players, encountered additional difficulties. During the war industrial workplaces welcomed women, but once the war was over, pressures mounted for women to retreat into the home. In the midst of the Cold War, as the United States sought to juxtapose its way of life with the Soviet Union, a more restrictive conception of femininity, one revolving around marriage, home, and family, once again won public favor. The revived cult of domesticity, along with a rising postwar homophobia that identified female athletics with lesbianism, dampened the enthusiasm for women's sports.[44]

CONCLUSION

For much of the twentieth century, women's sports can be separated into distinct spheres. One consisted of upper-class and upper-middle-class women. Private clubs provided homes for their golf, tennis, swimming, and other more "refined" sports. The schools and colleges offered a second sporting arena for women. At the college level the women were likely to come from the upper ranks of society as well, but high school sports, especially in smaller towns, included females from the other social strata. Within educational institutions, physical educators exercised a powerful influence over women's sports. They opposed both interscholastic and intercollegiate games for women. Industries, private promoters, and municipal recreation leaders supplied women with a third world of sport. Their sports programs, which often featured outstanding athletes and teams, tended to attract women from the working class. Although individual women bridged these three universes of sports, in most instances club, school, and industrial sports remained rigidly separated.

Considerations of sex and gender accompanied all aspects of women's sports. While reflecting the wider quest by the "new woman" at the turn-of-the century for greater freedom from Victorian constraints, "athletic girls" such as Eleanora Sears quickly encountered cultural limitations on their opportunities to pursue sports. The images if not the realities of the women sports heroes of the 1920s mirrored a more liberal conception of female sexuality, but the public continued to view sport in terms of men and masculinity. The Great Depression and World War II expanded opportunities for working-class women to play softball and industrial league basketball, but then the postwar era witnessed a general contraction in opportunities for women to enjoy equality with men in the world of sports.

NOTES

1. For the conceptualization and content of this chapter, I am especially indebted to Susan K. Cahn, *Coming on Strong: Gender and Sexuality in Twentieth Century Sport* (New York: Free Press, 1994), and Pamela Grundy, *Learning to Win: Sports, Education, and Social Change in Twentieth-Century North Carolina* (Chapel Hill: University of North Carolina Press, 2001). See also Cindy L. Himes, "The Female Athlete in American Society, 1860–1940," unpub. Ph.D. diss., University of Pennsylvania, 1984, and Allen Guttmann, *Women's Sports: A History* (New York: Columbia University Press, 1991). For late nineteenth-century attitudes, see Patricia Vertinsky, *The Eternally Wounded Woman: Women, Doctors and Exercise in the Late Nineteenth Century* (Manchester, UK:

University of Manchester Press, 1990; Urbana: University of Illinois Press, 1993). For historiography and theory, see the Spring 1994 issue of *Journal of Sport History*.

2. See esp. Himes, "Female Athlete," chap. 1, and Donald J. Mrozek, *Sport and the American Mentality, 1880–1920* (Knoxville: University of Tennessee Press, 1983), chap. 5.

3. Cahn, *Coming on Strong*, 15.

4. See esp. Himes, "Female Athlete," 117–21; James Whorton, *Crusaders for Fitness* (Princeton, NJ: Princeton University Press, 1982), 321–30; and Sarah A. Gordon, "'Any Desired Length': Negotiating Gender through Sports Clothing, 1870–1925," in Philip Scranton, ed., *Beauty and*

Business (New York: Routledge, 2001), 24–51. For the view that cycling had more substantial results in freeing women from Victorian restraints than mine, see Cahn, *Coming on Strong*, 15–16, and Patricia Marks, *Bicycles, Bangs, and Bloomers: The New Woman in the Popular Press* (Lexington: University of Kentucky Press, 1990), chap. 6.

5. Quoted in Cahn, *Coming on Strong*, 20–21.

6. Phyllis Hollander, *100 Greatest Women in Sports* (New York: Atheneum, 1976), 59.

7. Quotations in L.W. Banner, *American Beauty* (New York: Knopf, 1983), 157, and C.P. Gilman, *Women and Economics* (Boston: Small, Maynard, 1898), 308–09.

8. Quoted in Grundy, *Learning to Win*, 48.

9. Quoted in D.B. Van Dalen and B.L. Bennett, *A World History of Physical Education* 2d ed. (Englewood Cliffs, NJ: Prentice Hall, 1971), 451. For more detailed treatment of sports in the schools, see Himes, "Female Athlete," chaps. 3 and 4, and an illuminating essay, Pamela Dean, " 'Dear Sisters' and 'Hated Rivals': Athletics and Gender at Two New South Women's Colleges, 1893–1920," in Patrick Miller, ed., *The Sporting World of the Modern South* (Urbana: University of Illinois Press, 2002), chap. 3.

10. Quoted in R.N. Manley, *The Centennial History of the University of Nebraska* (Lincoln: University of Nebraska Press, 1969), 305.

11. Quoted in R.A. Smith, "The Rise of Basketball for Women in Colleges," *Canadian Journal of History of Sport and Physical Education* 1 (1970), 24.

12. *East Oregonian*, souvenir ed., September 17, 1925.

13. See Larry Englemann, *The Goddess and the American Girl: The Story of Suzanne Lenglen and Helen Wills* (New York: Oxford University Press, 1988), and the treatment by Cahn, in *Coming on Strong*, 47–51.

14. Quoted in "Decidedly Unconquerable is Mlle. Lenglen Tennis Champion," *Literary Digest* 62 (September 13, 1919), 80.

15. Paul Gallico, *Farewell to Sport* (New York: Knopf, 1938), 49–50.

16. *New York Times*, August 7, 1926.

17. For quotations and interpretations in this paragraph, see Himes, "Female Athlete," 224–37.

18. Gallico, *Farewell to Sport*, 239.

19. As quoted in Himes, "Female Athlete," 251.

20. W.O. Johnson and N.P. Williamson, *"Whatta Gal:" The Babe Didrickson Story* (Boston: Little, Brown, 1977), 132. See also Susan Cayleff, *Babe* (Urbana: University of Illinois Press, 1995).

21. Quoted in Cahn, *Coming on Strong*, 216.

22. See esp. ibid., 42–44, and Himes, "Female Athlete," 190–206.

23. Quoted in Ellen Gerber, "The Controlled Development of Collegiate Sport for Women, 1923–1936," *Journal of Sport History* 2 (1975), 11.

24. Cited in ibid., 3.

25. A.A. Sefton, *The Women's Division* (Stanford, CA: Stanford University Press, 1941), 44. For the classic statement of a leader in women's physical education, see Mabel Lee, "The Case for and against Intercollegiate Athletics," *Research Quarterly* 2 (May 1931).

26. See J.A. Beran, *From Six-on-Six to Full Court Press: A Century of Iowa Girls' Basketball* (Ames: Iowa State University Press, 1993).

27. Quoted in J.R. Tunis, "Women and the Sport Business," *Harper's Monthly* 159 (1929), 217. For a sophisticated discussion of the role of women's high school basketball in local communities, see Grundy, *Learning to Win*, chap. 5.

28. Quoted in Cahn, *Coming on Strong*, 90–91.

29. Ibid., 93, 206–28.

30. Tunis, "Women and the Sport Business," 214. For women's AAU basketball, see esp. Mary Jo Festle, *Playing Nice: Politics and Apologies in Women's Sports* (New York: Columbia University Press, 1996), chap. 2.

31. John Kord Lagemann, "Red Heads, You Kill Me!" *Collier's* (February 8, 1947), 65. See also William O. Johnson and Nancy Williamson, "All Red, So Help Them Henna," *Sports Illustrated* 40 (May 6, 1974), 76ff.

32. See esp. Cahn, *Coming on Strong*, 108–09, and Grundy, *Learning to Win*, 145–57.

33. Quoted in Mary Ellen Hanson, *Go! Fight! Win! Cheerleading in American Culture* (Bowling Green, OH: Bowling Green University Popular Press, 1995), 10. See also Grundy, *Learning to Win*, 246–55, 285–90; and Michael Oriard, *King Football: Sport and Spectacle in the Golden Age of Radio and Newsreels, Movies and Magazines, the Weekly and the Daily Press* (Chapel Hill: University of North Carolina Press, 2001), 280–88.

34. Quoted in Hanson, *Go! Fight! Win!*, 21.

35. Quoted in Grundy, *Playing to Win*, 246.

36. Quoted in Hanson, *Go! Fight! Win!*, 21.

37. Quoted in Grundy, *Playing to Win*, 247.

38. Ibid., 254.

39. Cited in Cahn, *Coming on Strong*, 141.

40. As quoted in B.G. Rader, *Baseball* (Urbana: University of Illinois Press, 1992), 158.

41. Ibid.

42. As quoted in Cahn, *Coming on Strong*, 150.

43. Ibid., 151.

44. See esp. ibid., chaps. 5–7.

14
THE SETTING OF ORGANIZED SPORTS SINCE 1950

"When the Dodgers left Brooklyn [in 1958]," recalled a fan 25 years later, "we lost our innocence forever. Love and loyalty, we were shattered to hear, were only so much mush to the people in power."[1] But one man in power, Dodger's owner Walter O'Malley, had his reasons. No matter that the Dodgers had been one of the most prosperous franchises in major-league baseball during the previous five years. Ebbets Field, the home of the Dodgers, seated only 35,000 fans, had parking places for only 700 cars, and was located in a decaying neighborhood. The future of baseball in Brooklyn, O'Malley said, depended upon the construction of a larger sports facility, one that included ample parking and that could be reached easily by motorists. While New York officials dallied, Los Angeles promised this and more. As a site for a new stadium, the city offered Chavez Ravine to O'Malley, 300 acres in downtown Los Angeles with easy access to several freeways. In addition, Los Angeles provided O'Malley with an uncontested media market in the nation's third largest metropolitan area.

The decision of O'Malley to transfer the Dodgers from the East to the West Coast exemplified two of the most fundamental external forces shaping the contours of organized sports in the post-1950 era. One was the rapid growth of new metropolises and the other was the new technological marvel of television.

THE SPRAWLING METROPOLISES

By the 1990s sprawling metropolitan areas, which consisted of one or more large cities, scattered suburbs, and satellite cities, become the homes for three out of four Americans. The 37 largest metropolises alone contained nearly half of the nation's population. Metropolises in the Sunbelt states of the South and Southwest grew faster than those in the Northeast. Los Angeles, San Francisco, Dallas–Ft. Worth, and Houston climbed into the top ten, pushing aside such older areas as St. Louis, Cleveland, Pittsburgh, and Baltimore.

Professional sports teams soon mirrored these changes. Aided by jet air travel, sports entrepreneurs moved to exploit the new population centers. They relocated existing teams and created additional franchises. In 1950 only 42 major-league professional franchises existed, and these were located mostly in a tier of industrial states that extended from the Northeast to the upper Midwest.

By 1990 the figure had swollen to over 100. As early as 1946 entrepreneurs had planted professional football teams in both Los Angeles and San Francisco. In the same year baseball's Pacific Coast (minor) League petitioned unsuccessfully for major-league status, but big-league baseball did not invade the Sunbelt until 1958 when the Brooklyn Dodgers and the New York Giants transferred to Los Angeles and San Francisco, respectively. By 1990 no major metropolitan area in the nation was without at least one big-league franchise.

In baseball, relocation preceded expansion. The owners first abandoned the smaller cities that hosted two teams. In 1953 the Boston Braves moved to Milwaukee, in 1954 the St. Louis Browns, to Baltimore, and in 1955 the Philadelphia Athletics to Kansas City, leaving behind the Red Sox, Cardinals, and Phillies. Then came the transfer of the Dodgers and the Giants to the Pacific Coast. In 1960 a congressional investigation that threatened to reverse baseball's exemption from the antitrust laws, the threat of competition from a proposed third major league (the Continental League headed by Branch Rickey), and the willingness of investors to pay $1.8 million (plus several million dollars for the purchase of players from other clubs) for a new franchise led both leagues to announce plans for expansion. By 1998, each big league had doubled—from 8 to 16—the number of its franchises. (For the expansion of professional football and basketball, see Chapter 15.)

By offering professional franchises subsidized playing areas, the sprawling metropolises often abetted relocation and expansion. To be "big league," cities thought they had to have a professional sports team. To attract such teams, cities increasingly had to provide potential franchises with generous terms. In the 1960s, 70s, and 80s, local governments went on a stadium-building binge. Of the 28 teams in the National Football League, for example, 26 played in city, county, or state-built facilities. In the early 1960s the price tag on a modest stadium ran to some $30 million, but Houston's Astrodome, the first stadium with a roof for all-season play, cost $45 million to complete in 1965. The cost of the Astrodome paled before that of the Louisiana Superdome, which mounted to at least $300 million before it was finished in 1975. To cover only the operating deficit of the Superdome cost Louisiana taxpayers $8 million annually.

As the cathedral represented the spirit of the Middle Ages and the great railroad terminal that of the nineteenth century, publicly financed sports stadia were seen as the quintessential symbol of the modern city by their supporters. Not only could the edifices serve as great cultural monuments, enthusiasts argued, but they could also stimulate downtown revitalization and lure tourist and investment dollars to the city. Several team owners seized the advantage that such thinking made possible. They presented cities with an ultimatum: either the cities build new stadia (or extend other specified subsidies) or the franchise would move elsewhere.

More than 20 percent of the new structures were built outside the downtown area, usually in a suburban satellite city but within easy access of freeways. For example, the Patriots football team moved out of Boston to Foxboro, Massachusetts, where they renamed themselves the New England Patriots; the Dallas Cowboys encamped at Irving, Texas; the Texas Rangers located at Arlington, Texas; both the football Giants and Jets departed from New York City to northern New Jersey; and the Detroit Lions moved to Pontiac, Michigan, 25 miles from downtown Detroit. Suburban facilities often permitted easier access to cars and to more affluent fans, while providing an escape from the congestion, dirt, and perils of the inner city.

Critics of public assistance for sports franchises responded that (1) cities should use the money for the resolution of more pressing problems, (2) building stadia or arenas in the suburbs simply encouraged the further decay of downtown areas, (3) corruption in financing and construction resulted in costs far exceeding original estimates and (4) in effect, all residents subsidized the entertainment of "the advantaged." Yet opponents rarely blocked stadium-building projects. In the late 1980s nearly two dozen of the largest 65 metropolitan areas built new facilities,

THE PONTIAC SIVERDOME The Pontiac Silverdome, located near Detroit Michigan, reflects the decline of the inner city and the growth of independent suburbs.
(General Motors Corp., Pontiac, Michigan)

many of which were the domed variety. Enthusiasm ran so high for stadia and arenas that several cities even built them before receiving assurance of a major-league franchise.[2]

The 1990s introduced yet another era of sports facilities. One feature of the new era was the building of "retroparks" for baseball. In 1992 Baltimore opened the first retropark, Camden Yards, which combined the fan intimacy of parks built early in the twentieth century with the latest high-tech razzmatazz. Camden Yards not only featured an asymmetrical playing area and natural grass, but also a view of downtown Baltimore, escalators, elevators, climate-controlled lounges, and luxury suites that could be leased for a minimum of $75,000 annually. A second feature of the new era was the naming of parks after corporations. Earlier parks might be simply called "municipal stadium," or "memorial stadium," or named after the team's owner, but in the 1990s and in the first years of the twenty-first century—for a price up to $50 million—arenas and stadia took on such corporate names as Networks Associates Coliseum (Oakland Raiders), Safeco (Seattle Mariners), PSINet (Baltimore Ravens), and Papa John's Cardinal Stadium (University of Louisville Cardinals).

A third feature of the new era was a growing reliance by professional sport franchises and colleges on the patronage of more affluent fans. In the 2001 season, the average household income of fans attending Baltimore Orioles games was $87,000. No longer could middle-class families afford to attend big-league ball games regularly. With more seating set aside for the rich in luxury boxes and ticket prices soaring, fans increasingly reflected the nation's rapidly escalating inequalities in income and wealth.

By 2000, the experience of attending a major sporting event had changed radically as well. Operating on the premise that the game itself could not hold the fan's attention, professional and college sports filled every moment of the fan's time with an unending profusion of images on big screens and a deafening infusion of prerecorded sound. Fans found themselves bombarded with loud music, big-screen replays, and big-screen commercials. A father had to forget about turning to his daughter to discuss the shortstop's remarkable stop of a hard-hit ball deep in the hole; she might not be able to hear him. Almost nothing in the experience of the game went unmediated. In vital respects attending a game resembled more and more what one saw on television, except that the music and ads were much louder.

THE INNER CITY AND THE SUBURBS

Decaying inner cities and fast-growing suburbs affected metropolitan leisure patterns in other ways. In the first half of the twentieth century, the lives of city dwellers had revolved mostly around the central business district. Even those residing in the suburbs used street railways to make their way downtown to work, shop, and find recreation. For amusement, the inner city offered shopping streets, restaurants, movies, indoor arenas, saloons, and for the pursuit of high culture, concert halls, and the theater. Baseball parks, football fields, and amusement parks, though located outside the central business district, could be cheaply and quickly reached by mass transit.

After World War II, the suburbs pulled both jobs and the more prosperous families away from the inner city. Soaring automobile sales, subdividers with a knack for building houses en masse, the construction of miles and miles of multi-lane freeways, and federal subsidies to new homeowners transformed cornfields and cow pastures into acres and acres of suburbs. In addition, manufacturers, retail outlets, corporate headquarters, and dozens of other businesses relocated along the beltways and the intersections of arterial highways. By the mid-1960s more jobs existed in the busy suburban rings than in the inner city. In short, the peripheral regions of cities became functionally independent of the older central business districts.

The creation of the independent suburbs in combination with television spelled disaster for inner-city commercial recreation. Only the poorer people, most of whom were blacks or Hispanics, remained in the city's core. Unless required to do so for employment, suburbanites rarely went downtown anymore. For example, one-fourth of the residents of a well-to-do Philadelphia suburb in the 1980s made their way downtown less than twice a month while another fifth did so less than twice a year. Without the patronage of the more affluent suburbanites, inner-city bars and restaurants closed their doors and movie attendance skidded downward. Attendance at major- and minor-league baseball, inner-city high school sports, and boxing and wrestling all dropped precipitously.[3] Although downtown renewal projects in the 1970s and 1980s partly reversed the tide, the relative decline of the city's original core seemed to be permanent.

For recreation, inner-city residents improvised as best they could. As with the working class of the past, ghetto leisure usually divided along gender lines. Women spent much of their spare time watching television, visiting on their front stoops, or, if it was Sunday, attending church services. Men watched television, too, but they were more likely than women to gather on street corners, in local bars, or in city parks. With restricted opportunities for recreation and inspired by the athletic stars they watched on television, ghetto youth spent far more time than their suburban counterparts in practicing and playing team sports. In particular, boys and young men devoted countless hours to "pickup" basketball games on outdoor courts. For many inner-city youth, developing expertise in sports seemed to offer one of the easiest, most lucrative, and most glamorous routes out of the ghetto.[4]

Nothing distinguished the independent suburbs from the inner city more than the automobile. Suburbanites drove their cars to their workplaces, schools, and shopping malls. The car became a supreme instrument of pleasure as well. Families drove them to drive-in restaurants, drive-in movies, and even drive-in churches, leading one historian to conclude that postwar suburban life could be summed up as a "drive-in culture."[5] Even working-class families now had available a highly flexible means of escaping on weekends, holidays, and vacations from the cities to the countryside. In addition to one or more cars used for convenience, families purchased record numbers of campers, pick-up trucks, jeeps, and other vehicles designed for recreation. For suburban teenagers of all classes, ownership of a car became a rite of passage; they customized their cars, transforming them into personalized art objects.

While the automobile pulled suburbanites back and forth between home and the outside world, television pulled one way—toward the home. "And so the monumental change began in our lives and those of millions of other Americans," recalled one man about the effects of his family's purchase of their first television set in 1950. "More than a year passed before we again visited a movie theater. Money that previously would have been spent for books was saved for TV payments. Social evenings with friends became fewer and fewer still." By 1956 three out of four families owned television sets; those families watched television on an average of 35 hours each week.

Novelty alone did not account for the new medium's magnetism; Americans persisted long afterward in spending a staggering amount of their free time watching television. A study 30 years later of Muncie, Indiana, found that the median viewing time for all families was 28 hours per week. The significance of such figures could not be dismissed by the argument that families had their sets turned on without really watching them. Viewers in Muncie, at any rate, could recall substantial amounts of program content.[6]

Television and the automobile, along with central heating, air conditioning, and more spacious houses and yards, contributed to a general shift in leisure from public places to the privacy of the home. Do-it-yourself projects, home repairs, and conquering the "crabgrass frontier" consumed more of the suburbanite's spare time. "No man who owns his own house and lot can be a Communist," observed one of the mass builders of suburban housing in 1948. "He has too much to do."[7] Indeed, for many, the house became a self-sufficient recreation center, or a "family playpen," as an anthropologist aptly put it. The enjoyment of children and "family togetherness," especially according to the popular media of the 1950s, became virtually a moral obligation.

Critics often charged that the suburbs were homogeneous, but in fact they were divided by educational levels, occupations, and race. Blue-collar working-class families cultivated a lifestyle distinct from white-collar families. In the past, both married and unmarried workingmen had spent much of their spare time in a homosocial milieu of saloons, billiard halls, lodges, union halls, and street corners. Similar patterns persisted, especially among younger, unmarried workers, in the postwar-era suburbs. Even married men frequently continued to gamble, hunt, and fish in all-male groups. But "night(s) out with the boys" became far less common. Husbands stayed home more with their families watching television, working on cars, or doing home repairs. Entire families loaded into cars or campers for weekend boating, swimming, or fishing excursions. Instead of neighbors or work mates, families more frequently joined relatives scattered over the larger metropolitan area for backyard barbecues and other social occasions. When younger men played softball or bowled, wives usually accompanied them as spectators or as participants. After the games, players and their families then retired together to a local bar or pizza parlor for food and refreshments.[8]

Suburban white-collar professionals occupied a quite different world of leisure. They entertained more in the home, had more social interaction with non-family members, and belonged to more voluntary associations than did their suburban counterparts. Country clubs grew in membership and numbers, though at rates slower than those in the 1920s or what might have been expected from increases in population and income. As a partial substitute for the country club, developers of expensive suburban housing sometimes provided residents with clubhouses, swimming pools, tennis courts, and golf courses. With jet travel at their disposal and infusions of additional income, the more affluent Americans ranged farther away from home for their amusements—to tennis ranches in the Sunbelt, to watering spots in Hawaii, the Caribbean, or the Mediterranean, and to ski slopes in the Rocky Mountains or the Alps.

THE NEW INDIVIDUALISM AND SPORTS

Merging with an expanding consumer capitalism, the counterculture of the tumultuous 1960s and early 1970s ushered in a new era of American cultural history. At its center was what may be described as a new individualism.[9] The new individualism entailed a "rights revolution." African Americans, women, youth, gays, Native Americans, Hispanics, welfare recipients, the handicapped, the elderly, and even consumers (among others) pressed forward claims for greater equality, relief from discrimination, and additional opportunities. In the past, the freedom for individuals to do as they wished had been hemmed in by custom, religious beliefs, and ties with others, but the new individualism called for a far more radical form of freedom. It entailed a view of life as an endless array of unfettered and ever-changing individual choices. Accordingly, individuals were or should be free to do as they wished, to buy consumer goods of their own choosing, to do what they pleased in their private lives (and to a substantial degree their public lives as well), and to make and break personal ties freely. In its ultimate formulation, the new individualism took as its primary commandment; each person should "do their own thing."

In the 1960s and early 1970s the new individualism, at least in its more radical forms, clashed with the world of organized sports. While the proponents of sport valued and rewarded self-sacrifice, self-restraint, and unquestioning obedience to authority, the new individualism prized fun, expressing one's self, and realizing fully one's individuality. Reflective of the new individualism were the results of a 1959 study of nine high schools. It found that membership in the "leading crowd" required boys to be athletes and girls to have sparkling personalities and good looks. But both boys and girls placed a high value on "having a good time." "A hedonism drains off the energies of most high school students," concluded James Coleman, the principal investigator.[10]

In the context of having fun and doing your own thing, the new, more expressive forms of individualism in the 1960s and early 1970s spawned a widespread critique of organized sports. "What has happened to the intrinsic fun in sports?" asked critics. Others challenged the central tenet of sports ideologues, the idea that sports built character. Within a range of only a few years a rash of books by professional athletes raised these and similar issues. NBA star Bill Russell examined race in professional basketball (1966); Dave Meggyesey, an All-Pro lineman with the St. Louis Cardinals, denounced the brutality, militarism, and inhumanity of the NFL (1970); Jim Bouton revealed the all-too-human frailties of his "heroic" New York Yankee teammates (1970); in 1969 Harry Edwards recapped the plight of African American athletes in *The Revolt of the Black Athlete;* and two years later Jack Scott summed up the varied expressions of discontent with the existing sports world in *The Athletic Revolution.* Still later, while athletic director at Oberlin College from 1972 to 1974, Scott sought to put his ideas in practice by hiring "liberated" coaches and giving the athletes a greater voice in decision making.

Not unexpectedly, the "athletic revolution" prodded a counterattack. Indeed, at least one prominent person seemed unable to comprehend the division between the sports world and the counterculture of the sixties. In the wee hours of the night, during a massive protest against his orders to invade Cambodia in 1970, President Richard M. Nixon visited with demonstrators who had made their way to Washington from colleges across the country. Rather then querying them about why they were demonstrating or taking issue with their positions, Nixon sought to find common ground with them by asking about the prospects of their respective college football teams.

Vice President Spiro Agnew was less sanguine. In an address at the First Annual Vince Lombardi Award Dinner in 1971, he reiterated the value of sport in inculcating discipline, restraint, ethics, and "manhood." He characterized the critics of sports as a minority and "out of touch with what is going on in our country today." To a degree, Agnew was right. But sports, as David Zang has argued, would never be the same after the cultural upheavals of the 1960s and early 1970s.[11] No longer would claims for the character-building value of sports go unchallenged. More and more Americans sought in sports, as they did in other dimensions of their lives, a means of self-fulfillment.

While there were abundant signs of a hungering for community in the final decades of the twentieth century, the dominant impulse among Americans was to turn inward. Turning inward entailed a breaking away from formal and enduring associations with others, with the past, with everything outside the self. Reflective of the turning to the self was a startling decline in the nation's associational life. Americans voted less frequently than in the past, participation in voluntary associations declined, and the divorce rate soared to more than half of all marriages. No imagery captured the tendency to disengage more compellingly than Robert Putnam's influential 1993 essay, "Bowling Alone: America's Declining Social Capital." While the total number of bowlers increased nearly 10 percent between 1980 and 1993, Putnam found that league bowling decreased by 40 percent. Enthusiasm for an unrestrained market and a growing hostility toward government were other integral components of the new individualism.

Yet, the new individualism did not entail the rejection of all ties beyond the self. Many Americans continued to vote, to belong to civic associations, to marry, and to be actively involved in their churches, synagogues, or mosques. Sports offered a potential means—though admittedly frequently tenuous and superficial—of making connections beyond the self. Without giving up the excitement and satisfactions found in the pursuit of personal fulfillment, millions of Americans sought "to go with the flow" by keeping abreast of major sporting events. "DON'T MISS THE DRAMA, EXHILARATION AND GLORY OF WAVING YOUR TICKETS AROUND THE OFFICE," read a full-page ad for the U.S. Open Tennis tourney in the *New York Times* in 2002.[12] In this instance the message was not so much that one now had the means to enjoy a major sporting event as it was a display of one "being with it." The proliferation of sports bars in the final two decades of the century even offered potentially face-to-face encounters among sports enthusiasts. Many better-off Americans sought ties beyond the self through the cultivation of a particular lifestyle. Hence, the elderly, regardless of their earlier occupations, ethnicity, or religious persuasions, might retire to a special village in Arizona devoted mainly to golf and convivial gatherings at the "nineteenth hole." Younger professionals might turn to tennis, golf, jogging, weight lifting, water sports, or patronization of all-sports bars to form their own lifestyle enclaves.

The growing enthusiasm for gambling seemed to reflect both the imperatives of the new individualism and a yearning for ties beyond the self. Once regarded by a substantial part of the population as not only a mockery of the work ethic but also of God, gambling offered millions a new form of excitement and potential enjoyment. Gambling achieved a new level of public respectability. Beginning in 1964 in New Hampshire, one state after another established state lotteries. In 1976 the Nevada Gaming Commission decided to permit legal sports gambling within the casinos; in 1990, through the state's 74 licensed sports books, bettors wagered $1.8 billion. Estimates placed this figure at about one-fourth of the total nationwide bets placed annually on sporting events. Although both professional and college sports moguls uniformly took rigid positions against gambling by all of those associated with their enterprises, betting boosted both interest in and attendance at sporting events.[13]

THE QUEST FOR SELF-SUFFICIENCY AND THE FITNESS CULT

A widespread quest for self-sufficiency accompanied the new individualism. As society became more rationalized and systematized and more people worked in bureaucracies, the importance of the individual seemed to diminish. As early as the 1960s corporations discovered pervasive problems of morale among executives. Rising absenteeism and declining rates of productivity, especially among middle managers, reflected a growing dissatisfaction with the anonymity and impotence of white-collar workers. To satisfy yearnings arising from feelings of powerlessness, meaningless work, loneliness, sexual deprivation, and the absence of material goods, many turned to arenas other than work to find greater sufficiency and personal fulfillment. They engaged in orgies of consumption, became converts to charismatic religions, experimented with vegetarianism, drugs, psychotherapy, and/or they became apostles of the new fitness cult.[14]

The fitness cult of the 1970s and 1980s differed significantly from the strenuous life movement of the early twentieth century. Then, members of the older Eastern elite had urged a strenuous life as a means of rejuvenating their class and thereby enhancing the nation's welfare. While social goals, especially becoming fit enough to meet the perceived threat of the Soviet Union, informed the President's Council on Physical Fitness organized in 1956, the council had a negligible relationship to the modern fitness movement. The new strenuosity focused upon the self rather than upon society. Unlike the earlier campaign for the strenuous life, the fitness crusade in the 1970s and 1980s included both sexes. Women not only took up vigorous exercise to look better, feel better, and to improve their health, but also as an assertion of self-sufficiency. By using physical prowess as a means of achieving equality with men as well as to oppose actual male oppression, physical fitness became a part of the larger women's liberation movement (see Chapter 19).

Recognition of the limits of modern medicine also provided an impetus to the quest for greater self-sufficiency through fitness. The antibiotic revolution of the 1940s and 1950s brought many contagious diseases under control, but not cardiovascular disease nor cancer, diseases that became the leading causes of death. The most effective way of countering these dreaded killers seemed to be turning to the self. White-collar professionals in particular began to practice a more abstemious lifestyle—exercising more, trying to control weight, drinking less, and ending their addiction to tobacco.

The transformation of physical activities into quantifiable units and the authority of scientific expertise encouraged the new strenuosity. While testing the fitness levels of thousands of potential pilots in the 1960s, Kenneth Cooper, an Air Force physician, developed measurable standards of ideal conditioning. Light calisthenics or short walks were not enough, according to Cooper. Only strenuous activities such as jogging, running, racquetball, cycling, swimming, or fast walking elevated the pulse rate to adequate levels. Cooper even told Americans exactly how far and fast they would have to run and walk in a given week in order to become "aerobically fit." By 1972 an estimated eight million Americans, including astronaut-hero John Glenn, followed Cooper's regimen for "aerobic" fitness, which included not only vigorous exercise but also the maintenance of careful personal records of pulse rate, blood pressure, weight, and the times taken to complete the exercises.

In the 1970s, as disillusionment mounted over the Vietnam War, the counterculture, leadership in high places, and the erratic performance of the economy, the enthusiasm for fitness increased. By the late 1970s, the number of Americans who claimed to exercise regularly had jumped to 20 million. As more and more white-collar employees replaced their two-martini lunches with jogging, swimming, and working out with exercise machines, YMCAs, YWCAs, and similar organizations experienced a sudden reversal in their long-term membership declines. The number of commercial health clubs multiplied from 350 in 1968 to more than 7,000 in 1986. Advertisers and manufacturers quickly moved in to exploit the new enthusiasm. Perhaps no sign of the times was more important than the decision to update the marketing of Barbie, "the ultimate yuppie doll," by including with the doll a workout center, complete with an exercise cycle, dumbbells, slant board, and a locker with towel.

The new strenuosity extended far beyond a desire to achieve simply physical fitness. After having been desk bound by day, "the new Spartans," as they were dubbed by *Time* magazine, sought intense physical experiences, even if it meant aching muscles, pounding hearts, and gasping lungs. While many jogged short distances only a few times weekly, an astonishing number of Americans took up regular long-distance running. In 1970, only 126 men entered the first New York marathon; but by the mid-1980s the organizers accepted 20,000 "official" entries from both men and women while rejecting thousands of others. By then hundreds of cities in all parts of the country scheduled marathons. As if running 26 miles were not enough exercise, the apostles of running invented the iron-man triathlon, which included a 2-mile swim, a 112-mile bicycle ride, and a 26-mile run. In 1986 more than a million Americans completed this grueling event. Apart from building or releasing additional sources of energy, improving one's sex life, and reducing anxieties, strenuous workouts, according to proponents, induced a mystical "runner's high," a trancelike euphoria that could become addictive. A distinctive runners' culture emerged, one that revolved not only around running, but also around clubs, special diets, in-group understandings and behaviors, running magazines, and a flourishing equipment industry.

The quest for fitness was often an integral component of a larger effort to reshape the body. To be sure, prosperous Americans had long been preoccupied with bodily beauty, but the postwar media's accent on youth gave the concern a new urgency. Weight lifting and other body-shaping exercises became more popular than ever before. Being fat in American became the greatest single sign of personal failure. "Eating has become the last bona fide sin left in America," concluded columnist Ellen Goodman in 1974.[15] Dieting had its negative side; a Gallup poll in 1986 estimated that three million Americans, most of them women, suffered from the eating disorders of anorexia nervosa and/or bulimia. If exercise and dieting failed to obtain the desired figure, the most affluent Americans increasingly resorted to plastic surgery.

Measurably positive results issued from the fitness crusade. The death rate from cardiovascular disease fell from 511 per 100,000 people in 1950 to 418 by 1985, though part of the decline was attributable to better medical treatment of cardiovascular patients. White-collar Americans smoked fewer cigarettes, drank less alcohol, and ate less red meat (beef and pork) while consuming more white meat (poultry and fish) than ever before.

Yet the positive effects could be easily exaggerated. A widely publicized Harris Survey in 1993 indicated that American health habits may have gotten worse during the 1980s. For example, fewer Americans watched their fat intake in 1993 than in 1983 and Americans exceeded recommended body weights in far greater numbers than the citizens in any other industrial nation. Children improved their scores little if at all on push-ups, high jumps, long jumps, endurance runs, and sprints. Although nearly half the adult population claimed to exercise regularly, probably less than one in ten exercised consistently enough to match the minimum levels specified by physical fitness experts. Blue-collar workers, in particular, rarely engaged in any form of systematic exercise.

In the late 1980s and in the 1990s the fitness movement apparently lost some if not much of its momentum. For many Americans buying exercise equipment and clothing represented a form of "propitiatory consumption," the purchase of items in the hope that the expenditure itself would convert good intentions into results. Participation rates in marathons fell, some evidence existed for believing that the "anorexia look" among women was waning in popularity, and public opinion polls reflected less negative views toward obesity than in the past. In the late 1980s, the media introduced the "couch potato" as a popular culture specie who conspicuously rejected the strenuous life. In the following decade obesity rates for both adults and children soared to new heights. Among people age 12 to 21, according to a report in 2000, 14 percent of them got no exercise whatever while in the 1990s the percentage of high school students enrolled in gym classes fell from 42 per cent to 29 percent.[16]

THE ADVENT OF TELEVISED SPORTS

Nothing was more central to the history of organized sports during the second half of the twentieth century than television. With the advent of television, the fans at home rather than those in the stadium or the arena became the ultimate arbiters of organized sports. To attract more television viewers and meet the demands of commercial sponsors, television directors employed multiple cameras, replays, slow-motion shots, flashy graphics, catchy music, and announcers to create a sporting experience unavailable to the fan in the stands. Likewise, to make their games more attractive television spectacles, the moguls of sports altered the nature of their games. For example, they changed game rules, permitted arbitrary timeouts for television commercials, and in most of the team sports established lengthy playoff systems for the national championships.

Television affected American sports in other ways. It contributed to the further nationalization and eventually even the globalization of sports. In earlier times, newspapers, magazines, movies, books, and radio had allowed Americans everywhere to learn about the feats of Babe Ruth, but television permitted millions to see instantaneously Pete Rose pursue Joe DiMaggio's record for hits in consecutive games. When fans could regularly see sports performed at the highest plateau of excellence on television, attendance at local sporting events frequently declined. Indeed, television made the future prosperity of professional sports increasingly dependent upon the creation of a broad-based national rather than local constituency. Thus pro football, the first sport to recognize fully the potentialities of the new media, staged the Super Bowl at neither team's home site and deliberately downplayed the traditional attachment of teams to cities. Finally, as television pumped additional millions of dollars into sports, professional athletes demanded a larger share of the revenues generated by sports.

During television's pioneer stage, that is, from 1938 (the first sports telecast)[17] to the early 1960s, technology limited the potential of televised sports. Before the common use of multiple cameras, color, replay, and slow motion, primitive television cameras more effectively captured the excitement of arena spectacles such as Roller Derby, wrestling, and prizefighting than outdoor games such as baseball and football. Television fans could easily follow two men whose combat was restricted to a small ring, but the small white baseball could sometimes hardly be distinguished from the white dots ("snow") on the black-and-white screens, and viewers, when they could see the hit ball, could rarely determine its precise location relative to the playing field. Because of its more concentrated action, football fared somewhat better, but the camera, located far from the playing field, could hardly capture the essence of sophisticated plays. Mud-covered and grass-stained uniforms sometimes made the teams indistinguishable.

In each of the arena sports, television contributed to a short-term boom and a long-term depression. Prizefighting was the most spectacular instance. In the late 1940s and early 1950s television lifted boxing into a new "golden age" only to deliver it a blow from which it never fully recovered. In 1944 the Gillette Safety Razor company signed a pact with Madison Square Garden to sponsor weekly telecasts of fights. In the 1950s the Gillette fights became something of a Friday night institution. Advertisers soon brought fights to television on the other nights of the week. Millions of Americans who had never seen a prizefight before became devotees of the ring. Fascinated fans even loved the Golden Glove bouts that usually featured the flailings of inept amateurs.

Then in the mid-1950s the happy union of television and boxing came apart. Old-time fight fans complained that television had created an entirely new form of entertainment. No longer did fighters bide their time until a proper opening occurred or soften up an opponent early in the match with nonlethal blows. Slugging replaced defensive finesse. Furthermore, to continue programming such a busy schedule of fights required an endless supply of winning fighters. "The big thing you were up against is that there had to be a loser, you know? And you couldn't bring a loser back on TV," explained Chris Dundee, a prominent fight promoter from Miami Beach, Florida. "The sponsors didn't want losers, just winners. And let's face it, the sponsors called the shots during the TV age of boxing."[18]

The voracious demand by television for fighters encouraged the monopolization of promotion by the International Boxing Club (IBC). By controlling the key arenas and through his connections with underworld figures, Jim Norris, the president of the IBC, drove independent promoters out of the fight game. Antitrust actions against the IBC, the convictions of Norris and mobsters associated with prizefighting for income tax evasion, and the televised hearings by a Senate committee on organized crime (which included revelations about boxing) darkened the reputation of a sport that had always had difficulty establishing a positive image.

In the late 1950s boxing's new golden age suddenly collapsed. Television and other at-home activities drove down live attendance and destroyed the once prospering smaller fight clubs. In 1948–49, 10 to 12,000 fans regularly watched the Friday night card at Madison Square Garden; by 1957, when the Garden had become little more than an oversized television studio, attendance had dropped to an average of a mere 1,200. By 1958, along "Cauliflower Row," as Eighth Avenue in New York City was known, nearly all the fight clubs had closed. In the early 1950s over 300 fighters had worked out of Stillman's Gym; by 1958, the number using the famous fight factory had dropped to below 90. Television wiped out over half of the fight clubs located in smaller cities. Likewise television ratings fell disastrously. In 1952, 31 percent of all households watching television had their sets tuned to prime-time fights; seven years later the figure had fallen to 10.6 percent. Apart from all the problems that beset prizefighting, boxing simply failed in head-to-head competition with other kinds of prime-time (evening) programming that the networks began developing in the late 1950s.

Initially, radio men, known for their "golden throats," handled television's announcing chores. Even though viewers could see the games for themselves, announcers tended to talk too much, employ too many cliches, and risk their credibility by resorting to hyperbole. Being enthusiastic fans themselves, employed by the networks or the home teams, and dependent upon the commissioners of professional sports leagues for approval, they rarely criticized players, managers or coaches, game officials, or team owners. Nor did they comment on racism or sexism in sports. By the 1960s dozens of athletes, ex-athletes, and even referees had joined or replaced radio men. While the diction of athlete-announcers sometimes bordered on incomprehensibility, producers believed that the athlete's inside knowledge added to the fan's enjoyment.

For baseball aficionados across the country in the 1950s, watching and listening to Jay Hanna "Dizzy" Dean on the CBS *Game of the Week* became virtually a weekend ritual. Apparently sensing the game could not always hold the viewer's attention, Dean himself took center stage, letting the game provide the background image for the spell of his personality. A former pitching star for the St. Louis Cardinals in the 1930s, Dean came to New York City in 1950 to do Yankee pregame shows on WBAD, the flagship station of the DuMont radio and television network. He was an "instant success" in New York, and in 1955 he joined Buddy Blattner, another ex-big leaguer, to do *Game of the Week*. Claiming to have attended a one-room school in Oklahoma only long enough to get into the "second reader," Dean enthralled viewers with his country drawl, unusual verbal conjugations, and uninhibited anecdotes. (When Dean heard the school teachers in St. Louis had complained about his syntax, he shot back: "Sin Tax. Are them jokers in Washington puttin' a tax on that too?")[19] When the game became unusually slow or boring, he might bawl out an impromptu version of the "Wabash Cannonball."

THE BATTLE OF THE NETWORKS

During the 1950s, none of the Big Three (NBC, CBS, and ABC) networks considered sports programming critical to their overall success. They put far more of their resources and talent into comedies, Westerns, and popular dramas. But in the early 1960s, ABC broke with this pattern. Having been long a laggard behind NBC and CBS, ABC gambled that increased sports programming would give its network greater visibility, bring in new local television stations as affiliates, and improve the audience ratings for all shows. The gamble paid spectacular dividends. Sports telecasts contributed substantively to ABC's sudden rise from third place in prime-time audience ratings in the 1950s to the top in the 1970s.

No single person was more responsible for ABC's success than Roone P. Arledge. After winning a television Emmy for producing the best children's program, "Hi Mom," in 1959 on NBC, Arledge joined ABC in 1960 to direct and produce the network's football games. Arledge was determined, as he put it, "to get the audience involved emotionally. If they didn't give a damn about the game, they still might enjoy the program."[20] To obtain more audience involvement, he attempted to capture the full ambience of the game setting. He used cranes, blimps, and helicopters to obtain novel views of the stadium, the campus, and the

CARICATURE OF ROONE P. ARLEDGE
More than any other single person, Arledge, the long-time director of ABC Sports, was responsible for major innovations in sports telecasting.

town; hand-held cameras for close-up shots of cheerleaders, pretty coeds, band members, eccentric spectators, and nervous coaches; and rifle-type microphones to pick up the roar of the crowd, the thud of a punt, or the crunch of a hard tackle.

Arledge made the crowd itself part of the performance. Once the fans perceived themselves as potential performers, they began to carry banners, run onto the playing field, and engage in unseemly antics to grab the attention of the television cameras. In the early 1970s shots of women in the stands stripping down to their bras and panties (usually local strippers seeking free publicity) aroused so much protest that ABC began to cut back on its coverage of some of the more bizarre forms of the off-the-field behavior.

Arledge also brought his talents to *The Wide World of Sports* and the Olympic Games. In 1961 he began production of *Wide World*, which was to win more Emmys than any other sportscast. A pioneer in stop-action filming, *Wide World* consisted of a potpourri of feats and games, including boxing matches, track meets, ski races, surfing, cliff diving, barrel jumping, wrist wrestling, and demolition derbies. The program was especially effective in stimulating public interest in winter sports. Although normally effusive in its enthusiasm for all sports, no matter how trivial, *Wide World's* occasional interviews by Howard Cosell of Muhammad Ali, Joe Namath, and other more or less controversial sports figures added spice to the telecasts. Arledge also turned the 1968, 1972, and 1976 Olympic Games into television extravaganzas.

One of Arledge's productions, *Monday Night Football*, outstripped all other regular sportscasts in popularity. Initiated in 1970, this prime-time sport show altered the Monday-night habits of a large portion of the American people. Movie attendance nose dived, restaurants closed, and bowlers rescheduled their leagues. Much of the success of *Monday Night Football* stemmed from Arledge's decision to hire Howard Cosell, already the most controversial sportscaster in the country as a commentator. (As part of the agreement for ABC to do the Monday night games, Arledge had refused to sign the traditional contract providing for "announcer-approval" by league officials.)

From the first telecast, Cosell, who had championed Muhammad Ali's resistance to the Vietnam draft and right to retain the heavyweight crown, sparked controversy. Cosell treated professional football with none of the reverence that his predecessors had bestowed upon the sport. By second-guessing the wisdom of head coaches, criticizing the decisions of officials, and lampooning the owners, Cosell claimed to "tell it like it is." Caustic, unctuous, polysyllabic, and given to making even the most trivial observation sound like something profound, analysts concluded that Cosell was a man the audience "loved to hate." Unlike any other broadcaster, Cosell was able to get away with simultaneously promoting, reporting, and criticizing an event packaged and merchandised by his own network.

Jarred by ABC's successes, in the 1970s and 80s CBS and NBC decided to do battle with the upstart network. The results (detailed in subsequent chapters) were (1) the money poured into sports by television in the late 1970s and early 1980s escalated at a pace far exceeding inflation or the nation's overall economic growth; (2) augmented in the late 1970s by competition from cable television, the quantity of sports available on the cool medium doubled, tripled, and then became practically omnipresent; and (3) to make their contests more attractive to television and capitalize upon the millions of dollars offered by the networks, all of the major sports made rule changes.

Apart from intense competition for the television rights to professional college football and basketball, major-league baseball, and the Olympic Games, the networks beamed a galaxy of "synthetic" or "trashports." "Legitimate sports, for the most part, have limited audiences," explained sportscaster Vin Scully. "But when you give it another dimension—entertainment—you capture a new breed of viewer."[21] In the 1960s ABC's *Wide World of Sports* pioneered in the telecasts of bizarre or unusual physical activities: high wire acts, the national logrolling championships, wrist wrestling championships, and a rattlesnake hunt in Keane, Oklahoma. In the 1970s, as the battle of the networks became more intense, the quantity of sports created especially for television increased. Allegedly to find out who was the best all-around athlete in the country, ABC first aired *The Superstars* in 1973. In that program, renowned athletes competed against one another in events outside their specialties.

The Superstars begot a large progeny of similar shows. At ABC, viewers soon witnessed *The Women Superstars*, *The World Superstars*, and *The Superteams*. NBC responded with *Dynamic Duos* and *US Against the World* (a celebrity Olympics). At CBS, *The Challenge of the Sexes* spawned *Celebrity Challenge of the Sexes*. One contest, a tennis match between Farrah Fawcett-Majors and Bill Cosby on *Celebrity Challenge*, drew a whopping 49 percent of the television audience. Since Majors was without even minimal tennis skills, one critic concluded that the astronomical rating must have resulted from men ogling the actress while she cavorted about in shorts. "The way we are going," asserted Curt Gowdy, a spokesman of the old school of sportscasting, "we'll see Secretariat racing a Wyoming antelope."[22] For a time, there seemed to be no end for the potential of trashsports, but in the early 1980s viewers tired of the made-for-television spectacles, and the networks responded by cutting back on their telecast of synthetic sports.

Syndicated sports shows, cable television, and communication satellites added vast new dimensions to the fight between the networks for supremacy in sports. From the earliest days of the new medium, independent producers had put together shows which would then be aired either by one of the major networks or by a special syndicated network of local stations. The launching of the first communications satellite in 1974 and the end of complex legal restrictions on cable television in 1977 paved the way for the so-called superstations and cable network systems. Fans of televised sports rejoiced at the formation of two sports networks: USA Network in 1975 and the Entertainment and Sports Programming Network (ESPN) in 1979. At first both networks concentrated on telecasting local contests or the more obscure college sports, but eventually ESPN landed contracts for college and professional football games as well as big-league baseball games. In the 1990s ESPN became part of a vast Disney media conglomerate that included the ABC network.

In the mid-1980s signs were present that the long romance between television and sports might be cooling. Network ratings told part of the story. Although millions continued to watch televised sports, ratings slipped downward. In particular, professional football, long the darling of the networks, suffered from declines. The networks faced increasing competition from superstations, cable television systems, VCRs, and video games for audiences, rights, and advertising dollars. Some long-time sponsors of televised sports, including car manufacturers and breweries, reduced their commitments or pulled out entirely. Video games began to offer some youngsters the same sense of action, speed, and power that they had earlier found in sports.

Yet, there was no persuasive evidence that the romance between television and sport had permanently chilled. In the 1990s and the first decade of the twenty-first century, total rights payments for sports resumed their upward climb. In 1997 two new all-sports cable networks formed. And in the same year, Australian media mogul Rupert Murdock began putting togther a huge global empire of televised sports. By the first decade of the twenty-first century, viewers even had the option of seeing separate cable channels devoted entirely to golf and to tennis.

AN ASSESSMENT OF THE MEDIA

Throughout the post-1950 era, televised sports occasioned debate. Everyone conceded that television could provide experiences unavailable to fans in the stands or to radio listeners. To keep viewers riveted to the screen, the directors provided quickly shifting images—from closeups to long-distance shots, from players to spectators, from spectators to cheerleaders, from live action to replays. Closeups, replays, and slow-motion shots could add to the fan's appreciation of beautifully executed plays. Perhaps for these reasons, a majority of Americans, according to a nationwide poll in 1978, preferred to watch sports (except baseball) on television rather than being in the stands.[23]

Yet, while conceding that television furnished viewers with experiences in some ways superior to those available to the live fan, critics argued that the medium ultimately trivialized and diluted the traditional sporting experience. Dilution and trivialization took the form of too much hype, too many "big plays," too many extraneous sensations, and too many games. By 1994 the number of possible playoff games for the championships in hockey could extend to 105, in basketball to 89, in baseball to 41, and in football to 11. Once the miracle of seeing major sporting events and well-executed plays become commonplace, viewers lost some of their enthusiasm. No longer did the sensations arising from the immediacy of the sporting event exert the same poignancy, the same urgency, or the same power to inspire.

The media contributed to the dilution and trivialization of the sporting experience in other ways. The sheer quantity of babble—the incessant, indiscriminate, and unnuanced—discussion of sports topics in the media threatened to overwhelm and diminish the fan's capacity to enjoy the sporting experience. Just as viewers and listeners were swamped with programs featuring polemical rather than well-conceived political debates, by 2000 fans could see or hear 24 hours of artificially induced outrage and endless discussions by ex-players, coaches, pundits, and other fans on subjects ranging from the inadequacies of the college football ranking system to the folly of paying baseball players too much money. That the patronage of such shows was so large suggested a widespread, indeed perhaps a desperate, hungering for some kind of ties beyond the self, even if ultimately of a superficial sort.

Television affected sports journalism as well. Although survivors of the literary tradition in sportswriting remained in the age of television, in the 1960s sportswriting took a new turn. Since presumably fans could see for themselves on television the drama transpiring on the field of play, reporters increasingly tried to cover dimensions of the contest hidden from the cameras. This usually meant seeking the opinions of others; thus postgame interviews of coaches and players became a kind of ritual. At worst, stories might consist of little more than quotations of game participants strung together; at best, the stories included analysis of important behind-the-scenes activities.

Other modern sportswriters, influenced by the Vietnam War and counterculture of the 1960s, attacked modern sports themselves. They sought to shatter the illusions surrounding sports and subject sports to the same close scrutiny as other important social institutions. They explored racism, sexism, drugs, religion, gambling, cheating, and violence in sports, as well as the business side. On occasion, the fan might find on the sports pages more about what happened in the courtroom, the boardroom, or the bedroom than what happened on the field of play.[24] But most fans cared little for news about social problems or business; they turned to the sports pages to escape news of wars, politics, assassinations, discrimination, and high finance.

CONCLUSION

The post-1950 era witnessed the far-reaching influences of television and population changes on American sport. Population growth, especially in the Sunbelt states, encouraged professional leagues to expand the number of their franchises and caused professional teams to relocate in cities that could promise them more patrons, subsidies, and/or media revenues. In the sprawling metropolises the traditional spatial pattern of urban leisure changed. Commercial entertainment in the inner city declined. Instead of seeking entertainment in the inner city, suburbanites turned to at-home, do-it-yourself projects. White-collar professionals even embarked upon a new physical fitness crusade. And all classes watched television. The new medium became the ultimate instrument not only in encouraging the privatization of leisure, but also in altering the general contours of organized sports.

NOTES

1. Jim Caplan, "Perspective," *Sports Illustrated* 58 (May 23, 1983), MW2. See also N.J. Sullivan, *The Dodgers Move West* (New York: Oxford University Press, 1987).

2. Steven A. Riess, *City Games* (Urbana: University of Illinois Press, 1989) examines the historical relationship between urban space and sports. See also Joseph Cuniglio, *The Names in the Games* (New York: Vantage 1978); Harrison Donnelly, "High Stakes of Sports Economics," *Editorial Research Reports*, April 8, 1988, 170–83; Charles C. Euchner, *Playing the Field* (Baltimore, MD: Johns Hopkins University Press, 1993); Tim Crothers, "The Shakedown," *Sports Illustrated* 82 (June 19, 1995), 76–82; and Michael N. Danielson, *Home Team: Professional Sports and the American Metropolis* (Princeton, NJ: Princeton University Press, 1997).

3. See data in B. G. Rader, "The Great Slump in Spectator Sports in the 1950s: The Case of the United States," in J.A. Mangan, ed., *Proceedings of the XI HISPA International Conference* (1985), 158.

4. See for example, Pete Axthelm, *The City Game* (New York: Harper's Magazine, 1970) and Rich Telander, *Heaven Is a Playground* (New York: Macmillan, 1976).

5. K.T. Jackson, *Crabgrass Frontier* (New York: Oxford University Press, 1985), chap. 14, and Robert Fishman, *Bourgeois Utopias* (New York: Basic Books, 1987).

6. B.G. Rader, *In Its Own Image: How Television Has Transformed Sports* (New York: Free Press, 1984), 35; Theodore Caplow et al., *Middletown Families* (Minneapolis: University of Minnesota Press, 1982); J.P. Robinson, *How Americans Use Time* (New York: Institute of Social Research, 1977), esp.172–79; and H.J. Gans, *The Urban Villagers* (New York: Free Press, 1962), 187–96.

7. W.J. Levitt, as quoted in Jackson, *Crabgrass Frontier*, 231.

8. See B.M. Berger, *Working-Class Suburb* (Berkeley: University of California Press, 1969), chap. 5, and David Halle, *America's Working Men* (Chicago: University of Chicago Press, 1984), chap. 2.

9. See Benjamin G. Rader, *American Ways: A Brief History of American Cultures* (Fort Worth, TX: Harcourt College Publishers, 2001), chap. 10.

10. Quoted in David W. Zang, *Sports Wars: Athletes in the Age of Aquarius* (Fayetteville: University of Arkansas Press, 2001), 23.

11. For Agnew quote, see ibid., xviii, and for Zang's conclusions, ibid., 165–68.

12. *New York Times*, June 9, 2002, viii, 20.

13. See Richard O. Davies and Richard G. Abram, *Betting the Line: Sports Wagering in American Life* (Columbus: Ohio State University Press, 2001); Richard O. Davies, "The Age of Jimmy the Greek: Sports Wagering in Modern America," *Nevada Historical Society Quarterly* (spring 1999), 21–45; and Garry Smith, "The 'So Do' Over What to Do about Sports Gambling: Sanitizing a Tainted Activity," in W.R. Eadington and J.A. Cornelius, *Gambling and Public Policy* (New York: Basic Books, 1991).

14. See esp. B.G. Rader, "The Quest for Self-Sufficiency and the New Strenuosity," *Journal of Sport History* 18 (1991), 255–67; M.S. Goldstein, *The Health Movement* (New York: Twayne, 1992); and R.J. Park, "A Decade of the Body: Researching and Writing about the History of Health, Fitness, Exercise and Sport, 1983–1993," *Journal of Sport History* 21 (1994), 59–82.

15. Quoted in Hillel Schwartz, *Never Satisfied* (New York: Free Press, 1986), 308.

16. Statistics from Jack McCallum, "Let's Get Physical," *Sports Illustrated*, (July 10, 2000), 25.

17. The long-accepted date for the first American sports telecast has been 1939, but a year earlier a college football game was telecast in Philadelphia. See NCAA Football Television Committee, *Football Television Briefing Book* (Shawnee Mission, KS, 1981), 1.

18. Quoted in W.O. Johnson Jr., *Super Spectator and the Electric Lilliputians* (Boston: Little, Brown, 1971), 92. On prizefighting, see also Barney Nagler, *James Norris and the Decline of Boxing* (Indianapolis, IN: Bobbs-Merrill, 1964); Jeffrey T. Sammons, *Beyond the Ring: The Role of Boxing in American Society* (Urbana: University of Illinois Press, 1988), chaps. 5–7; and Steven A. Riess, "Only the Ring Was Square: Frankie Carbo and the Underworld Control of American Boxing," *International Journal of the History of Sport* 5 (1988), 29–52.

19. Quoted in Rader, *In Its Own Image*, 57. See also Curt Smith, *America's Dizzy Dean* (St. Louis: C.V. Mosby, 1978), and on radio sports generally, Curt Smith, *Voices of the Games* (South Bend, IN: Diamond Communications, 1987).

20. Quoted in Johnson, *Super Spectator*, 161.

21. Quoted in Rader, *In Its Own Image*, 128.

22. Randall Poe, "The Angry Fan," *Harper's* 251 (1975), 95.

23. Don Kowet, "TV Sports: America Speaks Out," *TV Guide*, August 19, 1978.

24. For a biting analysis of sports journalism in the age of television, see Michael Novak, *The Joy of Sports* (New York: Basic Books, 1976), chap. 14. See also D.Q. Voigt, "From Chadwick to Chipmunks," *Journal of American Culture* 7 (1984), 31–37.

15
PROFESSIONAL TEAM SPORTS IN THE AGE OF TELEVISION

*A*t first no one expected the annual Super Bowl, a product of the National Football League and the American Football League merger of 1966, to exceed all other sports spectacles in popularity. Within only a half-dozen years of its founding, the Super Bowl enjoyed a larger national audience than horse racing's venerable Kentucky Derby or baseball's World Series. By the 1980s over half the nation's population watched the game on television. Only an occasional television special attracted so many viewers. Elaborate fanfare and ceremony accompanied the Bowls, and each was given its own Roman numeral, thereby elevating the pageant above the mundane and linking it with the spectacles of ancient Rome. Super Bowl Sunday became an unofficial national holiday, one that was more rigorously observed in many circles than Washington's Birthday, Independence Day, or even tippling on New Year's Eve.

Nothing suggested more dramatically than did the Super Bowl the relative decline of baseball and the astonishing growth in the popularity of professional football. Although millions continued to listen to baseball on radio, to follow the sport in their daily newspaper, and to watch games on television, in the post-1950 era baseball lost its preeminent position among American sports. By the late 1970s, professional football, a sport virtually unknown to millions prior to mid-century, overtook baseball in popularity—and basketball, once an equally obscure professional team sport, also won a growing following (see Figure 15–1).

THE WOES OF BASEBALL

In the post-1950 era baseball's elaborate superstructure all but collapsed. Literally thousands of semipro teams folded and minor-league baseball became a shell of its former self. The major leagues fared only somewhat better. Average game

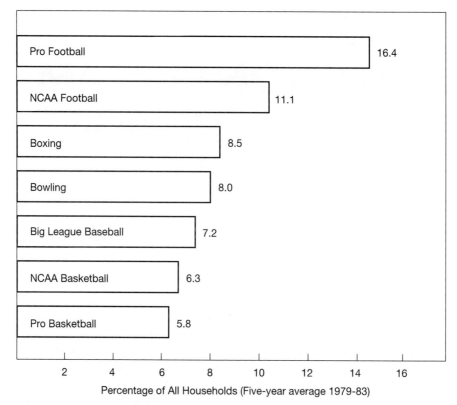

FIGURE 15–1   National television audience for sports
Source: A. C. Nielsen, *Televised Sports.*

attendance at big-league games remained below the marks achieved in the 1948–52 seasons until 1978, but even then lagged proportionately behind the population growth of metropolitan areas served by big-league franchises. Beginning in the mid-1960s the television audiences for regular season baseball games fell to nearly half of that of regular season professional football games.[1]

In large part, baseball's relative loss of fan support sprang from a general shift in urban leisure patterns. After World War II, growing slums surrounded many big-league parks. Responding in part to fears for their personal safety and for the security of their cars, the residents of independent suburbs hesitated to drive into the inner cities to attend games. In the summer, suburbanites chose to spend more of their spare time doing other things than watching baseball games. "Why should a guy with a boat in the driveway, golf clubs in the car, bowling ball and tennis racket in the closet, a trunkful of camping equipment, two boys in the Little League and a body full of energy left over from shorter working hours pay to sit and do nothing but watch a mediocre game?" asked W. Travis Walton of Abilene, Texas, in a letter to *Sports Illustrated* in 1958.[2] Apart from the intrinsic difficulties television had in capturing all of the dimensions of baseball, the sport's long season and many games (compared to football and basketball) meant that only a few games seemed crucial enough to attract large television audiences.

The problem of devising a satisfactory television policy also plagued organized baseball. In part, minor-league baseball succumbed to the greed of the big-league owners. The return of prosperity in the 1940s had stimulated a new boom in minor-league baseball. Annual attendance increased nearly threefold between 1939 and 1949, from 15 to 42 million—then came the invasion of television. Alone, the minor leagues could do nothing to stem the intrusions of big-league telecasts into their home territories. Threatened by antitrust action by the Justice Department and seeking to maximize their own broadcast revenues, in 1951 the major-league owners repealed their ban against their games being aired in minor-league territories.

Combined with the interest in competing leisure-time activities, the decision to allow unlimited telecasts spelled disaster for minor-league baseball. After 1951 nearly everyone who owned a television set could see the big leaguers play for free. Local minor-league heroes paled beside major-league superstars such as Henry Aaron, Willie Mays, Ted Williams, Bob Feller, and Mickey Mantle. Attendance at minor-league games fell from 42 million in 1949, before the advent of nationally televised major-league games, to 15 million in 1957 and 10 million in 1969. The number of minor leagues shrank from 51 in 1949 to 20 by 1970.

Until 1961, when Congress passed the Sports Broadcasting Act, major-league baseball was unable to develop a national television package for the regular season games that included all franchises. In 1954 the majors submitted to the Department of Justice a plan for a "Game of the Week" in which the commissioner of baseball would negotiate with the networks for the sale of national television rights of the member franchises, but the Justice Department advised that the proposal would violate federal antitrust laws. Organized baseball acquiesced without taking the issue to the federal courts; apparently the owners feared the possible loss of baseball's unique legal status. At any rate, the networks negotiated packages with individual clubs for national telecasts. Under such circumstances the fans enjoyed a bonanza of televised baseball in the late 1950s, but those clubs that could not land network telecasts (usually those located in smaller population areas) suffered from both declining attendance and a reduction in potential broadcasting revenues.

After the passage of the Sports Broadcasting Act of 1961, which exempted package contracts of professional sports leagues from the antitrust laws, the major leagues negotiated contracts with the television networks in which all clubs shared equally in the revenues. The size of the network contracts slowly drifted upward, paralleling the rate of inflation until 1983. In that year, an era when the networks were slugging it out for television rights for the major sports, baseball saw its payments from the networks suddenly increase to $4 million annually per club, more than four times what each franchise had received a year earlier. The 1990–93 package contracts with CBS and cable television shot upward again, totaling $14.4 million annually for each franchise, a figure comparable to the NFL.

But, unlike the NFL, each major-league franchise could negotiate local media rights as well. The franchises located in large market areas such as New

York (where the Yankees received $41 million in 1990) garnered far more from local television and radio than those in smaller cities such as Milwaukee, where the Brewers earned a mere $3 million from their local contract. These differences in club broadcast earnings resulted in much larger disparities in gross income among baseball franchises than in those of pro football.

As if these problems were not enough, the owners of big-league franchises also encountered increasing resistance from the players (see Chapter 20). Between 1972 and 1995 the players engaged in eight work stoppages resulting in the cancellation of 1,718 games. In the same years, salaries as a proportion of total operating costs also soared. No longer could the owners exercise unbridled authority over the professional game.

The formulation of a combined national/local television policy was not the only response of the big leagues to declining fan interest. As detailed in the previous chapter, the big leagues authorized the relocation and expansion in the number of franchises. To lure fans to their games, they also embarked upon the construction of new ballparks. In addition, they experimented with new forms of governance and in the 1990s began to redistribute some revenues from the richer to the poorer franchises. But, as in the past, the owners were reluctant to grant the commissioners extensive powers to govern the sport. And none of these measures brought about a full-scale recovery. As a proportion of the metropolitan areas serviced by the big-league franchises, attendance never again equaled the benchmark established in the 1948–52 seasons.

THE THREE ERAS OF RECENT BASEBALL HISTORY

On the playing field, baseball history in the post-World War II baseball fell into three distinct eras. In the first (from 1946 to 1969) the correlation between team success and the population area served by each club was stronger than ever before (see Tables 15–1 and 15–2). In those years, the New York Yankees captured an astonishing 15 flags in 17 seasons. Superior resources arising from larger attendance, more broadcast revenues, and skilled management accounted for the longevity of the Yankee dynasty. Casey Stengel, the erstwhile field manager of the Yankees from 1949 to 1960, had at his disposal so many good players that he platooned many of his hitters, using left-handed hitters against right-handed pitchers and vice versa. For similar reasons the Brooklyn-Los Angeles Dodgers franchise enjoyed almost equal success in the National League.

Near the end of the first era, the decade of the 1960s, baseball took a step that was a near disaster. Apparently to speed up games, the big leagues in 1963 instructed the umpires to call as strikes some pitches that had formerly been called as balls. With the new strike zone, offensive output dropped precipitously. Although batting averages had been slipping downward prior to 1963 (30 points between the mid-1930s and the early 1960s), in the 1962–63 seasons alone major-league run totals fell by 1,681, home runs by 297, batting averages by 12 points, and bases on balls by 1,345. Pitchers recorded 1,206 more strikeouts than in 1962. The 1963 totals

TABLE 15–1   National League Pennant Winners, 1946–1968*

Brook/ LA.	St. Louis	N.Y./ S.F.	Boston/ Milw.	Cinn.	Pitts.	Phil.	Chic.
1966	1968	1962	1958	1961	1960	1950	
1965	1967	1954	1957				
1963	1964	1951	1948				
1959	1946						
1956							
1955							
1953							
1952							
1949							
1947							

*Divisional play began in 1969.

TABLE 15–2   American League Pennant Winners, 1946–1968*

N.Y.	Boston	Cleveland	Baltimore	Chicago	Minnesota	Detroit	Phil./ K.C.
1964	1967	1954	1966	1959	1965	1968	
1963	1946	1948					
1962							
1961							
1960							
1958							
1957							
1956							
1955							
1953							
1952							
1951							
1950							
1949							
1947							

*Divisional play began in 1969.

became the standard for the next five years. At the very time that the nation seemed obsessed with power, baseball had transformed itself into a series of defensive contests reminiscent of the early twentieth century.

To reverse the damage caused by the 1963 decision, in 1969 the rulemakers lowered the pitching mound from 15 to 10 inches (thereby making the curve and the slider less effective) and ordered the umpires to reduce the size of the strike zone. Officially, the strike zone extended from the knees to the armpits, but to be certain of obtaining a called strike, pitchers now had to throw the ball between the knees and the belt. Moreover, in 1973 the American League replaced pitchers in the batting order with "designated hitters." These changes improved offensive output, though not to the levels of the pre-1960s.

Far greater team parity characterized the second age of post-World War II baseball history—the two-divisional era (from 1969 through 1993 each league had two divisions). During the two-divisional era, not a single team established a dynasty approximating the Yankees, Cardinals, or Dodgers of earlier times. Indeed, in the decade of the 1980s, only 3 of the 26 clubs failed to capture at least one divisional flag. Unlike earlier times, a home city's size was no longer as important in predicting team success.

The demise of dynasties arose from three main sources. In the first place, simply expanding the number of big-league franchises reduced the odds against a team winning the pennant. Second, in 1965 the major leagues implemented an amateur free agent draft which allowed clubs to draft (in reverse order of their standings in the previous season) the rights to negotiate with any unsigned amateur player. The draft decidedly reduced the advantages that the richer franchises had long enjoyed in the procurement of promising college and high school players. Finally, free agency, a right gained by veterans in 1976 to sign with whatever franchise they pleased, apparently encouraged rather than discouraged competitive balance.

The two-divisional era also witnessed a new kind of game on the playing field. It featured raw power, dazzling speed, and specialized pitching. The ballplayers were bigger and heavier than ever, and they reflected an expanded pool of new talent added by those of African and Latino descent. Quickness and strong arms allowed shortstops and second basemen to play far deeper than in the past. In the 1960s, with the introduction of increasing numbers of black and Caribbean basin players, the number of stolen bases shot upward. In the two-divisional era the base thieves broke all earlier records.

No departure from earlier managerial strategy was more striking than the use of relief pitchers. In the past managers had been tied to "the complete game mystique"; starters at the beginning of the century completed more than two-thirds of all games. Managers employed relievers only when their starters were manifestly struggling or when they had to be removed for a pinch hitter. But in the two-divisional era, the number of complete games pitched plummeted downward to less than one in ten. By the 1980s teams were beginning to develop relief specialists. In the eighth or ninth inning, regardless of how well the earlier pitcher had been doing, managers brought in their bullpen kings—"the closers."

The three-divisional era (beginning in the 1994 season) introduced the third age of post-World War II baseball history. In 1994 each league split into three divisions and the major leagues set up a new wild-card playoff system similar to professional football and in 1997 introduced limited interleague play. Most striking of all was a new offensive barrage and the return of dynasties. With a suddenness reminiscent of the 1920s, offensive output soared. Home runs were at the center of the new offensive explosion. All former marks fell. Ruth's seasonal record of 60 homers had stood for 34 years and Roger Maris's 61 home runs had remained unblemished for 37 years, but in two consecutive seasons (1998 and 1999), both Mark McGwire (70 and 65) and Sammy Sosa (66 and 63) easily obliterated these earlier feats. In the 2001 season Barry Bonds destroyed these marks by slamming out 73 home runs.

As with the offensive revolution of the 1920s, followers of baseball offered several hypotheses to explain the new hitting barrage. These included the introduction of a new "juiced" ball; a dilution in pitching talent occasioned by the expansion in the number of teams in 1993 and 1998; more hitter-friendly parks; lighter bats, umpires decreasing the size of the strike zone, which contributed to a new style of hitting; and hitters muscling up through weight training and dietary supplements. Of these, evidence points to the last three as the more plausible reasons for the new offensive breakthrough. In the first seasons of the twenty-first century, baseball sought to counter the upswing by increasing the size of the strike zone.

In the final years of the 1990s wide disparities in team performance reappeared. The Atlanta Braves, Cleveland Indians, and New York Yankees won five consecutive divisional titles (1995–99) and one of the three won eight of the ten league championships and four of the five World Series. At the top again were the Yankees. In 1999 the team posted the first set of consecutive World Series sweeps since the Yankees of 1938–39 and completed an incredible run of 18 victories in 19 postseason games. The following season, the team won its third straight World Series.

In the new era of competitive imbalance, nothing predicted team success or failure more accurately than the size of a team's payroll. Of the teams with the four highest average seasonal payrolls for the 1995–1999 era, only Baltimore failed to appear in every single playoff. In the 1990s the gap between the "haves" and the "have nots" widened. By 1999 the ratio between the seven teams with the highest payrolls was 2.6 times the seven with the lowest. Population of a team's host city no longer translated directly into additional revenues and higher salaries. New parks with luxury boxes, lucrative media markets, and rich owners (including the media giants of Disney which purchased the Angels, Time Warner, the Braves, Tribune Company, the Cubs, and Fox, the Dodgers) generated the additional funds that allowed some clubs to pay more for players than others. Players could be acquired or retained by the richer clubs: through the free-agency market; by simply paying higher salaries to players already assigned to the club; by obtaining players from clubs who could not afford arbitration awards; and by payment of higher signing bonuses (either through the amateur draft or to foreign players exempted from the draft).

BASEBALL OUTSIDE THE FOUL LINES

With memories of Kenesaw Mountain Landis's high-handed leadership still lurking in the background and by nature reluctant to relinquish authority to the commissioner's office, the owners themselves emerged as the primary shapers of baseball's history outside the foul lines in the second half of the twentieth century.

Working mostly behind the scenes, no owner was more powerful than Walter O'-Malley of the Brooklyn-Los Angles Dodgers. O'Malley not only moved the Dodgers to Los Angeles in 1959 but he also engineered baseball's first franchise expansions in 1961 and 1962, the choice of a series of complaint commissioners, and the negotiation of national television packages.

Within these constraints and the growing power of the Major League Baseball Players Association, commissioners struggled with limited success to operate baseball as an economic cartel. Bowie Kuhn, an O'Malley protégée who served as commissioner between 1969 and 1985, warred almost continuously with the faction-prone owners. Recognizing the need for more central direction, the owners assigned to the new commissioner, Peter Ueberroth, who was employed after his spectacular success in managing the 1984 Olympic Games in Los Angeles, more powers than any commissioner had enjoyed since Landis. By signing a lucrative television deal, aggressively merchandising big-league baseball, and by convincing the owners not to sign free agents, Ueberroth aided the big-league owners in turning substantial profits in the late 1980s. But, with Ueberroth's resignation in 1989, the owners in effect resumed complete command of baseball's operations.

In the 1990s and the opening years of next century, the owners wrestled with the yawning disparities in revenues among franchises. In 1996, for the first time in baseball history, the owners began a modest revenue-sharing program through what was called a "payroll tax." Four years later a Blue Ribbon Panel on Baseball Economics recommended revenue sharing up to 50 percent of local earnings from the media and sharply increasing the "luxury tax" on payrolls. The same year the owners rewrote the major-league baseball agreement or "constitution" and handed over to Allan H. "Bud" Selig, the newly appointed commissioner (in 1999), immense powers to "ensure an appropriate level of long-term competitive balance" between the teams. In 2002 the players agreed to both a payroll or luxury tax as well as the sharing of some local media revenues.

While professional baseball no longer occupied such an important place in the American psyche as it had in the past, in the late twentieth and into the early twenty-first centuries, a culture of memorabilia, magazines, Web sites, movies, games, and organizations flourished. Buying and selling baseball cards became a substantial business. Older fans attended fantasy camps where they could don big league uniforms and play alongside former big leaguers. Each February and March found a flood of annual baseball publications at newsstands, supermarkets, and bookstores. Dozens of Rotisserie Leagues allowed fans themselves to own and direct an imaginary big league team. *Eight Men Out* (1988), based on the Black Sox scandal, *Field of Dreams* (1989), *Bull Durham* (1988), and *A League of Their Own* (1992), based on the All-American Girls Professional Baseball League, were baseball movies that became box office hits.

Fans seemed to find in baseball, along with local historical preservation projects, downtown renewals, and the formation of neighborhood associations, a tie with the past and their local communities.[3] Some of the franchises themselves recognized this yearning; in the 1990s several teams moved out of their multipurpose domes and bowls into new ballparks that echoed more closely the past. Perhaps nothing reflected a craving for an older America than the enormous popularity of Ken Burns's lavish documentary *Baseball*, which, ironically, was released during a strike that prematurely ended the 1994 major league season. To Burns, baseball represented everything that was traditionally good about America.

THE EARLY DAYS OF PRO FOOTBALL

Professional football had modest origins. In the 1890s the tough mine and mill towns in western Pennsylvania and Ohio were the cradle for the infant sport. There, local clubs, often formed by the players themselves, began to pay some men a few dollars to risk life and limb to play on Sunday afternoons. A team representing the Panhandle Shop of the Pennsylvania Railroad in Columbus, Ohio, may have been typical of the pre-1920s teams. "The boys worked in the shop until four Saturday afternoon, got their suppers at home, grabbed the rattlers to any point within twelve hours' ride of Columbus, played the Sunday game, took another train to Columbus, and punched the time clock at seven Monday morning."[4] No leagues existed in the pre-1920 era and each team scheduled its own matches.

Unlike college football, the early ambience of the pro sport was ethnic, Catholic, and working class. Some rosters even included a few blacks and Native Americans. For almost a decade, Jim Thorpe, the hero of the 1912 Olympics and Carlisle Indian School football great, was the game's premier attraction. The playing of collegians and sometimes high school athletes under aliases, the practice by players of jumping from team to team during the season to maximize their pay, wagering, and charges of game fixing placed the sport outside of respectable middle- and upper-class circles.

Hoping to reverse the game's image and improve its profitability, representatives from mostly smaller Ohio cities gathered at the Hupmobile automobile agency showroom at Canton in 1920. There, led by Joseph F. Carr, a sportswriter, minor-league baseball owner, and manager of the Columbus football team, they formed a new pro league that became officially known as the National Football League in 1922.

Until the mid-1950s, NFL teams rarely earned profits. During the NFL's first 35 years, over 40 franchises joined the league, struggled, and then expired. The Great Depression of the 1930s wiped out all the franchises in smaller cities save Green Bay, Wisconsin. Major college games invariably outdrew the pro games. To many Americans, pay for play continued to carry a stigma. The league failed to attract many of the top college players. Even though the NFL signed such college heroes as Red Grange and Ernie Nevers in the 1920s, most college stars passed up the NFL; indeed, none of the first five Heisman Trophy winners (beginning in 1936) took up careers in the pros. In the early days, the newspapers, especially outside the cities hosting pro teams, all but ignored the NFL.

Yet the NFL somehow survived these handicaps as well as the ravages of the Great Depression and World War II. Creating a more offensive-oriented sport than the collegians may have been part of the reason. The pro rulemakers moved the hashmarks ten yards inside the sidelines and permitted forward passes from any spot behind the line of scrimmage (1933) and allowed free substitutions (1943). The adoption of two divisions in 1933 with a championship game at the end of the season also enhanced interest in the sport. The invention of the College All-Star Game in 1934, which pitted the NFL champion of the previous season against recently graduated college seniors, added to the respectability of the pro game, attracted large gates, and gained the attention of the nation's press. (Until the 1960s the All-Stars held their own against the pro champs, but beginning in the 1960s they won only one game—in 1963—before the series was abandoned in 1977.) In 1936, the NFL adopted a draft, which allowed teams the exclusive right to contract for the services of college players in reverse order of their league standing in the previous season. The owners hoped that the draft would equalize competition between clubs, but it also strengthened the owner's bargaining position with potential players.

At the conclusion of World War II, the fortunes of pro football improved. Though the NFL confronted an expensive war with a rival, the All-America Football Conference between 1946 and 1949, by 1950 NFL average game attendance had doubled. The All-America conference and the NFL signed more college stars to contracts than in the past. Paul Brown, owner-coach of the Cleveland Browns, a team that played in both conferences, introduced a series of offensive innovations, Brown invented the modern "pocket," in which the quarterback stands to throw, put coaches in the press box, and was the first coach to call all the plays from the sidelines. And on the horizon was television, which promised not only lucrative revenues, but the creation of a new body of fans for the sport.

THE MAKING OF PRO FOOTBALL

No one would have predicted in 1950 that pro football would shortly rival baseball for the affection of the American people. A New York Giants halfback, Frank Gifford, who came to the NFL in 1952, returned home to California after that first season and was asked by his friends: "Where have *you* been?"[5] But ignorance of the NFL among sport fans soon changed. By the mid-1960s, no other team sport even approximated professional football's popularity on television.

Superior management accounted for part of the NFL's success. The football owners had much in common. Nearly all of them were Irish Catholic in origin and shared the long history of financial tribulations that had beset the NFL. Unlike the savagely independent barons of baseball, they were far more willing to delegate authority to the commissioner's office. And unlike the baseball owners, they chose as commissioners men who had experience in the game's business side.

In the post-World War II era, both DeBenneville "Bert" Bell and Alvin "Pete" Rozelle provided the NFL with astute leadership. Appointed as commissioner in 1946, Bell, a former owner-coach of the Philadelphia Eagles, established the framework for the powerful NFL headed by Rozelle from the 1960s through the 1980s. The commissioners welded the NFL owners into a single economic cartel, one far more united than in any other professional team sport.[6] By the mid-1950s televised pro football was attracting millions of new viewers. Watching the games filled a gap in the lives of many Americans. On blustery fall Sunday afternoons men now had something to do besides take their dog for a walk or watch an array of "high brow" programs on television. Television helped the novice fan understand and appreciate the intricacies of the sport. As one fan put it: "You watched a game on television and, suddenly, the wool was stripped from your eyes. What had appeared to be an incomprehensible tangle of milling bodies from the grandstand made sense. [Television] created a nation of instant experts in no time."[7] The central requirement of the game—that the offense must move the ball ten yards in four plays or give it up to the opposing team—set up recurring crises, keeping the viewer's attention riveted to the little silver screen. The pause between plays permitted the viewer to savor the drama. If the situation were third down and long yardage, would the linebackers blitz? Would the quarterback throw or call a draw play?

Technological breakthroughs contributed to pro football's growing popularity. The perfection in the 1960s of instant replays and slow-motion shots allowed fans to experience the game in an entirely different way from that of the spectator in the stands. Instant replay (first used by CBS in 1963) and slow-motion shots could pinpoint a receiver running a pattern, the vicious blocking of an interior lineman, or the balletlike steps of a running back eluding would-be tacklers. Color television and artificial playing surfaces radically altered the appearance of games. The teams donned bright uniforms with the names of individual players on the backs and logos on their helmets. More than one viewer shared the judgment of critic Richard Kostelanetz, who declared that, compared with telecast games, "live games now seem peculiarly inept, lethargic, and pedestrian."[8]

One game, the 1958 championship tilt between the Baltimore Colts and the New York Giants, seemed to trigger the national mania for pro football that would reach unprecedented proportions in the following decade. With only seven seconds left in the game, Steve Myhra of the Colts calmly kicked a 20-yard field goal to tie the game, 17–17. For the first time in NFL history, the championship game went into a "sudden death" overtime. Some 30 million fans watched their screens intently as Johnny Unitas, the Baltimore quarterback, took "thirteen steps to glory," marching the Colts down the field for the winning touchdown. Television had enabled millions to share in the excitement of a classic sporting contest.

Television also played a key role in the making of a new league, the American Football League (AFL). Rebuffed in their efforts to obtain franchises in the NFL, in 1959 two millionaire Texans, Lamar Hunt of Dallas and K. S. "Bud" Adams of Houston, announced the formation of the new league. The AFL began play in 1960 with eight teams, four of which were in cities already occupied by the NFL. The AFL nearly went down at the outset; it lost an estimated $3 million in its first year, and the undercapitalized New York franchise, essential to the AFL's potential success, threatened to drive the entire league into bankruptcy. In 1960 Harry Wismer, former sportscaster and eccentric owner of the New York team, persuaded the AFL owners to sell the league's television rights to ABC as a package, each franchise sharing equally in the receipts. Although the AFL contract with ABC was modest, it helped keep the league temporarily afloat.

In the meantime, the NFL inaugurated its own new era. In 1959, Bert Bell died, and the NFL owners, after nine days of heated discussion, made the surprise choice of 33-year-old Pete Rozelle as their new commissioner. Rozelle had learned the game from the vantage point of business rather than as a player or coach; he had served as both chief publicity man and general manager of the Los Angeles Rams. He was to become the most remarkable commissioner in the history of professional sports. In due time, he so won the admiration of the owners that they delegated to him more authority than any other commissioner of a professional sport enjoyed.

The "Boy Czar" soon got an opportunity to test his skills. In 1961 the NFL signed a television pact with CBS similar to the one that the AFL had made with ABC, but in this instance a federal judge struck it down as a violation of federal antitrust law. Aroused by this adverse decision, professional sports leagues (including

CARICATURE OF ALVIN "PETE" ROZELLE Along with television, Pete Rozelle, the commissioner of the National Football League from 1959 to 1989, helped transform professional football into the nation's most popular televised sport.

major-league baseball) turned to Congress for relief. Package or pooled contracts, in which franchises shared equally in the receipts, were essential to the existence of modern sports leagues, the sports magnates argued in congressional hearings. Otherwise, Rozelle testified, the leagues could not avoid disparities in competition. None of the witnesses, however, noted that increased profits for all franchises would be likely to result from the monopolistic practice of pooled contracts.

Congress quickly passed and President John F. Kennedy signed the Sports Broadcasting Act of 1961. The act permitted the professional clubs to negotiate the sale of national broadcast rights as a single economic unit. The hasty action of Congress and the president clearly exhibited the clout of professional sport on Capitol Hill.

THE GOLDEN AGE OF PRO FOOTBALL

By any measure, the success of pro football from the 1960s to the early 1980s was staggering. Although owners refused to open their financial records to public perusal, apparently teams rarely lost money. "Any dummy can make money operating a pro football club," declared Al Davis, managing partner of the Oakland Raiders in 1978.[9] By the 1970s, each pro stadium regularly exceeded 90 percent of its capacity in attendance, even for preseason training games. The average audience for televised games leaped from 11 million in 1967 to nearly 20 million by 1977.

Two league policies virtually insured teams against financial failure. By giving visiting teams 40 percent of the gate receipts, the NFL avoided the gross disparities in revenues among franchises characteristic of major-league baseball and pro basketball. More importantly, the NFL split television revenues equally among the franchises. As Art Modell, the Cleveland Browns's owner, once happily quipped: "We're 28 Republicans who vote socialist."[10]

Much of the happiness of the owners sprang from escalating television contracts that the Sports Broadcasting Act of 1961 made possible. In 1964 Rozelle signed a $14 million pact with CBS that was nearly three times the contract of 1962. Little wonder that Arthur Rooney Jr., veteran owner of the Pittsburgh Steelers, exclaimed: "Pete Rozelle is a gift from the hand of Providence."[11] NBC, a loser in the 1964 bidding war for NFL rights, decided to gamble on the AFL by paying the new loop $42 million over five years.

NBC's generosity allowed the AFL to embark on a "battle of the paychecks" with the NFL for college stars. In 1965 the AFL signed the biggest prize of all, Joe Willie Namath, a slope-shouldered quarterback out of the University of Alabama, for the (then) astonishing sum of $420,000 for three years. Art Modell of the rival NFL hooted that the signing of Namath was merely a "theatrical stunt," but the high command of the New York Jets, headed by David "Sonny" Werblin, recognized the value of a player possessing both the athletic talent and charisma. Namath had both. In the first season with Namath at the helm, Jets ticket sales doubled. Soon other players received even higher contracts, making Namath's salary one of the best bargains in pro sports.

The rising costs of competition for player talent drove the leagues to the peace table in 1966. Under terms of the merger agreement, Rozelle became the sole commissioner, the combined league established a common player draft to end the bidding war, and the two leagues (or conferences as they were to be known after 1969) agreed to a NFL championship game to begin in 1967. Congress quickly passed a law exempting the merger from antitrust action. Senate Whip Russell Long and House Whip Hale Boggs, both from Louisiana, were chiefly responsible for guiding the legislation through Congress. Perhaps not coincidentally, only nine days after the Football Merger Act became law, the NFL awarded New Orleans an expansion franchise.

The American Football Conference, as it became known after the merger, soon caught up with the senior loop in the quality of play. Vince Lombardi's Green Bay Packers easily disposed of the first two AFC champions, but Super Bowl III in 1969 symbolically established the AFC's parity with the NFC. That year, Namath, leading the New York Jets of the AFC against the Baltimore Colts of the NFC, confidently predicted: "We'll win. I'll guarantee it." And the Jets did, 16–7. In the 1970s and 1980s, AFC teams dominated NFC rivals in interconference games.

Television contracts for the games of the combined leagues spiraled upward. In 1977, "Pete the Shark," as one of the network negotiators dubbed Rozelle, engineered a whopping $656 million, four-year package with the three major networks. Each team received nearly $6 million annually from the contract, nearly six times what they had obtained ten years earlier. But the 1977 contract paled beside the one of 1982. In the midst of an all-out battle among the networks for television rights to major sporting events, the three networks paid $14.2 million per team annually, a huge windfall for each NFL franchise. To put that figure in perspective, the annual television share of the Washington Redskins under the new contract exceeded the team's *gross* revenues for the previous season. Perhaps it was little wonder that some observers conjured up visions of pro football's becoming a studio sport. But in the mid-1980s, as the networks began to economize, the era of escalating television revenues seemed to be over. The NFL's 1987 contract with the three networks and ESPN called for the retention of the same total revenues that the teams had received from the 1983 agreement.

The long era of unity among the NFL franchise owners also began to waver. In 1984, against the wishes of the overwhelming majority of owners and Pete Rozelle, Al Davis moved his Oakland Raiders to Los Angeles. The federal courts upheld Davis's right to defy the league. Shortly thereafter the Baltimore Colts moved to Indianapolis and the St. Louis Cardinals, to Phoenix. Rozelle's power had diminished, and in 1989 he announced his retirement. In 1995, by signing separate contracts with corporate sponsors, Jerry Jones, the maverick owner of the Dallas Cowboys, assaulted the NFL's traditional concept of sharing revenues. The shifts in franchises and the defiance of Jones left in doubt whether the NFL would survive as a tight economic cartel.

The success of pro football in the post-World War II era evoked an unusual amount of speculation about the sport's larger significance. One point was certain. Pro football no longer attracted only workingmen and ethnics. According to national public opinion polls, the game appealed most to the "successful," to those who had a college education, lived in the independent suburbs, held jobs in the professions, and enjoyed incomes higher than the national average. Football more than baseball seemed to echo its fans' work experience. Most Americans now worked in large bureaucracies, corporations, or institutes. Football was a bureaucratic or corporate sport; 11 men acted in unison against 11 opponents. Football, unlike baseball, was time-bound; the ever-present clock dictated the pace and intensity of the game. And like modern work, football embodied rationality, specialization and coordination; the game required careful planning and preparation.

Yet football suggested that committees, systems, bureaucracies, and technologies were still the tools of men, not their masters. The long completed pass and the breakaway run reflected not only careful planning and long hours of practice, but also human potency, natural skill, and grace under pressure. The bone-crunching physicality of the game seemed to compensate for the widespread feelings of individual powerlessness in the 1960s and 70s. The game may have most attracted those who led lives of rigid self-control. But, as in all of human life, fate or luck could be decisive. Even the best-made plans and the best of human performance might fall victim to the unpredictable bounce of the oblong ball.

Many observers related football to the larger social upheavals of the 1960s and 1970s. To President Richard M. Nixon, perhaps the nation's most conspicuous football fan and a man obsessed with winning and losing, football was a miniature school of life, but without life's everyday ambiguities and moral dilemmas. Nixon believed football furnished a healthy antidote to the sixties' counterculture. He regularly placed long-distance calls to stadium locker rooms to congratulate winning teams. Intrigued by the strategy and tactics of the game, he even gave unsolicited suggestions for pass plays, including diagrams, to the head coaches of the Miami Dolphins and the Washington Redskins. He used the specialized vocabulary of football to describe his proposals for ending the Vietnam War and for dealing with the nation's economic problems. Some commentators, on the other hand, insisted that only a nation addicted to the violence of a sport like football could pursue a war as immoral and brutal as the Vietnam conflict.[12]

PACKAGING PRO FOOTBALL FOR TELEVISION

No other team sport was quite so responsive to the needs of television as pro football. "The product [we] provide, is, of course, simply entertainment," Pete Rozelle once confessed to a congressional committee.[13] At first, the NFL had refused to interrupt the flow of a game for commercials, but by the mid-1970s referees received signals from the television crews to call no fewer than 14 timeouts while each game was in progress. Commercials added at least 30 minutes to the length of each game. Traditionally, the NFL had all but ignored the hoopla which had long surrounded college football. But in the late 1970s pro teams urged fans to bring banners, pennants, and towels to wave during the games. By 1980 nearly every franchise hired skimpily dressed female cheerleaders to prance along the sidelines.

Even though the low-scoring, power football of the 1960s and early 1970s satisfied millions of spectators, in the 1970s the moguls of the NFL experimented with rule changes to make the game more exciting. Critics charged that the pro games had become too predictable; coaches seemed determined, above all else, to avoid costly mistakes. Some of the problem stemmed from more rapid improvements being made in defense rather than in offense. Since a football field consists of a rigidly defined and limited amount of space, the appearance of larger, speedier, and better-trained defensive players reduced offensive possibilities. Faced with stronger and quicker defensive players and required to keep their hands flat against their chests while pass blocking, offensive linemen, unless they violated the rules against holding, found it difficult to protect quarterbacks from defensive pass rushers. In 1975 alone, defensive players knocked 17 quarterbacks out of action.

To bring more offense to the game, the NFL adopted minor rule changes in 1972, 1974, and 1977, and a revolutionary set of changes in 1978. In 1978 the rulemakers permitted pass defenders to chuck, or bump, a potential receiver only once and allowed offensive linemen to extend their arms and open their hands to protect the passer. The next year, *Sports Illustrated* reported that "the offenses are going wild."[14] Within three years, passing yardage nearly doubled, and quarterback sacks fell to an all-time low. Gradually, however, defenses reversed the offensive barrage. Game officials began to permit more physical contact with receivers, coaches invented new pass defenses, and defensive players learned how to elude would-be pass-blockers more effectively.

As in baseball, for much of the late twentieth century team dynasties ruled the NFL. Vince Lombardi's Green Bay Packers won six conference titles and five championships, and the Dallas Cowboys (1966–1985) and the Oakland/Los Angeles Raiders (1965–1980) set NFL records for the most consecutive winning seasons. Until 1997, only four teams—the Cowboys, the 49ers, the Steelers, and the Packers—had won almost half of all the Super Bowls.

The NFL recognized that lopsided games, runaway races for the championships, and having the same teams repeatedly in the playoffs threatened to reduce interest in the sport. Hence, beginning in the 1970s, eight teams rather than four participated in the playoffs. A "wild-card" berth in the playoffs added excitement. Under this system, one team from each conference, the team that had the best record apart from the divisional champions, joined the divisional winners in the playoffs. In 1977 the NFL introduced the controversial "position" or "parity" scheduling. Based on their records in the previous season, parity scheduling pitted more of the weaker teams against each other and consequently more of the stronger teams against each other for regular season play.

While the new scheduling system virtually assured that three-fourths of the teams would have a crack at the playoffs up to the final few weeks of the season, it was not until the late 1990s and early years of the twenty-first century that dynasties seemed to disappear from pro football. Suddenly gone were the juggernauts of old; indeed winning the Super Bowl became pro sports' biggest crapshoot. Of the ten teams that played in the five Super Bowls of 1999 through 2003, only three had had a winning record in the previous season. Position scheduling had something to do with new age of competitive parity, but also contributing to a level playing field was a salary cap (that made it difficult to keep high-priced talent), free agency, revenue sharing, and the annual college draft.

As the NFL entered the twenty-first century, the sport could take satisfaction in being the only professional team game that continued to attract huge national television audiences. True, the popularity of the sport seemed to be declining among the young; for example the ratings for *Monday Night Football* fell 31 percent among 18- to 34-year-old men between 1992 and 2002. Overall television ratings were also down.[15] But, while both pro baseball and basketball featured network televised payoff games, only the NFL had the majority of its regular season games carried on network television. Furthermore, even a mediocre matchup on *Monday Night Football* frequently outdrew the final-round games of the National Basketball Association championships, and each year the Super Bowl remained among the most popular programs on television. The cost of owning a NFL franchise reflected the game's continuing prosperity. While the values of NFL and major-league baseball franchises had been roughly equal in the mid-1990s, by 2002 a typical NFL franchise was worth twice as much as its baseball counterpart.[16]

PROFESSIONAL BASKETBALL

Until the 1950s, professional basketball languished in the long shadows cast by college teams, Amateur Athletic Union fives, and the Harlem Globetrotters (an all-black quintet).[17] In the 1920s and 30s only a few barnstorming teams enjoyed more than short-term success. The New York Original Celtics, the most prosperous club of the 1920s, occasionally drew as many as 10,000 fans to Madison Square Garden. In the 1930s the New York Rens, an all-black five, and the Philadelphia Sphas, an all-Jewish quintet, fielded the strongest teams. In 1937 commercial concerns located in cities in the Midwest organized the National Basketball League; in 1949 it joined the Basketball Association of America (BAA) to form the National Basketball Association (NBA).

A turning point in the history of the pro game came in 1946 when a group of big-city arena owners decided to form the BAA. At first the owners saw BAA games only as fillers for vacancies in their winter schedule between the more profitable ice hockey and college basketball matches. Until 1951, for example, the New York Knickerbockers typically played less than half of their home games in the Garden.

Nor did the BAA teams initially compete seriously for the best college talent. Many of them opted to play in the National Basketball League, on AAU teams, or, if black, with the Harlem Globetrotters. Since the 1920s companies in towns where basketball enthusiasm ran high had formed powerful AAU teams composed mostly of college stars. Although they technically held regular jobs for the companies that they represented, these "amateur" players often earned more money than the avowed pros. Until 1950, when Boston drafted Charles Cooper of

Duquesne, no black played in the NBA. Apart from likely racial prejudice, the arena owners of the BAA did not want to offend Abe Saperstein, the owner of the Globetrotters, by raiding his near-monopoly on black talent. Saperstein's Globetrotters often drew larger crowds to their arenas than did their own league games.

In the 1950s pro basketball wiped out or absorbed some of the public following of its major rivals. The emergence of the powerful Minneapolis Lakers, led by towering George Mikan, strengthened the NBA's claim that the league featured the "best of basketball." In the 1950s the NBA began to recruit top black stars and the Globetrotters resorted increasingly to showmanship rather than playing serious basketball. Likewise, in the 1950s, the NBA began to outbid the AAU teams for players. Ironically, a point-shaving scandal in college basketball in 1950–51 also assisted the fledgling NBA. In the wake of the scandal most of the colleges canceled their games in the big city arenas. In these cities, fans either had to forego their hunger for basketball or attend pro games.

Yet problems remained. Indeed, even the teams in the larger cities continued to schedule some of their home games in high school gyms in smaller cities. Television produced only modest revenues; part of the reason was the failure of the NBA to field a strong team in New York City, where Ned Irish, the owner of the Knickerbockers, made many ill-advised trades and drafted players for their immediate publicity value rather than their potential. Because of his abrasive personality, Irish was unable to obtain assistance from fellow owners in building a stronger New York franchise. The NBA also had a problem in coping with low scoring and a rough-and-tumble style of play. Pressure from the fans and television induced the NBA in 1954 to adopt a 24-second rule. A team had to take a shot at the basket within 24 seconds or relinquish the ball to the opposing team.

Yet experience disclosed that the time-limit rule produced subtle, unforeseen difficulties. The new rule made it hard for fans to get excited about the game until the middle of the last quarter. Since it was difficult for a team to build up a lead and "sit" on it, to the fans it appeared that the players did not exert themselves fully until the last quarter. If a team did have a large lead in the final quarter of the game, then the last portion of the game was likely to be unexciting. On the other hand, if the score was close in the middle of the last quarter, then what transpired earlier seemed, in retrospect, to have been insignificant.

In the meantime the style of NBA play changed sharply. Apart from the jump shot, which became part of the standard repertoire of most players, Bob Cousy of the Boston Celtics introduced a razzle-dazzle style of guard play that featured pinpoint passing (even behind the back) and expert dribbling that foreshadowed the black playground style of the 1960s and 70s. Bill Russell, also of the Celtics, introduced a revolutionary style of play for the big center. Russell, who was exceptionally quick and agile, not only reduced the effectiveness of the opposing center, but also by playing in effect a one-man zone (zone defenses were technically illegal in the NBA), he clogged up driving lanes and prevented easy lay-ins. With Russell in the middle, Boston's other four players could gamble by pressing the ball everywhere, causing numerous turnovers without being victimized by easy shots. Russell's rebounding and precise outlet passes also ignited Boston's vaunted fastbreak offense. With Russell leading the way, Arnold "Red" Auerbach's Celtics captured nine NBA championships between 1957 and 1966. Before retirement in 1969, Russell, as coach of the Celtics, led the team to two additional championships.

Pro basketball shared in the largesse of the sports boom of the 1960s, though by no means as spectacularly as pro football. NBA attendance increased from less than two million in 1960 to ten million in the late 1970s. Network television, however, remained lukewarm toward the NBA. In 1962, NBC even dropped its coverage of regular season games, and in 1964 ABC paid a mere $750,000 for a package of Sunday afternoon regular season telecasts. While the NBA's fortunes with the media slowly improved, the newly founded American Basketball Association (1967), which had hoped to capitalize upon television to ensure its success, was unable to land a network contract. In 1976 it folded.

As in baseball and football, certain franchises tended to dominate championship play. In the 1970s, in the wake of the decline of the Boston Celtics dynasty, the NBA enjoyed a temporary era of competitive balance; eight different teams won championships. But from 1980 through 1988, with one exception, either the Boston Celtics or Los Angeles Lakers won all the championships. The market areas of the NBA franchise ranged from cities of a half million to nearly eight million. Furthermore, the gate-sharing arrangement favored the large market areas. But, although the home teams retained all gate receipts, the franchises shared the revenues from the NBA's package television contract. Long-term supremacy seemed to flow mainly from the ability of the Celtics and the Lakers to find the right combination of players rather than from distinct financial advantages.

Beginning in the mid-1980s, the NBA became the fastest growing and apparently the most financially successful of the professional team sports. The alienation of white fans because of the high percentage of blacks in the NBA apparently dissipated, for the NBA outstripped big-league baseball and the NFL in producing stars. Between 1979 and 1992, superstars Larry Bird and Earvin "Magic" Johnson emerged as the best-known athletes in the nation, and in the 1990s Michael Jordan may have replaced Muhammad Ali as the best-known athlete in the world. Only World Cup soccer games attracted as much international attention as the performance of the "Dream Team," which was virtually a NBA all-star team, at the Barcelona Olympics in 1992. According to a 1996 ESPN Chilton Sports poll, basketball was twice as popular as football among 12-to-17-year-olds. "Basketball is the MTV of sports," observed Sara Levinson, a former co-president of MTV who took over the NFL's market management in 1997. "The way TV covers basketball, with the quick cuts, the music overlaid—its much more like MTV [than football or baseball]."[18] Much of the credit for pro basketball's success went to David Stern, hired as the NBA's commissioner in 1984. Stern brought labor peace by guaranteeing the players 53 percent of the NBA's gross receipts, transformed the NBA arenas into advertising theme parks, and turned the NBA headquarters into a huge international star-making and marketing enterprise.

Yet, as the twenty-first century opened, the NBA began to lose some of its glamour. An effort in 2001 to speed up the pace of play and increase scoring by permitting zone defenses and requiring teams to move the ball across half court in eight seconds failed to improve dwindling television audiences. And, despite showcasing the talents of Lakers' Shaquille O'Neal and Kobe Bryant, the 2002 championship series between the Los Angeles Lakers and the New Jersey Nets received the second lowest television ratings in the 21-year span that the series had been a prime-time event. Part of the problem arose from a slumping economy and the failure of a star to step forward as a replacement of Michael Jordan. A few NBA players seemed especially prone to offend one or another segment of the public. In the season 2000–01 season alone, Rasheed Wallace of the Portland Trail Blazers acquired a record-shattering 42 technical fouls, Allen Iverson of the Philadelphia 76ers recorded rap lyrics that contained derogatory references to women and gays, and Jason Williams of the Sacramento Kings made offensive remarks against Asian Americans.

CONCLUSION

After the mid-twentieth century, baseball lost its predominant position among sports fans. In the first half of the century fans had not only given the game their attention in the summer months, but also continued to read and speculate about the game during the long, "hot stove" winter season. Only college football in the fall seriously diverted attention from the national game. By the close of the twentieth century, however, both professional football and basketball had firmly established their own seasons in the sports calendar. Intercollegiate football and basketball, subjects of the next chapter, likewise became major competitors for the attention and monies of sports fans.

As the twenty-first century opened, evidence pointed to the possibility that all three major professional team sports might be declining in popularity. At least partly due to the proliferation of alternative sources of entertainment, television ratings for pro sports dropped sharply from the mid-1990s to 2003. In particular, support of the pro team sports among the young seemed to be falling. The unrelenting bombardment of the senses with sound and visual data, the transformation of stadia and gyms into selling and advertising arenas, soaring ticket prices, and unrestrained exhibitions of greed and surliness among the players—these all entailed risks. They could and perhaps did detract from or diminish what it was about the sporting experience itself that so mesmerized fans.

NOTES

1. See Benjamin G. Rader, *Baseball: A History of America's Game*, 2d ed. (Urbana: University of Illinois Press, 2002); D.Q. Voigt, *American Baseball: From Postwar Expansion to the Electronic Age* (University Park: Penn State University Press, 1983); Bill James, *Bill James Historical Baseball Abstract* (New York: Villard, 1988); James E. Miller, *The Baseball Business: Pennants and Profits in Baltimore* (Chapel Hill: University of North Carolina Press, 1990) for general treatments. Attendance and

population data can be easily found in the annual editions of *Information Please, World Almanac,* and *Sports Illustrated's Sports Almanac*. On television audiences, see A.C. Nielson, *Televised Sports,* published annually. For the relative popularity of professional sports, see also Research & Forecasts, Inc., *The Miller Lite Report on American Attitudes Toward Sports* (Milwaukee: Research & Forecasts, 1983). For a provocative interpretation of baseball's woes, see Eric M. Leifer, *Making the Majors* (Cambridge, MA: Harvard University Press, 1996), and for an overview of professional sports and the American metropolis, see Michael N. Danielson, *Home Team* (Princeton, NJ: Princeton University Press, 1997).

2. *Sports Illustrated* 9 (September 1, 1958), 26.

3. Jules Tygiel in *Past Time: Baseball as History* (New York: Oxford University Press, 2000), chap. 9, entitled "Populist Baseball," argues that the new culture was a product of fans trying to take charge of their own baseball experiences.

4. H.A. March, *Pro Football*, 2d ed. (New York: Lyon, 1934), 65. For early pro football history, see Marc S. Maltby, *The Origins and Early Development of Professional Football* (New York: Garland, 1997); Robert W. Peterson, *Pigskin: The Early Years of Pro Football* (New York: Oxford University Press, 1997); Michael Oriard, *King Football: Sport and Spectacle in the Golden Age of Radio and Newsreels, Movies and Magazines, the Weekly & the Daily Press* (Chapel Hill: University of North Carolina Press, 2001), chap. 6; John M. Carroll, *Fritz Pollard* (Urbana: University of Illinois Press, 1992); John M. Carroll, *Red Grange and the Rise of Modern Football* (Urbana: University of Illinois Press, 1999); George Halas et al., *Halas by Halas* (New York: McGraw-Hill, 1979); and Paul Brown with Jack Clary, *PB: The Paul Brown Story* (New York: Atheneum, 1979).

5. Quoted in B. G. Rader, *In Its Own Image* (New York: Free Press, 1984), 83.

6. See ibid., chap. 8; Frank Deford, "Long Live the King," *Sports Illustrated* 52 (January 21, 1980), 100ff; and for a detailed analysis of the business side of the NFL, David Harris, *The League* (New York: Macmillan, 1986).

7. Quoted in Associated Press, *A Century of American Sports* (Maplewood, NJ: Hamond, 1975), 17–18.

8. Richard Kostelanetz, "Fanfare of TV Football," *Intellectual Digest* 3 (August 1973), 54. See also Joan Chandler, "TV and Sports: Wedded with a Golden Hoop," *Psychology Today* 10 (April 1977), 64–76; and Chandler, *Television and National Sport* (Urbana: University of Illinois Press, 1988), chap. 3.

9. Quoted *Sports Illustrated* 49 (July 24, 1978), 56.

10. Quoted in *Sports Illustrated* 51 (October 15, 1979), 24.

11. Quoted in Joseph Durso, *The All-American Dollar* (Boston: Houghton Mifflin, 1971), 58–59.

12. The literature is immense, but see esp. Murray Ross, "Football and Baseball in America," in J.T. Talamini and C. H. Page, eds., *Sports and Society* (New York: Little Brown, 1976), 102–13; Michael Novak, *The Joy of Sports* (New York: Basic Books, 1976), chap. 5; Allen Guttmann, *From Ritual to Record* (New York: Columbia University Press, 1978), chap. 5; Guttmann, *Sports Spectators* (New York: Columbia University Press, 1986), Part II; R.M. Collins, "Richard M. Nixon: The Psychic, Political, and Moral Uses of Sport," *Journal of Sport History* 10 (1983), 77–84.

13. Quoted in Rader, *In Its Own Image*, 149.

14. *Sports Illustrated* 51 (November 19, 1979), 26ff.

15. Paul Farhi, "It's a Whole New Ballgame," *Washington Post National Weekly Edition*, February 7–13, 2002, 11.

16. According to Frank Deford, "Suicide Squeeze," *Sports Illustrated* 97 (July 8, 2002), 70

17. For the early years, see Robert.W. Peterson, *Cages to Jumpshots* (New York: Oxford University Press, 1990), and for later ones Leonard Koppett, *24 Seconds to Shoot* (New York: Macmillan, 1968). For the Harlem Globetrotters, see Randy Roberts and James Olson, *Winning Is the Only Thing* (Baltimore, MD: Johns Hopkins University Press, 1989), chap. 2.

18. Quoted in John Seabrook, "Tackling the Competition," *New Yorker*, August 18, 1997, 42.

16
COLLEGE SPORTS IN THE AGE OF TELEVISION

*B*efore World War II, conference championships and the defeat of traditional rivals had satisfied all but the most rabid of college football fans. Only the military academies, Notre Dame, and to a lesser degree the Ivy League schools had more than regional followings. Even the New Year's Day bowl games were small-time affairs. But no longer. Television, jet air travel, regional consciousness, and shifting populations, among other considerations, prompted fans and college officials to seek a national standing for their teams. A team succeeded nationally only when it ranked high in the wire-service polls and, by the 1960s, appeared regularly on network television. To join the vaunted ranks of the wire-services' Top Ten required large sums of money, winning coaches, fancy athletic facilities, a national recruiting system, and a burgeoning bureaucracy.[1]

THE NCAA BECOMES A CARTEL

In managing college sports as a national, spectator-centered enterprise, the colleges faced a unique recruitment problem, one not shared by the professional leagues. Unlike the pros, the colleges had no draft; hence in theory some 120 colleges might compete for the same blue-chip football or basketball player. With the stakes so high, the temptation to cheat in recruiting and retaining top-flight athletes intensified. In part to solve this problem by equalizing and regulating the conditions of competition among the colleges for athletes and in part to improve revenues from television, the colleges turned to the National Collegiate Athletic Association (NCAA). In the 1950s the NCAA became a sprawling, frequently unwieldy, and not always effective economic cartel. As with other cartels that sought to control and equalize the costs of production, the colleges employed the NCAA to limit what its member schools could do to attract and retain athletes. No school, for example, could offer athletes more than a "full-ride" scholarship, which included the costs of tuition, board, room, and incidental expenses. In addition, the colleges turned to the NCAA to manage the new medium of televison.

The years from 1940 through 1953 marked a watershed in the evolution of the NCAA into an economic cartel. Prior to 1941 the colleges had limited the NCAA's authority to the making of playing rules for various sports, the supervision of certain national tournaments, and the assertion of principles. While frequently issuing statements condemning financial subsidies to players and unseemly recruiting, the NCAA could only resort to moral suasion to enforce its scruples. The colleges had accepted the basic premise that, being honorable institutions, they should police themselves. Yet the great football debates of the 1920s and 1930s had revealed the utter inadequacy of self-imposed restraints. While many Southern schools openly offered athletic scholarships, many Northern colleges continued to maintain at least the illusion of pure amateurism.

The first step in transforming the NCAA into a cartel came in 1940 when that organization's convention provided for the expulsion by a two-thirds vote of member schools that violated association rules. But practically speaking the provision was impotent. Despite rampant violations of its rules, the NCAA failed to expel a single institution. Indeed, with a resurgence of public enthusiasm for college football and basketball in the late 1940s, temptations to break the rules increased.

The colleges then decided to break with a fundamental principle of amateur athletics—the ideal that no athlete should receive monetary rewards simply for play. The so-called "sanity code" adopted in 1948 permitted the extensions of scholarships and jobs to athletes. But the sanity code *did* provide one major restriction: The grants or jobs had to be awarded solely on the basis of the athlete's demonstrated financial need.

Soon after the adoption of the sanity code, the colleges confronted a series of shocking revelations that forced them to reconsider all phases of intercollegiate sports. In 1950 the United States Military Academy acknowledged that all but two members of its varsity football team had been dismissed for cheating on examinations. The guilty cadets had stained the image of the mighty Army teams that had dominated college football for a decade. The next year, in 1951, the public learned that college basketball was the victim of the biggest scandal in the history of American sports. The New York District Attorney's office accused 33 players from seven colleges of "point-shaving"—keeping the margin of points between teams within a range called for by gamblers from whom the players received cash payments. Widespread revelations of illegal recruiting and under-the-table payoffs to football and basketball players by alumni, booster groups, and the colleges themselves soon followed. In 1953 the NCAA reported that Michigan State, which had fielded the nation's top football team in 1952, operated a huge "slush fund" from which football players were paid handsomely.[2]

The apparent failure of the sanity code as well as the apparently negative effects of unrestricted television on football attendance induced the colleges to extend additional powers to the NCAA. A showdown vote came at the 1950 NCAA convention when a motion to suspend seven colleges cited for noncompliance with the sanity code fell short of the necessary two-thirds vote. Through the American Council on Education, the college presidents even threatened to supplant the NCAA as a governing body for college sports.

The 1952 NCAA convention was a turning point in the history of the organization's evolution into a cartel. After having repealed the sanity code, the NCAA decided to permit the awards of *full scholarships based only on athletic ability* (or what are frequently today referred to as athletic scholarships). At the 1952 convention, the colleges also extended to the NCAA the power to impose sanctions upon colleges that violated the associations' legislation. For the 1952–53 seasons, the NCAA for the first time placed two colleges, Kentucky and Bradley, on probation. Finally, the 1952 convention adopted legislation governing postseason bowls, named a full-time executive director (Walter Byers, who held the post until 1988),[3] and established a national headquarters in Kansas City, Missouri (later moved to a suburb of Kansas City and still later to Indianapolis). With these 1952 actions, the colleges had taken the first steps toward converting the NCAA into a major athletic regulatory body. By abandoning two-platoon football (separate teams for defense and offense) in 1953, the NCAA also briefly (until 1965) checked some of the growing power that coaches wielded on the field of play.

Eager to obtain the publicity attendant on having their games televised, the colleges at first laid down no restrictions on telecasts. Each college negotiated its own contracts with television stations or networks. Perhaps in part due to the new medium of television many fans decided to stay at home and watch the games. Attendance at college games plummeted in 1950—to 1,403,000 below 1948 totals.

Alarmed college officials responded in 1951 by authorizing the telecast of only seven regular season games in each region and signing a national network football package for its schools with the Westinghouse Broadcasting Company. Although reports of possible Justice Department action against the NCAA for violation of the federal antitrust laws appeared in the press, the department took no action to prevent this form of economic collusion. Several colleges also threatened to ignore the NCAA. Notre Dame suffered the most from NCAA restrictions. If Notre Dame (given its large following) had signed a separate television pact with a national network, it could have earned much more than through the NCAA package.

While the colleges eventually agreed on a policy of limited telecasts and a package contract including all colleges, the results were mixed. Football attendance continued to lag behind 1948 figures for a decade. Since only those colleges (or conferences to which the colleges belonged) that had their games televised received funds from the networks, the medium contributed to a larger financial disparity among the colleges in their athletic budgets. On the other hand, the decision to grant to the NCAA control of television strengthened that organization's hegemony over college sports.

THE SOARING POPULARITY OF COLLEGE FOOTBALL

In the 1960s, television, an exciting style of football, postseason bowl games, and weekly press polls, all contributed to the soaring popularity of intercollegiate football. Annual attendance grew from 20 to 30 million in the 1960s and jumped another 10 million in the 1970s. While television ratings lagged slightly behind those of the pro game, they exceeded those of regular season major-league baseball games. Bowl games became major television spectacles. They grabbed almost as much attention as the World Series, the Super Bowl, or the Olympic Games.

The colleges introduced a new, wide-open style of offense. Clock-stopping rule changes allowed college teams to execute 27 more plays per game in 1968 than in 1964, and a study of the 1970 season found that colleges averaged 40 more plays per game than their pro counterparts. The adoption of two-platoon football in the 1960s permitted coaches to perfect more complicated offensive systems. It also resulted in the disappearance of one of the last pretensions of player centeredness in the sport—the tradition that the players rather than the coaches call offensive and defensive signals during play.

The 1960s produced record highs in scoring, passing, rushing, receiving, and kicking. Quarterbacks sometimes filled the air with 50 or more passes per game, figures that would have astonished football fans of the 1920s and 1930s. The "I formation," a popular offensive system developed by Tom Nugent at Maryland in the 1950s, permitted a team to combine both a potent running and passing attack. Perhaps even more remarkable were the triple-option formations that featured quarterbacks as an integral part of the running attack. Oklahoma's wishbone (invented by a Texas high school coach and adopted first at the college level by Darrell Royal at Texas) and Bill Yeoman's veer at Houston regularly produced more than 400 yards rushing per game. Many fans found the college game, with its explosive action, more exciting than the pros.

To accompany their games, the colleges added exciting half-time shows, featuring marching bands, baton twirlers, and card sections. Elaborate, animated card sections—apparently an invention of an University of Southern California student, Lindley Bothwell—first appeared in the early 1920s but did not become standard fare until the 1950s. The most remarkable change came in cheerleading. In the 1950s fans began to witness regularly the spectacle of briefly clad coeds leading cheers, doing fast, leggy can-cans, and other Broadway-like chorus-line routines. In the words of Michael Oriard "magazine covers and ads featured perky, sweater-popping cheerleaders, with skirts flying teasingly above the knee, perfect blends of [male] sexual fantasy and girl-next-door wholesomeness."[4] In the 1970s and 1980s the cheerleaders added difficult mixed-gender gymnastic moves to their more traditional exhibitions. By the end of the century, cheerleading at both the college and high school level had become fiercely competitive. Not only did men rejoin cheerleading squads, but at top levels cheerleading demanded far higher levels of athletic skills than in the past.

"Pseudoevents"—those created largely or solely by the media—also generated interest in the college game. Walter Camp had named mythical "All American" teams as early as the 1890s, but in the 1960s, the selection of all-star teams of college football players became something of a national ritual. The press services, magazines, broadcasters, and organizations of football fans chose not only all-American teams and all-conference teams, but also participants for East-West, North-South, Blue-Grey, and other all-star bowl games. The biggest individual prize became the Heisman Trophy, which had been awarded each year since 1936 by the Downtown Athletic Club of New York City in honor of a former coach and athletic director. After being subjected to an intensive selling campaign by sports information offices of the various colleges who put forth Heisman candidates, a group of sportswriters and sportscasters chose for the award the "outstanding" intercollegiate football player of the year.

The weekly press polls for determining the top teams in the nation furnished an additional source of excitement. Individual journalists had named national champions since the 1890s, but it was not until 1936 that Alan Gould, sports editor of the Associated Press, invented the weekly press poll. To determine the top 20 teams, the Associated Press polled about 50 writers and broadcasters nationwide. By establishing a board of college coaches to name the top teams in 1950, the United Press International (later replaced with the USA Today/ESPN

THE NATION'S NUMBER ONE FOOTBALL FAN *Here, President Richard M. Nixon awarded the National College Football championship to the University of Nebraska team of 1971. An avid fan, Nixon often placed calls from the White House to college and professional coaches and players.*
(Richard Voges)

coaches' poll) joined the polling game. The absence of a system for determining the relative strength of teams or a national champion made the polls a powerful symbolic substitute. By the 1960s, a college's standing in the weekly press polls was often more important to fans, players, and coaches alike than the defeat of a traditional rival or a conference championship.

Bowl games, though late arrivals to the college scene, eventually furnished an exciting climax to the regular season. The parent of college bowls, the Tournament of Roses (Rose Bowl), traced its origins back to 1902. In the depressed 1930s, boosters in Southern cities hoped to attract tourists and outside investors by founding the Orange (1933), Sugar (1935), Sun (1936), and Cotton (1937) bowls. Initially, the bowls offered little financial inducement to the top football-playing schools; the inaugural Orange Bowl, for example, paid each team a mere $1,000 to make the trek to Miami on New Year's day. Television changed that. In 1960 NBC paid the Rose Bowl half a million dollars for rights, but by 1983 the figure had escalated to $7 million. That the bowl games often determined the national champions added immensely to fan interest in the contests.

COED CHEERLEADERS Unlike the pre-World War II era, cheerleading in the age of televised sports frequently featured coeds doing Broadway chorus line routines.
(Nebraska State Historical Society)

College football's popularity strengthened the NCAA's bargaining position with the television networks. ABC, which held the regular season package from 1964 through 1981, increased its payments from $3 million to $29 million annually. Then, as with major-league baseball and pro football, the stakes escalated. Beginning in 1982, from a combined package extended by ABC, CBS, and the Turner Broadcasting System, the colleges received $74.3 million annually, more than twice what they had obtained two years earlier. But in 1984 the United States Supreme Court struck down the package contracts, declaring them in violation of federal antitrust law. Subsequently each college was free to negotiate its own television rights independent of the authority of the NCAA.[5]

The demise of the exclusive package contracts resulted in a hodgepodge of football telecasts originating from national networks, regional networks, and from local stations or cable companies. With the NCAA leaving the field entirely, the colleges scrambled for ways to maximize their televison revenues. Notre Dame promptly signed a contract with a national network, but the other colleges did not have sufficient followings to command such favorable terms.

In order to obtain more lucrative television deals, the colleges disbanded and reorganized traditional conference alignments. Rather than continue their independent status, previously powerful Penn State joined the Big Ten and Miami, the Big East. In 1994 the venerable Southwest conference folded entirely with Texas, Texas A&M, Baylor, and Texas Tech merging with the Big Eight to form the Big Twelve Conference. Dissatisfied with the power given to the individual bowl committees to determine the national championship and hopeful of increasing media revenues, in 1998 the big-time football powers (those comprising the six major Division 1-A conferences plus Notre Dame) established a Bowl Championship Series (BCS). A computer model that took into account the Associated Press media poll, the USA Today/ESPN coaches' poll, strength of schedule, and win-lost records determined the participants in the four championship bowls. While fans frequently took issue with the computer-derived choices, in 2001 ABC agreed to pay $400 million for television rights to the BCS bowls through the 2005 season.

JOINING THE TOP TEN

Becoming a member of the vaunted Top Ten teams in the nation required the generation of vast sums of money, lavish athletic facilities, a national recruiting system, and a burgeoning bureaucracy, in short, the full-scale professionalization of a college's athletic program. Success in joining the Top Ten began with a highly specialized, well-managed bureaucracy. In 1966 the ratio of players to coaches in college football stood at 30 to 1; seven years later, it was 8 to 1. Similar ratio changes occurred in other sports. Athletic directors who once performed multiple roles as business managers, sports information directors, fund-raisers, and coaches all but disappeared from the college scene. Almost no coaches or players applied their skills to more than one sport.

In season, athletes in basketball and football frequently spent up to 40 hours a week in practices, chalk talks, film sessions, and travel. Out of season, they typically engaged in programs of supervised weight lifting. In and out of season, a 1988 study by the NCAA revealed that athletes devoted an average of 30 hours a week to their sport and 26 hours studying and attending class. Such a regimen made it difficult to sustain the illusion that college players were first and foremost students and secondarily athletes.[6]

Pressures to join the Top Ten intensified efforts to recruit blue-chip athletes. "Recruiting, not coaching, is the name of the game," explained Oklahoma's Barry Switzer, the nation's most successful coach in the 1970s and 1980s. Oklahoma has "built its tradition with Texas high school players—and I am proud of it. We've got to get where the players are. Texas has 1,400 high schools playing football. There are just 200 in the entire state of Oklahoma."[7] Schools located in sparsely populated areas had to recruit nationwide, but in the 1970s, even the University of Southern California, which was situated in a rich pool of football talent, extended its recruiting effort to the entire nation.

Effective recruiting required a systematic, well-coordinated effort. Coaches spent hours poring over high school game films and some three months each year jetting about the country visiting high school athletes and their parents. Recruiters relied heavily upon personal contacts. Local alumni, especially if they were celebrities, often lent assistance to their alma maters. Colleges tried to appeal to the rising consciousness of ethnic, religious, racial, and regional concerns. Big-time football powers usually hired at least one black, one Irish American or another representative of a Catholic ethnic group, and one or more coaches who identified with a region outside the state in which the university was located. Once a prospective athlete arrived on campus, he might be greeted by the Bengal Babes, Hawk Hunters, Hurricane Honeys, or the Gater Getters, organizations of comely coeds recruited by athletic departments to act as official hostesses.[8]

Recruiters might promise prospective team members legal or illegal benefits. All major colleges offered athletic scholarships that consisted of room, board, and tuition. Without violating NCAA rules, a recruiter could also emphasize to a potential recruit the likelihood after graduation of joining the pro ranks or landing a good job, the quality of the school's coaching staff, the number of past bowl or past television appearances, or, more improbably, the quality of education offered by the college. Prospects could be shown special athletic dormitories (complete with a television set in each room, recreation rooms, a special dining hall, and a swimming pool), carpeted locker and shower rooms, the latest weight-training equipment, and a staff of private tutors to assist players in their academic programs. At the University of Oklahoma dormitory, known locally as the "Sooner Hilton," two athletes shared a suite consisting of a bedroom, living room, and private bath. On many campuses the players spent four years or more closeted only with fellow athletes.

Illegal inducement took several forms. Alumni and booster groups, often with the tacit approval or at least the knowledge of the coaching staff, might grant cash, cars, clothes, rent-free apartments, use of charge accounts, or high-paying jobs. One of the most common abuses was the sale by college athletes of tickets provided to them by athletic departments ostensibly for their families or close friends. But athletes often sold the tickets, sometimes generating more than a thousand dollars in income. To obtain the admission of an athlete with a poor academic record, coaches might tamper with transcripts. To make up deficiencies in college credits or grades, coaches might arrange for snap courses offered by regular faculty, by correspondence, or by college extension divisions.

Given the intense competition among colleges for top-flight athletes, the NCAA faced formidable enforcement problems. A thin line sometimes separated legal from illegal practices. Coaches often complained that minor infractions were impossible to avoid. Some of the rules seemed petty; for example, a coach could not technically treat his players to ice cream cones from a local Dairy Queen. The rules seemed to weigh heaviest against the poorer black players; for example, a coach or a booster could not buy such a player a round-trip airline ticket to return home for vacations.

Although the NCAA acted as police, prosecution, and judge, it had no subpoena powers. With an enforcement squad that grew to 15 full-time employees by 1988, it tried to police the complicated athletic operations of more than 900 colleges. Close observers of the college athletic scene, including coaches and athletes, estimated that only a small fraction of the total violations resulted in punishment. Even at that, more than half of the some 140 colleges playing big-time football in the post-1950 era were at one time or the other placed on probation.

Many colleges sought a quick entry to the Top Ten by hiring a coach with a proven record as a winner. To seize the opportunities, coaches broke their existing contracts with impunity. Such questionable ethics were consistent with the readiness with which colleges dismissed nonwinning coaches. Salaries of winning coaches soared. In 1982, Texas A&M stunned the college football world by luring Jackie Sherrill away from the University of Pittsburgh for $1.7 million over six years. A television show and boosters footed all but $95,000 of Sherrill's salary annually.

Rapidly escalating salaries in the 1990s made Sherrill's package look like a bargain. Wealthy boosters "can make it so attractive that even a high principled guy could be tempted to do anything to be in the top ten every year," asserted Donald B. Canham, director of athletics at the University of Michigan.[9] Lest their coaches misunderstood the stakes involved, the University of Nebraska in 1994 announced that their head football and basketball coaches would henceforth receive $50,000 bonuses for winning national championships.

Although in principle the NCAA equalized the conditions of athletic recruitment, glaring disparities in playing strength appeared throughout the era of televised sports. Year after year, many of the same teams dominated conferences and appeared regularly in postseason bowls. In the last half of the twentieth century, the same 15 colleges held more than 50 percent of the Top Ten positions in the Associated Press season-ending poll. Oklahoma and Nebraska led the parade by being chosen in the Top Ten 27 times, followed by Michigan (22), Alabama and Ohio State (21), Notre Dame (20), and Penn State (19). The Top Ten also increasingly mirrored the massive population shifts to the Sunbelt. Whereas 44 percent of Top Ten schools in the 1930s hailed from the Sunbelt, the figure exceeded 60 percent in the 1980s and 1990s. Further reflective of the shift was the enormous success of Florida's major universities—Miami, Florida State, and Florida—which among them during the last two decades of the twentieth century won or tied for seven national championships.

Disparities in competition arose from several sources. A few conferences imposed tougher standards than others. By refusing to grant athletic scholarships, the traditionally powerful Ivy League colleges dropped out of big-time football competition. In the 1960s and early 1970s the once-powerful Big Ten colleges fared poorly against nonconference foes. Until 1973, the conference had prohibited red-shirting (the practice of having a player sit out a season to gain more strength, size, and skills while on an athletic scholarship) and permitted only one team to go to a postseason bowl. Winning traditions, a skilled coaching staff, and ample revenues also played important parts in creating the disparities, but effective recruitment of superior athletes was the most significant key in establishing winning programs.

In the 1980s, colleges that did not belong to a conference (the "independents") and those located in the Sunbelt enjoyed the most success. For the 1981–91 seasons, independents won 8 of 11 national championships. Unlike conference teams, the independents did not have to share media receipts with conference schools. In the 1980s, Nebraska, for example, turned over almost $14 million in media money to fellow Big Eight schools while receiving less than $4 million in return. However, in the 1990s, a reconfiguration of television contracts forced the top independents (except Notre Dame with its separate national network contract) to join conferences.

COLLEGE BASKETBALL ENTERS THE NATIONAL ARENA

Until the mid-1930s, basketball had primarily been a local or regional sport. From its invention in the 1890s, it had attracted participants from diverse social groups and of both sexes. They played in community-based programs such as YMCAs, churches, and industrial leagues or on high school and college teams. Many more played informally in driveways, playgrounds, schoolyards, and gymnasiums. In a few places in the 1920s, notably Kentucky, Indiana, and Illinois, high school and college basketball caught on as a popular spectator sport. Yet, football remained the king of campus sports. College gymnasiums usually held only a few thousand spectators, the colleges scheduled few if any intersectional games, and coaching turnovers were frequent.

Perhaps architecture more than anything else converted college basketball into a sport that attained national attention. To capitalize upon the boxing craze of the 1920s, entrepreneurs in about a dozen Northeastern cities built large indoor arenas seating several thousand spectators. With the Great Depression and the decline in the popularity of boxing in the 1930s, the owners desperately sought other ways to make their arenas profitable. Intersectional college basketball games displayed potential in 1931 when Mayor Jimmy Walker of New York asked a group of sportswriters to organize tripleheaders in Madison Square Garden for the benefit of the city's relief fund. Despite the Depression, the "Relief Games" of 1931, 1932, and 1933 drew full houses.

One of the sportswriters who had organized the relief games, Edward S. "Ned" Irish, decided to stage his own college games in 1934. He rented the Garden, which held over 16,000 fans, paid the fees to visiting teams, and kept whatever was left over as a profit. To maximize interest among New York residents, Irish usually pitted strong local college fives against the most powerful rivals he could attract from other parts of the nation. The Garden games promoted by Irish served as a catalyst for the transformation of college basketball into a national spectator-centered sport.

Irish's games became a legend in basketball history. In 1936 he matched Long Island University, winner of 43 consecutive games, and Stanford University, led by tall (for that day) Angelo "Hank" Luisetti. Stanford won 45–31, but Luisetti was the bigger story. Luisetti scored 15 points—all on unorthodox one-handed shots—and became the nation's first basketball hero. His one-handed shots defied years of conventional coaching. "That's not basketball," sneered veteran City College coach Nat Holman. "If my boys ever shot one-handed, I'd quit coaching."[10] Yet the one-handed shot and its derivative, the jump shot, could be shot as accurately, more quickly, and with less danger of being blocked than the standard two-handed set shot. The new shooting styles, along with the elimination of the center jump after each goal in 1937, increased scoring and won the plaudits of fans.

From the late 1930s through the 1940s—World War II notwithstanding—New York was the hub of big-time college basketball. In 1938 the Metropolitan Basketball Writers' Association of New York organized the National Invitational Tournament (NIT) designed to determine the national championship team at the end of each season. The following year, the NCAA founded its own postseason invitational tournament, though until 1951 the NIT remained the premier college tourney.

After World War II, Ned Irish extended his promotion beyond the Garden to Philadelphia and Buffalo, thereby offering at least a three-game package to college teams venturing to the East. Irish also increased the number of doubleheaders to 25 or more per season. By 1950, when the Garden college program drew over 600,000 spectators, it had become every schoolboy's dream to play there one day. For both financial and publicity purposes, appearances at the Garden were obligatory for those college teams striving for national status. Never had the promise of basketball as a spectator sport looked more promising than in 1950.

Then disaster struck. In 1951 New York District Attorney Frank Hogan revealed that 32 players from seven colleges, including players from the strongest teams in the nation, had been involved in fixing point spreads. The Garden was not only the mecca of college basketball; it was also the "clearinghouse" for New York's sports gambling establishment. With the invention of the point spread by gamblers, basketball had become a hot attraction for bettors. Rather than picking a winning team or giving odds on favorites, the bettor wagered on how many points a particular team would win by. Such a system invited fixing, for a fixed team did not have to lose the game; it merely had to win by less than the quoted point spread. The revelations of the fixes shocked the entire country. Coinciding in time with the "fall" of China to communism, the commencement of the Korean War, Soviet detonation of an atomic bomb, and spectacular charges of treason in high governmental places, the basketball scandal contributed to a general climate of suspicion and mistrust.

The scandal had a far-reaching impact upon American sport. Apart from the apparent widespread immorality of college basketball players, the subsequent exposé revealed that many colleges, in their mad scramble for opportunities to play in the big city arenas and win national renown, engaged in the "illegal" recruitment and subsidization of players. For example, as many as 500 college players "worked" for munificent salaries in the Catskill resorts where they "incidentally" played basketball in organized leagues. College coaches and presidents reacted to the scandals and revelations of athletic subsidies with dignified horror. College officials announced that they would no longer permit their teams to compete in the big-city arenas.

The scandal ended the Garden's pivotal place in the financial structure of big-time college basketball. Irish's famed Garden doubleheaders collapsed. The scandal also wiped out the powerful basketball programs of New York's metropolitan colleges. After the scandal, the local colleges no longer attracted the best talent in the city; most of them went elsewhere. In the 1950s and 1960s, state universities began to fill the vacuum by building large fieldhouses themselves.[11]

THE RISING POPULARITY OF COLLEGE BASKETBALL

Despite the scandal of 1950–51 and an initial lack of interest in basketball by network television, when all levels of the sport were combined, it apparently outdrew football and baseball in live attendance. Estimates in the 1970s placed total annual attendance at 150 million per season. For sports fans, the basketball season bridged perfectly the gap between football in the fall and baseball in the spring. Competition from other forms of recreation was less intense in the winter months. Since the season was long, a team could easily play several games per week, the costs of fielding a team were small, and the sheer number of games exceeded those of football and baseball combined.

The sport appealed to all sizes and types of communities. In the small towns of mid-America, high school basketball often furnished a source of common pride, identity, and purpose, a shared experience equaled perhaps only when a natural disaster struck the community. At the other end of the spectrum, basketball flourished in the ethnic and racial enclaves of the sprawling metropolises. In fact, city basketball from the 1930s to the 1970s reflected the ascent of ethnic and racial groups from the ghettos. In the 1930s and 1940s, Irish, Jewish, and Italian athletes dominated the rosters of metropolitan high schools and colleges; in the 1950s, blacks began to replace the earlier ethnic groups. By the 1960s, the position of blacks in college and professional basketball had become so conspicuous that observers wondered if the sport was not especially suited to blacks, either because of physical or cultural reasons.[12]

New modes of play also helped account for the growing popularity of basketball in the post-1950 era. Player skills improved remarkably. By the 1970s, dozens of players six feet, six inches tall and taller had reached higher levels of coordination and dexterity than most of the shorter men of the pre-1940 era. In the 1940s, Robert Kurland of Oklahoma A & M, a towering defensive specialist, and George Mikan of DePaul, a prolific scorer, initiated the revolution in height. The next decade produced two more outstanding big men. Bill Russell of San Francisco demonstrated that the tall center could be a dominating force as a rebounder and defender, and Wilton Chamberlain, a center with the University of Kansas who stood over seven feet tall, showed that a big man could be almost unstoppable as a scorer. Rule changes to restrict the impact of the big men (defensive goal tending in 1944 and widening the free-throw lane in 1955) failed. Moreover, the fans loved the "playground style" of play led by the black players from the big-city ghettos, which featured individual moves, improvisation, and spectacular ball handling.

During the 1980s and 1990s college basketball moved from a game of control and finesse to a battle of strength and power. Whereas in the 1970s fans might see players moving smoothly through the free-throw lane, by the late 1980s cutters regularly encountered knees, elbows, and forearms. The game featured body-on-body contact, especially at the low post position. "It's like a rugby scrum out there," said Xavier coach Pete Gillen in 1991.[13] To gain a favorable position on the floor, bulk and strength became as important as height. By putting players on weight-lifting and dietary regimens, typical players were 10 to 20 pounds heavier than their predecessors of a decade earlier. In 2000 an effort by the basketball rules committee to curtail roughness failed to alter the fundamental character of the new style of play.

As an enterprise involved in the business of entertainment, college basketball resembled a scaled-down version of college football. While basketball did not generate as much revenue from spectators or television as college football, it cost much less to field a team. Since costs were modest, many more colleges tried to play big-time basketball. Like football, a high rating in the national press polls helped ensure a team a berth in the NCAA or NIT tourneys, a profitable season, and "free" publicity for the college.

In turn, the key to a successful team was the recruitment of blue-chip athletes. Unlike football, however, one or two super athletes might reverse the fortunes of an otherwise mediocre basketball team. Thus each year scores of coaches, many of whom were hired more for their recruiting ability than their coaching skills, sought the services of a dozen or so of the nation's most talented high school seniors. In order to make a special pitch to black athletes, nearly all big-time programs hired at least one black assistant coach. Given the intensity of competition for the more promising prospects, the basketball coaches tended to be even more flagrant in violating or ignoring NCAA rules than their football counterparts.

Until the 1990s, basketball could offer a relatively simple and inexpensive means by which an otherwise unknown smaller college could attract national attention. LaSalle, San Francisco, Cincinnati, Loyola Illinois, Texas Western, Georgetown, and Villanova all won national titles. In the post-World War II era, more than a score of smaller Catholic-affiliated colleges dropped football and placed the major part of their athletic resources into basketball. Between 1939 and 1987, 17 different Catholic institutions reached the final four of the NCAA playoffs.[14]

Certain institutions with well-established basketball traditions and well-known coaches nonetheless dominated conference championships and the top ten in the national polls.[15] In fact, between 1964 and 1975, the preeminence of the University of California at Los Angeles in college basketball far exceeded the performances of any college football team of the modern era. In that time John Wooden's UCLA team won ten NCAA championships in 12 years, including seven titles in a row. Inasmuch as the NCAA tourney format (where a single defeat eliminated a team) and the limit on the eligibility of a player to three years (after 1972 to four years) made such a feat appear to be virtually impossible, UCLA's success may have represented the most remarkable achievement in sport history. Wooden's first two championships seemed to be simply the products of astute coaching combined with superior athletes, but after 1965, UCLA was the beneficiary of several of the most promising players in the country. Two of the most spectacular big men to ever play the game—Lew Alcindor (1967–69) and Bill Walton (1971–74)—contributed directly to five of UCLA's ten championships.

During the late 1970s NCAA basketball began to emerge as a major television spectacle. To increase the size of the television audience, the NCAA spread the tournament over several weeks and expanded the number of participating teams to 64. During the 1990s the Final Four, as the miniseries tournament among the four surviving teams in the national tournament was dubbed, moved past the World Series in television ratings. Between 1987 and 1994 annual television income tripled, leaping from $49 million to more than $150 million. Then, in 1994, CBS agreed to the biggest sports contract in television history, to pay out $1.745 billion for the rights to the Final Four through the year 2002.

Beginning in the 1990s the possibility of smaller colleges reaching the NCAA's "Sweet Sixteen"—the final 16 teams in the national championship tourney—became increasingly remote. Indeed, the University of Nevada-Las Vegas in 1990 was the last small college team to win a national championship. During the 2000–02 seasons, 41 of 48 of those colleges making the final round of 16 were also members of the 68 colleges that comprised the Bowl Championship Series in football. Disparities in revenues seemed to be the key variable. "The BCS is turning Division I into haves and have-nots," explained San Diego State president, Stephen Weber.[16] The BCS schools in 2002 took in three times more money than all other Division I schools combined. This permitted them to provide bigger and better basketball facilities, to increase media exposure, and to spend more money on recruiting.

THE TRIPLE CRISES

Despite rising attendance and television ratings, college athletics in the 1980s confronted what Indiana University's President John Ryan aptly described in 1984 as "triple crises."[17] One crisis revolved around the integrity of college athletic programs, another around the academic performance of athletes, and the third around the exploding costs of college sports.

Beginning in 1980, a string of ugly stories leaped to the headlines of the nation's press, all revealing an utter disregard on the part of many college athletic programs for NCAA rules and regulations. In the Southwest reports indicated that Arizona State football players received credits for unattended, off-campus extension courses. Forgery and fakery wrecked the University of New Mexico basketball team. Then came even more startling news. Half of the Pacific-10 Conference schools admitted that they had "laundered" academic transcripts and granted false course credits to student athletes. In 1982 Charles "Digger" Phelps, respected Notre Dame basketball coach, charged that the "going underground" price for blue chip basketball players was $10,000 annually. An NCAA investigation verified that one football recruit received from boosters more than $10,000 in cash to sign with Southern Methodist while others obtained cash and cars. Perhaps it was little wonder that Walter Byers warned in 1984 that the situation was the "móst serious" that he had known during his 35 years as executive director of the NCAA. In 1986 national columnist George F. Will glumly concluded that American colleges were "our schools for scandal."[18]

For most colleges involved in big-time sports, the recruitment and retention of an athlete for four years of varsity eligibility seemed to come before concern about the player's opportunities in pro sports or whether the athlete obtained an education, let alone a college degree. The colleges recruited hundreds of scholastically handicapped youths who had elementary reading abilities; some were classified as having less than fourth-grade reading skills. Once the athletes were recruited, the athletic departments frequently insulated them against serious academic expectations. In the early 1980s, only one-third of the NFL players and even fewer NBA players ever earned college degrees. Handicapped by their earlier experiences and perhaps by special treatment within the colleges, black athletes had less chance of academic success than whites. By 2001, the situation had improved little, if at all; a comprehensive study sponsored by the Mellon Foundation found that athletes across the board performed less well academically than the average undergraduate.[19] Revelations of the apparent absence of concern for the ultimate fate of athletes damaged the moral image of the nation's colleges (see Table 16–1).

Recurring financial problems constituted the third crisis in college sports. In the 1960s and early 1970s, 42 colleges dropped football. Throughout the era of televised sports, nearly 90 percent of college athletic programs operated at a deficit. Notre Dame was, of course, an exception; in 1991, for example, it earned a profit of $32 million, most of which it turned over to academic programs. The costs of large athletic programs mounted from some $3 million in the mid-1970s to more than $12 million in the late 1980s. Inflation, nationwide recruiting, lavish

TABLE 16–1　Public Attitudes toward College Sports, 1989

	PERCENTAGE		
	Favor	Oppose	No Opinion
Do Division colleges place too much emphasis on sports programs?	68	25	7
Do colleges hold student athletes to high enough academic standards?	25	65	7
Do you think it's a common practice for colleges with big sports programs to make under-the-table payments to student athletes?	57	28	15
Do you think colleges should be permitted to pay cash to their student athletes or not?	18	76	7
Would you call yourself a college sports fan or not?	54	45	1

Source: Media General-Associated Press, as reported in *Lincoln* (NE) *Star,* April 3, 1989.

athletic facilities (typically more extravagant than those for the pros), large coaching staffs (again, larger than for the pro teams), stadium expansion, installation of artificial turf, construction of new arenas, and the expansion of women's athletics as a consequence of Title IX—all of these contributed to spiraling costs.[20]

In the 1980s, the colleges embarked on a wave of reforms designed to respond to the triple crises as well as to cap the momentum toward even costlier and more grandiose programs. To generate more revenue, many colleges increased ticket prices and added expensive private boxes ("skyboxes") to their stadia. The Presidents Commission, a body of 44 college presidents created in 1983, seized the reform initiative. The commission pushed through the NCAA a new set of tougher penalties for rule violators, including the "death penalty," which could cost a repeat offender its entire athletic program. The NCAA accepted the commission's recommendations for sharply curtailing the activities of boosters (boosters could not even phone or write prospects any more), ordered a reduction in the number of athletic scholarships and the size of coaching staffs, shortened the recruiting season by 60 percent, and cut the number of visits the coaches could make to potential recruits. To curtail the recruitment of academically questionable prospects, the NCAA in 1986 implemented Proposition 48, which mandated minimum test scores and high school grade point averages for entering athletes.[21]

The full impact of "the reformation" of the 1980s and 1990s remained to be seen. In perhaps the most drastic step in the cartel's history, the NCAA in 1985 levied the death penalty against Southern Methodist's football program, a program that had been guilty of NCAA violations in 11 of the previous 14 seasons. Proposition 48 reduced the number of academically marginal athletes, but it fell heaviest upon black athletes, especially those who came from the ghettos and received inferior educations. In 1996 the NCAA granted to Division 1-A universities—the big-time football playing teams—more power to govern themselves and in the next year the convention allowed Division I-A athletes to take paying part-time jobs year-round. The reforms did nothing to reduce disparities in competition. Indeed, the reforms may have had the effect of further curtailing athletic competition from newcomers and the more obscure institutions.[22]

CONCLUSION

In the post-1950 era big-time college programs operated in a national arena of competition. Although they continued to play most of their games with regional schools, nearly all of them tried to obtain national attention in the polls, play teams outside their region, and recruit on a nationwide basis. Dozens of colleges competed for the honor of having their football or basketball teams named to the Top Ten in the polls. With the stakes so high, temptations to cheat on NCAA rules escalated. During the 1990s and the early years of the twenty-first century, as the big-time schools sought to protect their interests from the other colleges playing sports, the future of the NCAA itself remained in doubt.

NOTES

1. See esp. A.A. Fleischer III et al., *The National Collegiate Athletic Association: A Study in Cartel Behavior* (Chicago: University of Chicago Press, 1992) and its bibliography. This chapter focuses on the NCAA's Division 1-A schools that sponsored what might be called "semiprofessional" teams. For the decade of the 1990s and since, the focus is even more specific—the so-called Bowl Championship Series (BCS) schools within Division 1-A. These are the 68 colleges (as of 2002) that could participate in football's BCS.

2. John Sayle Watterson, *College Football: History, Spectacle, Controversy* (Baltimore, MD: Johns Hopkins University Press, 2000), chaps. 11–12; D.S. Andrews, "The G.I. Bill and College Football," *Journal of Physical Education, Recreation and Dance* 55 (1984), 23–26; Jim Benagh, *Making It to #1* (New York: Dodd, Mead, 1976), 192–95; Charles Rosen, *The Scandals of '51* (New York: Holt, Rinehart and Winston, 1978).

3. On Byers, see Jack McCallum, "In the Kingdom of the Solitary Man," *Sports Illustrated* 65 (October 6, 1986), 64ff; and Walter Byers with

Charles Hammer, *Unsportsmanlike Conduct* (Ann Arbor: University of Michigan Press, 1995). For the official history of the NCAA, see Jack Falla, *The NCAA* (Mission, KS: NCAA, 1981).

4. Michael Oriard, *King Football: Sport and Spectacle in the Golden Age of Radio and Newsreels, Movies and Magazines, the Weekly & the Daily Press* (Chapel Hill: University of North Carolina Press, 2001), 185. See also Mary Ellen Hanson, *Go! Fight! Win! Cheerleading in American Culture* (Bowling Green, OH: Bowling Green University Popular Press, 1995), and Adrian Campo-Flores, "Cheerleading Gets Tough," *Newsweek* 132 (May 21, 2001), 150–151.

5. Quoted in W.O. Johnson Jr., *Super Spectator and the Electric Lilliputians* (Boston: Little, Brown, 1971), 90. On the NCAA and television, see also Falla, *NCAA*, chap. 6, Benjamin G. Rader, *In Its Own Image* (New York: Free Press, 1984), chap. 5, 122–23 and 164–69; and Ronald A. Smith, *Play-by-Play: Radio, Television, and Big-Time College Sport* (Baltimore, MD: John Hopkins University Press, 2001).

6. J.H. Frey, "The Organization of Amateur Sport: Efficiency and Entropy," *American Behavioral Scientist* 21 (1978), 367–68; *The Final Report of the President's Commission on Olympic Sports*, 2 vols. (Washington, DC: GPO, 1977), II, 345, 354; *Lincoln* (Nebraska) *Star*, November 30, 1988.

7. Quoted in *Lincoln* (Nebraska) *Star*, August 30, 1979.

8. See J.J. Rooney, *The Recruiting Game* (Lincoln: University of Nebraska Press, 1980) and Alexander Wolf, "The Fall Roundup," *Sports Illustrated* 67 (August 31, 1987), 46ff.

9. Quoted in Rader, *In Its Own Image*, 167.

10. Quoted in Zander Hollander, ed., *Madison Square Garden* (New York: Hawthorne, 1973), 76.

11. See Rosen, *Scandals of '51*, and Benagh, *Making It to #1*, 192–95.

12. See, for example, Martin Kane, "An Assessment of 'Black is Best,'" *Sports Illustrated* 34 (January 18, 1971), 72ff.

13. Phil Taylor, "Basketball," *Sports Illustrated* 75 (November 25, 1991), 57. On an effort to curb the rough style of play, see Alexander Wolff, "Crying Foul," *Sports Illustrated* 93 (December 11, 2000), 42–47.

14. See James Michner, *Sports in America* (New York: Random House 1976), 231–34, and Frank Deford, "A Heavenly Game," *Sports Illustrated* 64 (March 3, 1986), 58ff.

15. M.E. Canes, "The Social Benefits on Restrictions on Team Quality," in R.G. Noll, ed., *Government and the Sport Business* (Washington, DC: GPO, 1974), 89–90. Canes's data (90) indicate that between 1950 and 1965 basketball teams in the major conferences tended to win successive championships more frequently than football teams.

16. Quoted in *Lincoln* (Nebraska) *Journal Star*, March 26, 2002.

17. *Chronicle of Higher Education*, October 17, 1984, 23, 25.

18. See ibid.: "The Shame of College Sports," *Newsweek* 96 (September 22, 1980), 54; *New York Times*, March 16, 1982, A1, A22; *Wall Street Journal* (Midwest ed.), December 27, 1985; George Will "Our Schools for Scandal," *Newsweek*, September 15, 1986, 84; Harrison Donnelly, "College Sports Under Fire," *Editorial Research Report*, August 15, 1986, 590–608. For historical perspective on efforts to reform college sports, see John R. Thelin, *Games Colleges Play: Scandal and Reform in Intercollegiate Athletics* (Baltimore, MD: Johns Hopkins University Press, 1994).

19. James L. Shulman and William G. Bowen, *The Game of Life: College Sports and Educational Values* (Princeton, NJ: Princeton University Press, 2001). Other important findings of this sophisticated statistical study include (1) male athletes had SAT scores 94 points below their classmates; (2) winning teams did not translate into more money for academic programs either from alumni or state funds; (3) college sports contributed little to racial diversity on college campuses; indeed they may have perpetuated stereotypes of blacks as being less intellectually capable than whites. In 2002, *USA Today*, in a nationwide survey, found that the graduate rates of football and male basketball players at BCS schools were far below those of male undergraduates at the same institutions. *USA Today*, October 18, 2002, 3C.

20. See Watterson, *College Football*, 302–07, 334–36; *USA Today*, October 14–16, 1991, 1C–2C, 5C.

21. D.A. Williams, "Out of Bounds," *Newsweek on Campus*, September 1985, 8ff and *Lincoln* (Nebraska) *Star*, November 30, 1988.

22. See esp. Fleischer, *National Collegiate Athletic Association*, 144–47. In 1994, a Rand Corporation study found that, after an initial two-year decline following the adoption of Proposition 48, the number of blacks receiving athletic scholarships eventually exceeded pre-1986 levels. Furthermore, the number of all student athletes who graduated rose after the adoption of Proposition 48. See E.M. Swift, "Propping Up Student Athletes," *Sports Illustrated* 81 (December 5, 1994), 88. But see also the more recent evidence in Shulman and Bowen, *Game of Life*. In 2002, the NCAA dropped the combined SAT-score cutoff of eligibility for incoming college athletes to a mere 400, which in effect conditioned eligibility almost entirely on the athlete's high school grade point average. Such a decision, in the view of Alexander Wolff, invited grade inflation and the fixing of transcripts. See Wolff, "The Invisible Men," *Sports Illustrated* 97 (November 18, 2002), 29.

17
AMERICAN SPORTS IN A GLOBAL ARENA

As late as the 1948 Olympics, Bob Mathias won the gold medal in the decathlon, which was emblematic of the world's best athlete, after only a few months of training. Such a feat would never be possible again. Twenty-eight years later, in 1976, Bruce Jenner devoted four years of his life (and his wife's) to the single-minded pursuit of a decathlon gold medal. Each day, he worked out for six or seven hours. Driven not by the joy of play nor by patriotic sentiment, Jenner frankly acknowledged that he engaged in such arduous training only in anticipation of future financial gain. After winning at Montreal, he resolved never again to set foot on a track. By the 1970s even in the most traditionally relaxed sports, rigorous training and large sums of money were essential to success. For example, preparations for the 1983 America's Cup, in which a cup was the only tangible reward, cost yachtsmen in excess of $7 million. "I just a little bit deplore that you've got to work for two years—every working day—to prepare for a sailboat race," commented Robert Bavier, president of *Yachting* magazine.[1]

Such incidents heralded the arrival of a new stage in the evolution of sports with origins in the socially exclusive clubs of the nineteenth century. Well before 1950 spectators had played a key role in determining the character of track and field, golf, and tennis, but after the mid-twentieth century the possibilities of fabulous financial rewards for successful athletes in these sports escalated to undreamed-of heights. Under such circumstances, these sports at the championship level also severed most if not all of their connections with private clubs and dropped any lingering pretense to amateurism. Even youth sports programs began to resemble their professional counterparts more than before (see Chapter 20).

In addition, American sports, especially the former club sports, became increasingly inseparable from a global arena of competition. In earlier times, the wealthy and their sports had circulated back and forth between European and

American spas, but in the postwar era, a separate, highly commercialized universe of international sport came into existence. That German television in the 1990s paid more money for rights to tennis matches than American television was indicative of the growing globalization of sport. Champions in tennis, golf, and track and field played on world circuits, American basketball players joined professional fives in Europe, the Olympic Games became truly world spectacles, major league baseball expanded into Canada, Canadian football and hockey invaded the United States, the National Football League played exhibition games to capacity crowds in Barcelona, Berlin, London, and Mexico City in 1994, and in the same year the United States hosted soccer's World Cup. In the meantime, growing numbers of athletes from all over the world came to the United States to accept offers of college athletic scholarships.[2]

THE POLITICS OF THE OLYMPIC GAMES

Despite the experience of the 1936 Games and World War II, Olympic officials continued after the war to propound the principle that the Games should remain above the exigencies of politics and avarice. The International Olympic Committee (IOC) itself had changed little from the days of Pierre de Coubertin; a self-perpetuating aristocracy of counts, princes, barons, marquesses, and men of old wealth ruled the organization. Until the 1990s, no woman or active athlete sat on the IOC. "Sport," said Avery Brundage, the Chicago construction magnate who served as president of the IOC from 1952 to 1974, ". . . like music and the other fine arts, transcends politics. . . . We are concerned with sports, not politics or business."[3] Yet this nineteenth-century athlete-centered ideal of the Olympics never fully corresponded with reality. In the postwar years the gap between official Olympic ideology and practice widened. The Olympic Games became great international media spectacles. Not only athletes and nations, but also bureaucracies, business concerns, and even terrorists enlisted the Olympics in behalf of their special interests.

      The very structure of the Olympics worked against an athlete-centered orientation. By requiring that athletes compete as representatives of nations rather than as individuals, the Games inevitably became forums for international politics and the expression of national identities. In the postwar era the combatants in the Cold War and the new nations of the Third World were especially prone to use the Olympics to further their own international political goals. As the Games grew in size, cost, and the power to generate international attention, commercial considerations also shifted the focus away from the individual athletes. Financing the expanded games required ever larger sums from television, corporations, and governments. Corporate sponsors seized upon the Olympics to sell products. Finally, pressures from nation-states, and local organizing committees and the vast sums of money required to finance the Games forced the Olympic movement to place its emphasis upon the success of its organizations rather than the interests of the athletes.

The importance of external forces in shaping the history of the postwar Olympic movement first became manifest at the 1952 Games held in Helsinki, Finland. The 1948 Olympics, scheduled in war-ravaged London, had occurred with a minimum of commercialization and political friction. Although the Soviet Union did not send a team to the 1948 Games, Americans became alarmed when they learned that the Soviets would compete in the 1952 Games. To raise funds to counteract the "Red Menace" in 1952, the United States Olympic Committee (USOC) arranged for an Olympic Telethon starring Bing Crosby and Bob Hope. Hope set the tone for the American effort when he cracked: "I guess Joe Stalin thinks he is going to show up our soft capitalistic Americans. We've got to cut him down to size."[4]

Athletic rivalry between the two superpowers dominated the 1952 Helsinki Games. To the chagrin of the IOC, both countries devised ingenious self-serving scoring systems that allegedly demonstrated the athletic superiority of their respective social and political systems. Athletic success, the Americans and Soviets seemed to believe, would bolster national self-confidence, enhance the respect of allies and nonaligned nations, and demoralize the opposition. Little wonder that the athletes began to conceive of themselves as surrogate warriors in the Soviet-American battle for prestige and influence. Bob Mathias, the Olympic decathlon champion, captured the mood of the American team: "There were many more pressures on the American athletes [in 1952] because of the Russians than in 1948. They were in a sense the real enemies. You just loved to beat 'em. You just had to beat 'em. It wasn't like beating some friendly country like Australia."[5]

The degree to which the rivalry between the United States and the Soviet Union impinged upon the Olympics usually depended upon the intensity of the Cold War. Although conflict between East and West spilled over into the games at Melbourne in 1956, the United States and Soviet Union track officials announced a tentative agreement for an exchange of track meets to begin in Moscow in 1957. At the Rome Games of 1960 East-West goodwill abounded; Soviet and American athletes openly fraternized. The chairman of the Soviet Olympic Committee, Constantin Andrianov, was even moved to say, "Politics is one thing, sport another. We are sportsmen."[6] Yet apparently the poor showing of the highly touted American track and field team at Rome led President John F. Kennedy to enlarge the program of the President's Council on Physical Fitness. In the 1960s and 1970s regularly scheduled athletic competition between the Soviet Union and the United States became part of a wide-ranging program of cultural exchange between the two nations.

In the 1960s the apartheid (racial segregation) of South Africa replaced Soviet-American conflict as the main Olympic political issue. The newly formed black African states determined to use international sports as a lever to force change in South Africa's apartheid. The IOC barred South Africa from the 1964 Games, but reassured by promises that racism would be eliminated in South African sports, it voted by postcard to readmit the nation's team to the 1968 Games in Mexico City.

Almost all of the African nations and several Third World countries promptly withdrew from the Games. Black American athletes, led by San Jose

THE SOVIET JUNIOR OLYMPIC TEAM AT AN AMERICAN DEPARTMENT STORE In this photograph members of the Soviet Junior Olympic team examined sales items at a department store in Lincoln, Nebraska, suggesting the possibility that international sports competition could broaden understanding between nations. Yet political considerations often intruded, as when the United States boycotted the Olympic Games of 1980 and the Soviet Union, the Games of 1984.
(Nebraska State Historical Society)

State sociology instructor Harry Edwards, announced a probable boycott. With the 1968 Games seriously jeopardized and to save face, the IOC declared that the international climate of violence made it necessary to bar South Africa from the Games. In 1970 the IOC officially expelled South Africa from the Olympic movement; the nation was not readmitted until 1992, when it promised to end apartheid.

The political use of the Games reached grotesque proportions in the 1972 Munich Olympics when a group of Arab terrorists seized the Israeli compound and eventually killed nine Israeli athletes. The tragedy dripped with irony, because the West Germans had hoped to erase the ugly memories of Nazism only to have Jewish blood once again spilled on German soil. But this time the Germans were the would-be rescuers. After having scaled an eight-foot-high fence and capturing the Israeli compound, the terrorists made five demands for the release of the nine hostages, including the freeing of some 200 Arab guerrillas in Israel and elsewhere. The West German negotiators, guided by top Israeli government officials, refused to budge. In the meantime the terrorists postponed deadlines for the execution of the hostages. Television cameras positioned near the compound zoomed in on the hangmanlike visage of a terrorist in a stocking cap who seemed to symbolize the total prostitution of the Games to political ends.

West German and Israeli officials finally settled upon a desperate plan that was to culminate in an ambush of the terrorists at an airport near Munich. The plan failed. The terrorists killed all of the Israeli hostages, though German authorities captured three of the Arab guerrillas and killed the others. Despite the massacre, Olympic officials decided that the Games ought to continue. In the view of Richard Mandell, a witness of the 1972 Games, there was an additional irony. The martyred Israeli athletes "more deeply institutionalized the guilt on the part of outsiders that has been the basis for founding and maintaining the Jewish state; they stabilized a little more the always-threatened country."[7]

The Soviet Union's invasion of Afghanistan in 1979 suddenly reawakened the latent antagonism between East and West. Although the United States had not withdrawn from earlier Games to protest Soviet invasions of Hungary and Czechoslovakia, President Jimmy Carter quickly called for a worldwide boycott of the 1980 Games. Fearing Soviet expansion into the Persian Gulf region, American officials apparently believed that a boycott would serve as a moral condemnation of the Soviets, perhaps induce them to withdraw from Afghanistan, and deal a severe blow to Soviet prestige. Although only Canada, West Germany, and Japan, of the industrial states, cooperated fully with the American boycott, it was the first instance of one of the superpowers withdrawing from the Games.

In 1984 the Soviets retaliated by refusing to participate in the Los Angeles Games. With the absence of one or the other of the superpowers at the Games of 1980 and 1984, the Games lost some of their intrinsic excitement. With the collapse of the Soviet Union in 1989, the Cold War and its impingements on the games ended and, ironically, so did some of the excitement generated by the games. Indeed, except for 1996 when Atlanta hosted to Games, the American television audience for the Summer Games in the post-Cold War era sharply declined.

THE ESCALATION OF THE STAKES

Commercial considerations, though less sensational than political intrusions, also took on a growing importance for the Games. Avery Brundage visualized the Olympic movement as "a revolt against Twentieth Century materialism . . . a devotion to a cause and not the reward."[8] But such a noble sentiment hardly squared with the realties of the postwar era. Television alone was responsible for altering much of the commercial and financial structure of the Olympics. The medium transformed the Games into a genuine international drama, played upon national rivalries, and eventually became essential to their financial solvency.

The contracts between the American television networks and the Olympics grew slowly until the 1970s when they soared to astronomical heights. In 1988 Seoul received $300 million from NBC, $52 million from Japanese television, and $28 million from Western Europe for television rights; in the same year ABC paid $309 million for the rights to the Winter Games in Calgary, Canada. NBC then upped the ante to $705 million for the Summer Games of 2000 held in Sydney, Australia. But, despite a decade of falling television ratings—except Atlanta—NBC paid an astonishing $2.3 billion for the combined rights to the 2004 and 2008 Summer Games and the 2006 Winter Games.

ABC was largely responsible for transforming the games into major television spectacles. To its coverage of the 1968, 1972, and 1976 Games, ABC brought the technical expertise and ingenuity gained from producing *The Wide World of Sports* and college football. Apart from good Nielsen ratings, the networks believed that televising the Games enhanced their image and provided valuable "lead-ins" to their prime-time fall programming. For these reasons, the networks were willing to take at least limited financial losses from their telecasts.

Similar considerations led cities to host the Games. While up to 1984 costs to the host city always exceeded profits, cities believed that the Olympics offered unique opportunities for presenting themselves as showcases of modernity. The first cities since the Berlin Olympics to fully exploit these possibilities were the 1964 Winter Games at Innsbruck, Austria, and the Summer Games in Tokyo. While the Tokyo Games served as a stimulus for badly needed urban renewal, the Games also helped launch Japan as one of the world's top trading nations. Scheduling the 1988 Games in Seoul also reflected the growing power of the Pacific (Asian) Rim countries in world trade.

With its budget exploding in size, in the 1980s and 1990s the IOC became increasingly subject to control by multinational corporations. A decisive turning point in the growth of corporate power within the Olympic movement came with the 1984 Olympics. With only one bidder for the 1984 Games—Los Angeles—the IOC reluctantly altered its constitution so that it could sign a contract with a local organizing committee independent of the host city. By skillfully franchising sales of Olympic-related products, Peter Ueberroth, the manager of the games, raised millions of dollars from corporate sponsors. Altogether, the Los Angeles games produced a $200 million surplus, from which Ueberroth awarded himself a $475,000 bonus. Ueberroth's stunning success in making money from the games launched a mad scramble by other cities to tap into the lucrative corporate coffers. By 1997 no fewer than 11 cities sought to act as hosts of the 2004 Games.

With so much money at stake, scandal followed. To ensure that Salt Lake City would host the 2002 Winter Games, local boosters spent some $7 million in illegal gifts, travel, scholarships, medical care, jobs, and other perks to IOC members. In addition, according to an exposé published by *Sports Illustrated*, American taxpayers shelled out a staggering $1.5 billion in subsidies for the Salt Lake City Games. Beneficiaries included wealthy Utahans engaged in the development of housing, commercial property, ski resorts, and road construction. Had these dollars been divided up equally among the American athletes participating in the games, they would have each received $625,000 from the federal government. By contrast, taxpayers would have paid each athlete competing in the Atlanta Games of 1996 a mere $57,000.[9]

The growing dependence on televison and corporate monies further compromised the autonomy of the IOC. In 1985 the IOC signed the first of a series of marketing agreements with an entity called International Sports, Culture, and Leisure Marketing, which initially generated $95 million through 1988. Nine multinational corporations participated in what became known as TOP I ("The Olympic Program"). Twelve worldwide sponsors provided revenues to the IOC in excess of $350 million for TOP IV, which carried the program through 2004. While the TOP programs reduced the IOC's dependence on television revenues to about 50 percent, it meant that critical decisions within the Olympic movement were increasingly subject to, if not shaped by, the interests of global corporations.

AMATEURISM ABANDONED

Until the 1972 Games, Americans had for the most part accepted a hypocritical system of amateur athletics and an uncoordinated Olympics program. Except for a two-week interlude every four years, the media and most Americans simply ignored the Olympic Games. That changed in 1972. The Munich Games were the first to take over a network's entire prime-time schedule. Intrinsic drama, including monumental blunders (the failure of two American sprinters to show up for the second round of the quarterfinals of the 100-meter dash), the "theft" of the basketball gold medal from the Americans by the Soviets, sparkling heroes (American swimmer Mark Spitz and the tiny Soviet gymnast Olga Korbut), and tragedy (the seizure of the Israeli compound by Arab terrorists)—all riveted the American people to their television sets as nothing had done since the assassination of President John F. Kennedy and the murder of Lee Harvey Oswald in 1963. Television allowed viewers to become eyewitnesses to history in the making.

At both the 1972 Munich Games and the 1976 Montreal Olympics, television magnified the victories of the Soviet bloc countries, thereby making millions of Americans acutely aware for the first time of the deficiencies in their nation's Olympic effort (see Table 17–1). Americans had long complained that the Soviet bloc nations fully subsidized their athletes, thereby enjoying an advantage in Olympic competition.

Communist successes sprang from more than direct subsidies. Unlike the United States, the Communist nations made sport an integral part of state policy. They invested millions of dollars in sports centers, training programs, and research. East Germany, a nation of only 17 million people, won more gold medals in the 1976 and 1988 Summer Games than the United States with a population of more than 240 million. Despite the collapse of the Soviet Union, former Soviet republics (when combined) won more medals than the United States at the 1996 Games.

TABLE 17–1   Leading Olympic Medal Winners, Summer Games 1952–2000
(total medals)

Olympic Years	USA	Russia	E. Germany	W. Germany	Germany
2000	97	88	—	—	57
1996	101	63	—	—	65
1992	108	112	—	—	82
1988	94	132	102	40	—
1984	174	*	*	59	—
1980	*	195	126	*	—
1976	94	125	90	39	—
1972	93	99	66	40	—
1968	107	91	25	25	—
1964	90	96	—	—	50
1960	71	103	—	—	42
1956	74	98	—	—	26
1952	76	69	—	—	24

*Until the 1968 Games, Germany had a combined team. The USA and West Germany did not compete in the 1980 Games. The USSR and East Germany did not compete in the 1984 Games. In 1992, the former USSR athletes competed as the United Team and Germany again competed as one team.

In response to the poor showing of American athletes in 1972 and 1976, President Gerald Ford appointed a special commission to study the problem.[10] The resultant Amateur Sports Act of 1978 completely overhauled the American Olympic effort. To eliminate the long-standing disputes between the governing bodies of amateur sports for hegemony over the American Olympic program, the act empowered the USOC to act as a coordinating authority. This provision sharply trimmed the power of the once-powerful Amateur Athletic Union. Subsequently, the USOC set up permanent quarters in Colorado Springs, Colorado, for research and athletic training. For several months each year, promising Olympic hopefuls in several sports could train at Colorado Springs with all expenses paid.

The nation also moved closer to a complete and open subsidization of athletes competing in Olympic sports. Until the mid-1970s, amateur athletes could not technically benefit financially in any way from sports. However, nearly all the world-class athletes received some sort of subsidy. Those attending college usually enjoyed athletic scholarships and athletes in the military often received additional time off for training. Since at least the 1920s, promoters of track and field meets in both the United States and Europe had paid well-known athletes generous "travel" expenses to participate in their meets. In the 1960s, endorsements of sporting equipment became something of a worldwide scandal. Manufacturers offered Olympic participants free equipment plus cash payments to prominently display skis, vaulting poles, clothing, and shoes before the television cameras.

Practice and principle gradually came closer together. In 1974 the IOC modified its strict rules by permitting "amateur" athletes to receive their regular salaries when in training for international competition even though the athletes might not actually be working at a job. Additional changes in IOC rules and the Amateur Sports Act of 1978 allowed Olympic hopefuls to accept guaranteed appearance money, earn "Grand Prix" points on the international track circuit (which could be translated into dollars), serve as highly paid consultants to corporations, and even do television commercials without losing their eligibility. Suddenly, several of the world-class athletes in Olympic sports began to earn as much money as professional athletes in team sports.

Unlike avowed professionals, however, the Olympic track and field athletes could not receive the money directly. Funds first went to the national sports organization to which the athlete belonged. For example, The Athletic Congress (TAC), the governing body of track and field, placed athletes' earnings in a trust fund that could technically be tapped only for essential living and training expenses. But TAC was generous in its definition of living expenses, allowing athletes in effect to earn as much as they could. Such an artifice made it possible to retain the tissue-thin illusion of amateurism while in fact providing for a system of professional sports. In the meantime, the IOC ruled that each international sports governing body could determine its own rules of eligibility. Consequently, for example, the United States sent a nearly all professional basketball team (the Dream Team) to Barcelona in 1992.

TELEVISION AND THE ASCENT OF GOLF

In the era of televised sports, golf entered a new "golden era," or as some observers would put it, "the Age of Arnold Palmer." In the 1950s golf's ambience was still that of the country club and summer resorts, but in the 1960s golf rather suddenly experienced a revival of spectator interest. The number of active players and courses doubled, and the professional tour achieved unprecedented popularity and prosperity. In 1956 the television networks collectively carried only five and one-half hours of golf for the entire year, but by 1970 viewers could see nearly that much weekly, and earnings had soared to more than $6 million. Golf furnished the Associated Press "Athlete of the Decade" for the 1960s—Arnold Palmer.

Signs of the new golden age of golf were apparent in the 1950s. Ardent fans admired the precisionist play of Ben Hogan and Sammy Snead, perennial winners of major championships in the late 1940s and 50s. In the nation's capital, the new president, Dwight D. Eisenhower, unlike two of his golf-playing predecessors (William Howard Taft and Warren G. Harding) made no secret of his addiction to the game. To sharpen his putting skills, the president had a real green constructed outside his office. He played at every opportunity, with golfing pros, business tycoons, or entertainment celebrities, either in the Washington, D.C. area or at the Augusta, Georgia, National Course where club members built him a vacation cottage.

AMERICA'S DREAM TEAM *The triumph of America's "Dream Team" at the 1992 Barcelona Olympics signified the complete abandonment of the amateur tradition in Olympic sports. All except two of the players came from the ranks of the National Basketball Association, a professional league.*
(AP/World Wide Photos)

At the other end of the continent Hollywood celebrities took up golf with equal ardor. Often as part of a gimmick to hawk local real estate, Bing Crosby, Bob Hope, Perry Como, Danny Thomas, Andy Williams, and Jackie Gleason, among others, sponsored new professional tournaments. The association of golf with a popular president and a host of celebrities lent golf a glamour perhaps unequaled by any other sport.

Then in the 1960s came the potent combination of television and Arnold Palmer. Palmer brought to golf high drama and charisma. The son of a club pro from the Latrobe, Pennsylvania, Country Club, Palmer's first major victory came in the 1954 National Amateur; four years later he attained some national prominence by winning the Masters, the first of four triumphs on Bobby Jones's home course at Augusta. Then came the U.S. Open at Denver in 1960. Before a nationwide television audience on a searing afternoon, he established his reputation for the Palmer "charge," "a heart-attack approach to golf that demanded the situation look hopeless before one really begins to play." Entering the last round of the tourney while trailing by seven strokes and 14 players, Palmer exploded, scoring one birdie after another to finish with an epic 65, a score low enough to take the title.

Golf fans never forgot the 1960 Open, but Palmer added to his own legend by fashioning an incredible string of come-from-behind victories. Few experiences in sport equaled the sheer drama of the Palmer charge.

Not since the historic feats of Bobby Jones in 1930 had a golfer created so much national excitement. Golf fans loved Palmer and he reciprocated their affection. He acted and looked like a "regular guy" who needed the help of the fans. Palmer's face registered his emotions. He celebrated his good shots with a wide disarming grin and by raising his club high in the air as if to say "We did it" bad shots produced painful grimaces. Long after Palmer stopped winning many championships, "Arnie's Army," as the immense throngs who accompanied him were dubbed, continued to follow him around the course as he played.

He exuded trust and was an advertising agency's dream. His manager Mark McCormack, a Cleveland lawyer and a pioneer in the sports agent business, made Palmer into a one-man conglomerate, a corporation that produced and endorsed a galaxy of products, many of which were unconnected with golf. Even as late as 1987, when Palmer was more than 20 years past the prime of his career, estimates placed his earnings from product endorsements ($8 million annually) higher than those of any other athlete in the world.

In the mid-1960s Jack Nicklaus challenged Palmer's supremacy as a player but never his popularity. Nicklaus became the winningest golfer of all time. He won the U.S. Amateur twice, the Masters six times, U.S. Open three times, the British Open three times, and the PGA four times. His style of play amazed the world of golf. No one had ever been able to drive the ball so consistently down the fairway with distance, height, and accuracy. A stunned Bobby Jones acknowledged: "Jack Nicklaus plays a game with which I am not familiar."[11] Several tournaments even redesigned their courses to present Nicklaus with more formidable challenges.

Television was the other key to golf's new golden era. Although golf matches were expensive to telecast (more than double a NFL football game), the cameras could easily capture the bucolic scenery; even when most of the nation was blanketed with snow, viewers could be transported to sylvan, semitropical sites. Although televised golf was punctuated by numerous lulls and suffered from intrinsic difficulties in obtaining a proper perspective between the ball and the course, the drama of thousands of dollars riding on a single putt could produce a momentary intensity equal to any other sport. Even though television audiences consistently fell far below the major team sports, sponsors believed that televised golf attracted an ordinarily difficult-to-reach affluent, male clientele.

Television was mainly responsible for altering the economics and governing structure of pro golf. With growing infusions of money from television, the pro tour purses grew rapidly. By 1987 the leading money winner garnered more than a million dollars a year, and 21 players enjoyed lifetime tour earnings of more than $2 million each. Primarily to seize the opportunities made available by television, the touring pros in 1968 threatened to break away from the PGA, an organization comprised mostly of club pros. The warring factions finally reached a settlement; it called for the establishment of a separate division within the PGA (initially called the Tournament Players Division but later renamed the PGA TOUR) with its own commissioner. Although not backed by private promoters, the player-controlled PGA TOUR gained a large measure of control over the world's major tournaments.

Prize money and public exposure of women's professional golf lagged far behind that of the men's game. In 1946 a handful of women formed the Women's PGA (changed to Ladies Professional Golf Association in 1948). The LPGA sponsored the United States Women's Open from 1948 to 1953 when the USGA took charge of the tourney. Purses remained pitifully small. In 1948, for example, the ladies' tour consisted of only nine tournaments and Babe Didrikson Zaharias, the leading money winner, garnered only $3,400. As late as 1970, the women's tour offered only $345,000, divided among 21 events. Then television suddenly took an interest in the women's game. Nancy Lopez aided the sport, capturing the attention of the entire sporting world, when she reeled off five consecutive tour victories in 1978, a feat not accomplished since Arnold Palmer in the 1960s. Yet, it was not until a decade later that the woman's top earner received a half million dollars in prize money.

After a spurt of growth at the grass-roots level in the 1960s and 1970s, golf's popularity slowed in the 1970s. Some analysts blamed the "curse of slow play" for the slackened interest; critics said that slow play arose from amateur efforts to imitate the deliberate style of the pros that they watched on television.

AMATEUR GOLFERS *A sport long identified with the nation's upper classes. Television contributed to the growth of golf, as a popular spectacle in the post-World War II era.*
(Arlene Collins)

Regardless of the cause, on weekends at most courses playing 18 holes required five or more hours. Some golfers shifted to tennis or racquet ball where brisk matches could be played in an hour-and-a-half or less. Raging inflation in the 1970s slowed growth even more. Private clubs suffered financial squeezes, forcing them to close their doors or raise fees to new heights.

Popular participation increased again in the 1980s and 1990s. The construction of new courses by municipalities, resorts, and real estate developers expanded the number of venues for play. With the new public courses, the game no longer remained an exclusive preserve of white-collar professionals or the rich; growing numbers of blue-collar workers and professional women took up the sport. By 1994, businesswomen's beginner golf groups, something unheard of five years earlier, had sprung up in more than 90 cities. Although business golf remained largely a man's game, women in the corporate world found that an enthusiasm for golf enhanced their opportunities to get ahead. Whether at the office or on the course, playing golf seemed to ease their way into the corridors of economic power.[12]

Beginning in the late 1990s Eldrick "Tiger" Woods introduced yet another "revolution" in golf history. Never before had a golfer won so many tournaments while so young. In the 2000 season, at the age of 24, he won golf's Grand Slam and his earnings from tournaments alone totaled more than $9 million. Through 2002, he had won nearly 30 percent of all the PGA matches that he had entered, a stunning figure never before equaled in the history of pro golf. With his unprecedented level of play and a charisma equal to Palmer's, Woods singlehandedly sent the television ratings soaring. Woods's mixed ancestry (his father was one-quarter Chinese, one-quarter Native American, and half African American; his mother was half Thai, one-quarter Chinese, and one-quarter Caucasian) also extended the appeal of golf far beyond its traditional upper-middle and upper-class white clientele. In the opening years of the twenty-first century, Woods even challenged Michael Jordan's title as the world's most renowned athlete.

TENNIS—OPEN TO ALL

Patterns of competition in tennis, one of the last bastions of the player-centered era and one of the most conservative of sports, changed little from the 1930s to the mid-1960s. "Social climbers," more interested in using tennis as a means of earning a social reputation than in promoting tennis as a spectator sport, continued to dominate the management of the game. Consequently, the ambience of tennis remained stiff, formal, and pompous. The tennis establishment permitted and encouraged "shamatuerism" usually in the form of paying amateurs liberal "expense" allowances for appearing in tournaments. Most players could make more money by remaining nominal amateurs than they could by becoming avowed professionals.

Professional tennis could support only two or three players in a decent fashion. Beginning with the formula established by Bill Tilden in the 1930s, a handful of pro players embarked each year upon international tours, but these itinerant pros played in relative obscurity—in matches that the public often perceived as mere exhibitions. On the other hand, the absence of the best-known players in the great amateur tournaments at Forest Hills and Wimbledon robbed the tourneys of potential excitement. To be successful as a spectator sport, tennis needed to shed its "country club" image and develop a format which would feature classic confrontations between the world's greatest players, regardless of whether the players were professional or amateur.

"Open" tennis seemed to be a solution. In the 1950s Jack Kramer, winner at Forest Hills in 1946 and 1947 and Wimbledon in 1947 and the best-known figure in American tennis, launched an intensely personal campaign for the open game. Tournaments open to both pro and amateur players, with prize money, Kramer reasoned, would not only erase the blatant hypocrisy endemic to big-time amateur tennis but would also generate a renewed public interest in the sport. At the same time, tennis officials within the United States Lawn Tennis Association (USLTA) worried about falling tournament receipts and the drastic decline in the performance of American amateur players. Between 1953 and 1968 American men failed to capture even one singles title at Forest Hills; a series of great Australian players (Australia had a population approximately equal to New York City) dominated the sport.

The decision of an Australian, Rod Laver, winner of the Triple Slam—British, American, and Australian championships—to turn pro in 1963, when the game most needed a star gate attraction, and the establishment of a small but successful pro circuit in 1964 were important turning points in the movement for open tennis. While the USLTA wavered in its support for the open game, the British, French, and Australian associations joined the movement. Only the International Lawn Tennis Federation (ILTF), controlled by the national associations of the smaller nations, resisted the open game. By announcing that Wimbledon would be an open event in 1968, the British unilaterally defied the ILTF and thereby inaugurated a new era of tennis. The next year the United States championships at Forest Hills also opened its gates to the pros. Faced with a virtually united front of the largest tennis playing nations, the ILTF finally capitulated.

Open tennis, television coverage of the big tournaments, the emergence of a new set of American stars such as Stan Smith, Arthur Ashe, Jimmy Connors, Billie Jean King, and Chris Evert, plus burgeoning purses all contributed to a heightened public interest in tennis. Although television ratings remained below those of the team sports and golf, production costs were far less than the other sports and advertisers suspected that televised tennis matches reached an exceptionally affluent market. Between 1970 and 1973 the networks tripled the amount of time devoted to the sport and NBC paid a record $100,000 for the rights to televise each of eight World Championship Tennis tournaments. Televised tennis reached a peak in 1975. That year the networks telecast 50 matches and CBS paid $600,000—

a sum exceeding a NFL telecast—to cover a match between Jimmy Connors and John Newcombe.

Open tournaments with larger purses marked a decline in the monopolies of the national associations and the ILTF and the rise of a new set of private promoters. The promoters engaged in a vicious, cutthroat competition for profits. In 1970 Lamar Hunt, Texas millionaire and owner of the Kansas City Chiefs football team, bankrolled World Championship Tennis, which, for a guarantee, would provide pro tours anywhere in the world with a tournament of competing stars. The same year Jack Kramer established the Grand Prix, nominally under the jurisdiction of the ILTF, which awarded points to players for high finishes in major tournaments and prize money to top winners at the conclusion of the season. The top winners then played in a Masters tournament for bonus money. Largely because of the international character of tennis, neither the promoters nor the players established a single economic cartel to govern the sport.

Several observers forecast that tennis would replace football and golf as the major "growth" sport of the 1970s. The early years of the decade seemed to confirm their prediction. Apart from the professional games which were suddenly the beneficiary of unprecedented purses for tournaments, rich endorsement contracts, millionaire stars, and an abundance of television coverage, tennis became the "in" sport of upper-middle income groups. In the first three years of the decade sporting goods companies tripled, then quadrupled their sales of tennis gear; in 1973 the manufacturers, unprepared for the sudden boom, even ran short of balls. The demand for tennis instruction, especially in more or less exclusive social circumstances, reached new heights. John Gardiner, who started the country's first tennis ranch in 1957, pioneered in intensive instruction in a resort setting. Gardiner's program included professional instruction in basic strokes and tactics, the use of videotape replays, and rapid-firing ball-throwing machines. Hundreds of indoor tennis centers sprang up across the country. In 1961 only one indoor facility operated in the Chicago area; by 1974 there were 43 centers.[13]

But tennis never regained the momentum of the early 1970s. The construction of new resort and indoor facilities tapered off, the sale of tennis equipment slumped, and, except for Wimbledon and the United States Open, the networks cut back sharply on television coverage. "Unless there's better organization and focus," predicted NBC's Don Ohlmeyer in 1979, "[tennis] . . . is going to die on television in the 80s. There's eight million tournaments and only two that mean anything—Wimbledon and the U.S. Open."[14] Whether the manic court behavior of stars such as John McEnroe attracted or repelled fans was uncertain, but the failure of American men to do well in the late 1980s reduced the American television audience for the sport. Pete Sampras, Jim Courier, and Andre Agassi reestablished the preeminence of American men in the 1990s, but American television (though not the European media) remained lukewarm toward the sport.

As the new century opened, the Williams sisters (Venus and Serena of African American ancestry) seemed to be bringing a revolution to tennis similar to the one Tiger Woods brought to golf. At the completion of their finals played in Australia in 2003, they had played one another in four of the preceding five Grand

Slam tournament singles finals. They also easily captured the women's doubles title at Wimbledon. Television ratings for their matches frequently outstripped those of the men; indeed 50 percent more Americans watched their 2002 Wimbledon doubles final than the men's singles final. Their U.S. Open singles final against one another in 2001 drew more viewers than a competing top-20 football game between Notre Dame and Nebraska. As Woods had done with golf, the Williams sisters not only established a new level of play in women's tennis but also possessed unusual charisma.

CONCLUSION

In the second half of the twentieth century, track and field, golf, and tennis, sports whose antecedents extended back to socially exclusive clubs, reflected a more general trend toward the globalization of American sports. Just as Americans found their economy more intricately linked to the world economy and the media and foreign travel tying together the world's remotest outposts, some American athletes could sometimes earn more money by playing at foreign sites than at home. Likewise, increasing numbers of foreign athletes competed in the United States. Sports television became more internationalized as well. Television carried the Super Bowl to more than 50 nations, and ESPN, with the deregulation of European television in the 1980s and 1990s, began to furnish large amounts of sports programming to numerous cable and satellite systems there. Or take a more trivial but perhaps telling example of the influence of American sport abroad. In the summer of 1992 a visitor to a small Italian village witnessed 12-year-old boys sporting Michael Jordan shoes and T-shirts while playing basketball on a local school ground.

NOTES

1. *Newsweek*, (September 22, 1980), 11.

2. See a growing body of literature on the globalization of sports, such as John Bale, *The Brawn Drain: Foreign-Student Athletes in American Universities* (Urbana: University of Illinois Press, 1991); Rick Hoffer, "Foreign Legions: U.S. Colleges Are Recruiting Armies of Athletes From Abroad," *Sports Illustrated* 80 (June 6, 1994), 46–49; Allen Guttmann, *Games and Empires: Modern Sports and Cultural Imperialism* (New York: Columbia University Press, 1994): Joseph Maguire, *Global Sports: Identities, Societies, Civilizations* (Malden, MA: Blackwell., 1999); Walter Lafeber, *Michael Jordan and the New Global Capitalism* (New York: W.W. Norton, 1999); Alan Bairner, *Sport, Nationalism, and Globalization* (Albany: State University of New York Press, 2001);

Maaten Van Bottenburg, *Global Games* (Urbana: University of Illinois Press, 2001).

3. I.O.C., *The Speeches of Avery Brundage* (Lausanne: IOC, 1968), 67. For treatments of the Olympic games in this era, see Allen Guttmann, *The Olympics: A History of the Modern Games* 2d ed. (Urbana: University of Illinois Press, 2002); Guttmann, *The Games Must Go On: Avery Brundage and the Olympic Movement* (New York: Columbia University Press, 1984); Richard Espy, *Politics of the Olympic Games* (Berkeley: University of California Press, 1979); and P.J. Graham and Horst Ueberhorst, eds. *The Modern Olympics* (Cornwall, NY: Leisure Press, nd).

4. Quoted in W.O. Johnson, Jr., *All That Glitters Is Not Gold* (New York: G.P. Putnam's Sons, 1972), 223.

5. Quoted in Espy, *Politics of the Olympic Games,* 38.

6. Quoted in Johnson, *All That Glitters,* 236.

7. R.D. Mandell, *The Olympics of 1972: A Munich Diary* (Chapel Hill: University of North Carolina Press, 1991), 272.

8. Quoted in Johnson, *All That Glitters,* 24.

9. Donald L. Barlett and James B. Steele, "Snow Job," *Sports Illustrated* 95 (December 10, 2001), 78–98.

10. See *Final Report of the President's Commission on Olympic Sports,* 2 vols. (Washington, DC: GPO, 1977).

11. Quoted in Frank Deford, "Still Glittering after All These Years," *Sports Illustrated* 49 (December 25, 1978–January 1, 1979), 26.

12. See Ron Givens, "Hail the Size of Golf Balls," *Newsweek,* (August 18, 1988), 71, and Paul O'Donnell, "Look Who's No Longer Missing the Links," *Newsweek,* (March 14, 1994), 68.

13. Judson Gooding, "The Tennis Industry," *Fortune* 87 (June 1973), 124–33.

14. Quoted in *New York Times,* December 30, 1979, S7.

18
THE AFRICAN AMERICAN QUEST FOR EQUITY IN SPORTS

A symbolic turning point in the racial desegregation of American sports came on March 19, 1966. In the presence of 14,253 basketball fans at the University of Maryland's Cole Field House and before a nationwide television audience, number-one ranked Kentucky sought their fifth NCAA championship against upstart Texas Western College of El Paso. By 1966 nearly every major college team had been racially integrated, but at Kentucky their venerable coach, Adolph Rupp, had held out. Rupp recognized that black athletes had innate talent, but he thought blacks lacked the initiative, intelligence, and self-control to play basketball at the championship level. On the other hand, all five starters on the Texas Western Miners were black. Playing a ball-control offense, the Miners led all the way, winning by a score of 72 to 65.

An era had passed. Between the end of World War II in 1945 and the victory of Texas Western in 1966, overt racial segregation collapsed on many fronts. Even before the Supreme Court decision in 1954 (*Brown v Topeka Board of Education*) that began a process of undercutting the superstructure of Jim Crow laws and practices in the United States, both professional and college teams began to eliminate traditional racial barriers. By 1966, thousands of blacks played on teams in both North and South. In the early 1970s even Adolph Rupp began recruiting blacks. Yet the African American quest for equity in sports was not over. Despite claims to the contrary, race and racialist thinking continued to pervade the sports world, and, paradoxically, the striking successes of blacks in sports may have diverted public attention from the larger cause of racial justice.

THE ORIGINS OF DESEGREGATION

"Brooklyn announces the purchase of the contract of Jack Roosevelt Robinson from Montreal," read a terse press statement released by Branch Rickey, general manager of the Brooklyn Dodgers, on April 9, 1947.

The announcement revealed nothing of the larger significance of the event. It did not mention that Robinson was black, that he would be the first black to play in the major leagues since the 1880s, or that breaking the "color ban" in the national game might be of incalculable symbolic importance. No one knew that the racial integration of organized baseball would herald the beginning of a black breakthrough in many other sports, or that it would lead essayist George F. Will to conclude 40 years later that Robinson was "one of the two most important blacks

JACKIE ROBINSON AND BRANCH RICKEY In this publicity photograph, Jackie Robinson signed a contract offered by Branch Rickey to play professional baseball. By playing with first the Montreal Royals and then the Brooklyn Dodgers, Robinson broke a "color ban" that had existed in the major leagues since the 1880s.
(UPI/Corbis)

in American history."[1] (The other, according to Will, was Rosa Parks, who refused to move to the back of a Montgomery bus in 1955.)

In the wake of World War II overt racial segregation ended in other sports. Pro football reintegrated in the fall of 1946 when blacks joined the Los Angeles Rams in the NFL and the Cleveland Browns in the All-America Conference. In 1947 the Missouri Valley Athletic Conference dropped its racial bans; the next year more than a dozen blacks joined Valley Conference teams. In 1949 the American Bowling Congress opened its lanes to blacks. In 1950 two blacks joined the NBA and Althea Gibson played in the U.S. Open tennis tourney at Forest Hills. The PGA finally admitted the first black athletes in 1961, but then only as a consequence of a California court order.

The desegregation of sports arose from a combination of pressures: increasing agitation by blacks outside the world of sports, assertions of black political power, international circumstances, shifting attitudes of whites toward blacks, and quests for additional profits by sports entrepreneurs. Outside the sports world, resistance to segregation, especially by the rapidly growing number of blacks in the northern cities, had been mounting since the 1920s. In the 1930s Nazi racism exposed in glaring relief the contradictions between official American principles and actual racial practices. Not wishing to have American racial prejudice and discrimination publicized when the nation was about to wage war against Nazi Germany, President Franklin D. Roosevelt issued an executive order in 1941 banning discrimination in hiring "because of race, creed, color, or national origins" by the national government and its war-related contractors. But severe labor shortages in World War II did even more than the poorly enforced executive order to expand opportunities for blacks.

Urban blacks learned that trading black votes for black rights could be a highly effective tactic. Since the Northern cities lay in highly competitive, two-party states with large electoral votes, a solid bloc of black voters could tip the balance in elections. As early as 1942 in New York, a state in which black voters could decisively affect elections, the legislature passed the Quinn-Ives Act to ban discrimination in hiring. In New York City Mayor Fiorello LaGuardia established a special committee to study race relations, including the discrimination against blacks by New York's major-league baseball clubs. Obviously political circumstances in New York City were favorable to Rickey's assault on segregated baseball.

Inside the world of sports two black athletes—Jesse Owens and Joe Louis—both of whom had moved from the South to Northern cities as youths, enhanced black pride and won the admiration of many whites. The success of Owens, the hero of the 1936 Berlin Olympics, seemed to be the perfect answer to Nazi racism, but it also highlighted the existence of racial discrimination in the United States. The discrepancy between racial practice at home and propaganda against Nazi racism abroad was not lost upon American blacks or their white sympathizers. The career of Joe Louis, the victor in 1938 over the darling of the Nazis, Max Schmeling, revealed a similar incongruity.

The sharp decline in public interest in boxing after the retirement of Gene Tunney in 1928, the nonthreatening image of Louis, and the international tensions—all contributed to the circumstances that gave Louis a shot at the title and won him a large following. Five different men had held the championship between 1928 and 1937. Heavyweight boxing needed a new hero and Louis, with his superb boxing skills and powerful knockout punches, was, except for his race, the most likely candidate to fill the need. The promoters of Louis consciously determined to avoid the image problem that had beset Jack Johnson: They imposed a rigid code of personal conduct upon Louis. "The colored boy is clean, fine and superb, as modest and unassuming as a chauffeur or as the man who cuts and rakes the lawn once a week," declared a sportswriter.[2]

Louis also benefited immensely from the international climate of the 1930s. By defeating ex-champ Primo Carnera of Italy in 1935, at the very time that the Italian Fascist dictator Mussolini was blatantly overrunning defenseless Ethiopia, Louis won the plaudits of both white and black America. In 1936 Louis lost by way of a knockout to Max Schmeling, who had briefly held the crown after Tunney's retirement. One year after his humiliating defeat, Louis defeated James J. Braddock for the championship. In 1938 he again fought Schmeling, this time in a fight freighted with international tension. Only two months before the fight Hitler had annexed Austria. Approximately two-thirds of the people in the United States heard the fight on radio. Louis knocked out Schmeling in the first round. Louis further improved his standing among whites by voluntarily joining the Army in World War II. When he announced his retirement in 1949, he had held the heavyweight crown for nearly 12 years and had 25 defenses—both records for any weight divisions.

In view of the principle of nondiscriminatory hiring established in World War II, the passage of several state nondiscrimination laws, American condemnation of Nazi racism, and the heroics of Jesse Owens and Joe Louis, the continuation of racial segregation in baseball appeared to be at odds with a new phase in the history of white-black relations. During the 1930s urban black newspapers, a few influential white sportswriters, and the American Communist Party began to attack the ban. Not only would integration aid the "Negro cause," they claimed, but it would also open an enormous new pool of talent to big league clubs. Baseball spokesmen either denied the existence of a color ban or, contradictorily, suggested that integration would decimate the Negro leagues and therefore harm blacks. Since the teams in these leagues often played in major-league parks, the big-league owners also had a vested interest in their survival.

The shortage of major-league caliber white players during World War II set the stage for several attempts to arrange tryouts for black players; finally in 1945 a few blacks were asked to display their skills for the Dodgers, Boston Red Sox, and Boston Braves. But none of them were offered a contract. However, a year earlier, in 1944, Commissioner of Baseball Kenesaw Mountain Landis, who had secretly sabotaged efforts to integrate the national game, died. His replacement, former governor A. B. "Happy" Chandler of Kentucky, was far more sympathetic to baseball's integration.

RICKEY AND ROBINSON INTEGRATE THE NATIONAL GAME

In the meantime, unknown to the public, Branch Rickey, prepared to end base-ball's color ban. A devout Methodist, Rickey personally disliked segregation. But practical considerations also moved him; blacks playing in the Negro leagues represented a huge pool of potential talent for which the notoriously parsimo-nious Rickey would have to pay nothing. Rickey worked out a careful plan for the introduction of a black player into the major leagues. So that he could scout black talent without being detected, he announced the formation of a new all-black league. He sought a black athlete who would be assured of making the club and be able to wear a "cloak of humility" in the face of expected abuse from white players and fans.

Except for a rather hot temper and only one full season of experience as a professional player, Jackie Robinson fit Rickey's requirements perfectly. Robinson was familiar with the world of whites; he had attended UCLA for nearly four years, had been an army officer in World War II, and was an active Methodist, who did not smoke, drink, or womanize. Finally, he was a gifted athlete. He had starred in football, basketball, golf, track, and swimming at UCLA. In 1945 he played baseball for the Kansas City Monarchs of the Negro National League. After receiving assurances from Robinson that he would not retaliate against white in-sults, Rickey signed him to a contract to play for Montreal, a Dodger farm club in 1946. Robinson won the International League's most valuable player award and moved up to the parent club in 1947.

Jackie Robinson was an instant hero of blacks. "When times get really hard, really tough, He [God] always send you somebody," said Ernest J. Gaines's fictional heroine Miss Jane Pittman. "In the Depression it was tough on everybody, but twice as hard on the colored, and He sent us Joe [Louis] . . . after the war, He sent us Jackie."[3] At games in spring training, in the International League, and in the National League, blacks came out in droves to see Robinson play. Thanks largely to Robinson, five National League teams set new season attendance records in 1947. But racial integration spelled disaster for the black leagues. The Negro National League dissolved after the 1948 season and the Negro American League fielded only four teams in 1953 before expiring in 1960.

No uniform white reaction greeted Robinson. Before he arrived in Brook-lyn, southern players on the Dodgers circulated a petition demanding that Robin-son not be promoted to the majors, but organized opposition dissipated when Harold "Pee Wee" Reese, a southerner and the team captain, refused to sign, and Rickey agreed to trade discontented players to other clubs. A threat of wholesale suspensions by National League president Ford Frick stopped a rumor that the St. Louis Cardinals players planned to boycott games with the Dodgers.

At the personal cost of persistent headaches, bouts of depression, and smoldering anger, Robinson eased the way for his acceptance by publicly ignoring racial slurs. Instead of direct retaliation, he channeled his energies onto the base-ball field where he played magnificently. That Robinson had won over many whites became evident at the end of 1947 when he was ranked second only to popular singer Bing Crosby as the nation's most admired man. After completing the 1948 season, Robinson in effect declared his independence from Rickey's strictures. From then to the end of his career in 1956, he was as outspoken and as aggressive as the white players.

Baseball's example of apparent interracial harmony quickly became a weapon in the Cold War. In 1949, when Paul Robeson, a popular black singer and a former college football star, told a Paris audience that American blacks would never bear arms against the Soviet Union, the United States House of Representatives Un-American Activities Committee invited Jackie Robinson to repudiate Robeson's statements. Rickey urged Robinson to cooperate. Seated before the committee, the Dodger star denounced American racism. "I am not fooled because I've had a chance open to very few Negro Americans," Robinson said. But at the same time Robinson took issue with Robeson. "I've got too much invested for my wife and child and myself in the future of this country . . . ," he told the committee, "to throw it away for a siren song sung in bass."[4] The newspapers lavished praise on Robinson for his denunciation of Communism and Robeson, but they ignored or downplayed his critique of American racism. For the remainder of his life, Robinson remained painfully embarrassed by the use made of his testimony.

Robinson's successes did not result in the immediate full-scale integration of baseball. A few weeks after Robinson joined the Dodger organization, Rickey signed four other blacks, but no other team followed his example. The pace with which blacks joined major-league clubs was agonizingly slow; the Boston Red Sox did not employ a black player until 1959, 12 years after Robinson's debut in Brooklyn. By the early 1950s fears mounted among whites that blacks might dominate big-league baseball; many if not all clubs had unwritten understandings to restrict the total number of blacks. Driven in part by the profit motive, franchise owners tried to calculate whether increasing the number of black players would result in more wins and thereby increase attendance or whether it would adversely affect identification of whites with their teams and thereby reduce attendance and revenues. The net effect was that, in order to make team rosters, blacks had to outperform whites. Integration was uneven; in 1959 the National League had twice as many blacks as the American League.

The integration of intercollegiate sports was also slow. A few blacks had played on northern college teams as early as the 1890s, but their percentage was never proportionate to the nation's African American population. Moreover, until the 1940s, northern schools invariably agreed to bench their black players when playing in intersectional games. Until 1957, the National Collegiate Athletic Association barred black colleges from its tourneys. "The NCAA may mean National Collegiate Athletic Association to some people," concluded John McClendon, a black coach at North Carolina Central University in 1950, "but to us it means No Colored Athletes Allowed."[5]

Led mainly by students, a major push to integrate northern college athletic programs more fully got underway in the 1940s and 1950s. By selectively recruiting those blacks whom they perceived as best "fitting in" to the dominant white society or whom seemed destined for stardom, northern schools frequently practiced a kind of tokenism. During that era, several ugly racial incidents marred interregional college games, and white colleges in the Deep South continued to bar black players and frequently refused to play northern teams who fielded black players. Not until the mid-1960s, when the civil rights movement reached its heyday, did racial integration become commonplace in intercollegiate athletics.

MUHAMMAD ALI

Partly because of continued racial discrimination, black athletes, somewhat tardily, joined the larger civil rights movement. While Robinson had breached the color ban in the national game well before the momentous Supreme Court decision of 1954, black athletes were conspicuously absent from the "sit-ins" of the early 1960s, the Freedom Riders, and the March on Washington in 1963. Perhaps they had more to lose than nonathletes. By conforming to white expectations and the authoritarian structure of sports, a few blacks had clawed their way to athletic fame. To protest racism in sport or elsewhere might have jeopardized their newly won status. Nonetheless, a new stage of militancy in the civil rights movement in the mid-1960s, rising black expectations, and the controversy swirling around Muhammad Ali spawned a widespread black athletic revolt.

Initially, Ali's career furnished few indications that he would become a focal point of the massive social and cultural unrest of the 1960s. As Cassius Clay, he had won the light heavyweight gold medal at the 1960 Rome Olympic Games by defeating a more experienced Russian boxer. Asked by a Soviet reporter about racial prejudice in the United States, he responded with remarks that could have been authored by the State Department's press secretary. "Tell your readers we got qualified people working on that, and I'm not worried about the outcome," he said. "To me, the U.S.A. is still the best country in the world, counting yours." Ali soon began a rapid climb to the heavyweight championship. His good looks, enthusiasm, and loquacity attracted more than the usual attention given to an aspiring heavyweight. Ali exhibited a penchant for self-promotion; he told a reporter that "Cassius Clay is a boxer who can throw the jive better than anybody you will probably meet anywhere."[6] Before his fight with Sonny Liston for the heavyweight crown in 1964, he proclaimed, "I am the greatest!" Unlike the more reticent black athletes who had preceded him but reminiscent of Jack Johnson, Ali brought a more expressive, candid, self-indulgent black cultural style to the attention of the nation. His style would soon affect the behavior of other athletes, both black and white.

After his defeat of Liston, Ali shocked boxing fans by renouncing his "slave name" of Clay in favor of Ali and announcing his conversion to the Black Muslim faith. To counter its negative reputation for shady connections, the world of boxing had always tried to cloak its athletes in the mantle of orthodox religion, conventional morality, and patriotism. By rejecting Christianity and joining a militant black religious sect opposed to racial integration, Ali completely defied these conventions. Nearly all whites feared the Muslims; in a series of press and television reports the sect had been depicted as violent, disciples of black racial superiority, and as exceptionally disciplined. Ironically, the fact that Ali, consistent with his new faith, renounced coffee, liquor, drugs, and sexual liaisons with white women failed to allay white fears. Indeed, his palpable departures from black stereotypes may have intensified them.

Ali's proclamations of his conversion to Muslimism coincided with mounting social conflict. In the summer of 1964 riots broke out in Harlem, three white civil rights activists were murdered in Mississippi, and the Senate adopted the Gulf of Tonkin resolution, which opened the way for a large troop buildup in Vietnam. Ali became increasingly iconoclastic; he expressed an utter contempt for past boxing heroes, declaring them slow, inept, and ugly. His outrageous doggerel sometimes satirized American ideals. Ali's fight with Floyd Patterson, a former heavyweight champion, took on the character of a "holy war": Christian versus Muslim, loyal American versus one whose loyalty was suspect. Patterson, a recent convert to Roman Catholicism, was determined, as he put it, "to give the title back to America." Ali dashed all such hopes. He totally outclassed Patterson, mocking and humiliating him before the referee finally called a halt to the mismatch in the twelfth round. To militant black writer Elridge Cleaver, Patterson had been the "leader of the mythical legions of faithful darkies who inhabit the white imagination," while Ali was a "genuine revolutionary, the black Fidel Castro of boxing," who had inflicted "a psychological chastisement on 'white' white America similar in shock value to Fidel Castro's at the Bay of Pigs."[7]

When shortly thereafter Ali refused to be inducted into the army on religious grounds, was peremptorily on that account stripped of his livelihood by the custodians of boxing, and faced a possible prison term, he became one of the most powerful symbols of the troubled decade. While he was under suspension and while court appeals were being prepared, Ali may have become the best-known American in the world. He inspired blacks everywhere, as well as opponents to the war in Vietnam, participants in the counterculture, and civil libertarians. On the other hand, supporters of the war and adherents to traditional values found in Ali a highly visible target for their frustrations and anger.

Ali's actions placed other black athletes in an uncomfortable position. As a measure of the degree of their militancy, coaches and reporters repeatedly asked black athletes what they thought about Ali. Ali's aggressive anti-Christianity, his opposition to the war, his pronouncements against liquor, drugs, "race-mixing," and sex genuinely bothered many black athletes. Yet his bravery infused many others with additional courage. They began to ask: Had Ali been a white and a Christian, would his title have been taken from him? Would he have been indicted? Were black athletes as free as whites to develop their skills and fulfill their ambitions? Were they the victims of racism and exploitations? Ali's actions helped trigger a larger black athletic revolt.

THE BLACK ATHLETIC REVOLT

The most dramatic phase of the black athletic revolt arose in the "amateur" sports, especially track and field. In 1967, the year after Ali had been stripped of his title, Harry Edwards, a black sociology instructor at San Jose State College, inspired and organized a movement to boycott the 1968 Olympic Games. As a condition for their participation, the boycotters demanded that Ali's crown be reinstated, Avery Brundage be ousted as president of the IOC, South Africa and Rhodesia be barred from the Games, black coaches be added to the American team, and that the New York Athletic Club (NYAC) be desegregated.

The protestors first aroused national attention by boycotting the One Hundredth Anniversary Track and Field Games of NYAC held at Madison Square Garden in 1968. For many years the annual meet had been a showcase for black athletes who later starred on U.S. Olympic teams. The NYAC, now, according to one reporter, a "crusty old Irish-dominated club," refused to admit blacks and had only a few Jewish members. Surrounding the Garden, the demonstrators chanted "Muhammad Ali is our champ!" The boycott was a success. The Soviets pulled out and most black and many white athletes refused to compete in the event.[8]

Edwards enjoyed less success in organizing a boycott of the 1968 Olympics. While he obtained the support of prominent black civil rights leaders and broadened the purpose of the boycott to include a dramatization of the general plight of American blacks to the rest of the world, he could not generate universal support among the black athletes themselves. Apparently less than half of the black athletes likely to make the Olympic team favored the boycott. Consequently, Edwards made the boycott voluntary and recommended that those who decided to compete should protest in their own fashion. Lew Alcindor (who later, changed his name to Kareem Abdul Jabbar), the hero of ULCA's championship basketball team, passed up the games, but most athletes opted for participation. At the Games sprinters Tommie Smith, a gold medalist, and John Carlos, a bronze medalist, mounted the victory stand, and, while the National Anthem played, bowed their heads and raised their gloved fists in the air in a Black Power salute. The United States Olympic Committee quickly suspended Smith and Carlos from the team; the committee then gave them only 48 hours to leave Mexico.

While the Mexico City boycott fizzled, the success of the NYAC boycott, Ali's disbarment, and the Smith-Carlos demonstration helped mobilize an increasing militancy among black athletes. Between 1967 and 1971 racial protests occurred on at least 37 campuses. Since black athletes were especially conspicuous symbols on many campuses, they often experienced pressure from radical student groups—both black and white—to join various "liberation" movements. Often specific complaints touched off the revolts. To protest the Mormon Church's views toward blacks, black athletes at the University of Wyoming asked coaches to permit them to wear black armbands in a game against Brigham Young University. The head coach dismissed all the blacks from the team. In the course of the revolt, black athletes formulated a long list of more general grievances. Among them were "stacking," absence of black coaches, concern by the white coaches only for athletic performances and eligibility of black athletes (not their educations), expressions of racial prejudice by coaches and white teammates, and restrictions on personal freedom.

The sudden militancy of black athletes, joined by a few white athletes, shocked coaches everywhere. During the campus unrest of the 1960s, athletes had been the most conventional and conservative of all students; on several campuses they had led the physical beatings of radical demonstrators. To many coaches, the black protest exhibited a lack of gratitude for the opportunities offered by sports for blacks to escape the ghettos.

Moreover, coaches had traditionally exercised an unbridled authority over the public and private lives of their charges. Any relinquishment of that authority, they believed, would reduce the likelihood of winning. They were especially sensitive to symbolic challenges. Nothing irritated and frightened coaches more than the sight of long hair and beards: To them these styles signified personal license, the rejection of traditional manliness, and, in the instance of blacks, racial pride and rebellion. For a time, coaches everywhere issued orders against such symbolic challenges to their authority.

Yet the net effect of the revolt can easily be exaggerated. Reforms sometimes took the form of gestures rather than substance. Athletic departments hired black coaches, both to placate and recruit black athletes. As the popular culture as a whole adopted fashionably long hair and more liberal dress styles, most coaches compromised their codes of dress and appearance. The traditional crew cut of the athletes suddenly disappeared. The image of Ali softened. By the mid-1970s Wilfrid Sheed argued that even "the squares love him now. . . . His naughtiness seems almost old-fashioned by now and ready for the nostalgia bank."[9] By 1996, in a rite of expiation, the world applauded Ali, whose body was now wracked by Parkinson's disease, as he carried the torch and lit the cauldron that opened the Olympic Games in Atlanta. By then, Ali seemed the essence of reconciliation—the peaceful bringing together of black and white, old and young, and tradition and change. In the meantime, the token reforms, the rapid decline in general student and black unrest in the early 1970s, the built-in turnover of student athletes, and the changed cultural climate brought a quick end to the more radical aspects of the black athletic revolt.

CONTINUING DISCRIMINATION

In the final decades of the twentieth century, racial discrimination continued, albeit sometimes in new forms. Until at least the 1990s, blacks tended to be relegated to certain playing positions and excluded from others, a phenomenon known as "stacking." In 1976, for instance, 52 percent of the major-league outfielders were black, 4 percent of pitchers, 4 percent of catchers, none of the shortstops, 17 percent of the third basemen, 39 percent of the second basemen, and 50 percent of the first basemen. Stacking also existed in professional football. Blacks were more likely to be found playing at a wide receiver or running back position than at quarterback or in the middle of the offensive line. On defense, blacks usually constituted a majority of the cornerbacks and safeties, but few of them played linebacker positions.[10]

Sport sociologists speculated that white management discriminated in favor of whites when choosing players for "central positions," those positions that required more leadership, cooperation, coordination, and personal interaction between players. Perhaps this pattern was self-perpetuating, for blacks may have concluded that their chances of succeeding would be improved if they prepared themselves for noncentral positions. At any rate, by the late 1980s the incidence of stacking had diminished.

Nor did blacks receive equal rewards for equal performance or equal opportunities in sports-related activities. Until the mid-1980s, in all professional team sports blacks earned less in endorsements and off-season activities. The Equal Opportunity Commission reported in the fall of 1966 that black athletes appeared in only 5 percent of 351 commercials associated with New York sports events. Blacks in the 1970s and 80s enjoyed more success, though less than their numbers would warrant.

The 1993 "Racial Report Card" of the Center for the Study of Sport in Society at Northeastern University concluded that professional sports had achieved greater success in obtaining racial equity than society as a whole. While no black owned a professional franchise, the NBA had seven, the NFL two, and major-league baseball four black head coaches or managers. Blacks comprised 77, 68, and 16 percent, respectively, of the players in these leagues. (Big league baseball rosters also included 16 percent Latinos.) The colleges may also have been doing somewhat better, though not as well as the pros. In 1987 *Sports Illustrated* reported that of the nearly 300 Division I schools, there were two black athletic directors, three black head football coaches, and 29 black head basketball coaches. As of 2002, the situation had not changed much. Then there were only four head football coaches who were black, and only one of these, Tyrone Willingham of Notre Dame, was located at a major football power.[11]

Yet, by the 1990s, the endorsement opportunities, at least for black superstars, had shot upward at a fantastic rate. Michael Jordan, Magic Johnson, and Tiger Woods, along with such popular black entertainers as Oprah Winfrey, Bill Cosby, and Eddie Murphy, were examples of what the media described as "crossovers." Crossovers were blacks whose popularity crossed over racial boundaries; they were thus able to parlay their talent and charisma into exceptionally lucrative endorsement deals. According to the savants on Madison Avenue, the public, or at least the young, were colorblind when it came to athletes.

Nothing seemed to support their conclusion more than Michael Jordan's success in hawking Nike shoes. In 1985, the year that Nike introduced its Air Jordan shoes, sales rose by $28 million; five years later they exceeded $500 million and Jordan passed Arnold Palmer in all-time endorsement earnings.[12] Yet, whether crossovers substantiated an important shift in racial attitudes remained in doubt, for many white Americans seemed to be able to admire individual black athletes without changing their fundamental views on race.

HAVE SPORTS DAMAGED BLACK AMERICA?

"How Sport Has Damaged Black America and Preserved the Myth of Race"—this was the subtitle of John Hoberman's highly provocative book published in 1997.[13] To many blacks and whites, nothing could have been farther from the truth than Hoberman's conclusion. Merely examine the success of blacks in sports, they said. In the sports arena, one of the few occupational worlds in which performance alone counted for nearly everything, even a casual glance at the silver screen revealed a disproportionate (in terms of the general population) number of African Americans playing in the highly remunerative professional team sports of basketball, football, and to a lesser extent baseball. Interscholastic and intercollegiate team sports also seemed to offer individual blacks unusual opportunities to advance their lots. Others argued that sports had benefited blacks by expediting the collapse of Jim Crow. Due to a substantial degree to sports, they said, blacks had achieved a greater level of acceptability among whites than at any other time in American history.

But well before Hoberman's wide-ranging argument, Harry Edwards and other sport sociologists had questioned the notion that sports provided a sure-footed road to racial equality. They not only found evidence of discrimination within sports but also observed that the very success of African Americans in sports may have perpetuated a cruel hoax on thousands of ghetto youths. As the award-winning film *Hoop Dreams* (1995) documented, many young blacks dreamed of obtaining glory and money through sports, only to find their dreams dashed by cold reality.

One reality was that only a tiny percentage of all blacks (as well as whites) won spectacular rewards from sports. Upward mobility in sports entailed a savage winnowing process. Of some 700,000 boys who played high school basketball and one million who played interscholastic football each season, only 15,000 and 41,000, respectively, made it to the college ranks. The NFL drafted some 320 players each year of which perhaps 150 made the permanent rosters. Of those who did, their average playing career was about four seasons. The odds against a high school athlete, let alone all male students, making it all the way to the pros was thus astronomical, something like 15,000 to 1. Of those blacks unaware or oblivious to these facts, sports might actually hamper their upward mobility. Instead of preparing themselves for career alternatives, thousands of black youth (as well as many whites) might be spending an inordinate amount of time on sports.[14]

As early as 1971, the possibility of sports encouraging racial stereotypes surfaced when Martin Kane, a senior editor of *Sports Illustrated*, concluded that blacks as a group had distinctive physical features that gave them decided advantages over whites in certain sports. Harry Edwards promptly challenged Kane. Edwards insisted that the disparities in black-white numbers in certain sports (not all) and in their performances were culturally induced. Blacks believed that sports offered an unusual opportunity for upward social mobility.

Thus black youth on the whole spent more time in preparation for sports than their white counterparts.[15]

But the debate did not end there. In 1988, Jimmy "the Greek" Snyder, a 12-year veteran sportscaster on CBS's *The NFL Today*, reopened it when he told a local television interviewer in Washington, D.C., that black athletic superiority resulted from African Americans having been "bred to be that way since the days of slavery."[16] In the face of a lack of evidence to support his position and a widespread negative response, CBS promptly fired Snyder. The next year, Jon Entine and Tom Brokaw produced a documentary for *NBC News* that again raised the possibility that genetic differences accounted for the prominence of blacks in American sports. During the subsequent hullabaloo, Entine claimed that a "taboo" was stifling debate and inquiry into the subject. But critics, including those who conceded that there might be some merit to a genetic-based explanation of athletic performances, worried that such thinking could have pernicious consequences for African Americans. It could encourage the belief that the races might be endowed with unequal capacities in respects other than sports.

But Hoberman's main argument was not that genetics explained differences in performance; rather it was that the disproportionate numbers of blacks in sports encouraged racialist thinking and behavior. He insisted that, among African Americans themselves, there had developed a powerful "sports fixation." The fixation included an inordinate esteem for athletes and a concomitant absence of regard for intellectuals. The sports fixation contributed to a popular "black male style" which fused athletes, rappers, and criminals "into a single menacing figure who disgusts and offends many blacks as well as whites."[17] Furthermore, the success of the media and scholars in advancing the notion of the sports world as a kind of racial utopia had obscured and distracted attention from the larger struggle by African Americans for racial equality. Indeed, sports encouraged a general satisfaction with the racial status quo. While Hoberman's argument was difficult to verify empirically and prompted widespread and, in some cases angry, responses—especially among African American intellectuals—it was impossible to claim in its wake that sports since the mid-twentieth century had been an unmixed blessing for blacks or, for that matter, American society more generally.

CONCLUSION

Sports represented one arena, indeed a highly visible one, in which the nation's racial practices underwent fundamental changes during the second half of the century. Most of the team sports began the process of racial integration before the Supreme Court decision in 1954, yet the sports world initially remained on the periphery of the larger civil rights movement. Experiencing both rising expectations and frustrations, in the midst of the turbulent 1960s black athletes mounted their own revolt. In the 1970s and 1980s blacks, who constituted less than 20 percent of the population, became especially conspicuous at the upper echelon skill levels of both basketball and football. The extent to which their presence indicated fundamental changes in racial attitudes remains in doubt. What seems less problematic was the profound influence that black superstars exercised on black ghetto culture and white thinking about African Americans.

NOTES

1. George F. Will, "The Fuse that Lit the Fire," *Newsweek*, (April 13, 1987), 88. For Robinson and the early history of baseball's integration, see Jules Tygiel, *Baseball's Great Experiment: Jackie Robinson and His Legacy* (New York: Oxford University Press, 1983). For a bibliographical essay on the history of sports and race in America, see David Wiggins, *Glory Bound: Black Athletes in White America* (Syracuse, NY: Syracuse University Press, 1997), 279–87.

2. Quoted in A.O. Edmonds, *Joe Louis* (Grand Rapids, MI: William B. Eerdmans, 1973), 64. On Louis see also D. J. Capeci, Jr. and Martha Wilkerson, "Multifarious Hero: Joe Louis, American Society and Race Relations During World Crisis, 1935–1945," *Journal of Sport History* 10 (1983), 5–25.

3. Quoted in Tygiel, *Baseball's Great Experiment*, 196.

4. Ibid., 334. See also R. A. Smith, "The Paul Robeson-Jackie Robinson Saga and a Political Collision," *Journal of Sport History* 6 (1979), 5–27.

5. Quoted in Pamela Grundy, *Learning to Win: Sports, Education, and Social Change in Twentieth-Century North Carolina* (Chapel Hill: University of North Carolina Press, 2001), 188. See also Charles H. Martin, "Integrating New Year's Day: The Racial Politics of College Bowl Games in the American South," in Patrick Miller, ed., *The Sporting World of the Modern South* (Urbana: University of Illinois Press, 2002), 175–99; John Sayle Watterson, *College Football: History, Spectacle, Controversy.* (Baltimore, MD: Johns Hopkins University Press, 2000), chap. 16; and Michael Oriard, *King Football: Sport and Spectacle in the Golden Age of Radio and Newsreels, Movies and Magazines, the Weekly and Daily Press* (Chapel Hill: University of North Carolina Press, 2001), chap. 9.

6. For the Ali quotations, see "Through the Years with Ali," *Sports Illustrated* 45 (December 20–27, 1976), 111, 113. For other assessments of Ali's cultural significance, see Elliott J. Gorn, ed.,

Muhammad Ali (Urbana: University of Illinois Press, 1995); Gerald Early, ed., *The Muhammad Ali Reader* (New York: Rob Weisbach Books, 1998); and David W. Zang, *Sports Wars: Athletes in the Age of Aquarius* (Fayetteville: University of Arkansas Press, 2001), chap. 5.

7. Quoted in Gerard O'Connor, "Where Have You Gone, Joe DiMaggio?" in R.B. Browne et al., *Heroes in Popular Culture* (Bowling Green, OH: Bowling Green University Press, 1972), 87.

8. See Harry Edwards, *The Revolt of the Black Athlete* (New York: Macmillan, 1969), 64–70; Donald Spivey, "Black Consciousness and the Olympic Protest Movement," in Donald Spivey, ed. *Sport in America* (Westport, CT: Greenwood, 1985), 239–62; and Wiggins, *Glory Bound*, chaps. 6 and 7.

9. Wilfred Sheed, "Muhammad Ali—King of the Picture Gods," in Tom Dodge, ed., *A Literature of Sports* (Lexington, MA: D.C. Heath, 1980), 296.

10. "Scorecard," *Sports Illustrated* 69 (December 26, 1988–January 2, 1989), 24.

11. R.E. Lapchick and J.R. Benedict, "1993 Racial Report Card," *CSSS Digest* 5 (summer 1993), 1, 4–8; *Sports Illustrated* 68 (February 8, 1988), 9; Edward Wong, "The Mystery of the Missing Minority Coaches," *New York Times*, January 6, 2002, WK 5.

12. E.M. Swift, "The Black Athlete Revisited: Reach out and Touch Someone," *Sports Illustrated* 75 (August 5, 1991), 54–58.

13. John Hoberman, *Darwin's Athletes: How Sports Has Damaged Black America and Preserved the Myth of Race* (Boston: Houghton Mifflin, 1997), and Gerald Early, "Performance and Reality: Race, Sports and the Modern World," *Nation* (August 10/17, 1998), 11–20.

14. See J.J. Coakley, *Sport in Society*, 2d ed. (St. Louis: C.V. Mosby, 1978), chap. 11.

15. See ibid.

16. Quoted in Wiggins, *Glory Bound*, 194. Apart from chap. 9 of this book, see also Jon Entine,

Taboo: Why Black Athletes Dominate Sports and Why We Are Afraid to Talk about It (New York: Public Affairs, 2000); a review of Entine's *Taboo* by Paul Ruffins in *Washington Post National Weekly*, February 21, 2000, 32; Laurel R. Davis, "The Articulation of Difference: White Preoccupation with the Question of Racially Genetic Differences among Athletes," *Sociology of Sport Journal* 7 (1990), 179–87; Patrick Miller, "The Anatomy of Scientific Racism: Racialist Responses to Black Athletic Achievement," *Journal of Sport History* 25 (Spring 1998), 119–51; and S. L. Price, "What Ever Happened to the White Athlete?" *Sports Illustrated* 87 (December 8, 1997), 31–55. Also examine Mark Dyreson, "American Ideas about Race and Olympic Races from the 1890s to the 1950s: Shattering Myths or Reinforcing Scientific Racism?" *Journal of Sport History* 28 (Summer 2001), 173–215, which provides a comprehensive bibliography.

17. Hoberman, *Darwin's Athletes*, xix.

19
THE QUEST FOR EQUITY IN WOMEN'S SPORTS

*T*he quest by women for equity in sports was part of a far larger social upheaval that characterized the tempestuous 1960s and 1970s. Earlier, African Americans had inaugurated what would become a massive effort to unleash the chains of racial oppression, and in the 1960s youth rebelled against lingering Victorian restraints, "the establishment," and the coils of an unpopular war. Numerous other groups—women, Native Americans, Latinos, and gays—pursued their own freedom from oppression. Americans even sought emancipation from corporate arrogance, environmental pollution, and from government power seemingly gone berserk. Like the other liberation movements, the women's effort to obtain equity in sports achieved some sweeping changes, but it was only partly successful in altering deeply entrenched gender stereotypes.[1]

CONTINUING ISSUES IN WOMEN'S SPORTS

Although women had been playing organized sports for more than a half century, their contests evoked meanings distinctive from men's. The public almost invariably thought of women athletes in terms of the presence or absence of "femininity"; they tended to equate women's sports with expressions of beauty rather than strength. Sports themselves acquired gender connotations or designations. Nearly everyone, for example, considered football and boxing as exclusively men's sports while they branded water ballet and rhythmic gymnastics as appropriate women's sports.

Bowling illustrated how social class as well as sex could play a significant role in establishing the gender reputation of a sport. First gaining popularity in the 1890s and early 1900s, bowling quickly acquired a beer-drinking, rowdy, working-class ambience. As early as 1907 the World Bowling Congress scheduled a national tournament for both men and women. In 1916, women, who were mostly employed in industry, formed the Women's National Bowling Association (later to become the Women's International Bowling Congress); membership grew to about 5,000 within a decade. The organization by industries of thousands of women's teams and leagues among their employees during World War II reinforced bowling's long-time association with working-class culture.

In the postwar era, however, bowling's ambience and image began to change. While continuing as a popular sport of both working-class women and men, it won a growing following among middle-class suburban housewives. Aided by the use of automatic pinsetters that relieved them of the need to employ schoolboys during the day, proprietors built bowling alleys in the suburbs and made special pitches to women. They "sanitized" their alleys by replacing smoky bars and spittoons with beauty parlors, nurseries, and coffee shops. Bowling has "become the people's country clubs and it's the girls who have made it that way," declared an alley proprietor in 1960.[2]

In the meantime, the evolution of women's track and field during the 1930s, 40s, and 50s exemplified the triple interrelationships of social class, race, and gender. In the 1920s the women's version of the sport, which was usually community-based, thrived among ethnic working-class white and African American women; Babe Didrikson, the most renowned female track and field athlete, was of both blue-collar and recent ethnic origins. The AAU began to sponsor an annual national track and field event for women in 1924, the Olympics scheduled a five-event program for women in 1928, and Didrikson performed spectacularly at the 1932 Olympics. Yet, in the 1930s, media criticism, the opposition of women physical educators, and the financial exigencies of the Great Depression nearly drove white women completely out of the sport.

To a degree, black women filled the void. Though athletics among black women was far less common than among black males, up until the 1950s women frequently received more support in their sporting interests from black community leaders and educators than did their white counterparts. Conceptions of black womanhood were also less restrictive. Accustomed to an oppression that required multiple roles for survival, black women more often performed chores that white society assigned exclusively to men. Hence, black culture viewed evidence of physical and emotional strength among black women more positively. "The same crowd who came to see the guys play was there to see us play," remembered Mary Alyce Clemmons of playing high school varsity basketball in North Carolina in the 1930s.[3] Yet, in the 1940s and 1950s, in response to the black middle class, most black colleges and many black high schools discontinued varsity women's basketball.

In the promotion of black women's track and field, southern black educational institutions led the way. By the 1940s most of the segregated southern black high schools offered varsity competition in basketball and track and field to their female students. At the college level, Tuskegee Institute formed a track team in 1929 and began sponsorship of the Tuskegee Relays. With its athletes capturing 11 of 12 outdoor AAU championships between 1937 and 1948, Tuskegee reigned as the nation's premier women's track program for nearly two decades. During the 1950s Tennessee A & I (later Tennessee State) under the direction of Jessie Abbott assumed the leadership mantle; between 1956 and 1978, Tennessee State athletes captured 20 gold medals at the Olympic Games as well as 30 AAU titles.[4]

In the meantime, the Cold War between the United States and the Soviet Union focused renewed attention on women track athletes. While the U.S. men's team competed evenly or better than the Soviet men in the 1952 Olympics, Soviet women overpowered the American women. For the 1952 Games the American women's track team consisted of only ten athletes and a manager-coach; the team had no high jumper or discus thrower and only one hurdler, one shot-putter, one broad jumper, and one javelin thrower. In 1956 the situation had hardly improved when the United States again sent only ten women athletes to the Games; in contrast the Soviet team included women who held or shared world records in five of the nine women's events.[5]

Improving the performances of American women was not an easy task. Obviously many more girls and women needed to be recruited in the sport and provided with adequate training, but track had an unfeminine reputation and had been associated almost exclusively with black women. One tactic was for coaches and promoters of the sport to cultivate a more feminine image. For example, Tennessee State coach Edward Temple told reporters: "None of my girls have any trouble getting boyfriends. I tell them that they are young ladies first, track girls second." And, while *Ebony* magazine celebrated the feats of African American women athletes, it too noted "that a girl track star can be as feminine as the china-doll type."[6] In their efforts to revive track among white women, white athletic leaders resorted to similar strategies.

Enthusiasts for women's track may have enjoyed some success in reversing the pervasively masculine image of the sport. Wilma Rudolph, a triple gold medal winner at the 1960 Rome Olympics, won the universal plaudits of the media for both her performances and femininity. As *Time* magazine bluntly put it: "In a field of female endeavor in which the greatest stars have often been characterized by overdeveloped muscles and underdeveloped glands, Wilma (Skeeter) Rudolph has long, lissome legs and a pert charm." But, as Susan Cahn has perceptively observed, "like other black athletes, she was represented as a wild beast, albeit a gentle, attractive creature who could be [safely] adopted as a pet of the American public."[7] Furthermore, with the exception of Rudolph, images of masculinity continued to plague women's track and field athletes.

THE IMPETUS FOR CHANGE

The Cold War itself provided a major impetus for change in the world of women's sport. By the mid-1950s sports had become a major forum for the superpowers, the United States and the Soviet Union, to exhibit the prowess of their respective systems. In 1956, President Dwight D. Eisenhower established the President's Council on Youth Fitness, which proceeded to find that millions of American children were less fit than their British or Japanese cohorts. President John F. Kennedy picked up Eisenhower's mantle; "Our Olympic team and athletes," he said, "play a significant role in preserving our way of life."[8] With the Soviets winning more total medals than the United States in both the 1956 and 1960 Olympic Games and with the Soviet men beginning to catch up with of the American men in track and field in the late 1950s, pressures mounted to improve the performances of the nation's women athletes. The national media lent its support. Earlier it had accused Soviet women athletes of being unfeminine, but by the early 1960s national periodicals began to run articles that, in the words of Mary Jo Festle, "demonstrated that females could do athletics and still be beautiful."[9]

Confronted by these pressures and the fact that the AAU was proceeding to put more resources into women's athletics, women physical educators began a gradual retreat from their rigid opposition to an emphasis on elite athletes. In 1958, the USOC created the Women's Advisory Board consisting of representatives from the AAU, former women Olympic athletes, and sympathetic physical educators. Another turning point came in 1960 when Doris Duke Cromwell, heiress of the Duke tobacco fortune, donated a half million dollars to the USOC to promote women's athletics. With these funds, the women's board and the Division of Girls' and Women's Sports (DGWS) of the national physical education association set up a series of national institutes for the training of women athletes. Despite these steps, which encouraged an emphasis on top-flight athletes, most educators continued to hope that female performances on the Olympic team could be improved without the colleges and high schools committing themselves to varsity track programs.

The great cultural tumult of the 1960s and 1970s supplied an additional catalyst for change in women's sports. Members of the counterculture and advocates of a sexual revolution launched an all-out assault on the traditional restraints on physical freedom and the enjoyment of bodily pleasures. Although athletics was mostly peripheral to their concerns, their support of a vast expansion in the boundaries of proper female behavior spilled over into sports. Likewise, especially in the 1970s, the fitness industry began to seize upon the opportunities presented by women to expand their sales. To sell equipment, clothing, and services, they encouraged female fitness and athletics; they frequently equated athletics and fitness with appearance (see Chapter 14).

A revived women's rights movement also struck a responsive chord. In the same years that the civil rights movement intensified, opposition to the war in Vietnam mounted, and many of the nation's youth embarked upon experimental lifestyles, women began to demand the same opportunities as men to fashion their own destinies. Political pressures by women paid dividends. In 1963 Congress passed the Equal Pay Act and the Civil Rights Act of 1964 included women as well as blacks in its nondiscriminatory mandates.

Emboldened by women's involvement in the Olympics, the new cultural ferment, and political gains by women, a small band of women physical educators inched their way toward the establishment of full-fledged varsity sports programs for women. As early as 1941 Gladys Palmer of Ohio State University had organized a national golf tournament for college women, but the national body of women physical educators had quickly passed a resolution condemning her ventures into intercollegiate competition for women.

By 1964 the situation had markedly changed. That year the Division of Girls' and Women's Sports devoted an entire program at the national physical education convention to "Competition for the Highly Skilled Girls" and adopted a statement essentially reversing the 1923 platform on intercollegiate sports for women. Two years later a group of women within the DGWS formed the Commission of Intercollegiate Athletics for Women, which became the Association of Intercollegiate Athletics for Women (AIAW) in 1971. Threatened by the prospect of the NCAA entering the arena of intercollegiate sports for women, the commission scheduled its first set of national championships in 1969. Still, the women's sports leaders in the schools hoped for a program different from the men's, one that was less competitive and without athletic scholarships.

Then came Title IX of the Educational Amendments Act of 1972. Aided by women's lobbying efforts and pushed through Congress by Representative Edith Green of Oregon and Senator Birch Bayh of Indiana, both Democrats, Title IX in effect simply outlawed any sexual discrimination by school districts and institutions of higher education that received federal aid. Its provisions thus applied to nearly every school in the nation. If interpreted literally, the law would have required revolutionary changes in school sports. It also raised a dilemma: Should women support the principle of sexual integration of sports or a separate but equal doctrine? In the end, given the physical differences in the sexes that became more prominent in puberty, they usually opted for the latter, but Title IX did encourage sexually integrated physical education classes and experiments with integrated intramural sports programs.[10]

Most of the women in leadership positions, including those in the inner circles of the AIAW, continued to hope that women could implement Title IX while avoiding the pitfalls of the male model of intercollegiate sports. The AIAW initially opposed athletic scholarships. But a 1973 court case in which a woman athlete charged that the AIAW's prohibition on athletic scholarships was discriminatory forced the organization to permit athletic grants-in-aid. Soon afterward every major college began awarding women athletic scholarships. By the late 1970s the number and money value of women's scholarships (as compared to men's) became a principal test for compliance with Title IX.

The availability of scholarships firmly launched women's sports into the mainstream of big-time intercollegiate athletics. By the end of the 1970s women's basketball, in particular, began to resemble men's programs, even to the extent of widespread charges of the extension of illegal inducements to star players. Coaches, especially in women's basketball, also found their jobs imperiled when their teams lost too many games.

RISING HOPES AND EXPECTATIONS

Title IX was only one indication of the promise that characterized women's sports in the 1970s. While Title IX itself was limited to educational institutions, it stated a principle of sexual equity that could be applied throughout the world of sport. Even before the passage of Title IX, lawyers had begun to file suits on behalf of female high school students who sought opportunities to play on boys' teams when the schools offered no teams for girls' play. Legal pressure resulted in the sexual integration of Little League Baseball. In 1973 *Sports Illustrated* presented a three-part series that indicted sexism in sport and five years later *Time* magazine concluded that "the revolution in women's athletics is at full, running tide, bringing with it a sea change—not just in activities but in attitudes as well."[11]

Women's tennis in the 1970s gave focus to the "sea change." Traditionally, tennis had been an upper-class sport and a bastion of genteel sexism. Women had played the sport, but usually within the confines of genteel expectations of female behavior. In mixed doubles the male player played the most conspicuous and dominant role. Proper decorum, circumspection, and subordination had been imposed on women players, even though the emphasis placed upon winning by such players as Suzanne Lenglen and Helen Wills in the 1920s and Maureen Connolly in the 1940s had threatened to upset the delicate role assigned to women players.

In the 1960s and 70s Billie Jean King, a California player from a working-class family, led the crusade against sexism in tennis.[12] King was not only a superb player, but she was also confident, articulate, and assertive. She "gave soul" and "personalized" the "bringing of tennis—classiest of sports—to the people." She, more than any single person, helped erase the stiff formality and pomposity from the sport.

King led the women in demanding an end to gender inequities in pay. Although women's matches sometimes attracted audiences as large as those of the men, until the 1970s the prize money available to women was only about 10 percent of the men's purses. With the advent of open tennis several promoters, assuming that women could not draw financially rewarding gates, had dropped women from their tournaments. In response to their exclusion, in 1971 King and seven other players collaborated with Gladys Heldman to form the Virginia Slims, a separate circuit for women. At the urging of Heldman, the Philip Morris Tobacco Company decided to underwrite the circuit and promote it as part of the revived feminist movement.

The Slims acquired a substantial television contract and by 1975 awarded nearly a million dollars in prize money. By threatening to withdraw from Forest Hills and Wimbledon, the women also obtained far more equitable portions of major tournament purses. As an arena offering opportunities to women in professional sport, tennis was the most lucrative of all sports. In 1971 King became the first woman athlete to earn $100,000 in a single year; four years later Chris Evert won more than $300,000.

King's significance, like that of Muhammad Ali, extended far beyond the world of sport. Somewhat reluctantly, she became one of the most important symbols of the revived feminist movement of the early 1970s. Harassed by reporters for her frank pursuit of tennis as a profession and her decision not to have children, she insisted upon her right to be a full-time professional athlete. "Almost every day for the last four years," she told a reporter, "someone comes up to me and says, 'Hey, when are you going to have children?' I say 'I'm not ready yet.' They say, 'Why aren't you at home?' I say, 'Why don't you go ask Rod Laver why he isn't at home?' "[13] To those many Americans who held traditional notions of femininity such remarks seemed revolutionary. For a woman in sports to equate herself with a man inspired feminists and aroused the wrath of the movement's enemies. Other women's tennis players, including star Chris Evert whose public image was superfeminine, distanced themselves from the feminist movement. Part of Evert's appeal, Dave Anderson of the *New York Times* explained, was that "she always looked like a female."[14]

A 1973 tennis match between King and Bobby Riggs furnished a dramatic focal point for both the women's struggle for greater opportunity in sport, for gender role conflicts, and for the larger women's movement. By 1973 women had made substantial gains in acquiring equal purses in tournaments, but 55-year-old Bobby Riggs, a former triple-crown winner at Wimbledon (1939) and a long-time sports hustler, publicly claimed that women players were inferior to men and thus overpaid. He boasted that despite his age he could defeat the best of the women players. He first challenged King, but she refused, arguing that regardless of the outcome such a match could not benefit the cause of women's tennis.

Nonetheless, Margaret Court, another top-flight women's player from Australia, accepted Riggs's challenge. On Mother's Day, 1973, a nervous Court, who had recently become a mother—this fact became part of the match's hype—lost to Riggs, 6–2, 6–1. To the surprise of television producers, the audience rating for the match topped the WCT championship match played the same day.

The victory by Riggs, when reinforced by his flamboyant male chauvinism, appeared to jeopardize the advances made by women's tennis. King, as the militant leader of women in tennis, now relented to play Riggs. The offer of more than $100,000 in television rights and endorsements plus an additional $100,000 if she won may also have influenced her decision. Although the match itself and its accompanying circuslike atmosphere caricatured tennis as a sport and the quest for gender equity, no other single sporting event so compellingly dramatized the "Battle of the Sexes," as it was billed by the media. King confronted Riggs in Houston's Astrodome before a crowd of 30,472, the largest audience ever to attend a tennis match. Millions more watched on prime-time television which, via satellite, extended its coverage to 36 nations. King routed Riggs, 6–4, 6–3, 6–3. Ironically, though Riggs claimed to represent men and King women, it was King who played the more aggressive game. She served and volleyed while Riggs employed a stereotypical "women's style" of staying in the backcourt and hitting chips and lobs.

In the decade of the 1970s, one that witnessed a vast expansion of employment opportunities for women and an array of court decisions extending women's rights, evidence of improvement in women's sports came from quarters

BILLIE JEAN KING King was a leader of women's tennis both on and off the court. In the 1970s, she was the most important athletic symbol of the larger women's liberation movement.
(World Team Tennis)

other than tennis. Within five years after the passage of Title IX in 1972, nearly every college and high school in the country rushed to form varsity women's teams in a half dozen or more sports. By the end of the 1970s, the number of women playing intercollegiate sports had doubled and nearly two million girls participated in varsity high school sports, a sixfold increase from 1970–71. In 1976 women's basketball became an official Olympic sport, and, although professional women's softball and basketball leagues folded within a few years of their founding in 1976, during the 1970s a hopeful mood continued to prevail among the champions of women's sports.

RESISTANCE TO EQUITY IN WOMEN'S SPORTS

But not all was roseate. The NCAA and many athletic officials at both the intercollegiate and high school level sought to obtain the repeal of Title IX or at the least minimize its impact. College athletic directors insisted that equal funding for women would destroy the major revenue-producing sports of men's football and basketball. The destruction of these sports, they said, would not leave enough to fund either men or women's sports programs. Under the tutelage of its executive director Walter Byers, the NCAA launched a major lobbying effort at Congress and the Department of Health, Education and Welfare (HEW), the agency responsible for interpreting and enforcing Title IX. The NCAA failed to obtain the repeal of Title IX but did delay the laying down of Title IX regulations until 1975. HEW then gave schools until 1978 to comply with them.

Recognizing that the federal government was intent upon enforcing some version of Title IX, the NCAA decided on a new strategy in 1980. To conform with Title IX, its leaders reasoned, required that the NCAA sponsor women's as well as men's national championships. This led to a head-on conflict with the Association of Intercollegiate Athletics for Women. At the time the AIAW was already managing some 750 state, regional, and national championships for its 970 member schools. With the NCAA promising to offer more money and television coverage for national tourneys, the vast majority of the colleges abandoned the AIAW. With the loss of an antitrust suit against the male-dominated NCAA in 1984, the AIAW folded. With its collapse, women no longer exercised a predominant control over the direction of women's sports at the intercollegiate level.

In the same year (1984), the Supreme Court knocked the props from under the application of Title IX to women's sports. In its Grove City College decision, the court ruled that Title IX applied only to those specific programs that received federal funds. Since few women's sports programs obtained any of their funding directly from the federal government, the ruling potentially negated the revolution ignited by Title IX. Within a year after the decision, the Office of Civil Rights suspended 64 investigations, more than half of which involved college sports. But in 1988 the legal history of women's sports took another sharp turn. By an overwhelming majority, the Democratic-controlled Congress passed the Civil Rights Restoration Act over President Ronald Reagan's veto. It barred any institution that received federal aid from discriminating in any of their programs on the grounds of race, age, disability, or gender.

Still, the colleges managed to avoid—at least in the short run—gender equity in sports. Both the Jimmy Carter and the George Bush administrations refused to push hard for a literal interpretation or the strict enforcement of the restored Title IX. The results of both a NCAA and a *Chronicle of Higher Education* survey taken in 1992 found that the number of male varsity athletes outnumbered females two to one at Division I-A schools; huge discrepancies also existed in budgets. At Florida State University, for example, men received 63 percent of the scholarship monies. Nationally, women held less than half the coaching positions and only about a third of the administrative posts in women's athletics. Coaches of women's teams also received far less pay than did their male counterparts. A 1992 study reached similar conclusions about the overall state of high school sports.[15]

But the next year, in 1993, the Office of Civil Rights of President Clinton's administration sent shock waves through the college sports world when it laid down a new set of compliance guidelines. One rule required each college to maintain "proportionality," that is, for each college the number of varsity male or female athletes should approximate their proportions of the general student body. The only way such a goal could be achieved was either to eliminate or sharply reduce the size of football programs (which allowed 85 scholarships) or have women "overrepresented" in other sports. Indeed, apart from football, at most colleges women received more total athletic scholarships than did men. Referring to college football, Bobby Bowden, Florida State's head coach, begged: "Don't destroy the goose that lays the golden egg." If monies were taken from football, Bowden and others reasoned, then their teams would not perform as well and hence raise less revenue for other college sports. However, at most schools, football lost money. As Donna Lopiano, executive director of the Women's Sport Foundation, quipped: "There is a big fat goose [i.e., football] eating all the feed that could be used to feed all the other little geese."[16]

Upon its thirtieth anniversary in 2002, the controversy swirling around Title IX had not abated. Instead, it had intensified. This was mainly because many athletic directors argued that the proportionality rule forced them to eliminate men's programs. A suit (later dismissed) filed by the College Sports Council, representing coaches in men's wrestling, diving, and gymnastics, against the Department of Education reported that 171 college wrestling programs had been eliminated between 1981 and 1999. Opponents of proportionality frequently took a position similar to Maureen E. Mahoney, a *Sports Illustrated* writer, who said that it should not be presumed that women, "given the opportunity, will naturally participate in athletics in numbers equal to men." In comparison, she noted that such was not the case in collegiate dance where women far outnumbered men or in engineering where men far outnumbered women.[17]

However, defenders of proportionality insisted that, given the chance, women would participate in sports as avidly as men, that Title IX guidelines did not require absolute proportionality, and that, although the "gender gap" had been sharply reduced since 1972, there remained in 2002 a 4 to 3 ratio in favor of men over women in varsity sports. Athletic budgets revealed an even greater disparity: For every $1.00 spent on women's sports, there was $2.80 spent on men's sports. As of 2002, men's football and basketball received 72 percent of all athletic department expenditures. "What's clear," summed up Welch Suggs in an article for the *Chronicle of Higher Education*, "is that athletics directors [as opponents of proportionality] and advocates [of proportionality] aren't speaking the same language."[18] Athletic directors wanted to maximize incoming revenues by putting a major part of their resources into the most widely supported fan sports—men's football and basketball—while advocates of the strict enforcement of Title IX wanted to maximize opportunities for women to play varsity sports.

CONTINUING CULTURAL CONSTRAINTS ON WOMEN'S SPORTS

Inequities in funds and scholarships were not the only constraints on women's sports. Throughout the world of women's sports the long-time association between sport and masculinity lingered on. This was particularly true at the higher levels of competition. When the women, who comprised only 34 percent of the American squad at the Winter Olympics at Albertville, France, in 1992, won 82 percent of the medals, the media interpreted it as a defeat of the men. The Olympic

FLORENCE GRIFFITH JOYNER A hero of the Seoul Olympics in 1988, Griffith Joyner exuded a combination of self-confidence, muscularity, and traditional femininity.
(AP/World Wide Photo)

policy of mandatory sex testing (while lacking scientific reliability) also entailed the equation of athletics with masculinity. "I think they are just saying, 'You are so good, we can't believe you're a woman. So prove it,'" explained Olympic hepathlete Jane Frederick.[19]

Women athletes continued to experience pressures to reassure the public of their femininity. Even though sexual views in the late twentieth century had become far more tolerant than in the past, negative attitudes toward lesbianism and/or the expression of "manly" behavior persisted, especially in sports. First Martina Navratilova and later Billie Jean King lost millions of dollars in endorsements when they admitted having had lesbian relationships.[20] To ensure a heterosexual image, in 1989 the Ladies Professional Golf Association launched a campaign to sell the sexiness of its athletes; the campaign even included players modeling bikinis on Hawaiian beaches. Nothing brought home the tendency to sexualize the bodies of women athletes more vividly than the media's response to Brandi Chastain when she tore off her shirt (revealing a sport bra) in celebration of her winning goal in the 1999 World Cup championships. Reporters around the world interpreted the spontaneous act as a form of strip tease consciously performed by Chastain to titillate the masses.

Even more than in the past, women received mixed and confusing signals about their bodies. The ideal woman, explained sociologist Pirkko Markula,

*WOMAN SPORTSCASTER Lesley Visser of CBS interviewed Boris Becker at the 1990
U.S. Open Tennis Tournament. The employment of women sportscasters suggested a
weakening of the long-time association of sports with men and manliness.*
(Duomo Photography, Inc.)

should be "firm but shapely, fit but sexy, strong but thin." Images of the strong female athlete competed for public approval with images of superthin fashion models. "For every Mia Hamm [the star of the nation's World Cup soccer team winner in 1999]," explained columnist Ellen Goodman, "there are still dozens of supermodels. For every message of self-confidence there are still a stunning number of folks investing in feel-bad visuals."[21] The body of the ideal female popularized in the media was thinner than ever before. A 1992 study conducted by American University researchers of Miss Americas, *Playboy* centerfolds, and fashion models found that these women averaged 13 to 19 percent below the average weights of women of a similar age.[22] Both the fitness industry and the popular culture encouraged among women a preoccupation, one that sometimes endangered their health, with weight control.

CONCLUSION

Despite the failure of women to achieve equity in school and college sports, the presence of women in sports was far more pervasive and conspicuous at the opening of the twenty-first century than it had been three decades earlier. The fundamental incongruity that had long existed between sports and femininity apparently subsided; women, including schoolgirls, frequently reported that they had experienced no stigma from participation in sports. Indeed, a 1988 Women's Sports Foundation survey of parents found that 87 percent of them believed that sports was as important to their daughters as it was to their sons.[23] At the 1996 Olympic Games in Atlanta, women athletes even captured the media's center stage, in the same year two women's professional basketball leagues were launched; in 1997 three publishers announced plans for the publication of women's sports magazines, and in 1999 the United States's women soccer team captured the attention of the entire nation when it won the World Cup. Yet, while reduced, the dissonance between sports and womanhood had by no means been entirely eliminated.

NOTES

1. For general treatments of women's sports in this era, see Susan K. Cahn, *Coming on Strong: Gender and Sexuality in Twentieth-Century Women's Sport* (New York: Free Press, 1994), chap. 10; Mary Jo Festle, *Playing Nice: Politics and Apologies in Women's Sports* (New York: Columbia University Press, 1996); Allen Guttmann, *Women's Sports: A History* (New York: Columbia University Press, 1991), chap. 13 and 14; Reet Howell, ed., *Her Story in Sport* (Westport, NY: Leisure, 1982); and D. Margaret Costa and S. R. Guthrie, eds., *Women and Sports* (Champaign, IL: Human Kinetics, 1994).

2. Quoted in Cahn, *Coming on Strong*, 220.

3. Quoted in Pamela Grundy, *Learning to Win: Sports, Education, and Social Change in Twentieth-Century North Carolina* (Chapel Hill: University of North Carolina Press, 2001), 165. See also Rita Liberti, " 'We Were Ladies, We Just Played like Boys': African American Women and Competitive Basketball at Bennett College," in Patrick Miller, ed., *The Sporting World of the Modern South* (Urbana: University of Illinois Press, 2002), chap. 6.

4. Cahn, *Coming on Strong*, 117–22.

5. See, for example, Mary Snow, "Can the Soviet Girls Be Stopped?" *Sports Illustrated* 5 (August 27, 1956), 6.

6. Quotations from Cahn, *Coming on Strong*, 133, 134.

7. Ibid., 137.

8. Quoted in Festle, *Playing Nice*, 313, n42.

9. Ibid., 92

10. See ibid., chaps. 7 and 8, Cahn, *Coming on Strong*, Guttmann, *Women's Sports*; L.J. Carpenter,

"The Impact of Title IX on Women's Intercollegiate Sports," in A.T. Johnson and J.H. Frey, eds., *Government and Sport* (Totowa, NJ: Littlefield, 1985), 62–78; Joan Hult, "Women's Struggle for Governance in U.S. Amateur Athletics," *International Review of Sociology of Sport* 24 (1989), 249–63; Joan Hult, "The Female American Runner," in B.L. Drinkwater, ed., *Female Endurance Athletes* (Champaign, IL: Human Kinetics, nd), 1–39; Joan Hult, "The Philosophical Conflicts in Men's and Women's Collegiate Athletics," *Quest* 32 (1980), 77–94; Judy Jensen, "Women's Collegiate Athletics: Incidents in the Struggle for Influence and Control," in R.E. Lapchick, ed., *Fractured Focus* (Lexington, MA: Addison-Wesley, 1986), 151–61; Gail Maloney, "The Impact of Title IX," unpub. Ph.D. diss., State University of New York Buffalo, 1995.

11. Bil Gilbert and Nancy Williamson, "Sport Is Unfair to Women," "Are You Being Two Faced?" and "Programmed to be Losers" in *Sports Illustrated* on May 28, June 4, and June 11, 1973, respectively. Quotation from "Comes the Revolution," *Time* 111 (June 26, 1978), 59. For Little League baseball, see S.E. Jennings, " 'As American as Hot Dogs, Apple Pie and Chevrolet': The Desegregation of Little League Baseball," *Journal of American Culture* 4 (1981), 81–91.

12. See B.J. King with Kim Chapin, *Billie Jean* (New York: Harper & Row, 1974), and Festle, *Playing Nice*, chap. 6.

13. Quoted in Robert Lipsyte, *SportsWorld* (New York: Quadrangle/New York Times, 1975), 223.

14. Quoted in Festle, *Playing Nice*, 154.

15. Douglas Lederman, "Men Outnumber Women and Get Most of the Money in Big-Time Sports Programs," *Chronicle of Higher Education* 38 (April 8, 1992), 1, A37ff.

16. Quotations from "Battle of the Sexes," CNN Report, May 30, 1994.

17. Maureen E. Mahoney, "The Numbers Don't Add Up," *Sports Illustrated* 86 (May 5, 1997), 78. See also the critique of proportionality by Jessica Gavora, *Tilting the Field: Schools, Sports, Sex and Title IX* (San Francisco: Encounter Books, 2002).

18. Welch Suggs, "Title IX at 30," *Chronicle of Higher Education*, June 21, 2002, A 41. Also see data in this article plus the Associated Press story by Hal Bock reported in the *Lincoln* (Nebraska) *Journal Star*, June 23, 2002.

19. Quoted in Cahn, *Coming on Strong*, 264.

20. Yet, a 1993 Associated Press poll found Navratilova to be the "most popular active tennis player." As reported in the *Lincoln* (Nebraska) *Star*, May 17, 1993, she received 23 percent of the total votes cast in this category.

21. Quotations in Jay Coakley, *Sport and Society*, 7th ed. (Boston: McGraw, Hill, 2001), 208, and Ellen Goodman, "World Cup Win Only a Small Victory in the Struggle for Esteem," *Lincoln (Nebraska) Journal Star*, July 16, 1999.

22. As reported in *Lincoln* (Nebraska) *Star*, August 16, 1992. Women's gymnastics, a sport in which physical appearance could be crucial to winning at the world class level, witnessed the arrival of ever-more waiflike competitors. According to a special report by Merrell Noden in *Sports Illustrated* 81 (August 8, 1994), 58, "the average size of the women on the U.S. Olympic gymnastics team shrank from 5' 3", 105 pounds in 1976 to 4' 9", 88 pounds in 1992." Most of the women, Noden concluded, suffered from anorexia, a self-starvation eating disorder.

23. See Guttmann, *Women's Sports*, 217–18.

20
THE ATHLETES

*I*n the 1970s and perhaps the 1980s, the age of heroes seemed to be over. The titles of magazine articles struck ominous notes: "Where Have Our Heroes Gone?" "What's Happened to Our Heroes?" "Heroes: Do We Need Them?" "Death of Heroes," "Youth Heroes Have No Haloes," and "What Price Heroes?" Nearly every author particularly mourned the passing of sports heroes. "Where Have You Gone, Joe DiMaggio?" lamented Simon and Garfunkel in their hit song "Mrs. Robinson." CBS's popular television series *Sixty Minutes* did a special using the same title. Perhaps even more startling was the apparent decline of heroes among the young. In a 1977 survey of 1,200 junior-high-school students, the most common response to the question "Who is your hero?" was "None." Answers farther down the line in this and other polls revealed the devaluation of the traditional hero. When students did name heroes, they most often cited rock musicians, television's Bionic Man or Woman, and Evel Knievel, a television stunt man.[1]

The concern for the demise of heroes reflected in part mass nostalgia, the inclination of each generation to believe that those who held center stage in their youth were more noble than those who succeeded to such lofty positions later. Yet it also represented an important emotional response to genuine changes in the status, behavior, and images of athletes in the age of television. In professional sports, players achieved astronomical salaries, obtained long-term, no-cut contracts, organized labor unions, fomented strikes, and signed collective bargaining agreements, all of which shattered illusions that had long segregated the world of sports from the outside world. With journalism bent upon the full exposure of the private lives of would-be heroes, the American people learned that athletes were human, that they were prone to the frailties characteristic of young men or women who had suddenly become exceptionally well-paid celebrities.

HEROES OR MERELY CELEBRITIES?

In the post-1950 era, the images projected by athletes reflected not only their performances and behaviors but also the changing currents of society and culture at large. The athletic heroes of the 1940s and 50s, men such as Joe DiMaggio, Joe Louis, Mickey Mantle, and Willie Mays, became prominent during a widespread quest for national unity and personal security that had arisen out of the anxieties of the Great Depression, World War II, and the Cold War. Each hero, like many of their predecessors, had won a share of the American dream under adverse circumstances: DiMaggio came up from the fishing wharves of San Francisco, Louis from a Detroit ghetto, Mantle from the red-dirt country of Oklahoma, and Mays from the cotton patches of Alabama. Without the exposure of iconoclastic journalism or the full glare of television, these athletes seemed to have been nurtured on Frank Merriwell stories and traditional virtues. According to a 1958 story in the *New York Times Magazine*, professional ballplayers eschewed late hours, poker games, pinball machines, and chewing tobacco. They obeyed the Boy Scout Law, babysat, subscribed to the *Wall Street Journal*, and "would not think of tripping their mothers, even if Mom were rounding third on her way home with the winning run."[2]

But in the divisive 1960s and 1970s, sports idols no longer commanded universal reverence. As the quest for national unity and personal security gave way to struggles by individuals for personal liberation and fulfillment, to specific groups seeking a larger share of the promise of American life, and to other groups desperately trying to hold on to what they already had, athletes were less likely to be representatives of national values. Instead, each major social grouping claimed its own athletic champion. Muhammad Ali represented militant blacks, Billie Jean King militant females, Vince Lombardi, militant traditionalists, and Joe Namath a militant quest for freedom from traditional social constraints.

Professional football, as the nation's most popular sport, offered perfect heroes for two major segments of the American population in the 1960s. Those troubled by the cultural unrest of the decade idolized Vince Lombardi. As with Knute Rockne, tragedy cut short Lombardi's career; he died from cancer in 1969 at the age of 57. Like Rockne, Lombardi was a winner. Under Lombardi's guidance, the Green Bay Packers won 99 games, six conference titles, and five NFL championships. His Packers resembled a paramilitary organization. "He's the general and we're the privates," one of his players aptly said. But Lombardi brought to football more than the modern methods of cold, efficient rationality; he was an emotional man who laughed and wept publicly and thought of his team "as one big family." He implicitly condemned the counterculture. "Everywhere you look," he said, "there is a call for freedom, independence . . . [but] we must learn again to respect authority, because to disavow it is contrary to our individual natures."[3] "Broadway Joe" Namath, who was lionized both on and off the field, was the perfect antithesis of Lombardi. If Lombardi represented a father figure, then Namath symbolized the rebellious youth of the 1960s. Johnny Sample, a teammate of Namath's, said: "Our heroes were a new breed of players. Men like Joe Namath who wore their hair long and bragged about how good they were had replaced men like Johnny Unitas, the clean-cut All-America type."[4] Namath projected multiple, ultimately contradictory, images. On one hand, he seemed to be the hippie of the sports world: he wore long hair and a Fu Manchu mustache and could not abide schedules, strict discipline, authority, or Commissioner Rozelle. Yet he publicly apologized to Rozelle, shaved off his mustache for a price (a commercial on television), proudly wore a Persian lamb coat, and openly celebrated his indulgences— blonde "broads," alcohol, and parties. Supposedly putting to rest the ancient belief that sex the night before a big game impaired one's performance on the field of play, Namath was Hugh Hefner's quintessential playboy.

In the 1970s, the continuing war in Vietnam, the Watergate scandal, the inability of the federal government to solve such problems as inflation, unemployment, energy shortages, and pollution, the propensity of post-Watergate journalism to revel in the sordid details of the lives of would-be heroes all contributed to a decline in public confidence. Decisions by committees of experts, bureaucracies, and computers, some suggested, made the individual hero obsolete. The astronauts may have been the logical heirs of Charles A. Lindbergh, but their heroism was submerged in complex team efforts.

Television made mythmaking, which is essential to heromaking, more difficult than in the past. It reduced the distance between the potential hero and the hero worshiper. Physical distance had disguised imperfections and permitted fantasies; with television the fan could feel like a Lilliputian examining the craters in Gulliver's face. Television also produced a diffusion of images. Instead of a clear profile of the solitary hero generated by the imagination, television served up a bleary succession of endless candidates for heroism. In an age of multimedia roles, the line between the athletic hero and the celebrity tended to vanish.

Finally, reducing the performances of athletes to a tiny screen made them seem less noteworthy. On television, completing a long pass, returning a wide groundstroke on the tennis court, and scooping up a hard-hit ground ball looked deceptively easy. A wide-ranging survey on the attitudes of Americans toward sports in 1983 found that 45 percent of the respondents sometimes felt that, given the right training, they could do as well as the athletes on television. The figure shot up to a startling 74 percent among those aged 14 to 17 and was 25 percent even among those 65 and over. Given such perceptions, no wonder many spectators refused to elevate athletes into heroes.[5]

Several of the most successful athletes (when measured in terms of endorsement incomes) achieved oversized personas that had little to do with their feats on the field of play. No athlete exemplified the capacity to promote and profit from image making more effectively than Andre Agassi. While trailing behind Americans Pete Sampras and Michael Chang in world ranking as a tennis player during most of the 1990s, Agassi earned far more than the others from endorsements. In a society that had not succeeded in completely severing itself from Victorian strictures, Agassi, along with such icons as Madonna and Michael Jackson, reflected the co-option of the sixties' counterculture by corporate America.

THE ATHLETE AS A POPULAR CULTURAL ICON
Andre Agassi is shown here after his triumph at
the U.S. Open Tennis Tournament in 1994. His
celebrity status extended far beyond his athletic
triumphs. In a society that had not succeeded in
completely severing itself from Victorian strictures,
Agassi, along with such icons as Madonna and
Michael Jackson, reflected the co-option of the
sixties' counterculture by corporate America.
(Richard Drew, AP/World Wide Photos)

Advertisers tied Agassi's earrings, flowing hair, and bizarre clothing, when combined with his boyish charm, to immediate gratification, youthfulness, uninhibited instinct, playfulness, and liberation of the libido—all of which were conducive to consumption.

INTERLEAGUE COMPETITION FOR PLAYERS

The invasion of sports by the realities of the outside world contributed to a diminution of the aura surrounding athletes. In the past, the actors in sports dramas had often conveyed the impression that they hitched their own purposes to something larger than themselves, to something that demanded a special virtue, endurance, sacrifice, or courage. But in the 1960s athletes had become more politicized, and in the same decade talk and images of money began to invade the sports world as never before. In time, reports of strikes, free agents, and soaring salaries sometimes overwhelmed the stories of the games themselves.

Nothing contributed more to the demolition of the myth that sports were somehow insulated from the outside world than the process by which the professional athletes in team sports escaped their serflike relationships to owners. By striking down the reserve clause in baseball and similar player reservation systems in other sports, the federal courts released the players from perpetual bondage. The pro athletes organized unions, fomented strikes, and signed collective bargaining agreements. Beginning in the 1970s players' salaries suddenly escalated to undreamed-of heights. By then, players received incomes commensurate with celebrities in popular music, television, and the movies. Three conditions—the increased incidence of competition among franchises for player talent, the demise of the traditional player reservation systems, and the formation of player unions were mainly responsible for these radical changes.

In the past, direct competition for the services of players had been rare. Whenever team sports franchises could do so, they resorted to the reserve clause and the draft to avoid the rigors of bidding against one another for talent. Ordinarily this system broke down only when rival leagues formed. If leagues bid against one another for players, then salaries and fringe benefits improved. Yet historically such periods of open market competition had been brief. New leagues either had insufficient funds to compete for players, collapsed within a few years, or merged with an existing league. Players who jumped to a new league not only risked the possibility that the loop might fold but also the likelihood that the existing leagues would mete out harsh penalties if they wished to return.

Without interleague competition, players were in a poor position from which to bargain. Average salaries might not keep up with inflation or owner profits. For example, the actual purchasing power (income adjusted for inflation) of the big-league baseball players apparently declined between 1946 and 1963. Competition between the National Football League and the All-America Football Conference in the late 1940s pushed up the average football salary to about $8,000 by 1949. But, with the collapse of the All-America league in 1949, NFL salaries in the 1949–59 era grew more slowly than the rate of inflation.[6]

The rivalry between the NFL and the American Football League revealed even more dramatically the effects of interleague competition on player salaries. When the AFL signed a lucrative television contract with NBC in 1964, it obtained the financial means to launch a bidding war with the NFL for players. The salaries of the more prized veterans and draftees immediately skyrocketed. Joe Namath received $420,000 to sign a three-year pact with the New York Jets in 1964, but after the NFL-AFL merger of 1966 owners held the line on salaries and in 1968, Kenny Stabler, who had shattered all of Namath's passing records at Alabama, received only a $20,000 bonus and a $25,000 annual salary to sign with Oakland. In the late 1960s the salaries offered to new draftees fell from one-third to one-half. As late as 1968 one in five NFL players made less than $15,000 per season.[7]

Even after the players had formed a more effective union and the courts had struck down football's player reservation system, interleague competition continued to be the largest single determinant of NFL salaries. Throughout the post-1950 era, the signing of American players by Canadian Football League (CFL) teams exerted some pressure on NFL salaries. However, the CFL employed quotas to limit the number of American-born players on their teams and the Canadians never had the financial resources to compete with the NFL in an all-out war for talent. The players also benefited from the competition with the NFL furnished by the short-lived World Football League (1974–75) and United States Football League (1983–85).

The formation of the American Basketball Association (ABA) in 1967 caused professional basketball salaries to escalate temporarily as well. In an earlier era of no interleague competition for players (1952–57) the median salary increased one-third, but in a subsequent era of competition with the ABA (1967–71), NBA median salaries jumped from $25,000 to $40,000, or 60 percent.[8] Aware of the effect of the football merger of 1966 on player salaries, the NBA and the ABA athletes at first adamantly resisted a league merger. Finally, in 1975 the players approved the merger of the NBA and ABA, but only upon the condition that the classic forms of the draft and the reserve system be abolished.

THE PLAYERS ASSOCIATIONS

The cultural unrest of the 1960s, expectations of higher salaries stemming from the general prosperity of professional sports, and the almost simultaneous appointment of new executive directors of the player associations in baseball, basketball, and hockey helped induce a growing player militancy. In the 1960s and 70s the militancy led in two directions. One path led to the formation of more powerful player associations while the other led to the federal courts.

The players organized the most effective unions in baseball and basketball. With the teams playing many games and the number of players totaling only about 100, the basketball players knew each other better and could communicate more easily with each other than could football and baseball players. The high proportions of blacks in the NBA, many of whom had been inspired by the civil rights movement and common experiences of racial prejudice, and the selection of Oscar Robertson, a highly respected black superstar, as president of the Players Association, created a unity among the basketball players unmatched in any other professional team sport. The players hired Lawrence Fleisher, an experienced labor lawyer, to revamp their moribund association.

To the surprise of nearly everyone, the baseball players formed an equally, if not more, effective union. Many more men were involved (some 600) and for many years baseball players enjoyed the distinction of being the best-paid athletes in professional team sports. The team owners initially dominated the Major League Baseball Players Association (MLBPA), which had been founded in 1953. But in 1966 the players took a historic step by hiring a full-time executive director, Marvin J. Miller, a veteran employee of the United Steelworkers. "To a disinterested observer," concluded Robert H. Boyle in 1974, "Miller comes on like a David with an ICBM in his sling while the owners stumble around like so many befuddled Goliaths."[9] Ironically, the owners' undisguised contempt for Miller helped unite the players behind the MLBPA.

In the late 1960s and early 70s the MLBPA won a series of victories. The owners agreed to (1) increase minimum salaries, (2) adopt a grievance procedure

MARVIN J. MILLER Executive director of the Major League Baseball Players Association (1966–1983), Miller transformed the moribund association into a powerful agency of the players. (National Baseball Hall of Fame and Museum)

that led to outside arbitration rather than to the commissioner of baseball, (3) the right of players to have counsels or agents represent them in contract negotiations, and (4) a larger player pension fund. After having executed a successful strike in 1972, Miller won a major victory in 1973 when the owners agreed to accept salary arbitration, a procedure by which those players who had two years of experience in the majors could have their salaries decided by an "impartial" arbitrator. After having heard testimony by both sides about the player's performance and the salaries of other players whose performance was roughly equivalent, the arbitrator then chose one of two figures, one proposed by the player or one proposed by the owner, as the player's future salary. The twin forces of arbitration and free agency (gained by the players in 1976) drove up baseball salaries at astonishing rates (see Table 20–1).

Players had the most difficulty in organizing an effective union in the sport that prospered the most—pro football. This was partly because the football owners could more easily replace a player without damaging team performance. Secondly, unlike the baseball owners, who were notoriously divided within their ranks, the NFL acted as a close-knit economic cartel. Suffering from these handicaps, the National Football League Players Association (NFLPA) enjoyed less success than the baseball and basketball unions.

TABLE 20–1   Salary Average of Professional Athletes, Selected Years
(in thousands of dollars)

	1967	1975	1980	1985	1990	1995	2000
Major-League Baseball	$19	$46	$144	$371	$598	$1,111	$1,894
Basketball	$20	$107	$170	$325	$817	$2,010	$4,200
Football	$25	$42	$79	$194	$352	$714	$1,116

Source: U.S. Census, *Statistical Abstract of the United States*, annual editions; Major League Baseball Players Association; National Football League Players Association; National Basketball Players Association.

Organized in 1957, the NFLPA was essentially dormant until 1968. Even then, the association employed only one full-time person and he was without union experience. Yet, the union won small victories in both 1968 and 1970. Hoping in 1970 to secure a larger chunk of Rozelle's new $45 million contract with the television networks, the players exhibited a remarkable solidarity; only 21 of some 1,300 veteran players reported to the preseason camps. After a month-long lockout-strike during the preseason, the owners nearly doubled their payments to the players' pension and disability funds.

The next strike in 1974 was clearly a setback for the NFLPA. After the strike-lockout of 1970, the owners embarked on a systematic campaign to crush the players' association. Several owners took punitive action against the union's player representatives. During the strike of 1974, the NFL played the preseason games without the veteran players and threatened to dismiss striking players. "I have to think that there will be a terribly large turnover on our squad," remarked Wellington Mara, the owner of the Giants.[10] Unity among the players weakened, and in early August, led by Dallas Cowboys star, Roger Staubach, the veterans, especially the white players, began to cross the picket lines. The NFLPA suspended the strike, and a new agreement was not reached until 1977.

FREE AGENCY

While none of the player associations had been able to abolish the player reservation systems or player drafts through strikes or negotiations, between 1975 and 1977 the federal courts began to undercut the entire set of strictures on player freedom. But, instead of establishing a system of allowing players complete freedom to sell their services to the team of their choice, the player associations used the right of free agency as a bargaining chip in their negotiations with management. In each team sport, unions and owners eventually settled on modified draft and player reservation systems.

The first breakthrough came in basketball. In 1975, in the face of a challenge by the players, the NBA sought judicial approval of its draft and reserve systems. The following year the court denied their appeal and strongly hinted that the NBA's player control system violated antitrust law. Rather than take the issue to court, the NBA negotiated a contract in 1976 that permitted players to change teams. The team losing a player, however, would be compensated by the team that received the departing player.

Unable to control the upward spiral of salaries, in 1984 the owners negotiated a salary cap for each team. Limited initially to a total team salary of $3.6 million, salary caps restricted the possibilities of the owners making large offers to free agents. Nonetheless, the combination of interleague competition between 1967 and 1975 and the increased freedom for players to become free agents after 1975 spurred the salaries of basketball players to record highs (see Table 20–1).

The venerable reserve system in baseball fell in a more indirect fashion. In 1975 the MLBPA filed grievances on behalf of Andy Messersmith and Dave McNally alleging that, since the two athletes had played the previous season without a written contract, both were free agents. As provided by the agreement between the owners and the players, the issue went to an arbitration panel. By a vote of two to one the panel held that the two players were free agents. The owners promptly appealed the decision to a federal district court and the United States Court of Appeals. In both instances the courts ruled in favor of the players. Suddenly the reserve clause was extinct. Using the legal right of free agency as a bargaining wedge for other demands, the players' union proceeded to negotiate a series of contracts calling for a modified reserve system.

In the 1980s the free-spending baseball owners sought to achieve contracts with the MLBPA that would place a salary cap on arbitration awards and thus curb their own impulses to bid up salaries by signing free agents. If a team that gained a player as a free agent had to compensate the team that lost the player with a player or players of equal caliber or with money representing the player's value, it was assumed the owners would be far more reluctant to sign free agents. But the owners failed to obtain a compensation system that would have negated the effects of free agency on salaries. A seven-week strike over the amount of player compensation in 1981 resulted in a union victory.

Unable to negotiate a compensation system with the players' union that would have ended the bidding wars among themselves for free agents, the owners in 1985 reached a secret agreement. They suddenly stopped signing free agents. For the first time in recent baseball history, the ascent of salaries leveled off, but only temporarily. In 1987, an arbitrator found that the owners had violated their contract with the players by a "concerted conduct" to limit the market for free agents. He ordered compensation awards to those players who had become free agents during the time that the owners had practiced this restraint. In 1988, the owners resumed their bidding for free agents and player salaries soared in the early 1990s. In the 1994 negotiations, the owners insisted upon a salary cap, resulting in a season-ending strike that canceled the World Series for the first time in its history. In 1996 the owners and players reached a new agreement that placed some restraints on escalating salaries.

Until the late 1990s, the football players were less successful than baseball or basketball players in using free agency as a bargaining tool. Technically, football did not have a career-bound reserve system. A player could "play out" his option, that is, he could play for one year after his contract had expired and become a free agent. Hypothetically, at that point, he could look forward to bids for his services from other NFL teams. But if a free agent did sign with another team, the team had to grant compensation to the player's original team. If indemnity terms could not be agreed upon by the two teams involved, then Commissioner Pete Rozelle was empowered to make awards to the team losing a player. Under this so-called "Rozelle Rule," the commissioner could compensate the original team with current players, future draft choices, or both. Such a system reduced the prospects of signing free agents. Not knowing how much an indemnity might cost them and wishing to avoid open bidding for player services, the owners rarely signed free agents. In fact, until the abolition of the Rozelle Rule in 1975, Rozelle had awarded indemnities in only two instances.

In 1975 a federal court found the Rozelle Rule violated antitrust law, but it also permitted the NFL and the NFLPA to negotiate a player reservation system. In other words, any player reserve system would have to be the product of a contract negotiation rather than a unilateral decision of the owners. In 1977, in exchange for better pensions and insurance coverage, the NFLPA essentially bargained away free agency. Given the absence of open bidding for free agents, NFL salaries rose more slowly than those in basketball and baseball.

A FAN PROTESTING THE 1994–95 BASEBALL STRIKE To many fans, both the players and owners seemed to be more concerned with financial gain than the fate of America's national game. (AP/World Wide Photo)

In their 1982 negotiations the NFLPA decided upon a new ploy; the union demanded that 55 percent of the gross revenues of teams go to player salaries. A seven-week strike failed to obtain player demands, but competition with the United States Football League for players did force NFL salaries upward. In the 1987 negotiations the players decided to make free agency the main issue. A disastrous 24-day strike followed, which even left in doubt the future existence of the NFLPA. Finally, in 1993, after the owners had lost an antitrust suit filed by the players, the two sides reached a court-mandated settlement that provided for free agency and a salary cap. Resembling closely the labor agreement in pro basketball, the new accord promised escalating salaries for the football players but not of the dimensions of those unleashed in baseball (see Table 20–1).

THE IMPLICATIONS OF THE NEW STATUS

Given the salary explosion, unions, strikes, free agency, and the propensity of the media to expose all, the public did not perceive athletes in quite the same way as they had at mid-century (see Table 20–2). Sports fans worried lest the big salaries, the outside endorsements, and the long-term contracts destroy the players' drive to compete and damage the cooperation so essential to success in team sports. "Regardless of what the athlete says, if he has total security and is put in a tough sport, he may go through the motions and say, 'The hell with it. I've got mine,'" said Thomas Tutko, noted sports psychologist in 1978. Sports "are modeling greed, egotism, self-centeredness," continued Tutko. "We're modeling things that potentially threaten the fiber of the country. There's no such thing as loyalty to anybody."[11]

Many shared Tutko's grim conclusion. When running back Herschel Walker decided to pass up his senior year at the University of Georgia in 1983 and joined the professional ranks, *Newsweek* implored: "Say it ain't so, Herschel." For money, Walker had cut all ties with and responsibilities to his college. "He was so straight—the quintessential All-Everything," mourned *Newsweek*. "And everybody not only admired Herschel Walker, they believed. In the sublime order of

TABLE 20–2   Spectator Attitudes toward Professional Athletes, 1982
(in percentages)

	Agree	Disagree	Undecided
Athletes are overpaid.	76	20	4
Athletes are more dedicated to their own good than to the game.	50	42	8
Athletes should be tested for drugs before each game.	71	27	2

Source: Research & Forecasts, Inc., *The Miller Lite Report on American Attitudes Toward Sports* (New York, 1983).

things, he would finish out his record-shattering college career, gathering still more honors, the very perfect gentle scholar-athlete, and move with dignity into the professional game."[12] In a major cover story, *Time* magazine conveyed a similar sense of betrayal.

Other fans disliked the increasing incivility of the players. The assault on civility may have begun with Muhammad Ali, but when Ali asserted that he was the greatest, one sensed that he was mocking white America. No one detected a higher purpose in the conspicuous displays of churlish pouting and bad manners of dozens of other athletes. In the 1970s and 80s even the once sedate sport of tennis became the stage for the rude, vulgar, loud, and whining displays of John McEnroe. Television daredevil Evel Knievel, angered by the remarks of a sportswriter, proceeded to break the offender's arm with a baseball bat. The absence of restraint reflected in part a shift in American sensibility, but it also suggested that the athletes were uncertain about why they were celebrities. Was it their feats on the playing field or their uncivil behavior that captured the attention of the media?

The widespread use of drugs by athletes also bothered fans. While alcoholic beverages had long been (and continued to be) used to obtain "highs," athletes turned to other drugs to relieve pain and improve performances. Despite warnings of long-term, serious side effects, virtually every world-class weight lifter, shot-putter, and discus thrower turned to anabolic steroids. Revelations suggested that large numbers of linemen in both college and professional football also used the same drug. Many other athletes turned to the "glamour drug" of cocaine, which resulted in the shocking deaths of several well-known athletes. In 2002, sports fans learned of the widespread use of steroids by big-league baseball players. (Baseball was the only professional sport without a drug-testing program.)

Yet fans may not have been as disaffected with athletes as the critics charged. Grim predictions of a permanent decline in fan interest simply did not materialize. To a large degree the values and behaviors of the athletes reflected the changing values and behaviors of Americans as a whole. Rather than punish the teams and owners, after each of baseball's strikes the fans returned to the parks in record numbers. From time to time attendance and television ratings stagnated or fell, but then they invariably climbed upward again. Each of the major sporting events—the World Series, Super Bowl, college bowl games, the Final Four college basketball playoff games, and the winter and summer Olympic Games—broke records in either the 1980s or 1990s for both attendance and television ratings. And despite a fall in the licensing business as a whole, the sales of clothing and other gear with team names and logos grew 50 percent between 1988 to 1992. This trend continued into the early twenty-first century.[13]

While fans might be angered by the high salaries and behavior of the athletes, the players suffered from hidden costs. Careers were short, and athletes, at least those in pro football, faced the likelihood of permanent, disabling injuries as well. A questionnaire sent to 1,000 former NFL players in 1988 revealed that 78 percent of them suffered from physical disabilities related directly to having played football. Injuries, excessive weight gain (both during and after a player's career), high fat diets, and the use of steroids and other drugs, may have shortened life spans. Though no systematic study has been made of longevity in sports, the NFLPA claimed that of 78 vested players (those who played at least four seasons) who had died between 1960 and 1988, the average age had been a mere 38.2 years.[14]

YOUTH ATHLETES

In the post-1950 era the professional model of athletics increasingly extended to all levels of sports, including even the preadolescent and adolescent youth programs. Only the professional youth workers tried to stem the tide. They continued to adhere to the idea that games should be both nonspectator-centered and conducive to the physical, mental, and moral maturation of their young charges (see Chapter 7). But in the post-1950 era, as the inner cities decayed, the influence of the reformers in the YMCAs, YWCAs, city recreation departments, and schools declined. In the meantime, the programs of untrained adult volunteers, which were scaled-down facsimiles of professional sports, grew rapidly. Relative to time and place, professional physical educators continued to exercise some influence over high school sports, but, in the main, they too tended to take on the characteristics of the professional model.

In the post-1950 era, high school sports in the towns, smaller cities, and the independent suburbs prospered while those in the inner city declined. To prevent violent outbursts among fans and sometimes the players in the late 1960s and early 70s, some inner-city schools closed down varsity programs or scheduled contests only during the daytime hours. In terms of attendance as a ratio of population, the secondary schools in smaller towns fared much better than in the larger cities or in the independent suburbs. In the grim industrial and mill towns of Ohio and the desolate prairie towns of west Texas, no single activity exceeded the capacity of high school football in binding communities together. Basketball performed a similar role for Indiana towns.

In those places where interscholastic sports assumed important community functions, they invariably resembled collegiate or professional counterparts. One of the more extreme instances was Massillon, Ohio, an economically depressed steel mill city of some 30,000 people. In the 1980s, the varsity football team of Massillon-Washington High School had a booster club of 2,700 members, a lighted-stadium that held 20,000 spectators, and a 109-page *Official Football Media Guide*. The school also employed a statistician, a trainer, and a football information director—all full time—as well as a head coach and ten assistant coaches.[15]

High school football could be an equally serious enterprise for Texans. When Highland Park High School, located in a trendy suburb of Dallas, reached the Texas state football finals in 1985, the residents chartered nine Boeing 727s to shuttle themselves 300 miles to the championship games.[16] In a controversial book, Harold Bissinger, an investigative reporter with the *Chicago Tribune*, offered a vivid portrait of the 1988 football season in another Texas high school, the Permian High School Panthers of Odessa, which regularly drew 20,000 fans. While located in desertlike west Texas, dependent on ricocheting oil prices for their livelihoods, and wracked by racial tensions, Odessa's otherwise divided residents rallied behind a common cause—football—on Friday nights.

In Odessa, Bissinger found, high school football celebrated such traditional values as male toughness and female nurturence. Local boosters blamed losses on the failure of the coaches to be tough enough on the players. Boys who failed to hit hard enough, play with pain, or try to physically intimidate their opponents were described as "pussies." Girls anxiously sought to be chosen for the Pepettes, the senior girls' spirit squad. As a Pepette, each girl was assigned to an individual football player, expected to wear a jersey bearing his number, and to cater to his needs. However, a study of high school student culture in another small Texas town by Doug Foley, an anthropologist, reached conclusions somewhat at odds with those of Bissinger. Foley found that identity for most high school students was grounded more deeply in gender, class, and ethnicity than in sport participation.[17]

Long an important source of local identities, high school basketball began to emerge in the 1980s as a national spectacle. Beginning in 1918, the University of Chicago's famed coach, Amos Alonzo Stagg, had sponsored a national interscholastic tournament that gained considerable attention, but the tourney collapsed during the Great Depression of the 1930s. In the 1980s, *USA Today*, a popular nationwide newspaper, began to publish weekly high school rankings, and in December more than a dozen cities held tournaments that attracted teams from all parts of the nation. Most of the tournaments had local television contracts and some even had corporate sponsors. With national rankings and with tournaments in far-away exotic settings, the emphasis on winning inevitably increased. In some places, competition for star players resulted in scandals arising over the transfer of athletes from one school district to another. Other high schools permitted students to "redshirt"; they held back students for a year in school so that he or she could gain an additional year of athletic maturity.[18]

At the preadolescent level, the programs of adult volunteers in the post-World War II era grew phenomenally. Untrained volunteers founded the Pop Warner Football League in 1929 and Little League Baseball in 1939; for both, survival was doubtful until after World War II. In 1947, when the United States Rubber Company became the sponsor and financial angel of Little League, the league had only 60 teams and some 1,000 players. Then Little League suddenly took root, flourishing mostly in the small- and medium-size cities without municipal recreation programs and in the newly built independent suburbs. Within a decade nearly a million boys played on 19,500 teams in 47 states and in 22 nations abroad. Pop Warner grew almost as rapidly; by the 1970s it suited up a million players annually.[19]

Unlike earlier adult-managed youth programs, no ideology, unless it be the importance of winning, shaped Little League Baseball, Pop Warner football, and a dozen similar programs. Carl Stotz, the lumber company employee in Williamsport, Pennsylvania, who founded Little League, explained that he dreamed up the game in response to his own frustrations as a youth with unsupervised, chaotic play. The colorful team uniforms, use of a regular baseball, outfield

CONSOLING A LITTLE CHIEFS BASEBALL PLAYER, 1970 Not all coaches of pre-adolescent youths were as sensitive to the feelings of their charges as this coach apparently was.
(Peoria Journal Star)

fences, dugouts, and even a player draft system all provided for adult volunteers a vicarious experience of the unfulfilled fantasies of their own youth. Uninhibited by a theory of play, the volunteers tried to simulate professional team sports. Ironically, while several states prohibited state high school championships in football and usually strictly limited the number of miles a team could travel, eight- and nine-year-olds trekked all over the nation to play in such "midget" bowls as the Junior Liberty (Memphis), Junior Orange (Miami), Auto (Grosse Pointe, Michigan), and even the Honolulu Bowl. No national championships existed in high school baseball, but Little League Baseball held an annual World Series at Williamsport, Pennsylvania.

Critics, especially recreation professionals, frequently complained that the volunteers placed too much emphasis upon winning. Preadolescent youths had not matured enough, they argued, to engage in highly competitive games. Indeed, reports regularly surfaced in the media of apparent excesses. Untold numbers of preadolescents submitted themselves to a regimen of diet pills and low calorie diets in order to make weight limits in junior wrestling or junior football programs. The experience of coaching sometimes turned otherwise humane and reasonable men into angry, violent tyrants. "They want to win at any cost," reported Charles Ortmann, a former Michigan All-American who quit as chairman of a midget football program at Glen Ellyn, Illinois. "They tell their players, 'Go out there and break that guy's arm.' They won't even let all their kids play."[20] In terms of public attention out-of-control parents reached a tragic climax in 2000 when an angry hockey father in a Boston suburb assaulted and killed the father of another child athlete. According to the National Alliance for Youth Sports, the incidence of sports rage involving players, coaches, officials, and parents was rising. Because of parental behavior, some places had difficulty obtaining referees for child sports. "Fan rage, road rage, air rage—its all part of the same phenomenon," theorized New York sports psychologist Stanley Teitelbaum.[21] Some communities sought to counter the growing incivility by sponsoring sportsmanship classes or insisting that parents remain totally silent during play.

According to polls, an overwhelming majority of the parents of participants agreed that there was too much emphasis upon winning and not enough upon the physical and psychological development of their children, but at the same time they believed the benefits to the children outweighed the costs. In response to widespread criticism, several volunteer programs introduced reforms, such as requiring that all youngsters be permitted to play at least briefly. Yet the reforms failed to transform the main outlines of volunteer youth sports programs.

At the championship levels, the individual sports also became more serious for preteenage youth in the post-1950 era. Earlier, youth had rarely given tennis, track, gymnastics, figure skating, skiing, or swimming much of their attention or time. Perhaps during the summer months, they might take a few lessons at the country club to which their parents belonged or participate in a Y or city recreation program. Otherwise they simply played for fun or in a few meets scheduled over the summer.

But in the 1960s and 1970s television made celebrities of athletes such as Jimmy Connors, Chris Evert, Mark Spitz, and Olga Korbut. Within a decade following the 1972 Olympics, the level of competition in the individual sports took a sudden jump. In tennis, tiny teenage girls developed powerful, dependable ground strokes. Track and field records seemed to fall daily. The record time in swimming that won Mark Spitz the gold medal in the 100-meter race in the 1972 Olympics would not even have qualified him for the event in the 1980 Olympics. In diving, gymnastics, and figure skating, the execution of new, complex maneuvers (some of which were previously thought to be impossible) were necessary before one could even qualify to compete at the international level of competition.

Achievement of these advances came largely from early, systematic training. Those who aspired to national or international competition in individual sports had to begin as preadolescents, training three or four hours daily with careful supervision by individual coaches. On weekends and during the summer months, children engaged in regular competition, often embarking on long trips away from home. They might also live for varying periods at special athletic camps or compounds.

No one knew what the long-range effects of such rigorously focused childhoods might be. Disturbing reports occasionally surfaced of early "burnout," suicides, and aimlessness in later life. In particular, adolescent female tennis stars (including Tracy Austin, Andrea Yeager, and Jennifer Capriati) dropped out of the sport early for physical or psychical reasons. Likewise, several female gymnasts suffered from anorexia and severe adjustment problems later in life. The apparent employment of a "hit man" by figure skater Tonya Harding in 1994 to disable Nancy Kerrigan, her leading opponent, suggested the lengths to which competitors might go in order to claim victory. Yet such instances may have exaggerated the negative effects of early competition. Surveys of children competing at the national and international levels indicated that most of them performed well above average in their schoolwork and seemed better adjusted psychologically than nonsporting youth of a comparable age.

CONCLUSION

In the age of television, individual athletes remained central to the sporting experience. Athletes embodying traditional virtues such as Arthur Ashe, Chris Evert, Mary Lou Retton, Nolan Ryan, and Cal Ripken continued to have many admirers.[22] Other athletes represented new lifestyles or causes, for example, Billie Jean King, Joe Namath, and Muhammad Ali. Still others were prized for their spectacular exhibitions of special skills, for example, Michael Jordan, Joe Montana, and Wayne Gretzke. In all instances, the line between being a hero and a celebrity was sometimes indistinguishable. For instance, Bo Jackson, a marginally effective baseball player, and Andre Agassi, who failed to realize his full promise on the courts until late in his career, received far more media attention and endorsement earnings than their far more successful but less charismatic counterparts. Whether celebrity or hero, the athletes at the top of their professions continued to provide compelling models for countless Americans.

NOTES

1. See Gerard O'Connor, "Where Have You Gone, Joe DiMaggio?" in R.B. Browne et al., *Heroes in Popular Culture* (Bowling Green, OH: Bowling Green University Popular Press, 1972), 87–99; W.O. Johnson, "What's Happened to Our Heroes?" *Sports Illustrated* 59 (August 15, 1983), 32–42; and W.J. Bennett, "Let's Bring Back Heroes," *Newsweek*, (August 15, 1977), 8.

2. Gay Talese, "Gray-Flannel-Suit Men at Bat," *New York Times Magazine*, March 30, 1958, 15. See

also Peter Schrag, "The Age of Willie Mays," *Saturday Review*, (May 8, 1971), 15–17, 42.

3. Quoted in Leonard Schecter, "The Toughest Man in Pro Football," *Esquire*, (January 1968), 140. A widely shown 1968 sales training film entitled *Second Effort*, featuring Lombardi, and Howard Cosell's 1970 documentary, *"Run for Daylight,"* contributed to the Lombardi legend. See Jerry Kramer with Dick Schapp, *Instant Replay* (Cleveland: World, 1968); Michael O'Brien,

Vince (New York; Vintage, 1987), and L.T. Smith Jr., *The American Dream* (Bowling Green, OH: Bowling Green University Popular Press), 209–56, as examples of the literature inspired by Lombardi.

4. Quoted in O'Connor, "Where Have You Gone, Joe DiMaggio?" 95.

5. Research & Forecasts, Inc. *The Miller Lite Report on American Attitudes toward Sports* (New York: Research & Forecasts, 1983), 140. See also Benjamin G. Rader, *In Its Own Image: How Television Has Transformed Sports* (New York: Free Press, 1984), chap. 11.

6. Ralph Andreano, *No Joy in Mudville* (Cambridge, MA: Schenkman, 1965), 140; *Audible* 4 (July 1972), 3; and Leonard Koppett, *Sports Illusion, Sports Reality* (Boston: Houghton Mifflin, 1981), 52–53. For general accounts of labor relations in sport, see Kenneth Jennings, *Balls and Strikes* (New York: Praeger, 1990); James E. Miller, *The Baseball Business*, (Chapel Hill: University of North Carolina Press, 1990), Benjamin G. Rader, *Baseball* 2d ed. (Urbana: University of Illinois Press, 2002), chap. 14; Gerald Scully, *The Business of Baseball* (Chicago: University of Chicago Press, 1989); P.D. Staudohar, *The Sports Industry and Collective Bargaining* (Ithaca, NY: Cornell University Press, 1986); Andrew Zimbalist, *Baseball and Billions* (New York: Basic Books, 1992), chap. 1.

7. *Sports Illustrated* 28 (April 8, 1968), 20; *Audible*, 4 (July 1972), 1; *Audible* 5 (April 1973), 2.

8. J.G. Scoville, "Labor Relations in Sports," in R.G. Noll, ed., *Government and the Sports Business* (Washington, D.C.: GPO, 1974), 198.

9. R.H. Boyle, "This Miller Admits He's a Grind," *Sports Illustrated* 40 (March 11, 1974), 23.

10. *Sports Illustrated*, 41 (Aug. 12, 1974), 11.

11. *Sports Illustrated*, 49 (July 24, 1978), 44.

12. *Newsweek* (March 7, 1983), 82.

13. See Ben Brown, "Perceptions in a Battle with Economic Reality," *USA Today*, May 11, 1993, 8C.

14. As reported in the *Lincoln* (Nebraska) *Star*, June 28, 1988. See also William Nack, "The Wrecking Yard," *Sports Illustrated* 94 (May 7, 2001), 60ff.

15. Mark Russell, "Football Bores You?" *Wall Street Journal*, November 1, 1984, 1, 16

16. Paul Duke, Jr., "Teams Make Towns Winners . . . " *Wall Street Journal*, February 26, 1988, 4D, and A.W. Miracle Jr. and C.R. Rees, *Lessons of the Locker Room* (Amherst, NY: Prometheus Books, 1994).

17. H.G. Bissinger, *Friday Night Lights* (Reading, MA: Addison-Wesley, 1990); Doug Foley, "The Great American Football Ritual: Reproducing Race, Class, and Gender Inequality," *Sociology of Sport Journal* 7:2 (1990), 111–35.

18. See C.R. Barnett and David Helmer, "The Champs," *River Cities Monthly*, March 1980, 7–16; "Hoosier Madness," *Sports Illustrated* 3 (December 19, 1955), 23, 45–46.

19. See Kenneth Rudeen, "The Little League, Parts I and II," *Sports Illustrated* 5 (August 19–August 26, 1957), 56–62, 54–59, and "The World of Pop Warner Football," *Newsweek*, December 6, 1965, 102–03. For perhaps a typical division between old-stock and ethnic Americans over Little League, see Herbert Gans, *The Levittowners* (New York: Pantheon, 1967), 120–21.

20. John Underwood, "Taking the Fun Out of the Game," *Sports Illustrated* 43 (November 17, 1975), 92.

21. Pat Wingert and J.F. Lauerman, "Parents Behaving Badly," *Newsweek* (July 24, 2000), 47. See also William Nack and Lester Munson, "Out of Control," *Sports Illustrated* 93 (July 24, 2000), 86ff.

22. Perhaps no athlete received more praise from the media than Arthur Ashe. See, for example, Kenny Moore, "The Eternal Example," *Sports Illustrated* 77 (December 21, 1992), 17–26. See also Nick Trujillo, *The Meaning of Nolan Ryan* (College Station: Texas A & M University Press, 1994).

21
AMERICAN SPORTS: A CONCLUDING STATEMENT

*F*rom a broad perspective, American sports have evolved from the folk games of the colonial era to the highly organized sports of the age of television. Folk games arose from the daily routines of the people rather than from entrepreneurs of entertainment. Sometimes they combined work and play. Unwritten customs governed play; the way a particular game was played might vary radically from one place to another. The contestants rarely trained for or earned a living from their games. In most instances no sharp line separated the players from the spectators.

Although folk games were frequently transformed into organized sports in the nineteenth and twentieth centuries, such games never completely disappeared from American life. Children, as in the past, remained especially ingenious in designing games that could be executed within the constraints of the space and the number of players available. And varieties of informal bat-and-ball games, pickup basketball games, and impromptu games of running, jumping, and frisbee are reminiscent of early America's folk games.

In the middle decades of the nineteenth century, organized sports increasingly supplemented and to some degree replaced folk games. Entrepreneurs or the athletes themselves formed organizations, adopted written rules, extended competition beyond local areas, drew sharper distinctions between fans and players, attracted the attention of the media, and began to preserve records of their performances. The athletes trained more rigorously. Commercial boxing, wrestling, pedestrianism, and numerous other diversions became vital parts of the Victorian counterculture.

In addition, more "respectable" nineteenth-century Americans formed literally thousands of voluntary associations for the playing of games. Organized cricket, baseball, yachting, football, tennis, and golf, for instance, had origins in private, socially exclusive clubs. Although experiencing important changes since the nineteenth century, these sports retained forms familiar to Americans in the age of television.

In the 1890–1950 era organized sports became an entrenched feature of American society. For growing numbers of Americans, regardless of occupation, social class, ethnicity, or religious persuasion, their leisure experiences entailed the purchase of amusements. They bought tickets to prizefights, intercollegiate football games, and major-league baseball games. Organized sports thus became part and parcel of the larger consumer culture. Much of the traditional suspicion of sports dissipated. Indeed, Americans ranging from the old patricians to a generation of experts in play and the human body developed a powerful sporting ideology. Stressing the character-building functions of sports, they embarked upon a campaign to provide organized sports to the nation's youth.

In the post-1950 age of television, spectators in their homes rather than in the stands determined the main contours of organized sports. The sheer quantity of sporting experiences made available by television reached proportions unimaginable to previous generations. Television contributed as well to a growing nationalization, even globalization, of American sports. Intercollegiate sports entered a national arena of competition, and even preteenagers competed at championship levels internationally in gymnastics, tennis, golf, and ice skating.

Thus, in the opening decade of the twenty-first century, American sports comprise aspects of both the old and the new. Remnants of the old can be found everywhere. Children still play folk games; country clubs continue to serve as socially exclusive voluntary associations; prizefighting remains nearly as chaotic as it was during the age of John L. Sullivan; and the rules of major-league baseball differ little from what they were in 1900. Yet much is new. Everything is, or at the least seems, much bigger and more commercialized. With the advent of television, millions worldwide share sporting experiences instantaneously.

The importance of sports to contemporary American culture is manifest. It can be measured by the many hours that fans spend riveted to television screens, by the column inches in newspapers devoted to sports, to their presence in sports bars, and by samples of cocktail conversations. Novelists, poets, and dramatists increasingly turn to sports for motifs, and scholars are begining to execute minute investigations of the psychological, philosophical, and social significance of sports. As in the past, twenty-first-century sports mirror, sometimes reinforce, and sometimes challenge fundamental social divisions. Simultaneously sports have joined the electronic media, bureaucratic structures, and mass consumption as one of the new sinews holding together modern society.

INDEX